NEW APPROACHES TO EUROPEAN HISTORY

Women and Gender in Early Modern Europe

Second Edition

This is a major new edition of the most stimulating and authoritative textbook on early modern women currently available. Merry Wiesner has updated and expanded her prize-winning study; she summarizes the very latest scholarship in her chapters and bibliographies, adding new sections on topics such as sexuality, masculinity, the impact of colonialism, and women's role as consumers. Other themes investigated include the female life-cycle, literacy, women's economic role, artistic creation, female piety – and witchcraft – and the relationship between gender and power. The clear and helpful structure of the first edition remains: it reflects the tripartite division of the self – mind, body, and spirit – traditional in western philosophy. Coverage is geographically broad; the second edition includes longer discussions of the border areas, such as Russia, Ireland, and the Iberian peninsula. Accessible, engrossing, and lively, this book will be of central importance for courses in gender history, early modern Europe, and comparative history.

MERRY E. WIESNER is Professor and Chair of the Department of History at the University of Wisconsin-Milwaukee. She has published extensively on aspects of women's lives and gender structures in the early modern world; her books include *Gender, Church and State in Early Modern Germany* (1998) and *Christianity and Sexuality in the Early Modern World* (2000). She is also one of the authors of two books of sources and methodology for introductory history courses, one of the editors of *Becoming Visible: Women in European History*, 3rd edition (1998), and one of the editors of the *Sixteenth Century Journal*.

NEW APPROACHES TO EUROPEAN HISTORY

Series editors
WILLIAM BEIK *Emory University*
T. C. W. BLANNING *Sidney Sussex College, Cambridge*

New Approaches to European History is an important textbook series, which provides concise but authoritative surveys of major themes and problems in European history since the Renaissance. Written at a level and length accessible to advanced school students and undergraduates, each book in the series addresses topics or themes that students of European history encounter daily: the series embraces both some of the more "traditional" subjects of study, and those cultural and social issues to which increasing numbers of school and college courses are devoted. A particular effort is made to consider the wider international implications of the subject under scrutiny.

To aid the student reader scholarly apparatus and annotation is light, but each work has full supplementary bibliographies and notes for further reading: where appropriate chronologies, maps, diagrams, and other illustrative material are also provided.

For a list of titles published in the series, please see end of book.

Women and Gender in Early Modern Europe

Second Edition

MERRY E. WIESNER

University of Wisconsin-Milwaukee

CAMBRIDGE
UNIVERSITY PRESS

PUBLISHED BY THE PRESS SYNDICATE OF THE UNIVERSITY OF CAMBRIDGE
The Pitt Building, Trumpington Street, Cambridge, United Kingdom

CAMBRIDGE UNIVERSITY PRESS
The Edinburgh Building, Cambridge CB2 2RU, UK   http://www.cup.cam.ac.uk
40 West 20th Street, New York, NY 10011-4211, USA   http://www.cup.org
10 Stamford Road, Oakleigh, Melbourne 3166, Australia
Ruiz de Alarcón 13, 28014 Madrid, Spain

© Cambridge University Press 2000

This book is in copyright. Subject to statutory exception
and to the provisions of relevant collective licensing agreements,
no reproduction of any part may take place without
the written permission of Cambridge University Press.

First published 1993 and reprinted four times
Second edition 2000

Printed in the United States of America

Typeface Plantin 10/12 pt.   *System* QuarkXPress™   [HT]

A catalog record for this book is available from the British Library

Library of Congress Cataloging-in-Publication Data

Wiesner, Merry E., 1952–
    Women and gender in early modern Europe / Merry E. Wiesner.
      p. cm. – (New approaches to European history 20)
    Includes bibliographical references and index.
    ISBN 0 521 77105 6 (hb)
    1. Women – Europe – History. I. Title. II. Series
HQ1587.W54 2000
305.4′094 – dc21   00-022070

ISBN 0 521 77105 6   hardback
ISBN 0 521 77822 0   paperback

For Kai and Tyr

Contents

List of Illustrations   *page* x
Acknowledgments   xi

Introduction   1

1   Ideas and laws regarding women   13

Part I: Body

2   The female life-cycle   51
3   Women's economic role   102

Part II: Mind

4   Literacy and learning   143
5   Women and the creation of culture   175

Part III: Spirit

6   Religion   213
7   Witchcraft   264

8   Gender and power   288

Index   319

Illustrations

1 Abraham Bach, *Recipe for Marital Bliss, c.* 1680. Dorothy
  Alexander and Walter L. Strauss, *The German Single-Leaf
  Woodcut, 1600–1700* (New York, Abaris Books Inc., 1977),
  p. 61.   *page* 23
2 Melchior Lorch, *Allegory of Nature.* 1565. Walter L. Strauss,
  The German Single-Leaf Woodcut, 1550–1600, vol. II (New
  York, Abaris Books Inc., 1975), p. 609.   34
3 Anne Bonney as a pirate. Book illustration from *Historie der
  Engelsche zeerovers* (Amsterdam, 1725). Courtesy of
  Universiteitsbibliotheek Amsterdam.   69
4 Albrecht Dürer, *The Birth of Mary.* Staatliche Museen
  zu Berlin, Kupferstichkabinett.   80
5 Illustrations from Thomas Raynalde, *The Byrth of Mankynde*
  (London, 1545).   84
6 Geertruydt Roghman, *Woman Spinning.* Before 1650.
  Harvey D. Parker Collection, Courtesy, Museum of Fine
  Arts, Boston.   120
7 Dirk Vellert, *The School Room.* 1526. British Museum.   147
8 Anna Maria van Schurman, self-portrait, 1633. Engraving
  on copper. Kunstsammlung Veste Coburg.   161
9 Sofonisba Anguissola, *Lucia, Minerva, and Europa Anguissola
  Playing Chess.* 1555. Poznan, Museum Narodowe.   180
10 Judith Leyster, *The Proposition.* Mauritshuis, The Hague,
   inventory nr. 564.   183
11 Artemesia Gentilleschi, self-portrait. Royal Collection,
   Hampton Court. Copyright Her Majesty Queen Elizabeth II.   184
12 Lucas Cranach d. A., *Women Assaulting Clergy,* detail.
   After 1537. Staatliche Museen zu Berlin, Kupferstichkabinett,
   KdZ 4798.   221
13 Hans Baldung Grien, *The Witches.* 1510. Stadtgeschichtliche
   Museen Nürnberg, Kaiserstallung.   271

Acknowledgments

A study like this which attempts to survey the entire life experience of half the European population from Spain to Scandinavia over 250 years would not be possible without the kind assistance of a huge number of people. I would like first to thank the Regents of the University of Wisconsin, from whom I received a fellowship at the Institute for Research in the Humanities at the University of Wisconsin-Madison which allowed me a year off from teaching to write the first edition of this book. The comments and critiques of my colleagues at the Institute, particularly its director David Lindbergh, my *Doktorvater* Robert Kingdon, and my good friend Jane Schulenburg were invaluable. Much of the information from Germany comes from my own research in libraries and archives there over the years, which was supported by grants from the Deutsche Akademische Austauschdienst, the American Council of Learned Societies, and the graduate school of the University of Wisconsin-Milwaukee. My familiarity with women's writings in many languages was enhanced by a summer at the Center for Renaissance Studies at the Newberry Library, for which I would like to thank the Exxon Foundation. My experience there was not simply one of solitary scholarly pursuit, but was vastly enriched by discussions with Mary Beth Rose, Ann Roberts, and Diana Robin, who helped me think through many aspects of women's self concepts. My understanding of women's economic role and the relations between gender and work was greatly deepened by wonderful multilingual conversations at a study week sponsored by the Datini Institute in Prato, Italy and the people I met there: Liliane Mottu-Weber, Hilda Sandvik, Sølvi Sogner, Shulamith Shahar, Richard Smith, Brigitte Schnegg, Milagros Rivera, Renata Ago, Katerina Simon-Muscheid and Natalia Pushareva. Many of these scholars have continued to share their work with me, graciously summarizing research in languages that I don't read.

Because so much of this research is new, many studies have not yet been published, and I would like to thank Yael Even, Mary Elizabeth Perry, Daniel Kaiser, Valerie Kivelson, Ann Kleimola, Eve Levin,

Barbara Duden, Elizabeth Cohen, Sara Matthews Grieco, Howard
Adelman, Jane Bowers, Margo Anderson, James Amelang, Jodi Bilinkoff,
Alison Stewart, Craig Monson, Retha Warnicke, Hermoine Joldersma,
Anne Schutte, Gerhild Williams, Nancy Kollman, Phyllis Rackin, and
William Palmer for generously sharing their unpublished work with me,
and suggesting other people to whom I should write. Rudolf Dekker,
Anne Cruz, Elizabeth Rhodes, Margaret Hannay, Kristen Neuschel,
Monika Richarz, Frances Malino, Paula Hyman, Dora Dumont, Barbara
Becker-Cantarino, Margaret Atherton, Jill Bepler, and Gwynne
Kennedy also assisted me by referring to studies I might have missed, for
work in women's studies now appears in hundreds of journals, a great
triumph for the field, but a challenge for any researcher. No one can be
expert in a field this large, so I turned to many people whose expertise
in certain topics or areas is far greater than mine, and who willingly read
and commented on drafts of chapters: Barbara Duden, Jeffrey Merrick,
Jens-Christian Johansen, Carole Shammas, Grethe Jacobsen, Suzanne
Desan, Tom Broman, Susan Karant-Nunn, Jane Bowers, David
Lindbergh. The book would not have been the same without the expertise of Tom Friedrichs, who shot all of the illustrations. The editors of
the series, especially William Beik and the late Robert Scribner, were
also extremely helpful in both their criticisms and cheerleading.

Women's history has always prided itself on sisterly camaraderie and
the sharing of ideas. My own experience over the years has certainly
borne this out, and I have steadily relied on a wonderful network of historians of women for their letters, phone calls, e-mail messages, confer-
ence discussions, papers, bibliographic suggestions, and especially their
intellectual and emotional support over the years: Grethe Jacobsen,
JoAnn McNamara, Heide Wunder, Christina Vanja, Natalie Davis, Carol
Levin, Ulrike Strasser, Ulinka Rublack, Martha Howell, Lyndal Roper,
Sherrin Marshall, Susan Stuard, Eve Levin, Allyson Poska, Katherine
French, Larissa Taylor, Lisa DiCaprio, B. Ann Tlusty, Catherine
Pomerleau, Helmut Puff, Amy Leonard, Jessica Gerard, Gerhild Scholz
Williams, Stanley Chojnacki, Sharon Strocchia, Judith Brown,
Maryanne Kowaleski, Judith Bennett, Miriam Chrisman, Susan Karant-
Nunn, Beate Schuster, Susanna Burghartz, Barbara Hoffman,
Christopher Friedrichs, Anne Schutte. In addition, I would like to thank
the members of my Renaissance Women reading group: Margaret
Borene, Martha Carlin, Janet Jesmok, Gwynne Kennedy, Gretchen
Kling, Deirdre McChrystal, and Sandra Stark. Many of the insights of
all of my friends and colleagues are contained in the following pages, not
all of them amply credited, for they now seem so clear as to appear self-
evident, the mark of any important historical theory. The mistakes and

unclarities that remain are solely my own, and I can only hope that this network will maintain its usual kindness when pointing them out. I dedicated my first book to my grandmothers in sisterhood, and dedicate this to my sons, in the hope that the world they shape will be one where gender will make less of a difference, where cats will be cats.

Introduction

Both man and woman of three parts consist, Which Paul doth bodie,
soule, and spirit call...
Rachel Speght, *Mortalities Memorandum with a Dreame Prefixed* (London, by
Edward Griffin for Jacob Bloome, 1621), ll. 127–8.

Nothing more resembles a tomcat on a windowsill than a female cat.
Marie Jars de Gournay, *L'égalité des hommes et des femmes* (A la Reyne, 1622)

Within the last thirty years there has been an explosion of studies in
women's history. Historians have searched for new sources that reveal
the historical experience of women, and used traditional sources in inno-
vative ways. They analyze the distinctive experiences of individuals and
groups, and relate these histories to political, ideological, and economic
developments.

Interest in women's history has resulted from several different academic and political movements. Beginning in the 1930s, many historians
turned their attention from the traditional subjects of historical inquiry
such as public political developments, diplomatic changes, military
events, and major intellectual movements to investigating the lives of
more ordinary people. Instead of focusing simply on great dramatic
changes such as the French or Industrial Revolutions, these social historians investigated things that had changed much more slowly, or had, in
fact, stayed largely the same for centuries, such as people's diet and
underlying beliefs about the world. In the words of the French Annales-
school historians, leaders in this new approach, they were interested in
the *longue durée*, in economic and intellectual institutions and structures
which had shaped people's lives over a long period of time. Building on
this, during the 1960s some younger historians consciously developed
what they termed the New Social History, which differed somewhat
methodologically and ideologically from older social history. In terms of
methodology, New Social History often borrowed techniques developed
in other social sciences, such as quantitative analysis from economics or
the interpretation of symbols from anthropology. In terms of ideology,

New Social History was shaped by the civil rights, antiwar, student, and national liberation movements of the 1960s to be more overtly political, using historical investigation of past incidents of racial, class, or religious oppression in support of demands for change in present institutions and power structures.

The political movements of the 1960s also reinvigorated the feminist movement, as women involved in civil rights and antiwar causes discovered that even their most revolutionary male colleagues did not treat them as equals or consider their ideas or contributions as valuable as those of men. The feminist movement which began in the 1960s–often termed the "second wave" to set it apart from the "first wave" of feminism that began in the nineteenth century–included a wide range of political beliefs, with various groups working for a broad spectrum of goals, one of which was to understand more about the lives of women in the past. This paralleled a similar rise of interest in women's history which accompanied the first wave of feminism, from which emerged studies that are still influential.

Students in history programs in North America and Western Europe in the late 1960s and early 1970s, most (though not all) of them women, began to focus on women, asserting that any investigation of past oppression or power relationships had to include information on both sexes. Initially these studies were often met with derision or scepticism, not only by more traditional historians who regarded women's history as a fad, but also by some social historians, who were unwilling to see gender along with race and class as a key determinant of human experience. This criticism did not quell interest in women's history, and may in fact have stimulated it, as many women who were active in radical or reformist political movements were angered by claims that their own history was trivial, marginal, or "too political." By the late 1970s, hundreds of colleges and universities in the United States and Canada offered courses in women's history, and many had separate programs in women's history or women's studies. Universities in England were somewhat slower to include lectures and seminars on women, and continental universities slower still, with women in the 1990s still reporting that investigating the history of women can get them pegged as less than serious and be detrimental to their future careers as historians. Thus an inordinate amount of the work in women's history, including the history of continental women, has been done by English-speaking historians, though prospects for the next decade in continental Europe look a bit brighter.

Women's history therefore began in some ways as a sub-field of social history, but over the last thirty years it has widened to include investigations of intellectual, political, economic, and even military and diplomatic history. Historians of women have demonstrated that there is really no historical change that does not affect the lives of women in some way, though often very differently than it affects the lives of men of the same class or social group. This scholarship has called into question many basic historical categories and paradigms–class, modernity, capitalism, and even how historical periods are divided and designated. It has also become increasingly self-critical, putting greater emphasis on differences among women.

Building on studies of women, some historians during the 1980s shifted their focus somewhat to ask questions about gender itself, that is, about how past societies fashioned their notions of what it means to be male or female. They distinguished between sex–physical or biological differences between men and women–and gender–socially constructed differences–noting, as the anthropologist Gayle Rubin put it, "far from being an expression of natural differences, exclusive gender identity is the suppression of natural similarities." Historians studying gender often used and continue to use theories and methodology drawn from sociology, anthropology, and literary studies, and emphasize that gender structures are often contradictory, unstable, and frequently changing. This instability, combined with an emphasis on differences among women, has led a few historians to assert that there really is no category "woman" whose meaning is self-evident and unchanging over time. They note that what are usually described as the "biological" differences between men and women are themselves influenced by ideas about gender, with a single gender polarity (man/woman) so strong in western culture that individuals born with ambiguous genitalia are generally simply assigned to one category or another. In this view, gender determines sex rather than the other way around, or better said, there is no such thing as true sex difference, only gender difference. Most scholars do not go quite this far, though they recognize that the boundaries between what is understood as "biological" sex and what is "cultural" gender are not always clear.

The study of gender has not completely replaced the study of women, because we still have much more basic information about the lives of men than the lives of women, but it has resulted in new types of questions about the lives of men and relations between the sexes. Historians attuned to gender now study the construction of masculinity and men's experiences in history *as men,* rather than simply as "the history of man" without noticing that their subjects were men.

Along with a focus on the gendered nature of both women's and men's experiences, some historians have turned their attention more fully during the last decade to the history of sexuality. Just as interest in women's history has been part of feminist political movements, interest in the history of sexuality has been part of the gay liberation movement that began in the 1970s. The gay liberation movement encouraged the study of homosexuality in the past and present and the development of gay and lesbian studies programs, and also made both public and academic discussions of sexual matters more acceptable. Historians have attempted to trace the history of men's and women's sexual experiences–both homosexual and heterosexual–in the past, and, as in women's history, to find new sources that will allow fuller understanding. The history of sexuality has contributed to a new interest in the history of the body, with historians investigating how cultural understandings of the body shaped people's experiences of their own bodies and also studying the ways in which religious, medical, and political authorities exerted control over those bodies. This in turn has often led back to a focus on women, as female sexuality and the female body have generally been of greater concern to authorities than male sexuality.

Studies of gender, sexuality, and the body have been important parts of a more general trend in historical scholarship since the 1980s, often labeled the "linguistic turn" or the New Cultural History. Under the influence of literary and linguistic theory–often loosely termed "deconstruction" or "post-structuralism"–some historians focus their attention explicitly on the words and visual images of the past rather than on events, individuals, or groups. They study representation and meaning, with the most radical proponents of this approach arguing that these are all we can ever know; because all historical sources are produced by individuals with particular interests and biases, we can never know what actually happened and should simply analyze the sources as texts. "Reality," in this point of view, cannot be understood apart from the language in which it is expressed; for example, because women in the past perceived and described their bodies differently than do women today, those bodies really *were* different. Most historians do not take such an extreme approach, but instead treat their sources as referring to something beyond the sources themselves–an author, an event, a physical body–while recognizing that they do not present a perfect reflection. They do tend to use a wider range of literary and artistic sources than they did in earlier decades, and the boundaries between history, literature, and art history are becoming less sharp or disappearing altogether in the interdisciplinary field of Cultural Studies.

Whether social or cultural, research on women and gender has changed the way we approach and interpret nearly every historical development, including many of those of the early modern period (roughly

1500–1750). European history during those 250 years has traditionally been defined as a series of intellectual movements–the spread of Renaissance culture beyond Italy, the Protestant and Catholic Reformations, the Scientific Revolution–either viewed independently or placed within a political and economic context. The rise of the nation-state, both absolutist and constitutionalist, is generally viewed as the most important political development, and the growth of pre-industrial capitalism the most important economic change. Social historians have stressed the themes of growing geographic mobility, disparity between rich and poor, and social unrest.

Women's history of the early modern period, as of most periods, began by asking what women contributed to each of these developments, in a search for what Natalie Davis has termed "women worthies." Who were the great women artists/musicians/scientists/rulers? How did women's work serve capitalist expansion? What was women's role in political movements such as the English Civil War or other seventeenth-century revolts? Along with this, historians investigated what effects the developments of the early modern period had on women, a line of questioning that has resulted in the rethinking of several major historical issues. Joan Kelly, for example, began with a simple question, "Did women have a Renaissance?" Her answer of "No, at least not during the Renaissance" has led not only to more than two decades of intensive historical and literary research, as people have attempted to confirm, refute, modify, or nuance her answer, but has also contributed to the broader questioning of the whole notion of historical periodization. If a particular development had little, or indeed a negative, effect on women, can we still call a period a "golden age," a "Renaissance," or an "Enlightenment"? Can we continue to view the seventeenth century, during which hundreds or perhaps thousands of women were burned as witches on the European continent, as the period of "the spread of rational thought"?

Kelly's questioning of the term "Renaissance" has been joined more recently by a questioning of the term "early modern." Both historians and literary scholars note that there are problems with this term, as it assumes that there is something that can unambiguously be called "modernity," which is usually set against "traditional" and linked with contemporary western society. (Whether "modernity" is seen as a good thing or a bad thing depends on the commentator's view of contemporary society.) The break between "medieval" and "early modern" is generally set at 1500, roughly the time of the voyages of Columbus and the Protestant Reformation, but recently many historians argue that there are more continuities across this line than changes. Some have moved the decisive break earlier–to the Black Death in 1347 or even to the twelfth century–or have rejected the notion of periodization altogether. Women's historians, most prominently Judith Bennett, have been among those questioning the validity of the medieval/modern divide, challenging, in Bennett's words, "the assumption of a dramatic change in women's lives between 1300 and 1700" and asserting that historians must pay more attention to continuities along with changes. Most historians–myself included–continue to use the terms "medieval" and "early modern," however, though we are more conscious about our decision, and use them more as shorthand for certain periods than as value labels. There is also more scholarship that bridges 1500, but as yet there is no handy label to describe this period.

Both the original lines of questioning in women's history for this period–women's role in general historical developments, and the effects of these developments on women–continue, particularly for parts of Europe or groups of women about which we have as yet very little information: eastern Europe, Jewish women, peasant women in most parts of Europe, women's religious communities. They have been augmented more recently by quite different types of questions, as historians have realized the limitations of simply trying to fit women into historical developments largely derived from the male experience (an approach rather sarcastically described as "add women and stir"). Such questions often center on women's physical experiences–menstruation, pregnancy, motherhood–and the ways in which women gave meaning to these experiences, and on private or domestic matters, such as friendship networks, family devotional practices, or unpaid household labor. Because so little of this was documented in public sources during the early modern period, this research has required a great amount of archival digging and the use of literary and artistic sources.

This emphasis on women's private and domestic experiences has been challenged by some historians, who warn of the dangers of equating women's history with the history of the family or of accepting without comment a division between public and private in which women are relegated to the private sphere. They see a primary task of early modern historians as the investigation of how divisions between what was considered "public" and what was considered "private" were developed and contested. Some scholars hold that this period is one of the exclusion of women from many areas of public life and power at the very time larger groups of men were given access, though others emphasize that this exclusion was more theoretical than real. Linked to issues of public/private are questions about the symbolic role of gender, that is, how qualities judged masculine and feminine are differently valued and then used in discussions that do not explicitly relate to men and women, but that still reinforce women's secondary status. For example, Martin Luther's labeling of the pope as the "Whore of Babylon" has previously been viewed as an expression of his negative attitude about the papacy, and James I of England's description of himself as the "father of his country" as an expression of his ideas about his power vis-à-vis his subjects. These phrases are now also recognized as expressions of attitudes about women and gender relations, for the fact that both men use gendered language was not accidental. These investigations of the real and symbolic relations between gender and power have usually not been based on new types of sources, but have approached some of the most traditional types of historical sources–political treatises, public speeches by monarchs, state documents–with new questions.

All of these studies, and the ever-expanding amount of ongoing research, have resulted in four somewhat conflicting conclusions, each of which reinforces the need for still more research of all types. The first is that the historical experience of early modern women was much less uniform than we realized several decades ago. Women's experience differed according to categories that we had already set out based on male experience–social class, geographic location, rural or urban setting–but also categories that had previously not been taken into account–marital status, health, number of children. Historians are thus much less comfortable talking about the "status of women" in general without sharply qualifying exactly what type of women, or in what type of sources; we can make conclusions about, for example, the legal status of women in theoretical treatises, or the role of widows in a particular craft guild, but statements about the status of women rising or falling are too vague to have any meaning.

A second and related conclusion is that the role of gender in determining the historical experiences of men and women varied over time, and from group to group. For some people, such as the very poor, social class was probably more important than gender, though this "equality of misery" was certainly not much consolation to the women experiencing it. For the nobility and urban bourgeoisie, however, the early modern period appears to have been a time when, in the words of Rosemary Radford Ruether, "the perception of women as marginalized by gender became stronger than the perception of women as divided by class." How much this perception reflected reality and how it shaped reality are now being investigated for many areas of Europe.

A third conclusion is that almost every question that has been asked and is being asked about the female experience must also be asked about the male. The new scholarship on masculinity described above demonstrates that gender roles were just as prescribed for men as they were for women, and history which ignores the effects of "private" factors such as marital status, sexuality, and friendships in men's lives is incomplete. This new "men's history" is only in its infancy, and has been criticized both by traditional historians who see it as trivializing "great men and their ideas" and by some women's historians who view it as simply a way to refocus historical concern back where it has always been, on men.

Despite the criticism, studying men as men does seem a necessary outgrowth of the fourth conclusion, however, that, in the words of Joan Scott, "gender is a primary way of signifying relationships of power" and that people's notions of gender shaped not only the way they thought about men and women, but about their society in general. These ideas in turn affected the way they acted, but explicit and symbolic ideas of gender could also conflict with the way men and women chose or were forced to operate in the world. Thus the status of women *and* men was at once more varied and more shaped by their gender than most historians would have concluded thirty years ago.

I have attempted in this study to keep these conclusions in mind while providing an overview of what we have discovered about women's lives and the role of gender in early modern European society. The book begins with an introduction which examines ideas about women, and the laws that resulted from the notions of proper gender roles held by the dominant group in early modern society–educated men. This does not imply that women's experience was completely determined by intellectual and legal constructs, as the rest of the book will make clear, but simply the fact that male intellectual structures and institutions formed the most important frameworks for thought and action in early modern society. It also reflects the way the field of women's history has developed, because many of the early studies of women actually discussed male opinions and views, though sometimes the authors did not explicitly recognize this.

The main body of the book is divided into three sections which correspond to the three parts of the self traditional in Western philosophy–body, mind, and spirit. This tripartite division is particularly appropriate when studying women, who were often regarded as dominated by one part to the exclusion of the other two: married women and prostitutes by their bodies; learned women and artists by their minds; nuns and witches by their spirits. Perhaps because of this, early modern women who reflected on the condition of women in general such as Rachel Speght, the seventeenth-century English poet quoted above, emphasized that men were not the only ones with complex and multi-faceted selves.

Each of the three sections has two chapters: the section on the body a chapter on sexuality and the female life-cycle and one on women's economic role; that on the mind a chapter on literacy and learning and one on women and the production of culture; that on the spirit a chapter on religion and spirituality and one on witchcraft. The book ends with a single chapter on gender and power, which examines the public political roles of women, the relations between ideas about femininity, masculinity and social order, and the symbolic role of gender. This not only takes in the newest scholarly trends, but also stresses that a consciousness of gender as a social, rather than natural, construct, was already evident in some early modern thinkers. In the quotation above, for example, the French philosopher Marie Jars de Gourney succinctly and humorously states the insight of modern anthropologists and historians that gender identification involves the suppression of similiarities.

I hope that this book will not only provide you with information about the lives of early modern European women and men, but will also allow you to discover how a historical field develops and lines of inquiry connect and influence each other, how old assumptions are revised, and how totally new areas become accepted topics for historical inquiry. This field is growing very quickly in both descriptive studies and analytical interpretations, so quickly that the bibliographies in the first edition were already out of date when the book was published. For this second edition, I have updated every bibliography, and have made changes in each of the chapters. These changes vary from minor to substantive, for research in some areas, such as sexuality and masculinity, has been extensive, whereas other areas, such as education and work, have seen fewer new studies. Like the first edition, this is certainly not the final word, but an introduction and progress report.

Bibliography

There are several theoretical studies that underlie much of contemporary women's and gender history. The most important of these include: Joan Scott, "Gender: a useful category of historical analysis," *American Historical Review,* 91/5 (1986), 1053–75, which calls for a broadening of all history to include gender implications; several of the essays in Joan Kelly, *Women, History, and Theory* (Chicago, University of Chicago, 1984) which focus particularly on the relationship between class and gender and on women's experience in the Renaissance; several of the essays in Michelle Zimbalist Rosaldo and Louise Lamphere (eds.), *Women, Culture and Society* (Stanford, Stanford University Press, 1975) which discuss the issue of the public/private dichotomy; Gayle Rubin, "The traffic in women: notes on the 'political economy' of sex," in R. R. Reiter (ed.), *Toward an Anthropology of Women* (New York, Monthly Review Press, 1975), pp. 157–210, in which she proposes the idea of a "sex/gender" system of dominance and exchange; Rosemary Radford Ruether, *Sexism and God-Talk* (Boston, Beacon, 1983), which discusses historical and contemporary sexism in theological language.

Natalie Davis's survey of the writing of European women's history and suggestions for future research directions is still useful and provocative: "'Women's history' in transition: the European case," *Feminist Studies*, 3 (Winter 1975/76), 83–103. Gisela Bock's more recent discussion continues this and includes debates about the nature of gender: "Women's history and gender history: aspects of an international debate," *Gender and History*, 1 (Spring 1989), 7–30. For an excellent survey of trends in women's history around the world, see: Karen Offen, Ruth Roach Pierson, and Jane Rendell (eds.), *Writing Women's History: International Perspectives* (Bloomington, Indiana University Press, 1990). For analyses of recent theoretical developments, see Judith M. Bennett, "Feminism and history," *Gender and History* 1 (1989), 251–72; Sonya Rose, et al, "Gender history/women's history: is feminist scholarship losing its critical edge?" *Journal of Women's History* 5 (1993), 89–128; Mary Maynard, "Beyond the 'Big Three': the development of feminist theory into the 1990s," *Women's History Review* 4 (1995), 259–81. Sylvia Schafer and Merry E. Wiesner, *Women in the Curriculum: European History–Discipline Analysis* (Baltimore, National Center for Curriculum Transformation Resources on Women, 1997) provides both analysis and bibliography of developments in European women's history, primarily since 1990.

For debates about periodization, see Joan Kelly, "Did women have a Renaissance?" in her *Women, History, and Theory* noted above; Judith Bennett, "Medieval women, modern women: across the great divide," in Ann-Louise Shapiro (ed), *Feminists Revision History* (New Brunswick, Rutgers University Press, 1994) pp. 47–72 and "Confronting continuity," *Journal of Women's History* 9 (1997), 73–95 (with responses by Sandra E. Greene, Karen Offen, and Gerda Lerner); Gianna Pomata, "History, particular and universal: on reading some recent women's history textbooks," *Feminist Studies* 19 (1993), 7–50; Amanda Vickery, "Golden age to separate spheres? A review of the categories and chronology of English women's history," *The Historical Journal* (36/2) (1993), 383–414.

There are many collections of articles and surveys that discuss the history of women in Europe over a broad time period if you wish to gain a wider perspective. These include: Renate Bridenthal, Susan Mosher Stuard, and Merry E. Wiesner (eds.), *Becoming Visible: Women in European History*, 3rd ed. (Boston, Houghton Mifflin, 1998); Marilyn J. Boxer and Jean H. Quataert (eds.), *Connecting Spheres: Women in the Western World, 1500 to the Present*, 2nd ed. (New York, Oxford University Press, 1999); Bonnie S. Anderson and Judith P. Zinsser, *A History of Their Own: Women in Europe from Prehistory to the Present*, 2 vols., 2nd ed. (New York, Oxford University Press, 1999). Those that focus on a single country include: Lynn Abrams and Elizabeth Harvey (eds.), *Gender Relations in German History: Power, Agency and Experience from the Sixteenth to the Twentieth Century* (London: University College London Press, 1996); Natalia Pushkareva, *Women in Russian History: From the Tenth to the Twentieth Century*, trans. Eve Levin (Armonk, N.Y., M. E. Sharpe, 1997). For a collection of sources on European women, see Lisa DiCaprio and Merry E. Wiesner, *Lives and Voices: Sources on European Women* (Boston, Houghton Mifflin, 2000).

There are several surveys of women's lives in early modern Europe besides this one. Margaret King, *Women of the Renaissance* (Chicago, University of Chicago Press, 1991) and Olwen Hufton, *The Prospect Before Her: A History of Women in Western Europe* (London, HarperCollins, 1995) focus on most of western Europe. General studies with a specific national focus include: (for Spain) Ann M. Pescatello, *Power and Pawn: The Female in Iberian Families, Societies and Cultures* (Westport, Conn., Greenwood, 1976); (for England) Anne Laurence, *Women in England 1500–1760: A Social History* (New York, St. Martin's, 1994); Sara Mendelson and Patricia Crawford, *Women in Early Modern England 1550–1720* (New York, Oxford University Press, 1998); Jacqueline Eales, *Women in Early Modern England, 1500–1700* (London, UCL Press, 1998); Amanda Vickery, *The Gentleman's Daughter: Women's Lives in Georgian England* (New Haven, Yale University Press, 1998); (for Germany) Heide Wunder, *He Is the Sun, She Is the Moon: Women in Early Modern Germany*, trans. Thomas Dunlap (Cambridge, Harvard University Press, 1998); (for France) Wendy Gibson, *Women in Seventeenth-century France* (New York, St. Martin's, 1989); (for the Netherlands) Rudolf Michel Dekker, "Getting to the source: women in the medieval and early modern Netherlands," *Journal of Women's History* 10 (1998), 165–88. Natalie Zemon Davis analyzes the lives of three seventeenth-century women in *Women on the Margins: Three Seventeenth Century Lives* (Cambridge, Mass., Harvard University Press, 1995).

Two collections of sources for this period are: Kate Aughterson (ed.), *Renaissance Women: A Sourcebook: The Construction of Femininity in England 1520–1680* (London, Routledge, 1995); Monica Chojnacka and Merry E. Wiesner (eds.), *Ages of Woman, Ages of Man: Sources on European Social History 1350–1750* (London, Longman, forthcoming).

Collections of articles that focus solely or largely on the early modern period include: Mary Beth Rose (ed.), *Women in the Middle Ages and the Renaissance: Literary and Historical Perspectives* (Syracuse, N. Y., Syracuse University Press, 1986); Margaret Ferguson, Maureen Quilligan, and Nancy Vickers (eds.), *Rewriting the Renaissance: The Discourses of Sexual Difference in Early Modern Europe* (Chicago, University of Chicago, 1986); Mary Prior (ed.), *Women in English Society, 1500–1800* (London, Methuen, 1985); Jean R. Brink, Allison P. Coudert, and Maryanne C. Horowitz (eds.), *The Politics of Gender in Early Modern Europe*, Sixteenth Century Essays and Studies, 12 (Kirksville, MO., Sixteenth Century Journal Publishers, 1989); Marilyn Migiel and Juliana Schiesari (eds.), *Refiguring Woman: Perspectives on Gender and the Italian Renaissance* (Ithaca, Cornell University Press, 1991); Margaret MacCurtain and Mary O'Dowd (eds.), *Women in Early Modern Ireland 1500–1800* (Edinburgh, Edinburgh University Press, 1991); Natalie Zemon Davis and Arlette Farge (eds.), *A History of Women in the West. Vol. III: Renaissance and Enlightenment Paradoxes* (Cambridge, Mass., Harvard University Press, 1993); Jean R. Brink (ed.), *Privileging Gender in Early Modern England* (Kirksville, MO., Sixteenth Century Journal Publishers, 1993); Alain Saint-Saëns (ed.), *Religion, Body, and Gender in Early Modern Spain* (San Francisco, Edwin Mellen Press, 1991) and *Sex and Love in Golden Age Spain* (New Orleans, University Press of the South,

1996); Els Kloek, Nicole Teeuwen, and Marijke Huisman (eds.), *Women of the Golden Age: An International Debate on Women in Seventeenth-century Holland, England and Italy* (Hilversum, Verloren, 1994); Samuel H. Cohn, Jr., *Women in the Streets: Essays On Sex and Power in Renaissance Italy* (Baltimore, The Johns Hopkins University Press, 1996); Magdalena S. Sanchez and Alain Saint-Saëns (eds.), *Spanish Women in the Golden Age: Images and Realities* (Westport, Conn., Greenwood Press, 1996); Betty Travitsky and Adelle F. Seeff (eds.), *Attending to Women in Early Modern England* (Newark, University of Delaware, 1994); Lynne Tatlock and Christina Bohnert (eds.), *The Graph of Sex and the German Text: Gendered Culture in Early Modern Germany,* Chloe: Beiheft zum Daphnis, Vol. 19 (Amsterdam and Atlanta, Rodolpi, 1994); Valerie Traub, et al. (eds.), *Feminist Readings of Early Modern Culture: Emerging Subjects* (Cambridge, Cambridge University Press, 1996); Merry E. Wiesner, *Gender, Church and State in Early Modern Germany* (London, Longman, 1998); Hannah Barker and Elaine Chalus (eds.), *Gender in Eighteenth Century England: Roles, Representations, and Responsibilities* (London, Longman, 1998); Judith C. Brown and Robert C. Davis (eds.), *Gender and Society in Renaissance Italy* (London, Longman, 1998); Susan D. Amussen and Adele Seeff (eds.), *Attending to Women in Early Modern Europe* (Newark, University of Delaware Press, 1998); Susan Frye and Karen Robertson (eds.), *Maids and Mistresses, Cousins and Queens: Women's Alliances in Early Modern England* (New York, Oxford University Press, 1999); Lorna Hutson (ed.), *Feminism and Renaissance Studies.* Oxford Readings in Feminism (Oxford, Oxford University Press, 1999); Special issue of the *Sixteenth Century Journal* on gender in early modern Europe, 31/1 (2000). The bibliographies that follow each chapter will also refer you to additional collections of articles that have more specialized themes.

In addition to printed works, there are now many web sites and internet resources available to assist further research. Web sites are often ephemeral, but one that has strong institutional backing at this point is the Medieval Feminist Index at Haverford College, accessed through their home page at www.haverford.edu. Several e-mail discussion lists are:

H-Women (for women's history in general)
H-Frauen (for early modern women's history)
   (for both of these, subscribe through listserv@uicvm.uic.edu)
EMW-L (for work on early modern women in all disciplines)
   (subscribe through emw-l@umdd.umd.edu)
MedFem (for medieval women in all disciplines)
   (subscribe through medfem-l@u.washington.edu)

1 Ideas and laws regarding women

A woman, properly speaking, is not a human being.
> Jacques Cujas, *Observationes et emendationes*, 6.21 in *Opera omnia* (Lyons, 1606), 4, 1484.

Women then being the last of creatures, the end, complement and consummation of all the works of God, what Ignorance is there so stupid, or what Impudence can there be so effronted, as to deny her a Prerogative above all other Creatures, without whom the World itself had been imperfect.
> Cornelius Agrippa von Nettesheim, *De nobilitate et praecellentia sexus foeminei* (1529) in *Opera* (2 vols. Lyon, 1600? reprint Hildesheim: Olms, 1970), vol. 2; 533.

Women are created for no other purpose than to serve men and be their helpers. If women grow weary or even die while bearing children, that doesn't harm anything. Let them bear children to death; they are created for that.
> Martin Luther, *Sämmtliche Werke* (Erlangen and Frankfurt, 1826–57), vol. 20; 84.

There is nothing better on earth than a woman's love.
> Martin Luther, *Sämmtliche Werke* (Erlangen and Frankfurt, 1826–57), vol. 61; 212.

Ideas about women, particularly those of educated men, are in many ways the easiest thing to investigate when analyzing the experience of women in any culture. Educated men have been thinking and writing about women since the beginning of recorded history, trying to determine what makes them different from men and creating ideals for female behavior and appearance. Their ideas emerge in works of all types – religious literature, scientific treatises, plays, poetry, philosophical discussions – which have been preserved and read by subsequent generations. This not only makes them the most accessible source regarding women for modern historians, but also means that these ideas influenced all later periods. The works that contain them, especially religious, scientific, and philosophical writings, came to be considered authoritative and unquestionable, so that the ideas of educated men spread to the vast majority of women and men who could not record their own ideas, and served as the basis for law codes that attempted to regulate behavior. In fact, these ideas and opinions were often no longer recognized as such, but were regarded as religious truth or scientific fact, particularly when the laws that resulted from them led women to act in ways that conformed with male notions.

Before we explore the reality of women's lives in the early modern period, then, we must survey commonly held notions about women, many of which were inherited from classical and medieval writers, and from Jewish and Christian religious thinkers. Though they disagreed about many other things, the vast majority of religious and secular writers before 1500 regarded women as clearly inferior to men, and provided subsequent generations with countless examples of women's negative qualities. The fact that so many revered authorities agreed about "woman's nature" indicated to most people that they must be right. Only a few individuals recognized that the largely negative view of women in western culture resulted from the fact that almost all written records came from male authors and that a very different picture might have emerged had women also left records of their thoughts. Chaucer's fictional character, the Wife of Bath, states this clearly in the *Canterbury Tales:*

> My God, had women written histories
> Like cloistered scholars in oratories
> They'd have set down more of men's wickedness
> Than all the sons of Adam could redress.[1]

Her insight was not widely shared.

Ideas changed somewhat from 1500 to 1750 with the intellectual changes of the Renaissance, the religious reformations of the sixteenth century, and the development of science in the seventeenth century, when authorities of all types began to be questioned. Dissident voices, both female and male, expressing a more positive view of women began to be a bit louder, but negative views of women were also voiced more loudly, now based on new types of authority such as the natural sciences or comparisons of legal systems rather than on the views of Aristotle or the Bible. As we shall see, many of the legal changes of the period actually restricted, rather than increased, the ability of women to act independently.

---

[1] Chaucer, *Canterbury Tales,* trans. David Wright (London, Oxford University Press, 1985), p. 236.

Inherited traditions

Christianity was the most important source of ideas about women for early modern Europeans, and Christianity had, in turn, inherited many of its ideas from Judaism. There are two somewhat conflicting accounts of creation in Genesis, the first book of both Hebrew Scripture and the Christian Bible. In the first, God creates women and men at the same time, and in the second, a woman, Eve, is created out of the rib of the first man, Adam, after God decides Adam needs a mate. This account is the one that comes to be retold and portrayed visually much more often, so that medieval and early modern Europeans were much more familiar with it. It is also the one that goes on to describe the first human sin, in which Eve is tempted by a serpent to disobey God in order to gain knowledge, and then tempts Adam; their disobedience gets them expelled from the Garden of Eden and comes to be described in Christian doctrine as the "fall of man" or "the original sin." Most later Jewish and Christian commentators thus chose to view Eve, and by extension all women, as the source of evil and sin in the world, though there were also a few who held Adam equally responsible, and a very few who viewed him as *more* responsible because he was a man and should have been better able to withstand the temptation. (Their reasoning thus also expresses negative opinions of the relative merits of men and women.)

Jewish traditions and commentaries contained in Hebrew Scripture and later works continued to view women in a largely negative light. Women were totally excluded from the priesthood and from many religious duties, and were regarded as ritually impure for about half of each month because of menstruation. They were also viewed as unclean after giving birth, for forty days after the birth of a boy and eighty after the birth of a girl. They were responsible for some religious rituals within the household, but other parts of domestic religious life were carried out by men, so that no aspect of religious life was strictly female. The authors of Hebrew Scripture had a clear idea of the ideal woman; she was the mother of many children, up working before sunrise to provide food and clothing for her household, making no objections when her husband brought home concubines or a second wife, totally obedient and deferential. She was not passive, for Hebrew Scripture recounts the exploits of many women who carried out heroic actions to defend their households or Israelite society, but when the emergency had passed these women, such as Judith or Jael, returned willingly to their quiet domestic lives. It is perhaps no wonder that by the first century A.D. Jewish men included a special thank-you to God "who has not made me a woman" in their regular morning prayers. Along with Eve, Hebrew Scripture also describes other women whose actions helped create a negative stereotype for women: Delilah, whose sexuality could tempt even the strongest man; Rebekah, whose love for one of her sons led her to deceive her husband; Lot's wife (her name is not recorded) who was changed into a pillar of salt for disobeying God and her husband.

Christian ideas about women built on both the positive and the negative in Jewish tradition. Jesus himself spoke frequently to women and included them in his followers, sometimes to the embarrassment of his male associates. He preached that men and women were equally capable of achieving life after death, and that women as well as men should not let their domestic responsibilities come before their spiritual well-being. Many of his parables use women as positive examples, or relate things that would have more meaning for women, leading some contemporary scholars to view Jesus as a feminist. The untraditional nature of Jesus' ideas was quickly downplayed by many of his followers shortly after his death, however. The role of the twelve disciples, all of whom were male, was stressed in the books which became the Christian New Testament, and the role of his female followers, such as Mary Magdalene, was downplayed. Paul, whose letters form about half of the books of the New Testament and who in many ways transformed Jesus' teachings into a systematic set of beliefs, had a more ambivalent view about women's place; at one point he notes that there should be no distinction on account of gender in the Christian community, but says elsewhere that women should be silent in churches, though this latter statement is now held to have been written by another author and simply attributed to Paul.

Christianity gained followers very quickly, and as there was no central authority in the first centuries, an enormous range of ideas and practices developed. Women were very active in the early church. Some acted as missionaries or carried out priestly functions such as baptism. While most converts married, some rejected marriage in order to live a life not bound by domestic concerns and to devote themselves to contemplation or to the charity which was an important aspect of Christianity from the beginning. A few men and women decided to blend marriage and virginity, living in what were termed "chaste" or "spiritual" marriages in which the spouses either rejected sexual activity from the start or else renounced it sometime during the course of the marriage.

Many of these experiments were eventually rejected by church leaders as they attempted to make Christian teachings appear less threatening to Roman authorities, in order to gain still more followers and lessen the amount of persecution. Women were gradually excluded from church offices and priestly functions as the church became more hierarchical, using as its model Roman political structures which also excluded women from positions of authority. Chaste marriage was officially rejected, though popular accounts of saints continued to include such marriages. Virginity was accepted, however, and gradually came to be considered spiritually superior to marriage. Praise of virginity was often combined with denigration of women in the writings of the learned men whose ideas were most influential in the subsequent development of Christianity, however. These men, subsequently termed the Church Fathers, wrote harshly against women both to combat their own sexual urges and to restrict women's independent activities within the church. The second-century Church Father Tertullian, for example, linked all women with Eve, writing to women: "*You* are the Devil's gateway. *You* are the first deserter of the divine Law... *You* destroyed so easily God's image, man. On account of *your* desert, that is death, even the Son of God had to die."[2] He praised women who chose a life of virginity, but emphasized their dependence by terming them "brides of Christ" rather than the more active "virgins in the service of Christ" they chose to call themselves.

The most important early Christian philosopher, St. Augustine (354–430), asserted that the initial decision by Adam and Eve had ended human free will for all time, and also created sexual desire; he saw as proof of this the fact that men cannot control the actions of their sexual organs by virtue of their will or reason alone. After Augustine, even sexuality within marriage was considered sinful by most church leaders, and both clergy and laymen were warned against the temptations of women more emphatically. Augustine also saw female subordination as intrinsic in God's original creation, for only men were fully created in the image of God and women were intellectually, physically, and morally inferior. Augustine's contemporary St. Jerome (ca. 347–419/20) largely agreed, although both he and his female patrons asserted that women could move up the spiritual hierarchy by choosing a life of virginity: "As long as woman is for birth and children, she is as different from man as body is from soul. But when she wishes to serve Christ more than the world, then she will cease to be a woman and will be called man."[3]

[2] Tertullian, *De Cultu Fem.* 1,1 quoted in Rosemary Radford Ruether, *Religion and Sexism: Images of Women in the Jewish and Christian Traditions* (New York, Simon and Schuster, 1974), p. 157.

[3] Saint Jerome, *Commentaries on the Letter to the Ephesians*, book 16, cited in Vern Bullough, *Sexual Variance in Society and History* (Chicago, University of Chicago Press, 1976), p. 365.

The Greek philosopher Aristotle was the most influential non-Christian source for ideas in many fields up to the seventeenth century, which had very unfortunate effects for women. To Aristotle, women were imperfect men, the result of something wrong with the conception that created them – their parents were too young or too old, or too diverse in age, or one of them was not healthy. Nature always aimed at perfection, and Aristotle termed anything less than perfect "monstrous"; a woman was thus "a deformity, but one which occurs in the ordinary course of nature."[4] Aristotle was not sure exactly why imperfect men were required in the natural scheme of things, but decided that it must be because they performed a function necessary for men, so that his fundamental question about women was "What are women *for*?" whereas about men it was "What *is* man?" Aristotle did view the household and women's role within it as important, but because he regarded women as fundamentally intellectually inferior, he saw their primary function as procreation, not companionship. The philosopher Plato agreed, for he viewed the best love and friendship as that between men, and commented in one of his dialogues that originally all humans had been male, but some had been reborn as women when they proved to be cowardly and wicked. In his most important work, the *Republic*, Plato does include women among the group of people who governed the rest, but because he also abolishes the family for this group, these are women who, like celibate women in early Christianity, have rejected or escaped the traditional female role and become more like men.

Beginning in the twelfth century, theologians and religious writers generally called scholastics attempted to bring together the teachings of Aristotle and those of early Christian writers, creating one grand philosophical system. Thomas Aquinas, the most brilliant and thorough of the scholastics, synthesized classical and Christian ideas about women, stating that women's inferiority was not simply the result of Eve's actions, but was inherent in her original creation. Even in procreation her role was minimal, for the mother provided simply the material substance in the child, while the father supplied the active force. (An idea Aquinas drew largely from Aristotle.) Women needed male assistance in everything because of their physical and intellectual weakness, though they did have souls and so were responsible for their own salvation. Several other scholastics held slightly less negative views – Peter Abelard held that sexuality was God-given and could not therefore be sinful and Hugh of St. Victor stressed the importance of spiritual comradeship in

---

4 Aristotle, *Generation of Animals*, trans. A. L. Peck, Loeb Classics (Cambridge, Mass., Harvard University Press, 1943), Book IV, vi, p. 460.

marriage – but even these men did not view women as in any way equal to men. The opinions of the scholastics were expressed not only in complex philosophical treatises, but were communicated more broadly through public sermons and through the university lectures they gave.

At about the same time as the growth of scholasticism, a new emphasis on the veneration of Mary developed in western Christianity. During its early centuries, Christianity had not stressed the role of Mary because it wanted to differentiate itself from pagan religions with female goddesses. By the twelfth century, all of Europe was more or less Christian, and many churches began to be built which were dedicated to Mary; poetry and hymns were also written in her honor. Mary's peculiar status as virgin and mother allowed her to be honored as both pure and nurturing at the same time, and she came to be viewed as the exact opposite of Eve, creating a good woman/bad woman dichotomy that would become extremely strong in European culture. The effects of the cult of Mary on the actual status of women, or even on attitudes toward women, are ambiguous, however. Because Christianity taught that there was and would be only one savior, Mary represented an unattainable ideal for all other women, for no other woman could hope to give birth to the Messiah. Yet Mary was also not divine, so that she set a standard for female behavior in a way that Jesus did not for men. Some of the men most devoted to Mary, such as Bernard of Clairvaux, were also the harshest in their condemnation of all other women. Nevertheless, Mary did provide a female focus for veneration, and though official theology always stressed her role as obedient helpmate, in popular worship she was often viewed as one member of the Trinity, one no less powerful than God or Jesus.

Secular literature of the high and late Middle Ages also reflects male opinions of women. Beginning in the twelfth century, poetry and songs no longer celebrated simply the great military deeds of warriors and fighters, but also their passion and respect for women. An enormous number of romances, poems, and songs were written about what has come to be termed "courtly love," in which a knight swears loyalty to a lady, does great deeds in her honor, sings her praises, and so wins her love. Courtly love literature created many of the romantic conventions that have been part of popular and learned romance since then – the hero might die on his quest, or the lovers be separated by boundaries of social class – and generally described women as pure and virtuous. It thus presented a more positive view of women than religious literature, and actual women were involved in its production both as patrons of poets and as troubador poets themselves. We should not overemphasize its impact, however, because it is unclear whether the conventions of chivalry actually changed male behavior toward women very much. Even within the songs and poems, women often play a very passive role; they bestow handkerchiefs, but do not roam the world in search of dragons or villains, a passivity that continues in most contemporary romance literature. By the end of the Middle Ages as well, many writers of courtly love literature, such as Andreas Capellanus, also wrote cynical satires mocking chivalric conventions and bitterly criticizing women as devious, domineering, and demanding. Their misogyny matches that of the harshest clerical writers. Similar views of women also dominate most of the popular literature of the late Middle Ages, such as folk tales and songs. Women were often the central figures in popular stories and songs, where they represented either the positive or negative female stereotype: a patient Griselda, who put up with everything her sadistic husband did to test her loyalty, including apparently killing her children, or a shrewish wife who could only be tamed by physical violence.

The Renaissance debate about women

Toward the end of the fourteenth century, several writers in Europe decided to answer misogynist attacks on women directly, beginning a debate about women's character and nature that would last throughout the early modern period. Around 1380, Giovanni Boccaccio compiled a long list of famous and praiseworthy women, *De mulieribus claris,* describing women from classical history who were exemplary for their loyalty, bravery, and morality. This was the first such list since the Roman writer Plutarch's *Mulierum virtues,* and served as the model for scores of similar treatises by writers from many countries over the next 300 years, who would often add women from the Bible, Christian history, and more contemporary figures to their lists. Boccaccio's work and those modeled on it appear at first glance to be unqualified tributes to women, but they are actually more ambiguous, for the highest praise they can bestow on a woman is that she is like a man. In Boccaccio's words: "What can we think except that it was an error of nature to give female sex to a body which had been endowed by God with a magnificent virile spirit?"[5]

Christine de Pizan, the first female author to enter this debate, was not content simply to list illustrious women, but explored the reasons behind women's secondary status. She wrote a series of works in defense of women, the most important of which was the *City of Ladies* (1405), in

---

[5] Boccaccio, *Concerning Famous Women,* trans. Guido Guarino (New Brunswick, N.J., Rutgers University Press, 1963), p. 87.

which she ponders the question about why misogynist ideas are so widely held. She attacks these ideas in a sophisticated way, noting that the authorities usually cited in attacks on women are not only all men, but disagree among themselves and with reason and logic, that the language of the attacks is open to interpretation, and that they are often based on men's projection of their own fears and weaknesses. Instead of using extraordinary female counter-examples to argue against women's inferiority, she admits that women *are* inferior in many things, but that this comes from their lack of education, economic dependence, and subordinate status. Because she explicitly discusses the historical misrepresentation of women and recognizes the social and economic bases of women's weakness, Christine is sometimes termed the "first feminist." Others have seen this label as misleading because Christine does not use her analysis to call for social change, as will the feminist thinkers of the seventeenth century whom we will discuss in the last chapter of this book. If we keep in mind the time in which she wrote, however, we can view her conclusion that women's oppression and suffering made them better able than men to live virtuous lives in imitation of Christ not simply as a resigned acceptance of the realities of male power, but also as a positive affirmation of women's spiritual superiority.

Christine's work was not printed in France during the early modern period (though an English translation appeared in 1521) and most of the later defenses of women follow more closely the pattern set by Boccaccio, whose work was printed and translated frequently. Juan Luis Vives, Desiderius Erasmus, and Thomas Elyot, three important humanists, all viewed women as spiritually equal, and argued for the education of at least upper-class girls. None of them thought this spiritual equality should translate into political equality or even total mutuality between spouses, however, and their views of the most important human virtues were highly gender-specific. Men received the greatest praise for courage, wisdom, and power, and women, including female rulers, for piety, modesty, and obedience.

Cornelius Agrippa of Nettesheim, a German humanist, provided the most exhaustive and frequently pirated list of illustrious women in his *De nobilitate et praecellentia foeminei sexus… declamatio* (1529), and argued not simply that women were equal to men, but that they were superior. As the quotation that opens this chapter indicates, he cites as proof of this their place as the final act of God's creation, and then goes on to list other factors drawn from theology and biology. Eve was superior to Adam because she alone was created in the Garden of Eden, and she was made out of bone (Adam's rib), which was a material superior to the clay out of which Adam was formed; only women produce milk which nourishes human life, and only they have a natural process which rids the body of poisons (menstruation); Adam, not Eve, was responsible for bringing sin into the world, for God's commandment not to eat of the Tree of Knowledge had been given to Adam before Eve was created; the greatest human woman, Mary, far surpassed the greatest human man, whom Agrippa judged to be John the Baptist. Agrippa uses these reasons to argue that women can and should hold public office, but later writers who repeat his ideas lessen their impact by couching them as part of effusive praise for the female rulers to whom they dedicated their works, so it is difficult to ascertain their sincerity; Agrippa himself had written *De nobilitate* twenty years before he published it, deciding to publish only when a female monarch to whom he could write an appropriate dedication, Margaret of Austria, began to rule.

A number of the authors of defenses of women, such as Edward Gosynhille, an English hack writer, and Gedaliah ibn Yahya, an Italian Jewish historian, also wrote attacks on women, or, like Baldassar Castiglione in *The Courtier,* included both sides of the argument in a single work, so that it is difficult to gauge their actual opinions. This has led some modern analysts to view the entire debate about women as a literary game, an issue used by male writers and intellectuals to show off their rhetorical skills and classical or biblical knowledge but which did not reflect their actual opinions of women. The most extreme statements of female inferiority, such as the argument that women were not human beings which opens this chapter – made both in an explanation of the law of homicide written by Jacques Cujas, a French jurist, and in a theological treatise probably written by Valens Acidalius, a German scholar and physician – are judged to be so outrageous that their authors could have only meant them as satirical jokes.

Many of the attacks and defenses did use satire, and many of them were motivated by hopes of personal gain on the part of their authors, but this did not mean that the issue was simply an exercise for intellectuals. Beginning in the mid-sixteenth century, popular interest in the debate about women grew, leading to frequent translations and reprints of Latin works. Acidalius's treatise and some responses defending women were published as a pamphlet in German, Italian, and French, and Agrippa's longer work was translated into English, French, German, and Italian; both were reprinted for almost 200 years. Original vernacular works of all types also began to appear, particularly in England in the later sixteenth and seventeenth centuries. Edward Gosynhill probably wrote *The Schoolhouse of Women,* a humorous attack in rhyme in 1541, and *The Praise of All Women,* a sober defense, in the following year. Both of these provoked numerous satirical and serious answers for the rest of

1 Abraham Bach, *Recipe for Marital Bliss*, c. 1680. This woodcut was sold as a single sheet, to be read at home or hung on the wall. The qualitites on the part of the wife which merit a beating, according to the artist, are laziness, talkativeness, vanity, and lust for other men, and on the part of the husband drunkenness, laziness, and not supporting his family.

the century, the defenses usually catalogs of virtuous women based on Boccaccio and Agrippa and the attacks catalogs of women's vices; their main complaints included female pride, lasciviousness, obstinacy, desire for mastery, jealousy, talkativeness, vanity, greed, extravagence, infidelity, physical and moral inferority, and caprice.

In 1615 Joseph Swetnam published *The Arraignment of Lewd, Idle, Froward and Unconstant Women,* which was not very original in content, but very popular because of its humor and middle-class emphasis. This provoked three direct responses, all published under the name of female authors. Rachel Speght published *A Muzzle for Melastomus* (1617) under her own name, carefully refuting all of Swetnam's charges with biblical arguments and criticizing his grammar and logic. *Esther hath Hanged Human* (1617) appeared under the name Esther Sowernam (a clear play on Swetnam's name) and *The Worming of a Mad Dog* (1617) under the name Constantia Munda, both of which replied to Swetnam with invective and rational argument. Though the exact identity of these authors remains unknown, the spirit with which they wrote, the examples they use drawn from women's experience, the generalized nature of their attacks on men, and the fact that a male author would gain nothing from writing under a female pseudonym all argue for female authorship. Both attacks and defenses continued in England well into the eighteenth century, the latter frequently written by women, who became gradually more willing to publish their work under their own names.

In Italy, Laura Terracina, Moderata Fonte, and Lucrezia Marinella in the late sixteenth century all wrote vernacular defenses of women which directly refuted the works of misogynist writers; Marinella even pointed out the problems caused by the use of illustrious women as a disproof of female inferiority among many of the writers who considered themselves defenders of women. In France, Marie Jars de Gournay in *L'Egalité des hommes et des femmes* (1622) built on the arguments of Christine de Pizan to argue that the equality of men and women rested on divine law. Unfortunately, most of the other vernacular defenses of women by continental authors are not as sophisticated as these, and the serious and satirical attacks generally were republished more often and argued more forcefully. This was also the case with popular songs and stories that included examples of women's virtues and vices; misogynist sentiments find expression much more often than praises of women, and the praise of women that does appear is generally for qualities like obedience, piety, and submissiveness.

The debate about women also found visual expression in the early modern period, particularly in single-sheet prints which were hung in taverns or people's homes, again an indication that this was not simply a debate among intellectuals. Prints that juxtaposed female virtues and vices were very popular, with the virtuous women depicted as those of the classical or biblical past, and the vice-ridden dressed in contemporary clothes. The favorite metaphor for the virtuous wife was either the snail or the tortoise, both animals that never leave their "houses" and are totally silent, although such images were never as widespread as those depicting wives beating their husbands or hiding their lovers from them. Most of the prints, which people purchased to hang on their walls or were published as part of emblem books, portrayed the same negative stereotypes of women that the written attacks on women did; women are shown with their hands in men's purses, tempting men by displaying naked breasts, or neglecting their housework. Artists frequently portrayed misogynist stories involving classical figures, such as Socrates' wife Xantippe nagging him or Aristotle being so seduced by the beauty of Phyllis that he allowed her to ride him around a garden, so that these became part of popular culture as well as that of Europe's learned elite.

The debate about women's character and nature was not limited to pamphlets and prints which addressed it directly, but was also contained in works that considered larger topics, such as mystical writings or discussions of civil and natural law. Paracelsus, for example, a Swiss physician and alchemist, wrote that women had a special place in the cosmos because they bore children and were thus the end point of God's creative process; marriage was essential for both women and men because it was not simply a physical, but also a mystical union ordained by God. Mary, in his view, was more important than Christ as she was the heavenly wife of God, an idea taken up in the seventeenth century by German pietists. Legal scholars such as Jean Bodin included the standard list of female vices to prove that women were naturally inferior, and so should never be allowed to rule or hold public office: "Gynecocracy [rule by a woman] is squarely against the laws of nature that give men the strength, the prudence, the arms, and the power to command and take [these things] away from woman."[6] As we will see in Chapter 4, the debate about women also became part of the discussion of the merits of women's education, and, as we will see in Chapter 8, it was the springboard for considerations of gender, that is, considerations of what was distinctive about male as well as female experience. Writers of poetry, drama, and fiction also expressed their position in the debate through the female characters they created and the relationships between women and men they portrayed, but the best authors, such as Shakespeare, Milton, or Cervantes, recognized the complexity of the issue and so did

[6] Jean Bodin, *Six Books of a Commonweale* (London, 1606), p. 753.

not unambiguously support one side or another. The analysis of female characters and gender relations in the literature of the early modern period is an enormous, booming, and highly contentious field of literary criticism, and one best explored separately from our investigation of the lives of actual women.

Religious reformers of the sixteenth and seventeenth centuries

If the ideas about women expressed by writers of literature are a matter of debate among literary scholars, those held by religious thinkers in the early modern period are even more hotly disputed by contemporary scholars. One of the key reasons for this may be seen in the two quotations from Martin Luther which open the chapter. Many of the most important religious leaders of the period were not consistent, expressing strongly negative opinions of women at some points and very positive ones at others. Other leaders, such as John Calvin, expressed their view of women only obliquely while considering other issues, so that their opinions must be extrapolated and require a high degree of interpretation. Many contemporary scholars also have strong personal or religious convictions regarding certain religious leaders or the denominations they founded, so that it is sometimes difficult for them to accept the opinions they find. Despite the contradictions and ambiguities in the writings of religious thinkers, and the differences of opinion among modern scholars, however, there are some generalizations we can make about the impact of religious change on ideas about women.

Though they broke with the institutional structure and denounced many of the theological ideas of the Catholic Church, the Protestant reformers did not break sharply with the medieval scholastic theologians in their ideas about women. For Luther, Zwingli, Calvin, and the leaders of the English Puritans, women were created by God and could be saved through faith; spiritually women and men were equal. In every other respect, however, women were to be subordinate to men. Women's subjection was inherent in their very being and was present from creation – in this the reformers agreed with Aristotle and the classical tradition, though Luther in particular denounced the ideas of Aristotle on other matters and saw the scholastic attempt to reconcile Aristotle and the Bible as misguided. Most reformers accepted Eve's principle responsibility for the fall, and thought this had made women's original natural inferiority and subjection to male authority even more pronounced. The Protestants supported the Pauline teaching that women should be silent in church, though Calvin noted that this was determined by tradition and custom rather than divine commandment and so might be open to change; he did not see this change as happening in the foreseeable future or make any practical attempts to bring it about, however.

The Protestants did break with official Catholic teachings on the relative merits of celibacy and marriage, though some fifteenth-century writers had also thought that God had set up marriage and families as the best way to provide spiritual and moral discipline, so Protestant opinions were not completely new. Protestant writers championed marriage with greater vigor, however, and wrote large numbers of tracts trying to convince men and women to marry or advising spouses (particularly husbands) how best to run their households and families. It is in this pro-marriage literature that we find the most positive statements about women, for the writers recognized that many of their readers were former priests or monks who had been trained to regard marriage, sexuality, and women in general as destroyers of their spiritual well-being; Johannes Mathesius, for example, a Lutheran pastor, writes: "A man without a wife is only half a person and has only half a body and is a needy and miserable man who lacks help and assistance."[7] Many of the writers included lists of virtuous women drawn from Boccaccio or Agrippa, though, not surprisingly, they often included only those women who had been model wives. They use the story of Eve being created out of Adam's rib as proof that God wanted women to stand by the side of men as their assistants and not be trampled on or trod underfoot (for then Eve would have been created out of Adam's foot); these directives always mention as well, however, that women should never claim authority over men, for Eve had not been created out of Adam's head.

Protestant writers generally cite the same three purposes of marriage, in the same order of importance, that pre-Reformation writers did – the procreation of children, the avoidance of sin, and mutual help and companionship – though Calvin did view the last purpose as the most important. Some of them did interpret "mutual help and companionship" to have a romantic and sensual side, so there tends to be less of an antipathy toward sexuality (as long as it was within marriage) among Protestants than Catholics.

The ideal of mutuality in marriage was not an ideal of equality, however, and Protestant marriage manuals, household guides, and marriage sermons all stress the importance of husbandly authority and wifely obedience. This obedience, for almost all Protestants, was to take precedence over women's spiritual equality; a woman's religious convictions

---

[7] Johannes Mathesius, *Ehestand und Hauswesen* (Nuremberg, 1564), XIII, p. xx, ll. ii.

were never grounds for leaving or even openly disagreeing with her husband, though she could pray for his conversion. The only exceptions to this were some of the radical reformers, who did allow women to leave their unbelieving spouses, but the women who did so were expected to remarry quickly and thus come under the control of a male believer. Women were continually advised to be cheerful rather than grudging in their obedience, for in doing so they demonstrated their willingness to follow God's plan. Men were also given very specific advice about how to enforce their authority, which often included physical coercion; in both continental and English marriage manuals, the authors use the metaphor of breaking a horse for teaching a wife obedience. Though the opinions of women who read such works were not often recorded, we can tell somewhat from private letters that women knew they were expected to be obedient and silent, for they often excused their actions when they did not conform to the ideal. Such letters also indicate, however, that women's view of the ideal wife was one in which competence and companionship were as important as submissiveness.

The Protestant exhortation to marry was directed to both sexes, but particularly to women, for whom marriage and motherhood were a vocation as well as a living arrangement. Marriage was a woman's highest calling, even though it brought physical dangers and restraints on her freedom. Luther's words at the beginning of this chapter make this clear, as do those of the Tudor homily on marriage, which the crown required to be read out loud regularly in all English churches:

Truth it is, that they [women] must specially feel the griefs and pains of matrimony, in that they relinquish the liberty of their own rule, in the pain of their travailing [i.e., labor and delivery], in the bringing up of their own children, in which offices they be in great perils, and be grieved with many afflictions, which they might be without, if they lived out of matrimony.[8]

Despite their recognition of the disadvantages of marriage for women, however, most Protestants urged all women to marry, for they thought no woman had the special divine gift of freedom from sexual urges. Unmarried women were thus suspect, both because they were fighting their natural sex drive and because they were upsetting the divinely imposed order, which made woman subject to man. It is important to recognize, then, that the Protestant elevation of marriage is not the same as, and may in fact directly contradict, an elevation of women *as women*.

The opinions of Protestant leaders about marriage and women were not contained simply in written works, but were communicated to their

---

[8] Church of England, *The Two Books of Homilies* (Oxford, 1859), p. 505.

congregations through marriage sermons and homilies; because people in many parts of Europe were required to attend church, there was no way they could escape hearing them. Their opinions were also reflected in woodcuts and engravings which illustrated religious pamphlets, an important tool in the spread of Protestant ideas. The ideal woman appears frequently in both sermons and illustrations: sitting with her children, listening to a sermon or reading the Bible, dressed soberly and with her hair modestly covered. Negative depictions also appear: the nun who "parrots her psalter without understanding it... tortures her own body and creates her own cross, which God has not commanded";[9] the priest's concubine; prostitutes or women dressed extravagantly buying indulgences or expensive rosaries; disobedient wives being beaten by their husbands.

The Catholic response to the challenge of the Protestant reformers, usually termed the Catholic Reformation, included a response to the elevation of marriage. As with so many other issues, Catholic thinkers reaffirmed traditional doctrine and agreed that the most worthy type of Christian life was one both celibate and chaste. There was some disagreement about the relative importance of the three traditional purposes of marriage, with more liberal thinkers stressing the emotional bond between the couple more than procreation or the avoidance of sin, but in general there was a strong sense that all sexuality, including marital, was sinful and disruptive. The Catholic Church was much more vigorous in enforcing clerical celibacy after the middle of the sixteenth century, but accomplished this through stronger instilling of the virtues of celibacy in the seminaries and weeding out of unsuitable candidates for the priesthood rather than simply stressing the evils of women. Catholic leaders from the late sixteenth century on often recognized that women were useful allies in the fight to reconvert or hold areas to the Catholic faith, so did not openly express the type of harshly misogynist ideas that were common in early Christian thinkers or medieval theologians.

Catholic authors also realized that despite exhortations to celibacy, most women in Europe would marry, and so wrote marriage manuals to counteract those written by Protestants. The ideal wife they described was exactly the same as that proposed by Protestant authors – obedient, silent, pious – and their words give clear indication that they still regarded women as totally inferior. Fray Luis de Leon, for example, in the late-sixteenth century treatise *La perfecta casada (The Perfect Wife)*, comments:

[9] Georg Albrecht, *Der Hausstand* (Nuremberg, 1657), p. 1074.

When a woman succeeds in distinguishing herself in something praiseworthy, she wins a victory over any number of men who have given themselves over to the same endeavor. For so insignificant a thing as this which we call woman never undertakes or succeeds in carrying out anything essentially worthwhile unless she be drawn to it, and stimulated, and encouraged by some force of incredible resoluteness which either God, or some singular gift of God, has placed within her soul.[10]

Thus the opinions of learned Catholic authors about women, as well as marriage, tended to reaffirm traditional negative ideas, though the harshest criticisms were generally reserved for specific women who challenged male authority in some way rather than simply being addressed to women in general in the style of Tertullian or Jerome.

In Jewish opinion, like Protestant, all women should marry, and the qualities of the ideal wife had changed little since Old Testament times. According to Isaac ben Eliakim, the author of a Yiddish ethical manual written in the early seventeenth century and frequently reprinted, the ideal wife was thrifty, cheerful, obedient, never jealous, and always responsive to her husband's physical and emotional needs. Though this differs little from contemporary Christian opinion, the tone of the manual is a bit less dreary, commenting practically, "If you treat him like a king, then he, in turn, will treat you like a queen," rather than dwelling on obedience as a religious duty.[11]

The Scientific Revolution

As with religious reformers, most of the leading figures of the Scientific Revolution did not challenge inherited ideas about women, though they did dispute ancient and medieval authorities in many other fields. During the last half of the sixteenth century, female anatomy and physiology became a popular topic for medical authorities, who based their opinions somewhat on the recent actual anatomical experiments of Andreas Vesalius and Gabriele Fallopia, but more on the works of Aristotle, Hippocrates, and Galen which had just been reedited and reprinted, though the newest of these was 1,300 years old. The major dispute became one between Aristotelians and Galenists over the existence and function of female semen. Aristotelians generally held that women produce no semen or anything comparable, and so contribute nothing to the form,

---

[10] Luis de Leon, *The Perfect Wife*, trans. Alice Philena Hubbard (Denton, Tex., The College Press, 1943), p. 14.
[11] Reprinted in Jacob R. Marcus, ed., *The Jew in the Medieval World* (New York, Meridian, 1960, c. 1938), pp. 443–44.

intellect, or spirit of a fetus; their menstrual blood simply produces the matter out of which the fetus is formed. Galenists believed that women also produce semen which contributes to the form of the fetus, though they thought this was colder and less active than that of the male and that the father was still the more important parent. This female semen, in their opinion, also played a role in determining the sex of a child, while Aristotelians held that the father's semen alone determined this, though it was influenced by conditions at the time of intercourse; optimum conditions would always produce male offspring.

The Galenic view gradually gained more adherents, particularly as it made it much easier to explain why some children looked like their mothers, but some of Europe's leading scientists began to view the male semen as even more important than Aristotle had. William Harvey was in many ways a Galenist, for he thought that female humans, like chickens, produced eggs that did contribute materially to the child, but he thought the male sperm so powerful that it did not even need to touch this egg in order to fertilize it. He dissected large numbers of does just after coition and could see no sperm in their uteri, so determined that sperm could act at a distance, just like a magnet. Male semen not only fertilized the egg, but also "has such prodigious power of fecundation, that the whole woman both in mind and body undergoes a change."[12] Anton von Leeuwenhoek supported the Aristotelian position with what he viewed as physical evidence; using the newly developed microscope, he thought he could see preformed humans in sperm, and wrote that God had placed enough there to allow for the eternal perpetuation of the human species. He could see slight differences in them, which he attributed to sex, so maintained that the sperm alone determined the sex of the child. A few other scientists took an opposite preformationist position, arguing that humans are preformed in the female egg, rather than the male sperm. This "ovist" position was very threatening to the male scientific community, which reacted generally with ridicule, speculating on how many humans must have been within Eve's eggs to last until the end of time, particularly because each of these that was female had to contain all her future progeny ad infinitum. This is a problem in spermaticist preformationism too, of course, and contributed to the slow recognition that somehow both parents must be essential. The female ovum was not definitively identified until 1827, however, a remarkably late date considering its size relative to that of spermatazoa, which Leeuwenhoek had identified correctly in the 1670s.

---

[12] William Harvey, *Works*, trans. Robert Willis (London, Sydenham Society, 1847), p. 576

Though they disagreed about the mechanism of conception, Galenists and Aristotelians agreed about many other aspects of human anatomy and physiology. All believed in the existence of bodily humors, four fluids – blood, phlegm, black bile, and yellow bile – which were contained in the body. They viewed illness as caused by an imbalance in these humors, which was why the most common form of medical treatment was drawing blood, the only one of these humors for which the amount could be adjusted easily. (Black bile and yellow bile were never clearly identified, and the amount of phlegm the body produces is limited.) Though the humors were distinct, under certain conditions they could also transform themselves into a different humor, or into any other fluid that the body also produced, such as milk or semen. These humors were thought to correspond with the four elements – earth, air, fire, and water – and with the qualities of hot, cold, wet, and dry. These qualities varied from person to person, but were sex-related, with men generally believed to be hotter and drier and women colder and wetter.

Heat was viewed as the most positive of these qualities. It was the force within the body that could most easily change one kind of fluid into another, and it rose naturally toward the heavens and toward the brain, which explained why men, being hot and dry, were more rational and creative; women, being cold and wet, were more like the earth. Women's lack of heat was seen as the reason they menstruated (men "burned up" unneeded blood internally), did not go bald (men "burned up" their hair), and had wider hips and narrower shoulders (women did not have enough heat to drive matter toward their heads). Men's greater heat also meant they more often possessed qualities associated with heat – courage, honesty, reason, physical and moral strength. Early modern anatomists like Andreas Vesalius and William Harvey often quietly ignored the humoral theory because they could not discover any anatomical proofs of its existence, but still spoke about women's character and temperament being determined by their cold and moist nature. Not until the late eighteenth century would the idea of the psychological effects of the humors die out among learned Europeans, and not until the nineteenth did bloodletting completely lose favor as a medical procedure.

Galenists and Aristotelians thus agreed that men were superior, but Aristotelians tended to view human anatomy and physiology on a single scale, describing women as imperfect or misbegotten males, whose lack of body heat had kept their sex organs inside rather than pushing them out as they were in the more perfect male. Galenists generally viewed men and women as equally perfect in their sex, a view that became more common after 1600. They thus stressed that males and females complemented one another, and held that each sex desired the other mutually, whereas Aristotelians asserted that women desired men more because imperfect things always strive after perfection. The idea that women had a greater sexual drive than men did not die out in popular understanding with the triumph of Galenic ideas among learned writers, however, but remained constant until very late in the eighteenth century.

Another topic of great concern for scientists and medical writers was the nature and power of the uterus. Illness in women was very often attributed to the power of the uterus, particularly mental illnesses such as depression or irrational behavior; the word "hysteria" is, in fact, derived from the Greek word for uterus. Plato had proposed that the uterus was an independent animal that could smell and move on its own, an idea hotly debated in the sixteenth century; the ability to smell was generally rejected, but the notion of a "wandering womb" retained. Wombs were most likely to wander when they were not filled regularly through sexual intercourse and reproduction, and both male and female authors suggested various alternative remedies for single women and nuns. The uterus was also thought to be influenced by the moon and the maternal imagination, so that pregnant women in particular were advised to be aware of the stages of the moon and to avoid certain thoughts. Anger was regarded as particularly dangerous, for its "heat" could cause the woman's blood which normally nourished the fetus to destroy it instead.

The Scientific Revolution, which created a new view of the universe for educated Europeans, therefore did little to challenge existing ideas of the inferiority of women. In fact, some historians, most prominently Carolyn Merchant and David Noble, have argued that it deepened that inferiority by championing reason, order, control, and mechanical processes, all associated with men or defined as somehow masculine, while continuing to link women with irrationality, disorder, and nature. Membership in the new scientific societies that developed in the seventeenth century was limited to men; the purpose of the English Royal Society established in 1660 was expressly stated as the advancement of "Masculine Philosophy." Even contact with women through marriage was frowned upon, and many of the most prominent scientists, such as Pierre Boyle and Isaac Newton, remained unmarried and apparently chaste. Londa Schiebinger has pointed out that the acceptance of Galenic ideas of the complementarity of the two sexes, far from leading to greater egalitarianism, led instead by the end of the eighteenth century to the idea that gender differences pervaded every aspect of human experience, biological, intellectual, and moral; even the bones of the body demonstrated to most observers that women were destined to stay

OPIS SATVRNI CONIVNX
materque Deorum.

Die erd ist fruchtbar mit aller krafft
Gibt öl wein milcb most vnd gute safft.
Fiea föal frücbe awecbs früchte vnd thier
Artebendts vnd alles fleiscb speul von jr
Ein mutter erneort ir kinder klein
Mit zarten weiblichen brüsilein sein.

Vnd wie auch ein weib das scbwanger ist
Auch also die erd zu aller srui
Ecbr aut vnd sein alles geberet
Von irm leib vnd reicblicb erneret
Die gantze natur. Merck mit allem sleir
Gott zu ewigem lob ehr vnd prer.

home and raise children. Ideas about gender differences based in the
body were interwoven with those about racial differences as European
countries developed colonial empires: white women were viewed as most
likely to incorporate female qualities viewed as positive, such as piety
and purity, while non-white (especially Black) women were seen as
incorporating negative female traits, such as disobedience and sensual-
ity. White men, in this view, were more rational because of their sex *and*
their race, while non-white men were more likely to demonstrate negative or ambiguous male qualities such as anger or physical prowess.
Exactly how these two hierarchies intersected was a matter of dispute for
European thinkers, who also debated the ways in which class distinctions further complicated the picture. (We will return to this topic again
in Chapter 8.) In general, however, science provided much more "evidence" for the differences among people than for their similarities in the
early modern period; not until the twentieth century did it begin to provide as many arguments for the equality of men and women of all racial
and ethnic groups as for their essential inequality.

Laws regarding women

Ideas about women and "woman" in the abstract based on religion, biology, or tradition directly influenced the legal systems and law codes in
early modern Europe. It is important to recognize that laws are yet
another type of theory; like sermons and domestic guides, they describe
an ideal situation that their authors are trying to create, and do not
describe reality. To some degree, laws may be used as evidence that the

---

2   Melchior Lorch, Allegory of Nature, 1565. The poem beneath the
image reads:

The earth is fruitful with all power
Gives wine, milk, cider, and good juice
Birds, fish, plants, fruit and animals
Crawling or walking, all eat from her.
A mother nourishes her small children
With tender and fine feminine breasts
And like a woman who is pregnant
The earth also lets all
Who are born fine and good from her body
Eat from her and nourishes them all richly.
The whole earth does its best
To praise and honor God.

actions they attempt to prohibit or regulate are in fact going on, for, as legal historians have pointed out, lawmakers only feel it necessary to restrict actions that people are actually doing or which the lawmakers think they might contemplate doing. When surveying laws regarding women, however, we cannot carry this too far, because all lawmakers in early modern Europe, except for a few queens, were male; laws thus reflect male notions and worries more than real female actions.

Law itself changed significantly in the early modern period. Beginning in the thirteenth century in Italy and most of southern Europe, and in the sixteenth century in Germany and most of northern Europe (though not England), legal scholars encouraged governments to change their law codes to bring them into conformity with Roman law, a legal system based on the collection of laws and commentaries made by the Roman Emperor Justinian in the sixth century. Roman law was viewed as systematic and comprehensive, perfect for rulers who were attempting to bring political and judicial unity to their territories and get rid of the highly localized and often contradictory and conflicting law codes that had grown up in medieval Europe. Legal scholars who taught at universities and advised rulers came to regard law as an important tool for shaping society, and advised rulers to expand their law codes and prosecute those who broke these codes more vigorously. In areas of Europe that became Protestant, secular rulers took over the control of matters like marriage and morals from Catholic church courts, thus further expanding and centralizing their legal systems. The drive for comprehensiveness and uniformity also affected Catholic church courts, for the Council of Trent in the mid-sixteenth century cleared up many ambiguities in canon law, particularly in regard to marriage.

All of these changes had an impact on the legal position of women. Traditional medieval law codes in Europe had accorded women a secondary legal status, based generally on their inability to perform feudal military service; the oldest legal codes required every woman who was not married to have a male legal guardian who could undergo such procedures as trial by combat or trial by ordeal for her. This gender-based guardianship gradually died out in the later Middle Ages as court proceedings replaced physical trials, and unmarried women and widows generally gained the right to hold land on their own and appear in court on their own behalf. In most parts of Europe, unmarried women and widows could make wills, serve as executors for the wills of others, and serve as witnesses in civil and criminal cases, though they could not serve as witnesses to a will.

Thus limitations on women's legal rights because of feudal obligations lessened in the late Middle Ages, but marriage provided another reason for restricting women's legal role. Marriage was cited as the key reason for excluding women from public offices and duties, for their duty to obey their husbands prevented them from acting as independent persons; the fact that an unmarried woman or widow might possibly get married meant that they, too, were included in this exclusion. A married woman was legally subject to her husband in all things; she could not sue, make contracts, or go to court for any reason without his approval, and in many areas of Europe could not be sued or charged with any civil crime on her own. In many parts of Europe, all goods or property that a wife brought into a marriage and all wages she earned during the marriage were considered the property of her husband, a situation that did not change legally until the nineteenth century. In England, a married woman was not even considered a legal person under common law, but was totally subsumed within the legal identity of her husband; she could not accept a gift from her husband or make a will separate from him because they were "one person."

The husband's control of his wife's property could be modified somewhat by a marriage contract which gave her legal ownership of the dowry she brought into the marriage. The husband then had the use of this money, goods, or property as long as both spouses were alive, but she or her heirs were to receive the actual property or something of comparable value at his death. In many parts of Europe, widows were also assured of a certain portion of their husbands' estate, termed a dower, after his death, usually fixed by law or custom at one-third to one-half; this was hers to use for the remainder of her life, though it reverted to his heirs after her death, so was not legally regarded as belonging to her. Widows were generally free to manage this property as they wished, though the heirs could take them to court if they felt the widow was harming the value of the property.

Along with marriage contracts, late medieval and early modern cities and states began to offer other ways for wives to gain some legal and economic independence from their husbands, for political and legal authorities recognized that a wife's totally dependent legal position often did not fit with economic needs or social realities. In almost all city law codes beginning in the fourteenth or fifteenth centuries, married women who carried out business on their own, or alongside their husbands, were allowed to declare themselves unmarried *(feme [sic] sole)* for legal purposes. This meant they could borrow and loan money and make contracts on their own, though sometimes the amounts were still limited. They could also be jailed for debt or for violating civil laws. Wives were also gradually allowed to retain control over some family property if they could prove that their husbands were squandering everything through drink, gambling, or bad investments; such laws were described as protection for women and children, but they were also motivated by lawmakers' concerns to keep such families from needing public charity.

In addition to these exceptions provided through law codes, it is clear from court records that women often actively managed their dowry property and carried out legal transactions without getting special approval. Judges and officials were often willing to let women act against the letter of the law if the alternative would be financial problems for the family, or if they thought the law itself was harmful or unfair. In England two special courts, the Court of Chancery and the Court of Requests, were established specifically to make decisions case-by-case based on principles of equity, rather than a strict interpretation of common law. These courts heard all types of cases, but became particularly popular with married women in the sixteenth century, for they allowed them to bring cases independently, even against their husbands. These courts did provide relief for some women, though others were more likely simply to act and risk the consequences than to seek approval beforehand; it is clear that the legal provisions for exceptions in no way encompass all of women's actual legal and financial activities.

The proliferation of exceptions and the fact that women were often able to slip through the cracks of urban law codes began to bother jurists in many parts of Europe who were becoming educated in Roman law with its goals of comprehensiveness and uniformity. Roman law also gave them additional grounds for women's secondary legal status, for it based this not on feudal obligations or a wife's duty to obey her husband but on women's alleged physical and mental weaknesses, their "fragility, imbecility, irresponsibility, and ignorance," in the words of Justinian's code. Along with peasants and the simple-minded, women were regarded as not legally responsible for all of their own actions, and could not be compelled to appear before a court; in all cases their testimony was regarded as less credible than a man's. These ideas led jurists in many parts of Europe to recommend, and in some cases implement, the reintroduction of gender-based guardianship; unmarried adult women and widows were again given male guardians, and prohibited from making any financial decisions, even donations to religious institutions, without their approval.

Ironically, Roman law itself had not required unmarried adult women to have guardians, but had only known guardianship for children. Early modern jurists were thus selective in what they took from Roman law in regard to women, in general adopting clauses that placed women in a dependent or secondary position and neglecting those that gave women specific independent rights. This can be seen in changes in a mother's rights to her own children. Early medieval law codes had known only fatherly authority, but the concept of joint parental authority over children had grown gradually in the Middle Ages. This died out again with the reception of Roman law, for its concept of the absolute rights of the father *(patria potestas)* was cited frequently, and the control it gave mothers over their children was not; in many parts of Europe, women lost the right of guardianship over their own children if they remarried, or were only granted guardianship in the first place if they renounced remarriage at the death of the children's father.

Increasing restrictions on unmarried and married women continued throughout the early modern period. In 1731, for example, the Paris Parliament passed the *Ordonnance des donations,* which reemphasized the power of the husband over the wife; its provisions limiting women's legal rights later became part of the Napoleanic Code. Court records indicate that male guardianship was enforced, because fewer and fewer women appeared on their own behalf. Governments generally became less willing to make exceptions in the case of women, as they felt any laxness might disrupt public order. Customs of inheritance, though not specified by law, were also affected by notions of women's incapacity and ignorance, for in many parts of Europe daughters increasingly received only goods (movables) and no land (immovables) when they had brothers, whether land was normally divided between brothers (partible inheritance) or inherited as a block by the eldest brother (primogeniture). Daughters were required to renounce all claims to family land when they received their dowry, thus keeping land more closely within the patrilineage and taking away what had often been a source of great economic and legal power for upper-class women.

The spread of Roman law thus had a largely negative effect on women's civil legal status in the early modern period both because of the views of women which jurists chose to adopt from it and the stricter enforcement of existing laws to which it gave rise. Its impact on criminal law was less gender-specific, just as criminal law itself was. In general, women throughout Europe were responsible for their own criminal actions and could be tortured and executed just like men. Some mildness was recommended in the case of pregnant women, though generally this meant simply waiting until after delivery to proceed with torture. Women were often executed in a manner different from men, buried alive or drowned instead of being beheaded, largely because city executioners thought women would faint at the sight of the sword or ax and make their job more difficult. The wifely duty of obedience did enter into criminal law in a few instances, with both positive and negative effects for women. In England, a woman's marital status could affect her independent culpability for criminal actions, as women who were unmarried sometimes said they were in order to claim husbandly coercion in capital cases, which could keep them from being executed. On the other hand, women who killed their husbands were judged guilty of petty treason as well as murder, which would assure them of the death penalty. (Husband-murder does not appear to have been regarded as petty treason on the continent, though it was still judged as the most detestable type of murder.) In Spain, only in the sixteenth century did the state take over from the husband the right to punish his wife for adultery, and husbandly revenge was still allowed as long as he killed both his wife and her lover. In Germany, a wife was often included in her husband's banishment for criminal actions – including banishment for adultery! – while the opposite was not the case.

Along with concepts of feudal obligation, wifely obedience, and Roman law, one additional idea was essential in shaping women's legal rights in early modern Europe – the notion of honor. Honor in this period was highly gender-specific, and, in the case of men, class-specific. For upper-class men, honor still revolved around notions of physical bravery and loyalty, a link that was also accepted by journeymen and marginal groups such as professional criminals. For bourgeois and most working men, honor was primarily related to honesty, good craftsmanship, and integrity. For all women, honor was a sexual matter. In most parts of Europe, women of all classes were allowed to bring defamation suits to court for insults to their honor, and it is clear from court records that they did this frequently; such records also indicate that the worst thing a man could be called was "thief," or "coward" while for women it was "whore." Because of ideas of female sinfulness, irrationality, and weakness drawn from tradition, religion, and science, however, women, particularly those in the middle- and upper-classes, were never regarded as able to defend their own honor completely without male assistance. Lower-class women might trade insults or physically fight one another, but middle- and upper-class women were expected to internalize notions of honor and shame and shape their behavior accordingly, depending on male relatives to carry out any public defense of their honor. Male defense of female honor often took the form of laws and customs that might appear to protect women, but actually safeguarded their male family members. In Spain, for example, a woman whose fiancé had died after the engagement, but before the marriage, was granted one-half of the goods promised for the marriage, for a kiss was part of the betrothal ceremony, which made it extremely difficult for her to find another spouse; the property would allow her either to support herself in an unmarried state or perhaps find a partner who would not mind the fact that she "remained shamed," and would also free her father and brothers from having to support her. Similar motivations are behind laws that required rapists to compensate their victims, or the fathers of their victims, which are found throughout Europe. In Muscovy until the reforms of Peter the Great, elite women were totally secluded in separate quarters and did not mix socially with men at all; they rode in closed carriages even when going to church, and were veiled whenever they appeared in public. This was done in the name of family honor, but also kept family property in male hands as the women often did not marry and so did not receive a dowry.

As we will discuss more fully in Chapter 8, honor, along with order and the public good, were all concepts that in both theory and reality were closely linked not only to ideas about women, but also to ideas about men. The educated men whose notions we have concentrated on in this chapter were much less willing to generalize about their own sex than about the opposite one, but underlying all their ideas about women, and the laws that resulted from those ideas, were concepts about their own nature as men.

Bibliography

The literature on ideas about women is vast, and the following represent simply a few of the books and articles that are the most easily obtainable or most essential. Negative attitudes about women from the ancient period to the modern have been surveyed in Katherine Rogers, *The Troublesome Helpmate: A History of Misogyny in Literature* (Seattle, University of Washington Press, 1966), though there is no comparable long-term survey of positive attitudes. Jean-Louis Flandrin, *Sex in the Western World: The Development of Attitudes and Behaviors*, trans. Sue Collins (Chur, Harwood Academic, 1991) is also a useful general discussion from the point of view of a French early modern historian. For a lively, but also sharply critical study of Catholic ideas across many centuries, see Ute Ranke-Heinemann, *Eunuchs for the Kingdom of Heaven: Women, Sexuality and the Catholic Church* (New York, Doubleday, 1990).

For the Jewish tradition, Rachel Biale, *Women in Jewish Law: An Exploration of Women's Issues in Halakhic Sources* (New York, Schocken, 1984) and David Biale, *Eros and the Jews from Biblical Israel to Contemporary America* (New York, Basic Books, 1992). Several of the articles in Judith Baskin, (ed.), *Jewish Women in Historical Perspective* (Detroit, Wayne State University Press, 1991) also discuss ideas about women, as does Howard Adelman, "Images of women in Italian Jewish literature in the late middle ages," in *Proceedings of the Tenth World Congress of Jewish Studies*, Division B, vol. II (Jerusalem, World Union of Jewish Studies, 1990), pp. 99–106.

Surveys of women in the ancient world, including ideas about women, include: Sarah Pomeroy, *Goddesses, Whores, Wives, and Slaves: Women in Classical Antiquity* (New York, Schocken, 1975) and Elaine Fantham, et al., *Women in the*

Classical World: Image and Text (New York, Oxford University Press, 1994). More specific analyses of ideas in Athens include Eva Keuls, *The Reign of the Phallus: Sexual Politics in Ancient Athens* (New York, Harper & Row, 1985) and John J. Winkler, *The Constraints of Desire: The Anthropology of Sex and Gender in Ancient Greece* (New York, Routledge, 1990).

For ideas about women in early Christianity, see: JoAnn McNamara, *A New Song: Celibate Women in the First Three Christian Centuries* (New York, Haworth Press, 1983); Elizabeth S. Fiorenza, *In Memory of Her: A Feminist Theological Reconstruction of Christian Origins* (New York, Crossroad, 1983); Peter Brown, *The Body and Society: Men, Women and Sexual Renunciation in Early Christianity* (New York, Columbia University Press, 1988); Elizabeth Clark, *Ascetic Piety and Women's Faith* (Lewiston, Maine, Edwin Mellen, 1988); Elaine Pagels, *Adam, Eve and the Serpent* (New York, Random House, 1988); Joyce Salisbury, *Church Fathers, Independent Virgins* (New York, Verso, 1991).

For works that compare pagan and Christian ideas, see: Aline Rouselle, *Porneia: On Desire and the Body in Antiquity,* trans. Felicia Pheasant (London, Basil Blackwell, 1988); Kate Cooper, *The Virgin and the Bride: Idealized Womanhood in Late Antiquity,* (Cambridge, Mass., Harvard University Press, 1996); Deborah Sawyer, *Women and Religion in the First Christian Centuries* (London, Routledge, 1996); Bernadette J. Brooton, *Love Between Women: Early Christian Responses to Female Homoeroticism* (Chicago, University of Chicago Press, 1996). Ross S. Kraemer, *Maenads, Martyrs, Matrons, Monastics: A Sourcebook on Women's Religions in the Greco-Roman World* (Philadelphia, Fortress Press, 1988) is a wonderful collection of original sources in translation about women and religion in the ancient world, including pagan, Jewish, and Christian material.

Susan Miller Okin, in *Women in Western Political Thought* (Princeton, Princeton University Press, 1979), emphasizes the relationship between concepts of women and those of the family in Plato, Aristotle, Rousseau, and John Stuart Mill, and Arlene Saxonhouse, in *Women in the History of Political Thought from the Greeks to Machiavelli* (New York, Praeger, 1985) stresses the centrality and gendered nature of issues of public vs. private for all classical and medieval thinkers.

Women in the Middle Ages have recently been the focus a great many studies, most of which discuss ideas about women as well as women's actual situation. These include: Margaret Wade Labarge, *A Small Sound of the Trumpet: Women in Medieval Life* (Boston, Beacon, 1986), Penny Schine Gold, *The Lady and the Virgin: Image, Attitude and Experience in Twelfth Century France* (Chicago, University of Chicago Press, 1985); Angela Lucas, *Women in the Middle Ages: Religion, Marriage, Letters* (New York, St. Martin's, 1983); Nancy Partner, *Studying Medieval Women: Sex, Gender and Feminism* (New York, Medieval Academy, 1993); Henrietta Leyster, *A Social History of Women in England 450–1500* (London, Weidenfeld and Nicolson, 1995); Mavis Mate, *Daughters, Wives and Widows After the Black Death: Women in Sussex 1350–1535* (Rochester, Boydell & Brewer, 1998); Judith M. Bennett, *A Medieval Life: Cecelia Penifader of Brigstock, c. 1295–1344* (New York, McGraw-Hill, 1999). Recent collections include: Mary Erler and Maryanne Kowaleski (eds.), *Women and Power in the Middle Ages* (Athens, University of Georgia Press, 1988); James A. Brundage, *Sex, Law and Marriage in the Middle Ages* (London, Variorum, 1993); Katharina

M. Wilson (ed.), *Medieval Women Writers* (Athens, University of Georgia Press, 1984); Karma Lochrie, Peggy McCracken, and James A. Schulz (eds.), *Constructing Medieval Sexuality* (Minneapolis, University of Minnesota Press, 1996). Important studies of specific ideas or thinkers include: Kari Elisabeth Borreson, *Subordination and Equivalence: The Nature and Role of Women in Augustine and Thomas Aquinas*, tr. Charles H. Talbot (Washington, D.C., University Press of America, 1981); Marina Warner, *Alone of All Her Sex: The Myth and Cult of the Virgin Mary* (London, Weidenfeld and Nicholson, 1976); Pamela Sheingorn, "The holy kinship: the ascendancy of matriliny in sacred genealogy of the fifteenth century," *Thought* 64(1989), 268–286; Pierre Payer, *The Bridling of Desire: Views of Sex in the Later Middle Ages* (Toronto, University of Toronto Press, 1993); Christopher N. L. Brooke, *The Medieval Idea of Marriage* (Oxford, Clarendon Press, 1994); Dyan Elliott, *Spiritual Marriage: Sexual Abstinence in Medieval Wedlock* (Princeton, Princeton University Press, 1993).

Alcuin Blamires provides many examples of defenses of women from the fourth century through the fifteenth in *The Case for Women in Medieval Culture* (New York, Oxford University Press, 1997) and of both sides of this issue in *Woman Defamed and Defended: An Anthology of Medieval Texts* (New York, Oxford University Press, 1992). A similar study is Glenda McLeod, *Virtue and Venom: Catalogs of Women from Antiquity to the Renaissance* (Ann Arbor, University of Michigan Press, 1991).

All of the studies noted above focus on western Europe. For ideas about women in eastern Europe during the Middle Ages, see: Eve Levin, *Sex and Society in the World of the Orthodox Slavs, 900–1700* (Ithaca, Cornell University Press, 1989) and "Sexual Vocabulary in Medieval Russia," in Jane T. Costlow, Stephanie Sandler, and Judith Vowles (eds.), *Sexuality and the Body in Russian Culture* (Stanford, Stanford University Press, 1993), 41–52; Angeliki E. Laiou, *Gender, Society, and Economic Life in Byzantium* (London, Variorum, 1992) and *Consent and Coercion to Sex and Marriage in Ancient and Medieval Societies* (Washington D.C., Dumbarton Oaks Research Library, 1993); Liz James (ed.), *Women, Men and Eunuchs: Gender in Byzantium* (London, Rutledge, 1997).

Courtly love has recently been analyzed from a feminist as well as strictly literary viewpoint, especially in the work of Joan Ferrante, such as *Woman as Image in Medieval Literature* (1975; reprint Durham, N.C., Duke University Press, 1985). For courtly poetry by women authors, see Matilda Tomaryn Bruckner, et al (eds.), *Songs of the Women Troubadours* (New York, Garland, 1995).

Christine de Pizan is finally getting the attention she deserves in both translations and reprints of her work and biographical studies: Charity Cannon Willard, *Christine de Pizan: Her Life and Works* (New York, Persea, 1984); *The Book of the City of Ladies*, tr. Earl Jeffrey Richards (New York, Persea, 1982); *The Treasure of the City of Ladies or The Book of Three Virtues* (London, Penguin, 1985); Marilynn Desmond, *Christine de Pizan and the Categories of Difference* (Minneapolis, University of Minnesota, 1998); Rosalind Brown-Grant, *Christine de Pizan and the Moral Defence of Women: Reading Beyond Gender* (Cambridge, Cambridge University Press, 1999).

Interest in the Renaissance debate about women has led to many reprints and catalogs of texts, especially English ones: Francis Lee Utley, *The Crooked Rib: An*

Analytical Index to the Argument About Women in English and Scots Literature to the End of the Year 1568 (Columbus, Ohio University Press, 1944); Katherine Usher Henderson and Barbara F. McManus, *Half Humankind: Contexts and Texts of the Controversy About Women in England 1540–1640* (Urbana, University of Illinois Press, 1985); Joan Larsen Klein (ed.), *Daughters, Wives and Widows: Writings by Men about Women and Marriage in England, 1500–1640* (Urbana, University of Chicago Press, 1992); N. H. Keeble (ed.), *The Cultural Identity of Seventeenth Century Woman: A Reader* (London, Routledge, 1994); Susan Gushee O'Malley (ed.), *Defenses of Women: Jane Anger, Rachel Speght, Ester Sowernam and Constantia Munda*, The Early Modern Englishwoman: A Facsimile Library of Essential Works, 4.1 (New York: Scholar Press, 1996). Henricus Cornelius Agrippa, *Declamation on the Nobility and Preeiminence of the Female Sex*, ed. and trans. Albert Rabil, Jr. (Chicago, University of Chicago Press, 1996) is a new English translation of one of the strongest arguments for women by a continental writer, originally published in Latin in 1529. Hilda L. Smith and Susan Cardinale, *Women and the Literature of the Seventeenth Century: An Annotated Bibliography based on Wing's Short-title Catalogue* (New York, Greenwood, 1990) includes all books by, for, and about women printed in English from 1641 to 1700. The bibliographies that follow Chapters 4 and 5 include further references to modern editions and texts, especially those by women.

Along with textual reprints, there are also many good studies of the debate, some of which discuss writers from several parts of Europe: Joan Kelly, "Early feminist theory and the *Querelle des Femmes*, 1400–1789" in her *Women, History and Theory* (Chicago, University of Chicago Press, 1984); Constance Jordan, *Renaissance Feminism: Literary Texts and Political Models* (Ithaca, N.Y., Cornell University Press, 1990); Pamela Joseph Benson, *The Invention of the Renaissance Woman: The Challenge of Female Independence in the Literature and Thought of Italy and England* (University Park, Pennsylvania State University Press, 1992); Joy Wiltenburg, *Disorderly Women and Female Power in the Street Literature of Early Modern England and Germany* (Charlottesville, University Press of Virginia, 1992); Margaret Somerville, *Sex and Subjection: Attitudes to Women in Early-Modern Society* (London, Arnold, 1995). Ian Maclean, *The Renaissance Notion of Woman* (Cambridge, Cambridge University Press, 1980) analyzes the debate in philosophical, theological, medical, and legal writings, and provides the best overview of ideas about women through the sixteenth century; there is, unfortunately, nothing like it for the seventeenth or eighteenth centuries. Three interesting articles on lesser-known thinkers are Arlene Miller Guinsberg, "The counterthrust to sixteenth century misogyny: The work of Agrippa and Paracelsus," *Historical Reflections*, 8 (1981), 3–28; Gerhild Schulz Williams, "The woman/the witch: variations on a sixteenth-century theme (Paracelsus, Wier, Bodin)," in Craig Monson (ed.), *The Crannied Wall: Women, Religion, and the Arts in Early Modern Europe* (Ann Arbor, University of Michigan Press, 1992), pp. 119–38; Cornelia Niekus Moore, "'Not by nature but by custom': Johan van Beverwijck's *Van de wtnementheyt des vrouwelicken Geslachts* (Of the Excellence of the Female Gender)" *Sixteenth Century Journal* 25 (1994), 633–51. Studies of visual representations of the debate include: Sara F. Matthews Grieco, *"Querelle des femmes" or "guerre des sexes"? Visual Representations of Women in Renaissance Europe* (Florence, European University Institute, 1989); Keith Moxey, *Peasants,*

Warriors, and Wives: Popular Imagery in the Reformation (Chicago, University of Chicago Press, 1989); Ruth B. Bottigheimer, "Publishing, print, and change in the image of Eve and the apple 1470–1570," *Archives for Reformation History* 86 (1995), 199–235. Linda Woodbridge, *Women and the English Renaissance: Literature and the Nature of Womankind, 1540–1620* (Urbana, University of Illinois Press, 1984), Diane Purkiss, "Material girls: the seventeenth-century woman debate," in Clare Brant and Diane Purkiss (eds.), *Women, Texts and Histories, 1575–1760* (London, Routledge, 1992), pp. 69–101, Suzanne W. Hull, *Women According to Men: The World of Tudor-Stuart Women* (Thousand Oaks, Cal., Altamira Press, 1996) focus on England, while Sally-Ann Kitts, *The Debate on the Nature, Role, and Influence of Woman in Eighteenth-Century Spain* (New York, Mellen, 1995) looks at the debate in Spain. The bibliographies that follow Chapters 5 and 8 provide additional suggestions, especially about works written by female authors.

There are numerous studies of ideas about women and the family in English religious thinkers, including: Kathleen M. Davies, "The sacred condition of equality – how original were Puritan doctrines of marriage?" *Social History,* 2 (1977), 563–80; John K. Yost, "Changing attitudes towards married life in civic and Christian humanists," *American Society for Reformation Research, Occasional Papers,* 1 (1977), 151–66; Margo Todd, "Humanists, Puritans and the spiritualized household," *Church History,* 49 (1980), 18–34; Edmund Leites, "The duty to desire: love, friendship and sexuality in some Puritan theories of marriage," *Journal of Social History* 15 (1982), 383–408; Margo Todd, *Christian Humanism and the Puritan Social Order* (Cambridge: Cambridge University Press, 1987); Daniel Doriani, "The Puritans, sex, and pleasure," in Elizabeth Stuart and Adrian Thatcher (eds.), *Christian Perspectives on Sexuality and Gender,* (Leominster: Gracewing, 1996), pp. 33–52. There are fewer studies of continental religious thinkers available in English, but there are some. Steven Ozment, *When Fathers Ruled: Family Life in Reformation Europe* (Cambridge, Mass., Harvard University Press, 1983) and Scott Hendrix, "Masculinity and Patriarchy in Reformation Germany," *Journal of the History of Ideas* 56 (1995), 177–93 cover the ideas of a number of Protestant thinkers. Erika Rummel (ed.), *Erasmus on Women* (Toronto, University of Toronto Press, 1996) includes the writings of the most important Christian humanist. Merry E. Wiesner, "Luther and women: the death of two Marys," (pp. 123–137) and Daphne Hampson, "Luther on the self: a feminist critique," (pp. 215–224) both in Ann Loades (ed.), *Feminist Theology: A Reader* (London, SPCK, 1990) analyze Luther's thought. Susan Karant-Nunn, *"Kinder, Küche, Kirche:* social ideology in the wedding sermons of Johannes Mathesius," in Susan Karant-Nunn and Andrew Fix, *Germania Illustrata: Essays Presented to Gerald Strauss* (Kirksville, MO., Sixteenth Century Essays and Studies, 1991), pp. 121–40, discusses the ideas of a typical early Lutheran pastor, and Herman J. Selderhuis, *Marriage and Divorce in the Thought of Martin Bucer,* trans. John Vriend and Lyle D. Bierma (Kirksville, MO., Sixteenth Century Journal Publishers, 1998) analyzes the thought of a moderate reformer. For the ideas of the radical Protestant reformers, see: Joyce Irwin (ed.), *Womanhood in Radical Protestantism* (New York: E. Mellen, 1979); Lyndal Roper, "Sexual utopianism in the German Reformation," in her *Oedipus and the Devil: Witchcraft, Sexuality and Religion in Early Modern Europe* (London, Routledge,

1994); Beth Kreitzer, "Menno Simons and the Bride of Christ," *Mennonite Quarterly Review* 70 (1996), 299–318. Calvin's thought has received several excellent studies, including Mary Potter, "Gender equality and gender heirarchy in Calvin's theology," *Signs*, 11 (1986), 725–39, Jane Dempsey Douglass, *Women, Freedom and Calvin* (Philadelphia, Westminster Press, 1985) and John Lee Thompson, *John Calvin and the Daughters of Sarah: Women in Regular and Exceptional Roles in the Exegesis of Calvin, His Predecessors and His Contemporaries* (Geneva, Droz, 1992). Douglass's and Thompson's studies show how the traditional methods and sources of intellectual historians and theologians can be used to gain dramatically new insights; there is no comparable book-length study in English of any aspect of Luther's thought on women or gender. The bibliography that follows Chapter 6 includes further suggestions for readings in the area of women and religion.

Joan Cadden, *Meanings of Sex Differences in the Middle Ages: Medicine, Science, and Culture* (Cambridge: Cambridge University Press, 1993) analyzes medieval scientific ideas about gender, while David Noble, *A World Without Women: The Clerical Cultural of Western Science* (New York, Knopf, 1992) points out ways in which medieval misogyny carried over into modern science. Ideas about women that developed in the Scientific Revolution have been surveyed from a critical feminist perspective by Carolyn Merchant, *The Death of Nature; Women, Ecology and the Scientific Revolution* (New York, Harper & Row, 1980) and Londa Schiebinger, *The Mind Has No Sex? Women in the Origins of Modern Science* (Cambridge, Mass., Harvard University Press, 1989). Investigations of how preconceptions about women's nature and gender differences shaped "scientific" discoveries include: Hilda Smith, "Gynecology and ideology in seventeenth-century England," in Berenice A. Carroll (ed.), *Liberating Women's History: Theoretical and Critical Essays* (Urbana, University of Illinois Press, 1986); Maryanne Cline Horowitz, "The 'science' of embryology before the discovery of the ovum" in Marilyn J. Boxer and Jean H. Quataert (eds.), *Connecting Spheres: Women in the Western World, 1500 to the Present* (New York, Oxford University Press, 1987); Londa Schiebinger, *Nature's Body: Gender in the Making of Modern Science* (Boston, Beacon, 1993); Valerie Traub, "Gendering mortality in early modern anatomies," in Valerie Traub, et al. (eds.), *Feminist Readings of Early Modern Culture: Emerging Subjects* (Cambridge, Cambridge University Press, 1996); M. Walton, "Why can't a woman be more like a man? A Renaissance perspective on the biological basis for female inferiority" *Women and Health* 24 (1996); 87–95. The most thoughtful analyst of the intersection between racial and gender hierarchies in early modern Europe is Kim F. Hall; see her *Things of Darkness: Economies of Race and Gender in Early Modern England* (Ithaca, Cornell University Press, 1995) and "Culinary spaces, colonial spaces; the gendering of sugar in the seventeenth century," in Traub, *Feminist Readings*, 168–90. See also several of the essays in Margo Hendricks and Patricia Parker (eds.), *Women "Race" and Writing in the Early Modern Period* (London, Routledge, 1994).

Information about laws regarding women may be found in most surveys of the development of law, particularly those that focus on private law, and in general surveys of women's life. Specific studies of women's legal status generally limit themselves to one country or legal system, as it is difficult to generalize more broadly; such studies include: Pearl Hogreve, "Legal rights of Tudor women and their circumvention by men and women," *Sixteenth Century Journal,* 3 (1972), 97–105; Lucy A. Sponsler, "The status of married women under the legal system of Spain," *Journal of Legal History,* 3 (1982), 125–152; Maria Lynn Cioni, *Women and Law in Elizabethan England with Particular Reference to the Court of Chancery* (New York, Garland, 1985); Merry E. Wiesner, "Frail, weak, and helpless: women's legal position in theory and reality," in Jerome Friedman (ed.), *Regnum, Religio et Ratio: Essays Presented to Robert M. Kingdon,* Sixteenth Century Essays and Studies, Volume 8. (Kirksville, MO., Sixteenth Century Journal Publishers, 1987) pp. 161–69; Thomas Kuehn, *Law, Family, and Women: Toward a Legal Anthropology of Renaissance Italy* (Chicago: University of Chicago Press, 1992); M. Lindsay Kaplan, "Subjection and subjectivity: Jewish law and female autonomy in Reformation English marriage," in Traub, *Feminist Readings,* pp. 229–52; George Weickhardt, "Legal Rights of Women in Russia, 1100–1750," *Slavic Review* 55 (1996): 1–23. Studies that focus on women's actions in law courts include: Jenny Kermode and Garthine Walker (eds.), *Women, Crime and the Courts in Early Modern England* (London, UCL Press, 1994); Julie Hardwick, "Women 'working' the law: gender, authority, and legal process in early modern France," *Journal of Women's History* 9 (1997), 28–49; Tim Stretton, *Women Waging Law in Elizabethan England* (Cambridge, Cambridge University Press, 1998). Steven Ozment, *The Bürgermeister's Daughter: Scandal in a Sixteenth-Century German Town* (New York, St. Martin's, 1996) and Natalie Zemon Davis, *The Return of Martin Guerre* (Cambridge, Mass., Harvard University Press, 1983) both analyze single spectacular legal cases involving women. Elizabeth S. Cohen and Thomas V. Cohen, *Words and Deeds in Renaissance Rome: Trials before the Papal Magistrates* includes translations and analyses of cases involving female dependents, plaintiffs, and witnesses. Lyndal Roper, "Will and honor: sex, words, and power in Augsburg criminal trials," *Radical History Review* 43 (1989), 45–71; Nancy Shields Kollman, "Women's honor in early modern Russia," in Barbara Evans Clements (ed.), *Russia's Women: Accommodation, Resistance, Transformation* (Berkeley, University of California Press, 1991); Clare Brant, "Speaking of women: scandal and the law in the mid-eighteenth century," in Brant and Purkiss, *Women, Texts and Histories;* Laura Gowing, *Domestic Dangers: Women, Words, and Sex in Early Modern London* (Oxford, Clarendon Press, 1996) use legal cases to study issues of honor. Natalie Davis, *Fiction in the Archives: Pardon Tales and their Tellers in Sixteenth-century France* (Stanford, Stanford University Press, 1987) includes discussion of the ways in which early modern women manipulated stereotypes about women to gain pardons for homicide convictions.

Works that focus primarily on church courts include: Richard Helmholz, *Marriage Litigation in Medieval England* (Cambridge, Cambridge University Press, 1974); Richard M. Wunderli, *London Church Courts and Society on the Eve of the Reformation* (Cambridge, Mass., Harvard University Press, 1981); Michael M. Sheehan, *Marriage, Family and Law in Medieval Europe: Collected Studies,* ed. James K. Farge (Toronto, University of Toronto Press, 1996). The most important study of church law regarding many aspects of women's lives is James A. Brundage, *Law, Sex, and Christian Society in Medieval Europe* (Chicago, University of Chicago Press, 1987), which extends its scope into the sixteenth century.

Part I

Body

2   The female life-cycle

All the world's a stage,
And all the men and women merely players;
They have their exits and their entrances;
And one man in his time plays many parts,
His acts being seven ages...
        Jacques in William Shakespeare, *As You Like It,* Act II, Scene 7

All women are thought of as either married or to be married.
        Anonymous, *The lawes resolution of women's rights,* (London, 1632), fol. 6.

Beginning with the ancient Greeks, and perhaps earlier, western schol-ars debated about how many stages made up a man's life. Some argued for four, corresponding to the four seasons, some twelve, corresponding to the months and the signs of the zodiac, and some three, five, six, eight, or ten. The number that was increasingly accepted was seven, corre-sponding to the seven known planets (the planets out to Saturn plus the moon), and identified by St. Ambrose in the fourth century as infancy, boyhood, adolescence, young manhood, mature manhood, older man-hood, and old age. Discussions of the "ages of man" abounded in the Middle Ages and early modern period, and the stages were depicted in manuscript illuminations, stained-glass windows, wall paintings, and cathedral floors, so that people who did not read were also familiar with them.

The seven ages of man began with stages of physical and emotional maturing, and then were differentiated by increasing and decreasing involvement in the world of work and public affairs. As men moved from one stage to another, they were shown with different objects symboliz-ing changing occupations or responsibilities. For men, in only the third stage, adolescence, was sexuality a factor, and marriage or fatherhood were almost never viewed as significant.

Most written discussions of the ages of man never mention women at all; even Jacques, who begins by talking about men and women on the stage of life, goes on to describe a male life-cycle. People did talk less for-mally about the stages of a woman's life, however, and when they did it

51

was her sexual status and relationship to a man that mattered most, as the second quotation above makes clear. A woman was a virgin, wife, or widow, or alternately a daughter, wife, or mother. The visual depictions of the ages of man which show couples demonstrate the difficulties artists faced in trying to show stages in an adult woman's life, for though men are depicted as gaining status and authority in their occupations until old age, adult women of all ages are simply portrayed with spindles.

This difference in conceptualization both reflected and shaped social reality. For the vast majority of women in early modern Europe, the most important change in their lives was marriage. The choice of a spouse, whether made by themselves or their parents or a larger kin group, determined their social and economic status and place of residence. Though an early modern woman did not generally look to her husband for the same level of emotional intimacy and support that a contemporary western woman does, she certainly hoped that day-to-day life with him would be pleasant and that he would not physically or emotionally abuse her. Because divorce was either impossible or very difficult for women to obtain, and even living apart from an abusive spouse was illegal without court approval, the only possible relief from an unpleasant marriage was the death of a spouse, over which a woman, of course, had no control. It was the death of her husband, rather than any development in her own life, which moved a woman from one stage of life to another. Because this might happen at any age, and because remarriage meant a woman returned to the status of wife, the "ages of woman" correspond much less to her chronological age than the "ages of man" do to a man's. Though we might regard the early modern conceptualization of the female life-cycle as overly physical and marriage-oriented, lending too little credence to women's intellects or decisions, we will follow that conceptualization in this chapter, because corporeal accidents such as births and deaths not only shaped a woman's physical state, but her emotional health, economic position, opportunities for education, and status in the community.

Childhood and adolescence

The earliest studies of childhood in the early modern period, undertaken in the 1960s and 1970s, argued that childhood was not recognized as a distinct stage in life, and that children were raised harshly or regarded with indifference. These views were derived largely from child-raising manuals that advocated strict discipline and warned against coddling or showing too much affection and portraits of children which showed them dressed as little adults. This bleak view has been relieved somewhat in the last several decades by scholars using archival sources about the way children were actually treated; they have discovered that many parents showed great affection for their children and were very disturbed when they died young. Parents tried to protect their children with religious amulets and pilgrimages to special shrines, made toys for them, and sang them lullabies. Even practices that to us may seem cruel, such as tight swaddling, were motivated by a concern for the child's safety and health at a time when most households had open fires, domestic animals wandered freely, and mothers and older siblings engaged in productive work which prevented them from continually watching a toddler.

The attitudes about the relative value of men and women and the inheritance laws described in the last chapter led early modern parents to favor the birth of sons over daughters. Jewish women prayed for sons, and German midwives were often rewarded with a higher payment for assisting in the birth of a boy. English women's letters sometimes apologize for the birth of daughters. Girls significantly outnumbered boys in most orphanages or foundling homes, as poor parents decided their sons would ultimately be more useful; infants had a much poorer chance of survival in such institutions than among the population at large. An interesting exception to this is London, where more boys were abandoned than girls. Study of the London records from 1550 to 1800 indicates that infants were generally abandoned when they were more than a month old, rather than the several days that was common elsewhere in Europe, so that mothers may have become much more attached to them than they were at birth, and chose to abandon those children – the boys – who would be likely to receive better care and have a greater chance of survival. Infanticide statistics do not allow us to assess whether girls were more likely to be killed than boys, as court records generally simply refer to "child" or "infant," and the number of infanticides by the early modern period was not high enough to have affected the sex ratio among the population at large even if there was a greater likelihood for girls to be victims.

It is also very difficult to know how much differentiation by gender there was in the treatment of most infants and small children. Though society had sharply defined gender roles for adults, children were all dressed alike for the first several years of their lives (there is no early modern equivalent of the pink and blue dichotomy), and comments by parents about their small children show less gender stereotyping than is evident among many contemporary parents. It was when children began their training for adult life, at the age of four or five, that clear distinctions became evident. Girls of all classes were taught skills that they would use in running a household – spinning, sewing, cooking, care of domestic animals; peasant girls were also taught some types of agricultural tasks. As we will see in Chapter 4, they were much less likely than their brothers to be taught to read or to receive any formal schooling; the depictions of the ages of man which show both sexes portray the female in the second age spinning, and the male reading.

The onset of menstruation, termed menarche in modern English and "the flowers" in the sixteenth century, provided a girl with the clearest signal of bodily changes leading to adulthood. We know that the average age at menarche has declined in the western world for the last century, from about 15.5 in the 1890s to less than 13 today, but it is not clear that the average age in the early modern period was significantly higher than that in the nineteenth century. In fact, it may even have been lower, because age at menarche is affected by nutrition and other environmental factors, and many girls in the nineteenth century had a poorer diet and performed more physically debilitating work than those of earlier centuries. Somewhere around fourteen was probably about average, with poorer girls starting later than wealthier ones.

Because the actual biological function of menstruation had not yet been discovered, menstruation was viewed medically as either a process that purified women's blood or that removed excess blood from their bodies. As we saw in the last chapter, the humoral theory regarded all bodily fluids as related, and doctors recommended bloodletting as a treatment for disease in both men and women. Because of this, menstruation was not clearly separated from other types of bleeding in people's minds, and was often compared to male nosebleeds or hemorrhoids or other examples of spontaneous bleeding. Menstrual blood was thought to nourish the fetus during pregnancy, and because the body was regarded as capable of transforming one sort of fluid into another, to become milk during lactation. (In the same way, male blood was held to become semen during intercourse.) Semen and milk were not viewed as gender-specific fluids, however, for "virile" women who had more bodily heat than normal were seen as capable of producing semen, and effeminate men who lacked normal masculine heat were thought to lactate.

The cessation of menstruation (amenorrhea) was regarded as extremely dangerous for a woman, either because it left impure blood in her which might harden into an abnormal growth, or because it would allow excess blood to run to her brain, which would become overheated. (The opposite idea would be cited as a reason for barring women from higher education in the nineteenth century; education would cause all their blood to remain in their brains, which would halt menstruation and eventually cause the uterus to shrivel away.) Thus doctors recommended hot baths, medicines, pessaries placed in the vagina, and, for married women, frequent intercourse, to bring on a late menstrual period.

Menstruation was not simply a medical matter, however, but carried a great many religious and popular taboos, for though all bodily fluids were seen as related, menstrual blood was still generally viewed as somehow different and dangerous. Hebrew Scripture held that menstruation made a woman ritually impure, so that everything she touched was unclean and her presence was to be avoided by all. By the early modern period in Jewish communities, this taboo was limited to sexual relations and a few other contacts between wife and husband for the seven days of her period and seven days afterwards. At the end of this time, a woman was expected to take a ritual bath *(mikvah)* before beginning sexual relations again. Among the Orthodox Slavs in eastern Europe, menstruating women could not enter churches or take communion. Western Christian churches were a bit milder, but canon lawyers and other Catholic and Protestant commentators advised against sexual relations during menstruation. This was originally based strictly on the religious notion that women were unclean during this period, though during the sixteenth century the idea spread that this was medically unwise as it would result in deformed or leprous children. Menstruation was used to symbolize religious practices with which one did not agree, with English Protestants, for example, calling the soul of the pope a "menstruous rag." According to popular beliefs, menstruating women could by their touch, glance, or mere presence rust iron, turn wine sour, spoil meat, or dull knives. Though these ideas declined among educated Europeans during the seventeenth century, they are recorded well into the twentieth century among many population groups.

What women themselves thought of menstruation is more difficult to ascertain than male religious or medical opinion. One of the few direct comments by a woman comes from the autobiography of Isabella de Moerloose, published in Amsterdam in 1695, in which she writes that she asked her husband to sleep separately while she was menstruating because "the stink will cause thee to feel aversion for me." He would not allow it because he feared people might think they were Jews, though he, too, commented that he was "so terribly disgusted" by the smell.[1] Women's handwritten personal medical guides, small books in which they recorded recipes for cures and other household hints, include

---

[1] Isabella de Moerloose, *Gegeven van den Hemel door Vrouuwen Zaet...* (Amsterdam, 1695), quoted in Herman W. Roodenbuerg, "The autobiography of Isabella de Moerloose: sex, childrearing and popular beliefs in seventeenth-century Holland," *Journal of Social History* 18 (1985), 529.

recipes for mixtures to bring on a late menses and to stop overly-strong flow. Women turned to midwives and other women for help with a variety of menstrual ailments, and by the eighteenth century they also consulted male physicians. Physicians' case books from the early eighteenth century indicate that women worried most when menstruation ceased unexpectedly, especially if they thought something other than pregnancy was the cause. They requested the physician prescribe something to get the "flow" started again, because regular menstruation was a sign that all the fluids in the body were flowing as they should. Most women seemed to view menstruation not as an illness or a sign of divine displeasure, but as a normal part of life; only in the nineteenth century would normal menstruation come to be regarded as pathological. Though calling someone a "menstrual rag" was a serious insult, washing out one's own (or, if one was a servant, one's employers') menstrual rags were as much a part of women's lives as washing soiled infant clothing.

Sexuality

Learned opinion about menstruation was closely related with attitudes toward female sexuality in general, which were also a mixture of medical and religious opinion. In medical terms, male sexuality was the baseline for any perception of human sexuality, and the female sex organs were viewed as the male turned inside out or simply not pushed out. The great sixteenth-century anatomist Vesalius depicted the uterus looking exactly like an inverted penis, and his student Baldasar Heseler commented: "The organs of procreation are the same in the male and the female... For if you turn the scrotum, the testicles and the penis inside out you will have all the genital organs of the female."[2] This view of the correspondence between male and female sexual organs survived the Renaissance discovery of the clitoris, with scientists simply deciding that women had two structures which were like a penis. This idea meant that there was no precise nomenclature for many female anatomical parts until the eighteenth century because they were always thought to be congruent with some male part, and so were simply called by the same name.

The fact that the female sex organs were inside was viewed as a sign of female inferiority, of women's colder and damper nature which had not produced the heat necessary to push them out. The parallels between the two could lead to unusual sex changes, for many medical

[2] Baldasar Heseler, *Andreas Vesalius' First Public Anatomy at Bologna 1540: An Eyewitness Report*, ed. Ruben Eriksson (Uppsala, Almqvist and Wiksells, 1959), p. 181.

doctors throughout Europe solemnly reported cases of young women whose sex organs suddenly emerged during vigorous physical activity, transforming them into men; there are no reports of the opposite, however. Because female sex organs were hidden, they seemed more mysterious than male organs to early modern physicians and anatomists, and anatomical guidebooks use illustrations of autopsies on women's lower bodies as symbols of modern science uncovering the unknown.

Judging by early modern sex manuals, female sexuality was also viewed negatively in popular opinion. Two of the most frequently published were *Aristotle's Master-Piece,* in English, first published in 1684, and *Venus Minsieke Gasthuis,* published in French and Dutch in Amsterdam in the 1680s. Both of these link female sexuality in text and illustrations with animals, and see women as sexually insatiable, as witnessed by their ability to have multiple orgasms. Unlike the spermaticists' view of the essentially passive role of women in procreation, these manuals regard female orgasm as necessary for procreation, for only through this would female "seed" be released. (Yet another example of female experience being simply extrapolated from male.) This idea was common throughout Europe in the early modern period, which was unfortunate for women who were raped, as pregnancy was widely viewed as proof that the woman had had an orgasm, signaling her enjoyment of the experience, which proved it wasn't rape. This supposed connection between female orgasm and procreation allowed the manuals to go into great detail about ways to heighten sexual pleasure, while still claiming moralistically to be guides for happy marital life.

The negative view of female sexuality portrayed in medical texts and sex manuals was enhanced by religious opinion. Orthodox Slavs in eastern Europe had the most negative opinion, seeing all sexuality as an evil inclination originating with the devil and not part of God's original creation; as in the rest of Europe, women were viewed as more sexual and the cause of men's original fall from grace. Even marital sex was regarded as a sin, with the best marriage an unconsummated one; this led to a large number of miraculous virgin births among Russian saints, and to the popular idea that Jesus was born out of Mary's ear, not polluting himself with passage through the birth canal.

Western Catholic opinion did not go this far, but displayed an ambivalent attitude toward sexuality. Sex was seen as polluting and defiling, with virginity regarded as the most desirable state; members of the clergy and religious orders were expected, at least in theory, to remain chaste. Their chastity and celibacy made them different from, and superior to, lay Christians who married. On the other hand, the body and its sexual urges could not be completely evil, because they were created by God;

to claim otherwise was heresy. Writers vacillated between these two opinions or held both at once, and the laws that were developed in the Middle Ages regulating sexual behavior were based on both of them. In general, early modern Catholic doctrine held that sexual relations were acceptable as long as they were within marriage, not done on Sundays or other church holidays, done in a way that would allow procreation, and did not upset the proper sexual order, which meant the man had to be on top. (What has since been termed the "missionary position.") Spouses were held to enjoy a mutual right to sexual intercourse (the "marital debt"), which would even excuse intercourse when procreation was not possible; it was better, for example, for a pregnant or menstruating woman to allow her husband to have intercourse with her if refusing this would cause him to turn to a prostitute. Sixteenth-and seventeenth-century Catholic authors adopted a more positive view of marital sex than their medieval predecessors, regarding sexual pleasure, even fantasies and variant positions, as acceptable as a prelude to procreative intercourse.

The Protestant reformers broke clearly with Catholicism in their view that marriage was a spiritually preferable state to celibacy, and saw the most important function of marital sex not as procreation, but as increasing spousal affection. Based on his own experience, Luther stressed the power of sexual feelings for both men and women, and thought women in particular needed intercourse in order to stay healthy. This approval of *marital* sexuality did not lead to a lessening of the notion that female sexuality in general was dangerous, however. Luther termed prostitutes "stinking, syphilitic, scabby, seedy and nasty" tools of the devil, sent to bewitch his students and other unmarried men, and in his mind prostitutes were not the only women with such power. He commented:

For girls, too, are aware of this evil [lust] and if they spend time in the company of young men, they turn the hearts of these young men in various directions to entice them to love, especially if the youths are outstanding because of their good looks and strength of body. Therefore it is often more difficult for the latter to withstand such enticements than to resist their own lusts.[3]

Western Christian authors and officials thus generally agreed that sexual relations were permissible as long as they were marital and "natural," though interpretations of the latter varied. Jewish authorities agreed, seeing procreation as a commandment of God, though marital sex still

---

[3] *Luther's Works,* ed. Jaroslav Pelikan, vol. 7: Lectures on Genesis (St. Louis: Concordia, 1965), p. 76.

made one ritually impure. Popular ideas about sexuality, and especially those of women, are more difficult to assess than official ones. Many historians have viewed traditional popular culture in Europe as unrestrained, celebrating at least male sexuality with bawdy stories, obscene songs, and, after the development of the printing press, a range of pornographic literature. They see the sixteenth and seventeenth centuries as a period when state and church officials attempted with some success to impose their ideas on the rest of the population and repress this freer sexual expression.

It is difficult to say whether this popular acceptance of sexuality ever fully included women, however. Many songs and stories that extol the exploits of male lovers are deeply misogynist, and express a fear of rampant female sexuality similar to that found in the writings of learned authors. Women who showed too much independence, sexual or otherwise, are generally punished in popular literature, and sometimes even killed. For example, a mid-sixteenth century German song titled "Song of how one should beat bad women" included the verses:

> Now will I sing so gaily
> Hit thy wife on the head
> With cudgels smear her daily
> And drink away her dress…
> Her body be sure well pound
> With a strong hazel rod;
> Strike her head till it turns round,
> And kick her in the gut.[4]

The women who are viewed positively in early modern popular literature are generally saintly virgins who guard their chastity at all costs, or sweethearts and wives who remain loyal to one man.

Since most of these works are anonymous, we can't say for certain whether any represent the views of lower-class women, but if they do, women had internalized the negative view of their own sexuality propounded by male authors. Written works known to be by women stem mostly from the middle- and upper-classes, and rarely include any discussion of sexual feelings.

Because using literature is so problematic, another way to approach female sexuality is to investigate those women who deviated from accepted norms of behavior. All early modern societies attempted to control sexual behavior through a variety of means, from secular and

---

[4] "Ein Tagweyss/wie man die bösen weyber schlahen sol" quoted and translated in Joy Wiltenburg, *Disorderly Women and Female Power in the Street Literature of Early Modern England and Germany* (Charlottesville, University Press of Virginia, 1992), p. 121.

church courts to popular rituals designed to humiliate those perceived as deviant. Court records can give us an idea of at least what types of acts communities felt it most important to control. Because the consequences of sexual misconduct became visible within the bodies of women, they appeared more frequently than men in the courts that handled moral behavior, which confirmed people's notions that women were more sexual.

The vast majority of cases involving sexual conduct were for premarital intercourse, termed fornication. This has been best studied for England, where researchers in various counties have found that between one-fifth and one-third of brides were pregnant upon marriage in the sixteenth and seventeenth centuries, and up to one-half in the eighteenth. Much of this was because by the sixteenth century, the marriage ceremony involved several stages, a contract between the two parties agreeing to get married, and then, often much later, a formal ceremony in the church. Though officially the couple was not married until after the church ceremony, if they had agreed to marry or were regarded simply as seriously courting, sexual relations between them were not condemned in the popular mind and they might never be prosecuted for fornication. The same was also true in Norway, where 40 to 50 percent of first children were born within eight months of marriage, but it was not true in Scotland, where people never regarded sex as a normal part of courting. The contract was supposed to be somewhat formal, with witnesses and a clear understanding on the part of both parties about what they were doing, but breach-of-promise cases indicate that the two parties often had a very different understanding of what had been agreed upon.

It was often very difficult for unmarried women to avoid sexual contacts. Many of them worked as domestic servants, where their employers or employers' sons or male relatives could easily coerce them. They worked in close proximity to men (a large number of cases involved two servants in the same house) and were rarely supervised or chaperoned. Female servants were sent on errands alone or with men, or worked by themselves in fields far from other people; though notions of female honor might keep upper-class women secluded in their homes, in most parts of Europe there was little attempt to shield female servants or day-laborers from the risk of seduction or rape.

Once an unmarried woman suspected she was pregnant, she had several options. In some parts of Europe, if she was a minor her father could go to court and sue the man involved for "trespass and damages" to his property. The woman herself could go to her local court and attempt to prove there had been a promise of marriage in order to coerce the man to marry her. This might also happen once her employer or acquaintances suspected pregnancy. Marriage was the favored official solution, and was agreed upon in a surprising number of cases, indicating that perhaps there had been an informal agreement, or at least that the man was now willing to take responsibility for his actions. In cases where marriage was impossible, such as those involving married men, the courts might order the man to maintain the child for a set period of years. This worked best in Scotland, where 65 percent of the men accused of fathering illegitimate children admitted to it, though this meant they might have to pay more than half their annual wages for several years to support the child.

The woman might also charge the man concerned with rape. Rape was a capital crime in many parts of Europe, but the actual sentences handed out were more likely to be fines and brief imprisonments, with the severity of sentence dependent on the social status of the victim and perpetrator. The victim had to prove that she had cried out and made attempts to repel the attacker, and had to bring the charge within a short period of time after the attack had happened. As noted above, her pregnancy might be used as disproof that a rape had occurred, but not all jurists accepted the notion that conception proved consent. Charges of rape were fairly rare, which suggests that it was underreported, but examinations of trial records indicate that rape charges were usually taken seriously, with judges and lawyers rarely suggesting the woman herself provoked the attack. Women bringing rape charges were often more interested in getting their own honorable reputations back than in punishing the perpetrator, and for this reason sometimes requested that the judge force their rapists to marry them. We may have difficulty understanding why any woman would do this, but it was often the easiest way for a woman who was no longer a virgin to establish an honorable social identity as a married woman.

Many women attempted to deny the pregnancy as long as possible. Early modern clothing styles, with full skirts and aprons, allowed most women to go until late in the pregnancy without showing clear visible signs. A woman might attempt to induce an abortion, either by physical means such as tying her waist very tight or carrying heavy objects, or by herbal concoctions which she brewed herself or purchased from a local person reputed to know about such things. Recipes for what we would term abortificients were readily available in popular medical guides, cookbooks, and herbals, generally labeled as medicine which would bring on a late menstrual flow, or "provoke the monthlies." As we noted above, both doctors and everyday people regarded regular menstruation as essential to maintaining a woman's health, so anything that stopped her periods was dangerous. Pregnancy was only one possible reason, and a woman could not be absolutely sure she was pregnant until she quickened, that is, felt the child move within her. This was the point at which the child was regarded as gaining a soul to become fully alive – that is what "quickening" originally meant – so that a woman taking medicine to start her period before quickening was generally not regarded as attempting an abortion. Whether any of these medicines would have been effective is another matter, however. Some of them did contain ingredients that do strengthen uterine contractions, such as ergot, rue, or savin, but these can also be poisonous in large doses. It was very difficult for women to know exactly what dosage they were taking, for the raw ingredients contain widely varying amounts of active ingredients and their strength depends on how one prepares them, so that it was very likely that a woman would take too little to have any effect or too much and become violently ill or die.

Penalties for attempting or performing an abortion after the child had quickened grew increasingly harsh during the early modern period. In the Holy Roman Empire, aborting a "living" child was made a capital offense in 1532, with death to be by decapitation for men and by drowning for women. Midwives were ordered "when they come upon a young girl or someone else who is pregnant outside of marriage, they should speak to them of their own accord and warn them with threats of punishment not to harm the fetus in any way or take any bad advice, as such foolish people are very likely to do."[5] Abortion was very difficult to detect, however, and most accusations of abortion emerged in trials for infanticide, in which a mother's attempts to end her pregnancy before the birth became evidence of her intent. (Contraception was even harder to detect, and though religious and secular authorities all opposed it, there were almost no cases in which it was an issue.)

In most cases women resigned themselves to having the baby even if they could not get married, often leaving their normal place of residence to have it with friends or relatives, though it was illegal in many parts of Europe to harbor an unmarried pregnant woman. The consequences of unwed motherhood varied throughout Europe, with rural areas that suffered labor shortages being the most tolerant. In Scotland, for example, unmarried mothers had to do a public penance which could be very humiliating, but then they were officially regarded as "purged" of their sin, and apparently were able to gain employment even with their child.

---

[5] Prussian court record from 1746, quoted in Ulrike Gleixner, *"Das Mensch" und "der Kerl": Die Konstruktion von Geschlecht in Unzuchtsverfahren der Frühen Neuzeit* (Frankfurt, Campus, 1994), p. 158. My translation.

In rural Norway, about one-quarter of the unwed mothers married men other than the father of their child one to six years after giving birth, and the others managed fairly well. Even in areas where the stigma attached to giving birth out of wedlock was strong, such as England, some women gave birth to two or three children without marrying, and Peter Laslett has discovered that certain families were particularly prone to unwed parenthood among both their female and male members.

For many unmarried women, however, pregnancy meant disaster. this was particularly the case for pregancies in which the father was the woman's married employer or was related by blood or marriage to her, for this was adultery or incest rather than simple fornication and could bring great shame on the household. Women in such situations were urged to lie about the father's identity or were simply fired; they received no support from the wife of the father, whose honor and reputation were tightly bound to her husband's. Even when the man was accused of rape, his wife would stoutly defend him, asserting, as one village woman did that "he always acted honorably during the 23 years that they have been married, so this person [the pregnant maid] must have seduced him into doing this."[6] A pregnant woman fired by her employer was often in a desperate situation, as many authorities prohibited people from hiring or taking in unmarried pregnant women, charging them with aiding in a sexual offense if they did.

Women in such a situation might decide to hide the birth. They gave birth in outhouses, cowstalls, hay mounds, and dung heaps, hoping that they would be able to avoid public notice, and took the infant to one of the new foundling homes which had opened during the fifteenth or six-teenth centuries in many cities, or killed it. Before the sixteenth century, church and secular courts heard very few cases of infanticide, as jurists recognized that physicians could not make an infallible distinction between a stillbirth, a newborn who had died of natural causes, and one who had been murdered. This leniency changed in the sixteenth century, when infanticide became legally equated with murder in most areas of Europe and so carried the death penalty, often specified as death by drowning. A French royal edict promulgated in 1556 carried this even further, requiring all unmarried women to make an official declaration of their pregnancy and decreeing the death penalty for any woman whose infant died before baptism after a concealed pregnancy or deliv-ery, whether or not there was evidence of actual infanticide. A similar

---

[6] 1578 Memmingen ordinance, quoted in Merry E. Wiesner, *Working Women in Renaissance Germany* (New Brunswick, N.J., Rutgers University Press, 1986) p. 62.

statute was passed in England in 1624 and in Scotland in 1690, and in various German states throughout the seventeenth century.

These stringent statutes were quite rigorously enforced. More women were executed for infanticide in early modern Europe than any other crime except witchcraft, and in some areas the percentage of accused who were executed was much higher than the percentage of accused witches; in Geneva, for example, 25 women out of 31 charged with infanticide during the period 1595–1712 were executed, as compared with 19 out of 122 charged with witchcraft. In Belgium women found guilty of infanticide were generally also accused of witchcraft – the reasoning being that only the devil could lead a mother to kill her child – and executed in gruesome ways, such as being impaled on a stake and then buried alive, or having the offending hand cut off before being drowned. In England the conviction rate went down after 1680 when women successfully argued that they had not intended to kill the child because they had prepared linen for it, or had killed it accidentally or through ignorance. Women were still executed for presumed infanticide in Scotland until 1776, however.

Midwives were enlisted to help enforce the statutes. They were to report all births, and attempt to find out the name of the father by asking the mother "during the pains of birth." If an accused woman denied giving birth, midwives or a group of women from the village examined her to see if she had milk or showed other signs of recent delivery; in the case of foundlings, they might be asked to examine the breasts of all unmarried women in a parish for signs of childbirth. Though always justified with comments about a rising tide of infanticide, sometimes this surveillance of unmarried women bordered on the pornographic; an eighteenth-century German physician suggested, for example, that all unmarried women between the ages of 14 and 48 should be viewed monthly at a public bath to see if their bodies showed any signs of pregnancy. Midwives also examined the bodies of infants for signs that they had drawn breath. Courts were intent on gaining confessions, occasionally even bringing in the child's corpse. Records from a 1549 trial in Nuremburg report: "And then the midwife said, 'Oh, you innocent little child, if one of us here is guity, give us a sign!' and immediately the body raised its left arm and pointed at its mother."[7] The unfortunate mother was later executed by drowning.

Execution for infanticide was the most extreme result of premarital sexual activity for women, but women also suffered for much less serious actions. In many southern European cities, women charged with

[7] Nuremberg State archives, quoted in ibid., p. 71.

fornication or even unseemly behavior such as flirting or physically demonstrative conduct might be locked up in institutions established by church or city authorities for repentant prostitutes and other "fallen women." Such houses, often dedicated to Mary Magdalene, also began to admit women who were regarded as in danger of becoming prostitutes, generally poor women with no male relatives; the ordinances stated explicitly that the women admitted had to be pretty or at least acceptable looking, for ugly women did not have to worry about their honor. Many of these asylums were started by reforming bishops or leaders of religious orders, and some began to admit a variety of other types of women along with prostitutes, such as girls who had been raped, women whose husbands threatened them, attractive daughters of prostitutes, poor young widows, or young women regarded as in danger of losing their sexual honor. These various types of residents were supposed to be separated, and those still "honorable" taught a trade and given the opportunity to earn a dowry; in practice the residents were often housed together. Their founders of such asylums also supported the establishment of orphanages and foundling homes (termed *ospizi* in Italy), in which unwed mothers were required to leave their children (and in which they might be required to work as wet-nurses for other infants along with nursing their own). All of these institutions were attractive charities for those interested in moral reform, and were sometimes also supported by taxes on registered prostitutes and courtesans.

In such asylums, the women did not take vows and could leave to marry, but otherwise they were much like convents, with the women following a daily regimen of work and prayer. Some of them stressed penitence and moral reform while others were more purely punitive, closer to prisons than convents. The latter were seen as particularly appropriate for women who refused to change their ways; who – in the words of the reforming nun Madre Magdalena de San Gerónimo, "insult the honesty and virtue of the good ones with their corruption and evil" and as "wild beasts who leave their caves to look for prey" spread "family dishonor and scandal among all the people." Madre Magdalena recommended the establishment of a special women's prison to King Philip II of Spain in 1608 "where in particular the rebellious incorrigible ones will be punished."[8]

---

[8] Madre Magdalena de San Gerónimo, *Razón, y forma...* (1608) translated and quoted in Mary Elizabeth Perry, "Magdalens and Jezebels in Counter-Reformation Spain," in Anne J. Cruz and Mary Elizabeth Perry (eds.), *Culture and Control in Counter-Reformation Spain* (Minneapolis, University of Minnesota Press, 1992), pp. 135–6.

This mixture of punishment and penitence may be seen very clearly in the Parisian women's prison of the Salpêtrière. In 1658, Louis XIV ordered the imprisonment there of all women found guilty of prostitution, fornication, or adultery, with release only coming once the priests and sisters in charge determined the inmate was truly penitent and had changed her ways. Imprisoning women for sexual crimes marks the first time that prison was used as a punishment in Europe rather than simply as a place to hold people until their trial or before deportation. Such prisons later became the model for similar institutions for men and young people – often specifically called "reformatories" – in which the inmate's level of repentance determined to a great degree the length of incarceration. (This, of course, is still true for prisons and "reform schools" today.) Once men and boys as well as women and girls were locked up, however, sexual crimes were no longer the basis of the majority of incarcerations the way they were in the earliest women's prisons.

Premarital sexuality was also controlled through less formal means, such as the discussions among a woman's neighbors and acquaintances about her reputation and honor. Such discussions show up in court records when they led to charges of slander, in which, as we saw in the last chapter, the most serious accusation for a woman was to be termed a "whore," and most sexual slander directed at men – terms like "cuckold," "whoremaster," or "pimp" – actually involved the sexual activities of the women ostensibly under their control. Concern for their sexual honor combined with a clear recognition of the consequences of premarital pregnancy made women themselves the most effective controllers of their sexual conduct. Courts were only successful in imposing standards that most members of the community already accepted, as witnessed by their largely unsuccessful campaign against intercourse between engaged persons. Many women took a more pragmatic view of their honor than church and state authorities did, however, recognizing that it could often be redeemed for a price (such as a dowry) and thus had material as well as moral aspects.

So far I have been discussing women's heterosexual relations which were viewed as in some way deviant. What about homosexual relations? This is a topic that is only beginning to be studied, and many surveys of homosexuality focus exclusively or almost exclusively on men. In part this is a function of the sources, for there are many more references to male homosexuality in the prescriptive literature of the medieval and early modern periods than to female. Jewish tradition from Biblical times through the early modern period prohibited female homosexuality, but the punishment was much less than for male. The New Testament makes no clear mention of it, though medieval Christian commentators including Augustine and Aquinas interpreted a vague reference in Paul's Letter to the Romans to refer to it. Guides to priests and monks about what penances to set for various sins specifically refer to female homosexuality, generally setting lower penances than for male, though higher if the women involved were nuns or used dildos. Among the Orthodox Slavs in Eastern Europe, female homosexuals were accused of praying to female spirits and charged with paganism as well as deviant sexual behavior; female homosexuality therefore carried with it an anti-Christian component which male homosexuality did not. In western Europe, some authors commented that witches engaged in female-female sex, though this was not a standard charge against women accused of witchcraft. In 1532, female homosexuality was explicitly listed as a capital crime in Germany, though two years later an English statute prohibiting same-sex sexual relations made no mention of women at all.

These somewhat contradictory attitudes toward female-female sex stemmed in large part from misunderstandings about female anatomy combined with male bias on the part of commentators and lawmakers. Though the more enlightened sex manuals such as *Aristotle's Masterpiece* mentioned the role of the clitoris in female orgasm, male authors could not imagine satisfying sex without penetration. For many of them, there was simply no sex without penetration, so that they regarded female homosexuality as a kind of masturbation. It is, in fact, classed with masturbation as a lesser sin by many clerical commentators, for whom only male-male sex, bestiality, and heterosexual anal intercourse are major sins. Scientific writers such as Ambroise Paré interested in biological anomalies began to report in the sixteenth century about women in other parts of the world, usually the Near East or Africa, with clitorises so enlarged they could penetrate, and included these women in their discussions of monsters and prodigies. (These reports may have been motivated by learning that women in these areas underwent clitorodectomies, which led European men to assume the women's clitorises must have been overly large.) European women charged with female-female sex began to be examined for signs of enlarged clitorises, and termed "tribades" or "fricatrices," words of Greek and French origin which meant women who enjoyed rubbing.

Though there may have been some women whose clitorises were as large as those imagined in travel literature and anatomical texts, a more realistic way for women to effect penetration was to use a dildo or similar device. Women using dildos show up in early modern pornography in both text and illustrations, but pornography reflects fantasies (largely male, as were its authors in this period) rather than reality, so we cannot use it as an indication of the frequency of the practice. Dildos also show up in a few actual cases of female-female sex, and their use was uniformly condemned as far worse than female-female sex without one. A woman using a dildo was, of course, taking the male role, and most authorities regarded such gender inversion as much more serious than female homoeroticism. (In the same way, many punishments for male homosexual activity were more severe for the man who took the passive role because he was perceived as letting himself become feminized.)

The lack of understanding regarding female-female sex was generally accompanied by a lack of concern on the part of most authorities. Actual trials or accusations of female-female sex which made it into the written records are extremely rare, particularly considering the all-female milieus in which many women lived, worked, and slept, and the late age of marriage and high percentage of women who never married in some parts of Europe. Though references to female-female sex do emerge in legal and literary sources, because it did not produce children who would need to be supported, authorities were generally less concerned than they were about heterosexual fornication, particularly if both women were young and of the same social class.

Of the small number of cases involving female-female sex which actually came to trial, most involved transvestite dress or women who had otherwise usurped male prerogatives, such as the abbess Benedetta Carlini in Italy who took on the persona of a male angel to engage in sexual relations with another nun. Many of the women who were discovered dressed in men's clothing were serving as soldiers and sailors, and reported that they dressed as men primarily to gain the greater opportunities and mobility available to men, rather than for sexual reasons. Catalina de Erauso, for example, fled as a teenager from the Spanish convent where she had lived since she was four, reworked her habit into a shirt and breeches, and took off for South America. She described her various adventures in her memoirs, and, at least in her own writings, drinking, gambling, and brawling were the most significant aspects of her male identity. A few cross-dressing women actually married other women, however, including Maria of Antwerp (1719–81) who was arrested twice for marrying a woman. In her trial, she described herself not as a woman who was sexually attracted to women, but as a man in a woman's body, indicating perhaps that, like those who arrested her, she had difficulty figuring out how to describe sexual love between two women. Maria of Antwerp was exiled, and in several other cases in which cross-dressing women married other women the judges recommended that the transvestite partner be executed. In all of these cases, the "wife,"

3   Anne Bonney as a pirate, a book illustration from *Historie der Engelsche zeerovers*, 1725. Bonney was one of the women who chose to dress in men's clothing to live a more independent life, and became an almost mythic figure. Besides highly romanticized portrayals such as this, there were also songs and stories written about her life and adventures.

that is, the woman who remained in women's clothing, received a milder punishment, another indication that gender inversion was viewed as more threatening than female-female sex alone.

Maria of Antwerp had difficulty describing herself as a woman attracted to another woman, but other early modern women did not, though they generally expressed their emotions in sentimental and sensual, rather than explicitly sexual, terms. Recent studies of women's letters, poetry, diaries, and drama reveal passionate attachments and close friendships to other women, both among the female characters they create and between themselves and other actual individuals. Such "romantic friendships," as they came to be termed in the eighteenth century, were expressed physically through kissing and caressing, but did not necessarily include genital sex. This has led some analysts to deny that they were "lesbian" – a word that came into common usage only in the nineteenth century – but more recent scholarship has stressed that the notion of a "sexual identity" as heterosexual or homosexual is also more recent than the early modern period and a focus only on genital sexual acts misrepresents how women expressed erotic feelings in earlier centuries. Early modern female authors were familiar with the Platonic ideal of spiritual love and close friendship and with literary forms such as the elegy in which passion was expected, but this does not mean that their writings were simply a literary exercise accidentally addressed to another woman. Thus along with court records, literary references in works by women are providing increasing evidence about same-sex relationships and feelings, such as those expressed by Lady Mary Chudleigh in "To *Clorissa*" (1703):

> O'let our Thoughts, our Interests be but one,
> Our Griefs and Joys, be to each other known;
> In all Concerns we'll have an equal share,
> Enlarge each Pleasure, lessen ev'ry Care;
> Thus, of a thousand Sweets possest,
> We'll live in one another's Breast:
> When present, talk the flying Hours away,
> When absent, thus, our tender Thoughts convey:
> And, when by the decrees of Fate
> We're summoned to a higher State,
> We'll meet again in the blest Realms of Light,
> And in each other there eternally delight.[9]

---

[9] Lady Mary Chudleigh, "To *Clorissa*," in Robert W. Uphaus and Gretchen M. Foster (eds.), *The "Other" Eighteenth Century: English Women of Letters 1660–1800* (East Lansing, Mich., Colleagues Press, 1991), p. 148.

Marriage

For the majority of women in early modern Europe, sexual desires and relations did not lead to charges of fornication, infanticide, or deviancy, or to romantic poetry, but were simply one part of the institution that most shaped their lives – marriage. Marital patterns and customs varied widely throughout Europe, but in all places and at all times the vast majority of women and men married at least once, and society was conceived of as a collection of households, with a marital couple, or a person who had once been half of a marital couple, as the core of most households.

Marital patterns varied according to region, social class, and to a lesser degree religious affiliation. The most dramatic difference was between the area of northwestern Europe, including the British Isles, Scandinavia, France, and Germany, and eastern and southern Europe. In northwestern Europe, historians have identified a marriage pattern unique in the world, with couples waiting until their mid- or late twenties to marry, long beyond the age of sexual maturity, and then immediately setting up an independent household. Husbands were likely to be only two or three years older than their wives at first marriage, and though households often contained servants, they rarely contained more than one family member who was not a part of the nuclear family. In most of the rest of the world, including southern and eastern Europe, marriage was between teenagers who lived with one set of parents for a long time, or between a man in his late twenties or thirties and a much younger woman, with households again containing several generations. The northwestern European marriage pattern resulted largely from the idea that couples should be economically independent before they married, so that both spouses spent long periods as servants or workers in other households saving money and learning skills, or waited until their own parents had died and the family property was distributed. (Why this idea developed only in northwestern Europe has not been fully explained.) This period of waiting was so long, and the economic requirements for marriage set so high, that many women did not marry until they were in their thirties, and a significant number never married at all.

The most unusual feature of this pattern was the late age of marriage for women. Women entered marriage as adults and took charge of running a household immediately. They were thus not as dependent on their husbands as were, for example, upper-class women in early modern Italian cities, where the average age of marriage for men was over thirty and for women fifteen. They were not under the authority of their mothers-in-law the way women were in eastern European households where younger couples lived with the husbands' parents. Did this also mean that women had a greater say in who they married? This has been a hotly debated question lately, particularly for England, which provides the most sources in the form of family letters, diaries, and statistics regarding marriage. Miriam Slater and John Gillis have argued that kin networks and a woman's immediate family continued to play the major role. Slater's evidence comes largely from the upper classes, where she finds complicated marriage strategies to cement family alliances; Gillis's comes from the lower classes, where neighbors and public authorities also helped determine whether a couple would marry, the neighbors through pressuring courting couples and public authorities by simply prohibiting marriage between individuals regarded as too poor. Historians who have focused on the middle classes, such as Sara Heller Mendelson, Linda Pollock, and Alan Macfarlane, assert that though couples may have received advice or even threats, they were largely free to marry whom they wished.

In some ways this debate sets up a false dichotomy because both sides tend to focus on cases in which there was clear and recorded conflict between individuals and family or community. In the vast majority of marriages, the aims of the woman involved and her parents, kin, and community were the same; the best husband was the one who could provide security, honor, and status. Therefore even women who were the most free to choose their own husbands, such as widows or women whose parents had died, were motivated more by what we would regard as pragmatic concerns than romantic love. This is not to say that their choice was unemotional, but that the need for economic security, the desire for social prestige, and the hope for children were as important emotions as sexual passion. The love and attraction a woman felt for a man could be based on any combination of these.

The link, rather than conflict, between social and emotional compatibility was recognized explicitly by Jewish authorities. Jewish marriages in most parts of Europe continued to be arranged throughout the early modern period, and the spouses were both young. Authorities expected love to follow, however, and described the ideal marriage as one predestined in heaven. Judaism did allow divorce, which was then sometimes justified on the grounds that the spouses had obviously not been predestined for each other.

One of the key ideas of the Protestant Reformation was the denial of the value of celibacy and championing of married life as a spiritually preferable state. One might thus expect religion to have had a major effect on marriage patterns, but this is very difficult to document, in large part because all the areas of Europe that became Protestant lie within northwestern Europe. There were a number of theoretical differences. Protestant marriage regulations stressed the importance of parental consent more than Catholic ones, and allowed the possibility of divorce with remarriage for adultery or impotence, and in some areas also for refusal to have sexual relations, deadly abuse, abandonment, or incurable diseases such as leprosy; Orthodox courts in eastern Europe allowed divorce for adultery or the taking of religious vows. The numbers of women who actually used the courts to escape an unpleasant marriage were very small, however, and apparently everywhere smaller than the number of couples who informally divorced by simply moving apart from one another. Women more often used the courts to attempt to form a marriage (i.e., in breach of promise cases, or to renew a marriage in which their spouse had deserted them), than to end one. The impossibility of divorce in Catholic areas was mitigated somewhat by the possibility of annulment and by institutions that took in abused or deserted wives; similar institutions were not found in Protestant areas.

Social class had a larger impact than religion on marital patterns. Throughout Europe, rural residents married earlier than urban ones, and were more likely to live in complex households of several generations or married brothers and their families living together. They also remarried faster and more often. Women from the upper classes married earlier than those from the lower, and the age difference between spouses was greater for upper-class women. Women who had migrated in search of employment married later than those who had remained at home, and married someone closer to their own age.

Along with significant differences, there were also similarities in marriage patterns throughout Europe. Somewhere around one-fifth of all marriages were remarriages for at least one of the partners, with widowers much more likely to remarry than widows and to remarry faster. The reasons for this differ according to social class; wealthy or comfortable widows may have seen no advantage in remarrying, for this would put them under the legal control of a man again, and poor widows, particularly elderly ones, found it very difficult to find marriage partners. Women of all classes were expected to bring a dowry to their marriage, which might consist of some clothing and household items (usually including the marriage bed and bedding) for poor women, or vast amounts of cash, goods, or property for wealthy ones; in eastern Europe the dowry might even include serfs or slaves. This dowry substituted in most parts of Europe for a daughter's share of the family inheritance, and increasingly did not include any land, which kept land within the patrilineal lineage. Laws regarding a woman's control of her dowry varied throughout Europe, but in general a husband had the use, but not the ownership, of it during his wife's lifetime, though of course if he invested it unwisely this distinction did not make much difference. Women could sue their own husbands if they thought they were wasting their dowries, however, and courts in many areas sided with the women, taking control of the dowry out of the husbands' hands. This was clearly something done only as a last resort, however, as it meant a woman had to admit publicly her husband was a wastrel or spendthrift. During the late medieval period, women appear to have been able freely to bequeath their dowries to whomever they chose, but in many parts of Europe this right was restricted during the sixteenth century to prevent them from deeding property to persons other than the male heirs.

This increasing legal emphasis on the male lineage paralleled an increasing concern among male religious, literary, and political writers with the authority and role of the male head of household, as we have seen in Chapter 1. At the same time, Puritans and some other Protestant writers also stressed the wife's authority over children and servants and the importance of mutual affection between spouses. But what about actual marital relations? Did husbands and wives show more or less affection for one another than modern couples? Which injunction was followed more in practice, that of husbandly authority or that of mutual respect? Studies that address these questions have been undertaken for various parts of Europe for the last twenty years, but little consensus has developed. Lawrence Stone took a very negative stance, viewing the early modern family as patriarchal and authoritative and relations between spouses and parents and children as cold and unfeeling. Most work since then has modified this position, using a variety of sources. Michael MacDonald has discovered that many people turned to physicians in seventeenth-century England because of serious depression suffered at the loss of a spouse or child. He and other historians have used a variety of sources to discover that people, particularly women, expected a marriage to include affection and companionship and were very distressed when it did not. Examples of tyrannical husbands and of mutually caring relationships both abound, with the safest generalization that which also seems the most obvious – marriages appear to have been most egalitarian when husband and wife were near in age, of the same or relatively the same social class, when the woman had brought some property or cash to the marriage as her dowry, and when her birth family supported her in disputes with her husband.

Marriage not only brought a woman into a relationship with her husband, but also with her husband's family, and often a new neighborhood and community; it also transformed her relationship with her birth family. Despite the increased emphasis on patrilineality, women in most parts of Europe continued to think of themselves as still belonging to their birth families, or as belonging to two families at once. Women's wills often bequeathed items and cash to their sisters or nieces, and provided for masses to be said for members of their birth as well as marital family; women sometimes chose to be buried with their birth families rather than their husbands.

Marriage was the clearest mark of social adulthood for both women and men; for men marriage often meant that they could now be part of the governing body of their village or town, a role from which unmarried men were excluded, and for women that they would have authority over dependent members of the household. Middle-class urban women also began during the early modern period to redefine what it meant to be a "housewife." In part this was a response to their exclusion from productive labor outside of the household, which we will discuss in the next chapter, and in part a response to the increased emphasis on the family and marriage, particularly in Protestant areas. In fact, it was the wives of Protestant pastors who were often the leaders in a town in the creation of this expanded domestic role. Medieval urban "housewives" had had very little time for purely domestic labor; cooking was simple, cleaning tasks were few, and many domestic tasks such as baking and laundry were hired out. This began to change in the sixteenth and even more in the seventeenth centuries, when foodstuffs were more likely to come into households in a less finished state and middle-class households contained more consumer goods that needed cleaning and care. Of necessity, the time spent by middle-class women on domestic tasks expanded, particularly as things which had been unavailable or unimportant in the Middle Ages – glass windows, a stone floor instead of a dirt one, several courses at dinner – became important signs of middle-class status. Now the ideal wife was not simply one who showed religious virtues such as piety and modesty, but also economic ones such as order, industriousness, and thrift. We are used to thinking about the early modern period as a time of growing prosperity among the middle classes; the fruits of that prosperity, what we would term the "bourgeois life-style," were determined and to a large degree created by middle-class married women.

But what about women who could not or chose not to get married? In eastern Europe, with a much earlier average age at first marriage, the number of women who never married was very small, and most of them were in convents. In southern Europe, wealthy or middle-class women who chose not to marry or whose parents could not raise a dowry large enough to obtain an appropriate husband also ended up in convents, whose standards about austerity were often not very high so that the women lived the same comfortable life-style they would have on the outside. In 1552 in Florence, for example, there were 441 male friars and 2,786 nuns, out of a population of 59,000; the difference between the two numbers results not from women's great religious fervor, but from a staggering increase in the size of the dowry required for a middle- or upper-class woman to marry. Historians are currently debating the cause of this dowry inflation, and it was decried at the time by moralists who rightly saw it as preventing people from marrying. Families were unable to control it, however, and so placed their daughters in convents instead of trying to find husbands for them, because convent entrance fees were much lower than dowries.

Entrance fees for convents were too high for poor women, however, and, as noted above, special institutions were opened in Italian cities by the Catholic Church and municipal governments for young, attractive unmarried women to allow them to earn a dowry and thus perhaps a husband. Women whose marriage chances were seen as unlikely in any case were also often sent to convent-like religious institutions, where they did not take formal vows and worked at spinning or sewing to support themselves. Unmarried poor women also worked as domestic servants for their entire lives, living in the household of their employer and so under his control.

In the cities of northwestern Europe, the number of unmarried women had been significant since the Middle Ages, and did not decrease in the early modern period. Demographers estimate that between 10 to 15 percent of the northwestern European population never married in the early modern period, and that in some places in some eras this figure may have been as high as 25 percent, making this more important than late marriage as a check on population growth. Cities attracted unmarried women with the possibility of employment as domestic servants or in cloth production, a situation reflected in the gradual transformation of the word "spinster" during the seventeenth century from a label of occupation to one of marital status. The types of employment open to unmarried women or widows left without resources were generally poorly paid, which we can see from the fact that households headed by widows and unmarried women were always the poorest in any city; unattached women often had to live together in order to survive.

In the late Middle Ages, city governments worried about how to keep unmarried women and widows from needing public support, and in the sixteenth century, cities began to view women living independently as a moral, as well as an economic problem. They were "masterless," that is, not members of a male-headed household, at a time when greater stress was being laid on the authority of the husband and father, and so were perceived as a possible threat to the social order. Laws were passed forbidding unmarried women to move into cities and ordering unmarried female servants who had left one domestic position to leave the city, should they refuse to take another one. In some cases grown, unmarried daughters were ordered to leave the household of their widowed mothers to find a position in a male-headed household if their mothers could not prove need for them at home. Suspicion of unmarried women was not completely new in the sixteenth century, for medieval religious groups such as the Beguines had also experienced it, but this was the first time actual laws had been enacted against secular unmarried women. Both Protestant and Catholic authorities increasingly viewed marriage as the "natural" vocation for women – for all women in Protestant areas and for most women in Catholic areas – so that women who did not marry were somehow "unnatural" and therefore suspect.

Women themselves sometimes internalized the stigma attached to never being married. This was particularly true for middle- and upper-class Protestant women, who in only a few parts of Europe had convents as an alternative. The funeral sermons of unmarried women, for which the women themselves often chose their own Biblical texts and wrote the biographical segment, explain that the deceased was not simply a person who had lost out in the marriage market, but one who had fulfilled her Christian duties in other ways than being a wife or mother, such as taking care of elderly parents or serving the needy. Middle-class unmarried women in England took part in philanthropy, and in the eighteenth century began to teach in schools that were slowly opening for poor children, a field they would come to dominate in the nineteenth century.

Not all women agreed that marriage was preferable, however. The opposite opinion was expressed most eloquently by Anna Bijns, a sixteenth-century Antwerp poet:

> How good to be a woman, how much better to be a man!
> Maidens and wenches, remember the lesson you're about to hear
> Don't hurtle yourself into marriage far too soon.
> The saying goes: "Where's your spouse? Where's your honor?"
> But one who earns her board and clothes
> Shouldn't scurry to suffer a man's rod.
> So much for my advice, because I suspect –
> Nay, see it sadly proven day by day –
> 'T happens all the time!
> However rich in goods a girl might be,
> Her marriage ring will shackle her for life.
> If however she stays single
> With purity and spotlessness foremost,

Then she is lord as well as lady. Fantastic, not?
Though wedlock I do not decry:
Unyoked is best! Happy the woman without a man.[10]

Pregnancy, childbirth, and motherhood

Very shortly after marriage (and in many cases before marriage, as we
have seen) most women in early modern Europe were pregnant. In all
religious traditions, the procreation of children was viewed as one of the
most important functions of marriage – or the most – and childless couples were viewed with pity. Childlessness hit women particularly hard,
because despite the fact that many people regarded the man as the
source of all the active forces in the creation of a child and the woman
simply the vessel, childlessness was invariably seen as the woman's fault.
This is one of the reasons that suggestions about how to promote fertility through diet, exercise, potions, and charms were extremely common
in midwives' manuals and advice books for women. Childless men could
test their fertility outside of marriage with little public condemnation
(though not officially condoned, adultery if one's wife was barren was
rarely punished), but childless wives did not have this opportunity.

Determining whether one was pregnant was not an easy matter, however. The cessation of menses opened up the possibility, but midwives'
manuals and women's private medical guides cautioned women against
regarding this as a clear sign, because it may also have been due to other
medical conditions. Nausea, breast enlargement, and thickening around
the middle also pointed toward pregnancy, but only at quickening – that
is, when the mother could feel the child move within her body which
usually happens during the fourth or fifth month – was the mother
regarded as verifiably pregnant. Until the late eighteenth century on the
Continent and the nineteenth century in England, quickening was also
viewed as the point at which a child gained a soul, so that charges of
abortion could not be brought against a woman who had not yet quickened. This legal definition affected the way that women thought about
their own pregnancies, for they did not describe a miscarriage before
quickening as the end of a pregnancy or the death of a child, but as the
expulsion of blood curds or leathery stuff or wrong growths. Pregnancy
was not a condition affirmed externally and visually the way it is today
with home pregnancy tests and ultrasound screenings, but internally

---

[10] Anna Bijns, "Unyoked is best! Happy the woman without a man," trans. Kristiaan P. G.
Aercke, reprinted in Katharina M. Wilson (ed.), *Women Writers of the Renaissance and
Reformation* (Athens, University of Georgia Press, 1987), p. 382.

and tactilely, with only the mother able to confirm that quickening had happened.

Once a woman suspected or knew she was pregnant, she received a great amount of advice. The sixteenth century saw the publication of the first midwives' manuals in most European languages, which contained advice for prenatal care for the mother as well as the handling of deliveries. These manuals were reprinted and pirated for centuries, and new ones published in the seventeenth century, but their advice for expectant mothers changed little. Much of what they advise is still recommended today: pregnant women should eat moderately of nourishing foods, including a good amount of protein, and avoid foods that make them nauseous or that are highly spiced; they should moderate their drinking and avoid strong liquors; they should get regular exercise but avoid strenuous lifting; they should wear low-heeled shoes and loosen their lacing or corsets. The advisability of sexual intercourse during pregnancy was debated, as was the practice of letting blood from pregnant women. Many of their suggestions have to do with the mental, rather than strictly physical well-being of the expectant mother, and stem from a strong belief in the power of the maternal imagination. Both learned and uneducated people in early modern Europe believed that what a woman saw or experienced during pregnancy could affect the child. The desire to drink red wine or eat strawberries might lead to children with red birthmarks; being frightened by a hare or longing to eat hare caused harelip; sudden frights might cause a miscarriage or deform the fetus in some way. Birth defects were regularly attributed to bad experiences during pregnancy, or to a woman's frequent contact with animals.

As the time of the birth approached, a woman began to make preparations. She decided which friends and neighbors she would invite to assist her, a matter taken very seriously; witchcraft accusations occasionally stemmed from the curses and anger of a neighbor who had not been invited. If she lived in a town where the services of professional midwives were available, the mother chose which midwife would direct the birth. If she lived in a rural area, she would generally contact a woman known to be experienced in handling childbirths, for midwives who had undergone some theoretical training in childbirth procedure were rare in the countryside. In rural areas where church approval was needed to practice midwifery, village women simply chose one of their number as the most experienced, and then gave her name to the church authorities.

Until the mid-seventeenth century, and until the twentieth in many parts of Europe for most women, childbirth was strictly a female affair. The husband was not present unless his wife was dying, and male med-

4   Albrecht Dürer, *The Birth of Mary*. Though ostensibly the depiction of the birth of Mary, in reality Dürer's engraving portrays a typical sixteenth-century birth scene, with a number of women bustling
about, the baby being bathed and the tired midwife asleep by the bed.

ical practitioners took little interest in delivery. Male physicians were only called in if the child or mother or both were dead or dying, so their presence was dreaded.

This began to change in France in the mid-seventeenth century, where some male barber-surgeons began to advertise their services for childbirth as well, and the use of "man-midwives" came to be fashionable among the wealthy. At first the techniques of these men differed little from those of educated urban female midwives, for both read the same books and had the same concepts of anatomy and the birth process, but gradually the training of male midwives improved as they took part in dissections and anatomical classes, from which women were excluded.

Male midwifery spread to England, where sometime in the seventeenth century the forceps was invented by the Chamberlen brothers, who kept its design a family secret for nearly a century and then revealed it only to other male midwives. The forceps allows a midwife to grasp the head of a child who has become lodged in the birth passage and pull it out, a procedure that is not usually possible with the hands alone and had been accomplished earlier only on dead children with hooks stuck in their mouths or eyes. A higher level of training and more use of instruments made male midwives appear more scientific and "modern" to middle- and upper-class English and French women, though there was still a strong sense of the impropriety of male practitioners touching women in childbirth among rural residents and lower-class urban dwellers, who could not pay the fees demanded by male midwives in any case. Male midwives were not very common in the early modern period in Germany, and were not found at all in eastern and southern Europe, where female urban midwives were much more likely to be granted access to formal training in female anatomy and physiology than they were in France or England. In northern Italy in particular, midwifery schools were founded in the mid-eighteenth century to teach women anatomy, though most midwives continued to be educated through apprenticeship.

Once labor had begun, the women assisting transformed the room, or in small houses the bed, into a "lying-in chamber," according to local traditions of what was proper. In many parts of Europe, air was viewed as harmful to the mother, so doors and windows were shut and candles lit. Special objects felt to be efficacious in speeding delivery were brought in, such as amulets, relics of saints, or certain herbs. Special prayers were offered, prayers that were often the most resistant to change when the religious allegiance of an area changed. The women prepared broth or mulled wine (termed "caudle" in England) to nourish the mother through the delivery, and arranged the swaddling clothes for the infant.

The actual techniques of delivery varied widely, even within the same town. Some midwives and mothers preferred to use a birthing stool, a special padded stool with handles which tipped the mother back slightly; other mothers lay in bed, kneeled, stood, or sat in another woman's lap. The level of intervention also varied from midwife to midwife. Some immediately began vaginal massage and tried to speed the birth along by making the mother change positions or pulling on the child as it emerged; such midwives also often pulled on the afterbirth to be sure it all emerged quickly, a technique that could be very dangerous as too vigorous pulling can cause the uterus to become detached from the abdomen or even emerge. Others might wait for days during a very difficult labor before attempting to interfere. The most skillful and best-trained midwives took a middle route, intervening only when they thought it necessary, which was usually a case of abnormal presentation. If the child was emerging feet or knees first (breech), it could usually be delivered, but if it emerged arm- or face-first it generally needed to be turned. Until the invention of the forceps, the best way to do this was to reach inside the uterus and grasp the feet, turning the child by the feet to effect a feet-first birth (this technique is termed podalic version). Midwives' manuals beginning in the sixteenth century recommend this, and records of births handled by professional midwives throughout the early modern period indicate they handled this technique successfully.

There is currently great debate about how to assess the level of skill of early modern midwives. They have been viewed on one hand as drunken bunglers and licensed torturers and on the other as representatives of traditional female culture in which birth was a natural process, successfully handled in all but a tiny proportion of cases and the cause for group celebration. Some researchers assert that the early modern period saw childbirth as pathological, routinely associated with illness and death, while others state that it was not medicalized until the eighteenth century. All of these views are probably true to some degree. Urban midwives were highly supervised and regulated beginning in German cities in the sixteenth century and slightly later elsewhere, were generally literate and had received both theoretical and practical training; their level of skill was highly regarded, as rural noblewomen called for them at every childbirth. Rural midwives did not until the eighteenth century have much opportunity for training, and are sharply criticized in the guides and diaries written by their urban colleagues. Childbirth was an event with many meanings, at once a source of joy and the cause of deep foreboding. Most women experienced multiple childbirths successfully, but all knew of or had even watched someone die in childbed. Using English statistics, it has been estimated that the maternal mortality rate in the past was about 1 percent for each birth, which would make a lifetime risk of 5 to 7 percent. Women knew these risks, which is why they attempted to obtain the services of the midwife they regarded as the most skilled. The fact that they took such care is probably the best indication that the talent and competence of one's midwife could make a significant difference.

Though we have very few records from midwives themselves, those that exist can give us a glimpse of both their activities and their self-concept. Catharina Schrader (1656–1746) was a professional midwife in the Netherlands who kept notebooks of all of her cases between the years 1693 and 1745, more than 3,000 in all. When she was in her eighties, she decided to pull all of her most complicated cases into a single book, dedicating it to the women she had delivered. Her discussion of one difficult delivery reads:

1711 on 10 February I was fetched to Nijkerk to Wattse Jennema, whose wife was called Alltie Jouwkes. She wanted me to attend to her, but didn't call for me. And fetched a midwife from Morra, who tortured her for three days. She turned it over to the man-midwife, doctor Van der Berrg. He said, he must cut off the child's arms and legs. He took her [the mother] for dead. And he said, the child is already dead. Then I was fetched in secret. When I came there her husband and friends were weeping a great deal. I examined the case, suspected that I had a chance to deliver [her]. The woman was very worn out. I laid her in a warm bed, gave her a cup of caudle, also gave her something in it; sent the neighbors home, so that they would let her rest a bit. An hour after her strength awakened again somewhat. And I had the neighbors fetched again. And after I had positioned the woman in labour, [I] heard that the doctor came then to sit by my side. I pulled the child to the birth canal and in half of a quarter hour I got a living daughter. And I said to the doctor, here is your dead child, to his shame. He expected to earn a hundred guilders there [about 10–20 times what Schrader usually earned]. The friends and neighbors were very surprised. The mother and the child were in a very good state.[11]

Midwives were responsible for the spiritual as well as the physical well-being of the children they delivered. In both Catholic and Protestant areas, they were allowed to perform emergency baptisms on children they thought might die, and midwifery ordinances contain careful instructions on how to do this properly. By the middle of the eighteenth century in Catholic areas they were also instructed to baptize a fetus that had miscarried and to perform a Caesarean section on any pregnant woman who

[11] Hilary Marland, *Mother and Child were Saved: the Memoirs (1693–1745) of the Frisian Midwife Catharina Schrader* (Amsterdam, Rodopi, 1987), pp. 62–4.

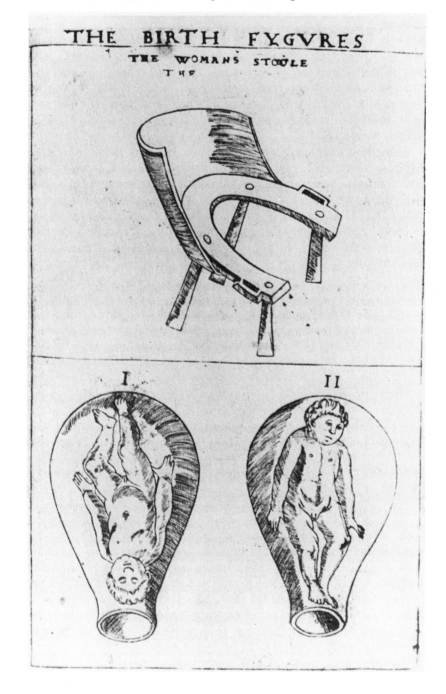

had died in order to baptize the fetus within her. This intensification of concern with a midwife's spiritual duties among Catholics led in some areas to a decreasing concern with the physical care of mother and child; one study from a small city in Germany where Catholics and Protestants lived side-by-side has revealed that the postpartum death rate of Catholic mothers and infants (handled by Catholic midwives) was significantly higher than that of Protestants (handled by Protestant midwives) of the same social class during the period 1650–1800.

Mothers of all religions in Europe recognized that the dangers of childbirth might be intensified when children were born too close together, and attempted to space births through a variety of means. Many nursed their children until they were more than two years old, which acted as a contraceptive, for suckling encourages the release of the hormone prolactin, which promotes the production of milk and inhibits the function of the ovaries. They sought to abstain from sexual relations during the time of their monthly cycle regarded as most fertile, though this "rhythm method," based on an incorrect view of the menstrual cycle, was even less effective than that practiced in the twentieth century. Judging by the frequency with which such practices were condemned, couples regularly attempted to restrict fertility through coitus interruptus, magical charms, and herbal potions; the first of these was the most effective. Condoms made from animal intestines or bladders were available to those who could afford them by the mid-sixteenth century, but they were originally designed to protect men from veneral disease carried by prostitutes and were only slowly seen as a possible means of fertility control for married couples. All of the methods that could be effective – abstinence, coitus interruptus, condoms – required the cooperation of the woman's husband, of course.

The experience of childbirth did not end with actual birth. In most parts of Europe, mothers were advised to undergo a period of "lying-in" after the birth, in which they sharply restricted their activities and contacts with the outside world. Although this was difficult for many rural and poor women, religious taboos which made a recently delivered mother impure meant that such restrictions were often followed

---

5 These illustrations from Thomas Raynalde, *The Byrth of Mankynde*, 1545, a popular English midwives' manual, depict a standard birthing stool, with handles at the sides for the mother to grasp, and early modern ideas of a baby *in utero*; they had originally appeared in a German midwives' manual, and were frequently reprinted in manuals in other languages throughout Europe.

even when they were economically disadvantageous. Early modern Russia had perhaps the strongest taboos, for Orthodoxy taught that everything associated with childbirth, including the midwife, attendants, place, and even the child was defiled. Not until her ritual of purification, which occurred forty days after birth, was anyone supposed to eat in the woman's company; baptism was often delayed until the same day so that the newborn remained impure and could nurse from its impure mother. Judaism and Catholicism had a similar ritual of purification, though contacts with the mother were not so sharply restricted. Her movements outside the home were, however, which meant a Catholic woman could not attend her child's baptism; in Italy the midwife who carried the child was the only woman normally present at a baptism. In some parts of Catholic Europe, this purification ceremony was seen as so important that it was performed over the coffin of a woman who had died in childbirth.

Protestants rejected the idea that women needed to be purified after giving birth, but Anglicans and some continental Protestants retained the ceremony, commonly called churching, terming it instead a service of thanksgiving. In some Lutheran areas, churching was required of all married mothers and forbidden to those who gave birth out of wedlock, another mark of the distinction between honorable and dishonorable women. Among Anglicans, unmarried women who had given birth were only to be churched if they named the father and wore a white sheet signifying their penitence during the service. Churching was violently opposed by English Puritan men in the seventeenth century as a Catholic holdover, but many Puritan women continued to demand it, as did English women well into the twentieth century even if they never attended other church services. We may view churching and similar ceremonies as stemming from clerical hostility toward the female body and childbirth, but there is evidence that early modern women rejected this interpretation and instead regarded churching as a necessary final act of closure to a period of childbirth. A woman attended her churching in the presence of the women who had been with her during the birth, including the midwife, and many of the rituals that were part of churching were of popular, rather than ecclesiastical, origin. Women objected when pastors sought to change the ritual in any way; one report from Abingdon in England in 1668 noted that "women refuse to be churched because they have not their right place, and midwives are excluded... from their women, who always used to sit together."[12] Churching is, in fact, only

[12] Quoted in David Cressy, *Birth, Marriage and Death: Ritual, Religion, and the Life Cycle in Tudor and Stuart England* (London, Oxford, 1997), p. 227.

one of many popular rituals and beliefs surrounding birth which did not die out in the eighteenth century. Evidence gathered in the mid-twentieth century indicates that people continued to regard a woman who had recently given birth as unlucky, and prohibited her from touching wells or stalls or visiting her neighbors.

The vast majority of women during the early modern period nursed their own children, often until they were more than two years old and on demand rather than on a set schedule. Women who could not produce their own milk and middle- and upper-class women in many parts of Europe relied on wet nurses, the very wealthy hiring the nurse to come into their own homes, and the rest sending the child to the home of the wet nurse, often for two or three years. Though by the eighteenth century this practice came to be viewed by moralists like Rousseau as a sign of the heartlessness and decadence of wealthy women, it actually stemmed from the fact that nursing was incompatible with many of their familial and social duties. Wealthy women were pressured to produce many heirs, and people seem to have been aware of the contraceptive effects of lactation; they were advised that nursing would ruin their physical attractiveness; they were taught that sexual intercourse would corrupt their milk and that their first duty was to their husbands. The decision to hire a wet nurse was often made not by the woman herself but by her husband, who made a contract with the wet nurse's husband for her services.

Wet nurses were chosen with great care, with those from rural areas who had borne many healthy children favored. Psychological and moral qualities were also taken into consideration, for it was thought that an infant gained these through the nurse's milk; after the Reformation, for example, parents inquired about the religious affiliation of any prospective nurse, for Catholic parents feared the corruption caused by Protestant milk, and vice versa. The wet nurse and her husband had to agree to refrain from sexual relations during the period of the contract, for it was thought that pregnancy tainted a woman's milk.

Along with the children of the wealthy, wet nurses also cared for the children of the poor; communities hired wet nurses to suckle foundlings and orphans, and by the eighteenth century working women in some parts of Europe hired wet nurses so that they could work longer hours without stopping. Many of these poor children died, as did many of the wealthy, some no doubt because of neglect or carelessness, but also because the wet nurses themselves were generally poor and took on more children than they had milk; in many cases these women had sent their own infant to an even poorer woman in order to take on children to nurse in the first place. These deaths led wet nurses to be called "angel-killers" by eighteenth-century writers advocating maternal nursing, but it is difficult to document whether infant mortality rates were actually higher for the children in their care than they would have been otherwise; for orphans or foundlings, there was no other option anyway, and evidence clearly indicates that mortality among children put to nurse went up when dry nursing (feeding infants with flour gruel or pap sucked off a rag) was substituted for wet nursing.

Wet nurses often became very fond of the children they suckled, and were reluctant to return them to their parents, sometimes remaining with the children as servants or companions into adulthood. Some historians have speculated that children in early modern Europe also suffered emotional distress because of the wet-nursing system; frequent changes in wet nurses, the absence of their biological mother, and permanent separation from the wet nurse at weaning could prevent small children from forming good relationships with women. Because infant feelings affect later psychological development, wet nursing has been seen as contributing to negative ideas about women, particularly their fickleness and changeability. The irony of these possible consequences is the fact that, until the mid-eighteenth century, it was husbands who made the decision about how a child would be nursed. Only at that point did some middle- and upper-class women begin to assert their right to nurse their own children, and the rate of maternal nursing among these social groups increased.

Motherhood is, of course, an emotional and intellectual experience as well as a physical one, and, in sharp contrast to the theories of contemporary historians about parental coldness, early modern mothers generally became deeply attached to their children. Even those forced to abandon them for economic reasons could be torn apart by the decision, as this noted pinned to a foundling left in 1709 indicates:

This child was born the 11th of June 1708 of unhappy parents which is not able to provide for it; therefore I humbly beg of you gentlemen whosoever hands this unfortunate child shall fall into that you will take that care that will become a fellow creature and if God makes me able I will repay the charge and redeem the child with thanks to you for her care... pray believe that it is extreme necessity that makes me do this.[13]

The deaths or illnesses of their children often led women into depression or even suicidal despair, and those who showed no attachment to their children were viewed as mentally disturbed.

---

[13] St. Martin in the Fields parish examination book, quoted in Valerie Fildes, "Maternal feelings re-assessed: child abandonment and neglect in London and Westminster, 1550–1800," in her *Women as Mothers in Pre-industrial England* (London, Routledge, 1990), p. 153 (spelling modernized).

Women's concern over their children became particularly acute during their own illnesses, leading a number of middle- and upper-class women to write advice books for their children in case they should die. Dorothy Leigh in *The Mother's Blessing* (London, 1616) commented that "motherly affection" led her to risk public censure by writing, and Elizabeth Grymeston opened *Miscelanea, Meditations, Memoratives* (London, 1604) with the comment:

My dearest son, there is nothing so strong as the force of love; there is no love so forcible as the love of an affectionate mother to her natural child: there is no mother can either more affectionately show her nature, or more naturally manifest her affection, than in advising her children out of her own experience, to eschew evil, and incline them to do that which is good.[14]

These books include much more advice about personal and family matters such as the choice of a spouse than do similar books written by men; a guide for her son written by Elisabeth, the widowed ruler of Braunschweig in Germany, includes long discussions of his role as a father as well as a ruler, a concern not found in similar "mirrors of princes" written by male rulers.

Widowhood and old age

Widowhood and old age are usually linked in the modern world, but they were not necessarily in early modern Europe, for women became widows at all ages, and might easily be widowed several times during their lives. The death of a spouse brought a more dramatic change in status for women than it did for men, for their link to the world of work was often through their husbands, so that his death affected their opportunities for making a living while the death of a wife did not. We can see this distinction in the fact that the word for "widower" in most European languages derives from the word for "widow," whereas the more common pattern is for the female designation to derive from the male – princess from prince, actress from actor. The word "widower," in fact, does not enter common usage until the eighteenth century, when people began to think about the loss of a spouse more as an emotional than an economic issue.

In many parts of the world women who became widowed returned to their birth families or entered the household of a brother or brother-in-law, but in most areas of Europe widows became heads of households

---

[14] Elizabeth Grymeston, *Miscelanae, Meditations, Memoratives* (London, 1604), quoted in Betty Travitsky, *The Paradise of Women: Writings by Englishwomen of the Renaissance* (New York, Columbia University Press, 1989), p. 52 (spelling modernized).

themselves and were forced to find some way to survive and to support their dependent children. Not surprisingly, widowhood generally brought a decline in a woman's economic status, with the poorest households in towns and villages those headed by elderly widows. During times of economic hardship, crime by widows, mostly petty theft, increased, though authorities tended to treat them less harshly than other malefactors.

Though widowhood often brought economic adversity, it also gave women a wider range of action throughout most of Europe. Widows who had inherited money or property from their husbands or who had received their dowry back at his death were usually quite free to invest it or dispose of it as they wished; records from rural England and Germany indicate that widows frequently engaged in moneylending. Aristocratic widows were often very active managing their families' business affairs, and identified the rights and privileges attached to their position as *theirs,* and not simply belonging to them in trust for their sons. The widows of some officeholders in France and Germany could inherit the office and the income that went with it, and artisans' widows could inherit their husbands' shops, though these inheritance rights were restricted beginning in the sixteenth century, as we will see in the next chapter. Widowhood could also place a woman in a position of great power over her children, deciding the amount of dowry for her daughters and assisting her sons in gaining positions of political influence.

Thus the fact that widows were not cared for within extended families was in some ways cruel, but it also meant that a greater share of the population was active economically through work or investing than in parts of the world where widows simply retreated into the household of a male family member. The prominence of widows was not new in early modern Europe, but had begun in the High Middle Ages, leading some historians to speculate that this was one of the factors in the dramatic expansion of the European economy which occurred at the same time. (The ability of an economy to grow is closely linked, along with other factors, to the size of the workforce; medieval and early modern widows' participation in economic life bolstered the European economy in the same way that the entrance of huge numbers of married women with children bolstered the U.S. economy in the 1970s and 1980s.)

Because nuclear households were the norm among most classes in most parts of Europe, there was really no alternative to allowing widows more economic and social independence than any other group of women, for they were the maintainers of a family unit. They were still very disturbing to notions of male authority, however, both because they were economically independent and because they were sexually experienced women not under the tutelage of a man. Thus remarriage was often seen as the best solution to the problem of these women who were neither "married or to be married." Remarriage was also troubling, however, for this lessened a woman's allegiance to the family of her first husband and could have serious economic consequences for the children of her first marriage, and might also give a wealthy widow what was seen as an inappropriate amount of power over her spouse. Early modern laws regarding widows often reflect this ambivalence. In many parts of Europe laws made remarriage more attractive by requiring a widow to have a male guardian co-sign all financial transactions, even religious donations, and giving him power over her own children. The same law code might also make it less attractive by stipulating that a widow could lose all rights over her children through remarriage, including the right to see them. Not wishing to contemplate either the independence or remarriage of their wives, lawmakers were thus attempting somehow to keep a widow dependent on the family of her first husband.

In actual practice, whether a widow remarried or not was more determined by her economic and personal situation than by laws or theoretical concerns. Younger widows remarried much more readily than older ones, and widows with few children more readily than those with many. (The opposite is true in the case of widowers; those with many children were most likely to remarry, and to remarry quickly.) Widowers were far more likely to remarry than widows; French statistics from the seventeenth century indicate that 50 percent of widowers remarried, while only 20 percent of widows did so. For very poor widows or those with many children this low rate of remarriage stemmed from the fact that they were less attractive on the marriage market than single women, but for middle- and upper-class women it was often the result of their choice; the "lusty widow" who wants to remarry as quickly as possible is a common figure in early modern literature, but studies indicate that women who could afford to resisted all pressure to remarry and so retained their independence.

Widowhood was a clear legal status, but "old age" in the early modern period is harder to define. For women, the best marker might be menopause, which usually occurred somewhere in a woman's forties; the mean age at which women in northwestern Europe bore their last child was forty. Generally a woman's fertility lessened as she grew older, and attempts at contraception appear to have increased in England and France by the late seventeenth century among older couples. Because life expectancy was less than it was today, however, even if a woman stopped having children before forty she still had children in her household for most of her later years of life. Older women (and men) whose children had all left home generally continued to live on their own as long as possible. Evidence from England indicates that middle-class children were more likely to assist their elderly parents by providing them with servants so that they could stay in their own households rather than taking them in; the elderly lived with their married children only among the poor. Though we often romanticize earlier periods as a time when the elderly were cherished for their wisdom and experience, this was not necessarily so. In many parts of Europe, parents made formal contracts with their children to assure themselves of a certain level of material support (e.g., "twelve bushels of rye and a place by the fire"), and public welfare rolls included many elderly whose children were still in the area but were not supporting them.

Older women were generally more in need of public support than older men, in part because their spouses were less likely or able to care for them than were the wives of older men, who were generally younger or had no way to leave an ailing spouse. Younger relatives were also more willing to take in elderly men than women; older women often formed joint households with other older female relatives or simply acquaintances to pool their resources and expenses, a practice almost unknown among men. The higher percentage of elderly female welfare recipients may have also been partly due to the fact that there were simply more older women than men around. Despite the dangers of childbirth, female life expectancy seems to have been gradually growing longer than male throughout the early modern period; by the eighteenth century in France, female life expectancy at birth was about thirty-four and male about thirty-one.

Aging brought physical as well as economic changes, and there is evidence that these were viewed as more of a problem for women than men already in the sixteenth century. Post-menopausal women were widely believed to experience increased sex drive, which might even lead them to seek demonic lovers in order to satisfy themselves. They were held to emit vapors from their mouths which could cause nursing women's milk to dry up or animals and children to sicken. They were thought to be especially concerned with the lessening of their physical attractiveness, for a Spanish physician's remedies to combat wrinkles were all directed to women.

Women themselves do not discuss wrinkles or sexual frustration, but complain about more serious types of age-related infirmities. Though she lived to be sixty-five, Allesandra Strozzi, a wealthy Florentine, described herself as old at forty-two because of her frequent pregnancies and many illnesses. Poorer women of course shared these problems, and added to them the effects of hard physical labor which often continued through pregnancies and illnesses. Shakespeare has Jacques in *As You Like It* describe the seventh (and last) age of man as "second childishness and mere oblivion"; old women, often caring for both an even older spouse and children who were not yet grown, did not have the luxury of being able to lapse into such a state.

As we investigate the female life-cycle in early modern Europe, it may appear at first glance that little had changed since ancient times, and that, in fact, little has changed since. Hasn't women's experience always been more influenced by the condition of their bodies – menstruating, pregnant, lactating, menopausal – than men's? Haven't most women married and had children, with those who did neither or only one without the other regarded as somehow deviant? Haven't men always tried to control female sexuality and regarded the female body as inferior because it lacked a penis? The answer to all these questions is yes, which is why it remains extremely important in analyzing the history of women in any period to pay attention to the physical and social life-cycle. The new scholarship on men as men and on masculinity, which we will explore in the final chapter, has begun to take these issues into account as well, but this scholarship is – to use an appropriate metaphor – very much in its infancy.

Though many aspects of the female life-cycle appear to be true across time, our investigation has also demonstrated ways in which early modern women's experience differed dramatically from that of contemporary western women. Bodily processes – menstruation, sexual arousal, fertility cycles, pregnancy, menopause – are now regarded almost solely as physical matters, to be controlled and affected by hormones, drugs, and other medical treatments; to a large degree they have lost their religious or magical meaning. Through this medicalization, women have achieved greater control of these processes – they can now prevent conception or achieve it outside the womb, establish regular menstrual periods, and limit the discomfort of menopause – yet they have also lost connections with what these processes used to mean to women. Women have also achieved greater control of their social life-cycle; they can often choose to accept or reject men as sexual partners or husbands, choose how many children to have, choose to remain unmarried or widowed without sinking into poverty. This greater range of choice is threatening to many people, however, including many women, who long for what they perceive as the "traditional" female roles of the period we have been discussing and attempt to restrict contemporary women's choices through legislation or social pressure. One of the key elements in this view of women's traditional role is the idea that paid employment and economic activities outside of the family were largely the province of men, an idea we will test in the next chapter.

Bibliography

Many of the studies on which this chapter is based focus on the early modern family. For an overview of the issues and a large bibliography, see my "Family, household, and community," in Thomas A. Brady, Jr., Heiko A. Oberman, and James D. Tracy (eds.), *Handbook of European History 1400–1600* (Leiden, E. J. Brill, 1994), pp. 51–78.

The two studies that first set out a rather bleak view of family life, and against which most later scholarship has reacted, are: Philippe Ariès, *Centuries of Childhood: A Social History of Family Life,* trans. Robert Baldick (New York, Vintage, 1962) and Lawrence Stone, *Family, Sex, and Marriage in England 1500–1800* (London, Penguin, 1977). Books that examine upper-class families include: Randolph Trumbach, *The Rise of the Egalitarian Family: Aristocratic Kinship and Domestic Relations in Eighteenth-Century England* (New York, Academic Press, 1978); Miriam Slater, *Family Life in the Seventeenth Century: The Verneys of Claydon House* (London, Routledge, 1984); Christiane Klapisch-Zuber, *Women, Family, and Ritual in Renaissance Italy* (Chicago, University of Chicago, 1985); Kate Mertes, *The English Noble Household, 1250–1600* (London, Basil Blackwell, 1988). Middle-class family life is surveyed in Alan Macfarlane, *Marriage and Love in England, Modes of Reproduction 1300–1840,* (London, Basil Blackwell, 1986); Sara Heller Mendelson, *The Mental World of Stuart Women: Three Studies* (Brighton, Harvester, 1987); Sherrin Marshall, *The Dutch Gentry, 1500–1650: Family, Faith and Fortune* (New York, Greenwood, 1987); Margaret Hunt, *The Middling Sort: Commerce, Gender, and the Family in England, 1680–1780* (Berkeley, University of California Press, 1996). Lower-class families are discussed in John Gillis, *For Better, for Worse: British Marriages 1600 to the Present* (Oxford, Oxford University Press, 1985). Books that include information from all classes include: Jean-Louis Flandrin, *Families in Former Times: Kinship, Household and Sexuality,* trans. Richard Southern (Cambridge, Cambridge University Press, 1979); James Traer, *Marriage and Family in Eighteenth Century France* (Ithaca, Cornell University Press, 1980); Michael Mitterauer and Reinhard Sieder, *The European Family: Patriarchy and Partnership from the Middle Ages to the Present,* trans. Karla Oosterveen and Manfred Horzinger (Chicago, University of Chicago Press, 1982); Ralph Houlbrooke, *The English Family 1450–1700* (London, Longman, 1984); Lawrence Stone, *Road to Divorce: England 1530–1987* (Oxford, Oxford University Press, 1990); Mary Abbott, *Family Ties: English Families 1540–1920* (London, Routledge, 1993); Anthony Molho, *Marriage Alliance in Late Medieval Florence* (Cambridge, Mass., Harvard University Press, 1994); Trevor Dean and K.J.P. Lowe (eds.), *Marriage in Italy, 1300–1650* (Cambridge, Cambridge University Press, 1998); Martha C. Howell, *The Marriage Exchange: Property, Social Place, and Gender in the Cities of the Low Countries, 1300–1500* (Chicago: University of Chicago Press, 1998).

Hans Medick and David Sabean (eds.), *Interest and Emotion: Essays on the Study of Family and Kinship* (Cambridge, Cambridge University Press, 1984) includes a number of essays on family relationships, particularly those between generations, and Mary Chan, *Life into Story: The Courtship of Elizabeth Wiseman* (London, Ashgate, 1998) provides a fascinating case study, with documents, of one contested marriage. Other useful collections of articles that explore the family in various cultures and time periods, including early modern Europe, are: Robert I. Rotberg and Theodore K. Rabb (eds.), *The Family in History: Interdisciplinary Essays* (New York, Harper, 1971); Charles Rosenberg (ed.), *The Family in History* (Philadelphia, University of Pennsylvania Press, 1975); Jack Goody, Joan Thirsk and E. P. Thompson (eds.), *Family and Inheritance: Rural Society in Western Europe, 1200–1800* (Cambridge, Cambridge University Press, 1976); Robert I. Rotberg and Theodore K. Rabb (eds.), *Marriage and Fertility: Studies in Interdisciplinary History* (Princeton, Princeton University Press, 1980); Robert Wheaton and Tamara K. Harevan (eds.), *Family and Sexuality in French History* (Philadelphia, University of Pennsylvania Press, 1980); R. B. Outhwaite (ed.), *Marriage and Society: Studies in the Social History of Marriage* (London, Europa Publications, 1981); Jean Dupaquier, et al. (eds.), *Marriage and Remarriage in Populations of the Past* (New York, Academic Press, 1981); Peter Laslett and Richard Wall (eds.), *Household and Family in Past Time* (Cambridge, Cambridge University Press, 1983); Richard Wall, Jean Robin and Peter Laslett (eds.), *Family Forms in Historic Europe* (Cambridge: Cambridge University Press, 1983); Richard M. Smith (ed.), *Land, Kinship, and Life-Cycle* (Cambridge, Cambridge University Press, 1984); David Kertzer, et al. (eds.), *The Family in Italy from Antiquity to the Present* (New Haven, Yale University Press, 1991); David Herlihy, *Women, Family and Society in Medieval Europe* (Providence, Berghahn Books, 1995); André Buguière, et al. (eds.), *A History of the Family,* 2 vols. (Cambridge, Mass., Harvard University Press, 1996). The *Journal of Family History,* which began publication in 1976, includes many other relevant articles.

Engagement and wedding ceremonies have been explored most fully in: Susan C. Karant-Nunn, *The Reformation of Ritual: An Interpretation of Early Modern Germany* (London, Routledge, 1997) and David Cressy, *Birth, Marriage and Death: Ritual, Religion, and the Life-Cycle in Tudor and Stuart England* (Oxford, Oxford University Press, 1997); see also Lyndal Roper, "Going to church and street: weddings in Reformation Augsburg," *Past and Present* 106 (1985), 62–101 and several of the essays in Robert Forster and Orest Ranum (eds.), *Ritual, Religion and the Sacred: Selections from the Annales* (Baltimore, The Johns Hopkins University Press, 1982).

Women who remained unmarried are discussed in the essays in Judith M. Bennett and Amy M. Froide (eds.), *Singlewomen in the European Past* (Philadelphia: University of Pennsylvania Press, 1998) and in Jens-Christian Johansen, "Never married women in town and country in eighteenth-century Denmark," in John Henderson and Richard Wall (eds.), *Poor Women and Children in the European Past* (New York, Routledge, 1994), pp. 196–206; Virginia Cox, "The single self: feminist thought and the marriage market in early modern Venice," *Renaissance Quarterly* 48/3 (1995), 513–81; Christine Adams, "A choice not to wed? Unmarried women in eighteenth-century France," *Journal of Social History* 29 (1996), 880–93. The best study of the ideas of women about their own bodies is Barbara Duden, *The Woman Beneath the Skin: A Doctor's Patients in Eighteenth-century Germany* (Cambridge, Mass., Harvard University Press,

1991). Another fascinating survey of popular attitudes toward the female body and the process of childbirth is Jacques Gélis, *History of Childbirth: Fertility, Pregnancy and Birth in Early Modern Europe* (Boston, Northeastern University Press, 1991). Patricia Crawford, "Menstruation in seventeenth-century England," *Past and Present* 91 (1981), 65–79 also covers both popular and learned ideas.

Childhood has been a topic of great interest, though not all works on the subject are careful about making gender distinctions, and the experience of boys has often left more sources than that of girls. David Hunt, for example, uses sources that relate only to the upbringing of the future King Louis XIII of France in his *Parents and Children in History: The Psychology of Family Life in Early Modern France* (New York, Harper, 1970). More recent studies which achieve a better balance include: Hugh Cunningham, *The Children of the Poor: Representations of Childhood since the Seventeenth Century* (Oxford, Oxford University Press, 1981); Linda Pollock, *Forgotten Children: Parent-Child Relations from 1500 to 1900* (Cambridge, Cambridge University Press, 1983); C. John Sommerville, *The Discovery of Childhood in Puritan England* (Athens, University of Georgia Press, 1991); Rudolf Dekker, *Childhood, Memory and Autobiography in Holland: From the Golden Age to Romanticism* (London, Macmillan, 1999). Michael Mitterauer, *A History of Youth* (Oxford, Oxford University Press, 1992) and Katherine J. Lewis, Noël Jane Menuge, and Kim M. Phillips (eds.), *Young Medieval Women* (Phoenix Mill, Sutton, 1999) both investigate young women's experiences. *The History of Childhood Quarterly,* which began publication in 1973, always contains the newest research on the topic.

Some studies of the family focus primarily on domestic life, including Wayne Franitz, *Paragons of Virtue: Women and Domesticity in Seventeenth-Century Dutch Art* (Cambridge: Cambridge University Press, 1993) and Alison Sim, *The Tudor Housewife* (London: Sutton Books, 1998).

Motherhood has been explored from many angles in the essays collected in Valerie Fildes (ed.), *Women as Mothers in Pre-industrial England* (London, Routledge, 1990) and Naomi Miller and Naomi Yavneh (eds.), *Mothers and Others: Female Caregivers in the Early Modern Period* (London, Ashgate, 2000). The stresses associated with motherhood, along with other types of mental anguish, are investigated by Michael McDonald in *Mystical Bedlam: Madness, Anxiety and Healing in Seventeenth-century England* (Cambridge, Cambridge University Press, 1981). Peter C. Hoffer and N.E.H. Hull, *Murdering Mothers: Infanticide in England and New England 1558–1803* (New York, New York University Press, 1981); Mark Jackson, *New-Born Child Murder: Women, Illegitimacy and the Courts in Eighteenth-Century England* (Manchester, Manchester University Press, 1996); René Leboutte, "Offense against family order: infanticide in Belgium from the fifteenth through the early twentieth centuries," *Journal of the History of Sexuality* 2 (1991), 159–85; David I. Kertzer, *Sacrified for Honor: Italian Infant Abandonment and the Politics of Reproductive Control* (Boston: Beacon, 1993) examine the legal, economic, and social factors affecting women charged with killing or abandoning their infants or small children. Toni Bowers, *The Politics of Motherhood: British Writing and Culture, 1680–1760* (Cambridge, Cambridge University Press, 1996) looks at the symbolic role of motherhood, and Jacqeuline Marie Musacchio, *The Art and Ritual of Childbirth in Renaissance Italy* (New Haven, Yale University Press, 1999) at visual representations of childbirth.

The physical side of giving birth, and the role of the midwife who assisted, is discussed in the essays in Hilary Marland (ed.), *The Art of Midwifery: Early Modern Midwives in Europe and North America* (London, Routledge, 1993) and in Audrey Eccles, *Obstetrics and Gynaecology in Tudor and Stuart England* (London, Croom Helm, 1982). Nina Rattner Gelbart, *The King's Midwife: A History and Mystery of Madame du Coudray* (Berkeley, University of California Press, 1998) tells the story of one dynamic midwife who sought to teach obstetrical skills to rural midwives throughout France, and Hilary Marland, *Mother and Child were Saved: the Memoirs (1693–1745) of the Frisian Midwife Catharina Schrader* (Amsterdam: Rodopi, 1987) provides an excellent discussion and translation of the diary of a Dutch midwife. Adrian Wilson, *The Making of Man-Midwifery: Childbirth in England, 1660–1770* (Cambridge, Mass., Harvard University Press, 1995) discusses the gradual entry of men into obstetrical care.

The debates surrounding and the practices of maternal breastfeeding and wet nursing are surveyed in Sara Matthews Grieco, "Breastfeeding, wet nursing and infant mortality in Europe (1400–1800)" in *Historical Perspectives On Breastfeeding* (Florence, UNICEF International Child Development Centre, 1991), pp. 15–62; George Sussman, *Selling Mother's Milk: The Wet-nursing Business in France 1715–1914* (Urbana, University of Illinois Press, 1982); Valerie Fildes, *Breasts, Bottles and Babies: A History of Infant Feeding* (Edinburgh, Edinburgh University Press, 1986), which focuses primarily on the period 1500–1800; Ruth Perry, "Colonizing the breast: sexuality and maternity in eighteenth-century England," *Journal of the History of Sexuality* 2 (1991), 204–34.

Because widows appear independently in many sources, it is often easier to find information about them than married women, so they have been the objects of a number of studies, including Sandra Cavallo and Lyndan Warner (eds.), *Widowhood in Medieval and Early Modern Europe* (London, Longman, 1999); Barbara Diefendorf, "Widowhood and remarriage in sixteenth century Paris," *Journal of Family History* 7 (1982), 379–95; Sherrin Marshall Wyntges, "Survivors and status: widowhood and family in the early modern Netherlands," *Journal of Family History* 7 (1982), 396–405; Barbara Todd, "The remarrying widow: a stereotype reconsidered," in Mary Prior (ed.), *Women in English Society 1500–1800* (London, Methuen, 1985), pp. 54–92. For a slightly earlier period see the essays in Louise Mirrer (ed.), *Upon My Husband's Death: Widows in the Literature and Histories of Medieval Europe* (Ann Arbor, University of Michigan Press, 1992).

The process of aging itself in both women and men is only beginning to be studied, but several helpful discussions are: Robert Jütte, "Aging and body image in the sixteenth century," *European History Quarterly* 18 (1988), 259–90; Lois W. Banner, *In Full Flower: Aging Women, Power and Sexuality* (New York, Knopf, 1992); Joel T. Rosenthal, *Old Age in Late Medieval England* (Philadelphia, University of Pennsylvania Press, 1996); Sherri Klassen, "Old and cared for: place of residence for elderly women in eighteenth-century Toulouse," *Journal of Family History* 24 (1999), 35–52; Lynn Botelho and Pat Thane (eds.), *Old Women in England, 1500 to the Present* (London, Longman, 1999).

The examination of the history of sexuality is even newer than the history of women or the family; the *Journal of the History of Sexuality* began publication only in 1990. This is an incredible growth field at the moment, however, and the following is just a suggestion of what is available. For more references, especially on the control of sexuality, see the bibliographies in my *Christianity and the Regulation of Sexuality in the Early Modern World: Regulating Desire, Reforming Practice* (London, Routledge, 2000), which discusses the impact of Christian ideas and institutions on sexual norms and practices throughout the world.

There are several general collections on early modern sexuality, which bring together the work of historians, art historians, and scholars of literature: Robert Purks Maccubbin (ed.), *'Tis Nature's Fault: Unauthorized Sexuality during the Enlightenment* (Cambridge, Cambridge University Press, 1987); James Grantham Turner (ed.), *Sexuality and Gender in Early Modern Europe: Institutions, Texts, Images* (Cambridge, Cambridge University Press, 1993); Richard Burt and John Michael Archer (eds.), *Enclosure Acts: Sexuality, Property, and Culture in Early Modern England* (Ithaca, Cornell University Press, 1994); Jacqueline Murray and Konrad Eisenbichler (eds.), *Desire and Discipline: Sex and Sexuality in the Premodern West* (Toronto, University of Toronto Press, 1996); Louise Fradenburg and Carla Freccero (eds.), *Premodern Sexualities* (New York, Routledge, 1996).

Sexuality, both within and outside marriage, has been approached from a wide variety of viewpoints. Martin Ingram, *Church Courts, Sex and Marriage in England 1570–1640* (Cambridge, Cambridge University Press, 1987) uses legal documents, as do G. R. Quaife, *Wanton Wenches and Wayward Wives: Peasants and Illicit Sex in Early Seventeenth Century England* (New Brunswick, Rutgers University Press, 1979), Thomas Max Safley, *Let No Man Put Asunder: The Control of Marriage in the German Southwest* (Kirksville, MO., Sixteenth Century Publishers, 1984) and Guido Ruggiero, *Binding Passions: Tales of Magic, Marriage and Power at the End of the Renaissance* (New York, Oxford University Press, 1993). Peter Laslett, *Family Life and Illicit Love in Earlier Generations* (Cambridge, Cambridge University Press, 1977) and the essays in Peter Laslett, et al. (eds.), *Bastardy and Its Comparative History: Studies in the History of Illegitimacy and Marital Non-Conformism in Britain, France, Germany, Sweden, North America, Jamaica and Japan* (Cambridge, Mass., Harvard University Press, 1980) use quantitative as well as qualitative sources. The essays in Jacqueline Murray (ed.), "Sexuality in the Renaissance," a special issue of *Renaissance and Reformation/Renaissance at Réforme* 24 (1988) approach sexuality from a largely literary perspective, and Bette Talvacchia, *Taking Positions: On the Erotic in Renaissance Culture* (Princeton, Princeton University Press, 1999) uses literary and artistic materials. Thomas Laqueur, *Making Sex: Body and Gender from the Greeks to Freud* (Cambridge, Mass., Harvard University Press, 1990) traces ideas about sexuality and the body in scientific and philosophical writings and argues that sex, along with gender, is culturally determined and can't be viewed as innately biological. Popular ideas about sexuality and the control of fertility are explored in Angus McLaren, *Reproductive Rituals: The Perception of Fertility in England from the 16th to the 19th Century* (London, Methuen, 1984) and Orest and Patricia Ranum (eds.), *Popular Attitudes toward Birth Control in Pre-industrial England and France* (New York, Harper, 1972).

Angus McLaren, *A History of Contraception* (Oxford, Oxford University Press, 1990) is the best survey of the issue over a broad time frame. Two excellent studies that use a wide range of sources to explore border areas of Europe are Eve Levin, *Sex and Society in the World of the Orthodox Slavs, 900–1700* (Ithaca, Cornell University Press, 1989) and Rosalind Mitchison and Leah Leneman, *Sexual and Social Control: Scotland 1660–1780* (London, Basil Blackwell, 1989). The essays in Edward Muir and Guido Ruggiero (eds.), *Sex and Gender in Historical Perspective: Selections from Quaderni Storici* (Baltimore, The Johns Hopkins University Press, 1990) cover a number of topics including menstruation, sexual honor, and the control of reproduction in early modern Italy, and are written by Italian scholars whose work is not often translated into English. Though it focuses on a slightly earlier period, Guido Ruggiero, *Boundaries of Eros: Sex Crime and Sexuality in Renaissance Venice* (Oxford, Oxford University Press, 1985) is the best study to date which integrates ideas about sexuality with more general cultural and political attitudes.

Violence against women and the control of women's sexuality are becoming increasingly common topics of investigation. See: Philip F. Riley, "Michel Foucault, lust, women and sin in Louis XIV's Paris," *Church History* 59 (1990), 35–50; Lynda E. Boose, "Scolding brides and bridling scolds: taming the woman's unruly member," *Shakespeare Quarterly* 42 (1991), 179–213; Margaret Hunt, "Wife beating, domesticity, and women's independence in eighteenth-century London," *Gender and History* 4 (1992), 10–29; Susan Dwyer Amussen, "'Being stirred to much unquietness': violence and domestic violence in early modern England," *Journal of Women's History* 6 (1994), 70–89; Joanna M. Ferraro, "The power to decide: battered wives in early modern Venice," *Renaissance Quarterly* 48/3 (1995), 493–512; Miranda Chaytor, "Husband(ry): narratives of rape in the seventeenth century," *Gender and History* 7 (1995), 378–407; Ulinka Rublack, "The public body: policing abortion in early modern Germany," in Lynn Abrams and Elizabeth Harvey (eds.), *Gender Relations in German History: Power, Agency and Experience from the Sixteenth to the Twentieth Century* (Durham, Duke University Press, 1997), pp. 57–79; Garthine Walker, "Rereading rape and sexual violence in early modern England," *Gender and History* 10 (1998), 1–25. Several studies have paid particular attention to the way women and men portray themselves or are portrayed in cases involving sex and gender relations: Frances E. Dolan, *Dangerous Familiars: Representations of Domestic Crime in England 1550–1700* (Ithaca, Cornell University Press, 1994), Laura Gowing, *Domestic Dangers: Women, Words and Sex in Early Modern London* (Oxford: Clarendon Press, 1996), and three essays by Elizabeth S. Cohen, "No longer virgins: self-presentation by young women of late Renaissance Rome," in Marilyn Migiel and Juliana Schiesari (eds.), *Refiguring Women: Perspectives on Gender and the Italian Renaissance* (Ithaca, Cornell University Press, 1991), pp. 169–92, "'Courtesans' and 'whores': words and behavior in the streets of early modern Rome," *Women's Studies* 19 (1991), 201–8, and "Honor and gender in the streets of early modern Rome," *Journal of Interdisciplinary History* 22 (1992), 597–625. Art historians have also begun to focus on images of sexual violence: Diane Wolfthal, *Images of Rape: The "Heroic" Tradition and its Alternatives* (Cambridge: Cambridge University Press, 1999); Yael Even, "Commodifying images of sexual violence in sixteenth-century Italy," *Source* (forthcoming) and

"Daphne (without Apollo) reconsidered: some disregarded images of sexual pursuit in Italian Renaissance and Baroque art," *Studies in Iconography* 18 (1997), 143–59.

Many studies of homosexuality in the early modern period focus exclusively or almost exclusively on men. Same-sex relations between women have been investigated in: Theo van der Meer, "Tribades on trial: female same-sex offenders in late eighteenth-century Amsterdam," *Journal of the History of Sexuality* 1 (1991), 424–45; Emma Donoghue, *Passions Between Women: British Lesbian Culture 1668–1801* (London, Scarlet Press, 1993); Betty Rizzo, *Companions Without Vows: Relationships Among Eighteenth-century British Women* (Athens, University of Georgia Press, 1994); Valerie Traub, "The (in)significance of 'lesbian' desire in early modern England," in Susan Zimmerman (ed.), *Erotic Politics: Desire on the Renaissance Stage* (London, Routledge, 1992); Patricia Simons, "Lesbian (in)visibility in Italian Renaissaance culture," *Journal of Homosexuality* 27 (1994), 81–122; Ros Ballaster, "'The vices of old Rome revisited: representations of female same-sex desire in seventeenth- and eighteenth-century England," in Suzanne Raitt (ed.), *Volcanoes and Pearl Divers: Essays in Lesbian Feminist Studies* (London: Onlywomen Press, 1995), pp. 13–36; Harriet Andreadis, "Sappho in early modern England," in Ellen Greene (ed.), *Re-Reading Sappho* (Berkeley, University of California Press, 1997), pp. 105–21 and "The erotics of female friendship in early modern England," in Susan Frye and Karen Robertson (eds.), *Maids and Mistresses, Cousins and Queens: Women's Alliances in Early Modern England* (New York, Oxford University Press, 1999), pp. 241–58; Margaret Hunt, "English lesbians in the long eighteenth century," in Bennett and Froide, *Singlewomen*, pp. 270–96; Randolph Trumbach, *Sex and the Gender Revolution, Volume I: Heterosexuality and the Third Gender in Enlightenment London* (Chicago, University of Chicago Press, 1999); Lillian Faderman, *Surpassing the Love of Men: Romantic Friendship and Love between Women from the Renaissance to the Present* (New York, William Morrow, 1981) includes a brief discussion of the period. Judith C. Brown, *Immodest Acts: The Life of a Lesbian Nun in Renaissance Italy* (New York, Oxford University Press, 1986) investigates the case of an abbess accused of falsifying visions and engaging in homosexual relations with another nun. Rudolf M. Dekker and Lotte C. van de Pol, *The Tradition of Female Transvestism in Early Modern Europe* (New York, St. Martin's, 1989) examine several hundred Dutch cases of women accused of dressing in men's clothing, some of whom were sexually attracted to other women, and Catalina de Erauso, *Lieutenant Nun: Memoir of a Basque Transvestite in the New World,* Michele and Gabriel Stepto (ed. and trans.), (Boston, Beacon/Press, 1995) presents a fascinating autobiographical text of the Spanish nun who purportedly went to the New World dressed as a soldier. Brigitte Eriksson, "A lesbian execution in Germany, 1721: the trial records," *Journal of Homosexuality* 6 (1981), 27–40 and Patricia Crawford and Sara Mendelson, "Sexual identities in early modern England: the marriage of two women," *Gender and History* 7 (1995), 362–78 both discuss cases in which women married women. For discussions of the clitoris, see Valerie Traub, "The psycho-morphology of the clitoris," *GLQ: A Journal of Lesbian and Gay Studies* 2 (1995), 81–113 and Katherine Park, "The rediscovery of the clitoris," in David Hillman and Carla Mazzio (eds.), *The Body in Parts* (New York, Routledge, 1996), pp. 170–93.

General essay collections or monographs which include studies of both women and men in the early modern period are: Salvatore Licata and Robert Petersen (eds.), *Historical Perspectives on Homosexuality* (New York, Haworth, 1981); Martin Duberman, Martha Vicinus, and George Chauncey, Jr. (eds.), *Hidden From History: Reclaiming the Gay and Lesbian Past* (New York, Meridian, 1989); Tim Hitchcock, *English Sexualities, 1700–1800* (London, Macmillan and St. Martin's, 1997). For a slightly earlier period, see E. Ann Matter, "My sister, my spouse: women-identified women in medieval Christianity," *Journal of Feminist Studies in Religion* 2 (1986), 81–93 and Jacqueline Murray, "Twice marginal and twice invisible: lesbians in the Middle Ages," in Vern L. Bullough and James A. Brundage, *Handbook of Medieval Sexuality* (New York, Garland, 1996), 191–222. The best and most up-to-date bibliography on early modern homosexuality in Europe may be found on the web site of my colleague Jeffrey Merrick: www.uwm.edu/jmerrick.

3   Women's economic role

Alas! Our labors never know no end,
On brass and irons we our strength must spend;
Our tender hands and fingers scratch and tear:
All this, and more, with patience we must bear.

The Poems of Mary Collier, The Washerwoman of Petersfield (Petersfield:
W. Minchin, 1739), p. 10

God in Heaven, who gave me soul and body, reason and understanding, for which I have to thank him daily, gave me my skill at healing. I
heal out of charity for the poor and needy... [as is] done by honorable
women not only here but also in other cities just as large and important
as Memmingen. Such are fine things for women to do.

Elisabeth Heyssin, a medical practitoner in Memmingen, Germany, 1598,
quoted in Merry E. Wiesner, *Working Women in Renaissance Germany*
(New Brunswick, Rutgers University Press, 1986), pp. 51–2

At that time I was busied in the merchandise trade, selling every month
to the amount of five or six hundred Reichsthalers... My business pros-
pered, I procured my wares from Holland, I bought nicely in Hamburg
as well, and disposed of the goods in a store of my own. I never spared
myself, summer and winter I was out on my travels, and I ran about the
city the livelong day.

Glickl bas Judah Leib, *The Memoirs of Glückel of Hameln,* trans. Marvin
Lowenthal (New York, Schocken, 1977), p. 179.

Including a separate chapter on women's economic role in some ways
contradicts recent feminist scholarship and other revisions of both traditional and Marxist economic history, which persuasively argue that work
and other economic activities cannot be detached from the family and
political and social institutions. This revisionist scholarship reminds us
that, to be accurate and inclusive, an analysis of economic life in any
period must include reproductive as well as productive activities; reproduction is defined not simply as childbearing, but as the care and nurturing of all family members, which allowed them to take part in
productive labor. This is especially true for pre-industrial societies in
which production often went on in the household, for all family members took part in both productive and reproductive labor. Thus women's

childbearing, discussed in the last chapter, may properly be considered an economic activity. It is also important to recognize that in early modern Europe a family's economic status might be more dependent on its access to royal or noble favors than on anything we would recognize as labor. The training of upper-class girls and young women in decorum and dancing which we will examine in the next chapter was carried out by families not for the girls' own enjoyment, but to allow them to catch a royal eye and perhaps gain a lucrative post for a family member; service at court was therefore also an economic activity.

Thus we need to keep in mind a broad understanding of "economic," but we can also distinguish certain activities as *primarily* economic without misrepresenting how early modern society operated or how people thought it operated. These activities fall under two basic categories, work and the control of property. This chapter will examine women's activities in each of these areas, exploring their labor in the countryside and cities, and their management and manipulation of property through money-lending, purchasing, investment, and bequests.

Work identity and concepts of work

Though the actual work that men and women performed in the early modern economy was often very similar or the same, their relationship to work and work identities were very different. Male work rhythms and a man's position in the economy were to a large degree determined by age, class, and training, with boys and men often moving as a group from one level of employment to the next. Female work rhythms were also determined by age and class, but even more so by individual biological and social events such as marriage, motherhood, and widowhood, all of which were experienced by women individually and over which they might have little control. Women often changed occupations several times during their lives or performed many different types of jobs at once, so that their identification with any one occupation was not strong. As we saw in the last chapter, a man's stages of life were often differentiated by his place in an occupational or professional hierarchy, while a woman's depended on her marital status. Popular rituals such as festivals and processions strengthened men's identification with their profession, with men and boys celebrating or marching as an occupational group, often wearing distinctive clothing. Women had no similar rituals to mark their solidarity with other women performing the same types of work; their rituals revolved around family or neighborhood events such as births and funerals, further encouraging them to identify with the family rather than with an occupation. The only exceptions to this appear to be midwives in some cities, who required new midwives to provide a celebratory meal for the entire group, and female members of the few all-female guilds in a handful of cities, who bequeathed tools and property to other members of their all-female guild.

Women rarely received formal training in a trade, and during the early modern period many occupations professionalized, setting up required amounts of formal training and a licensing procedure before one could claim an occupational title. Thus in the Middle Ages both male and female practitioners of medicine were often called "physicians," but by the sixteenth century though women still healed people, only men who had attended university medical school could be called a "physician." This professionalism trickled down to occupations that did not require university training; women might brew herbal remedies, but only men could use the title "apothecary." Professionalization did not simply affect titles, but also the fees people could charge for their services; a university-trained physician, for example, could easily make ten times the annual salary of a female medical practitioner.

Religious opinion and the language of laws and records also made it difficult for women to see themselves as members of a certain occupation. In their desire to remove the distinction between clergy and laity, Protestant writers described all occupations as "vocations" for men, that is, activities to which a man could be called by God and be blessed through his labor; for a woman, however, the only possible vocation was wife and mother. Advice manuals and sermons by Protestant clergy, and later in the sixteenth century by Catholic clergy as well, all viewed whatever productive labor a woman did as simply part of her domestic role of being a helpmate to her husband and an example for her children. This idea also permeates secular laws, tax records, and the ordinances passed by guilds and other occupational groups beginning in the fifteenth century. When a woman performed an activity, such as sewing clothes, it was defined as "domestic work" or as "housekeeping," even if those clothes were not for her own family's use; tax records note that the woman had an income, but neglect to mention how she received it. When men did the same activity, also in their own homes, it was regarded as "production"; only very rarely do tax records fail to mention explicitly what this production was. Thus the gender of the worker, not the work itself or its location, marked the difference between what were considered domestic tasks and what was considered production.

City and state governments often suggested that guilds and other occupational groups overlook the production of a small number of items by widows and other poor women because this was not really "work," but simply "support," and the women would otherwise need public assistance. Guilds generally agreed to accept this fiction unless the woman was so successful that her products were favored over those of guild members; they then argued that she had overstepped the boundary into production and should be prohibited in the same way any male non-guild member would be. Women themselves also used this language, rarely asking for the right to work or produce, but simply to "earn my meager piece of bread... as a lonely widow... so that I and the poor infant mouths I have to feed may be supported."[1]

During the early modern period, gender also became an important factor in separating what was considered skilled from what was considered unskilled work. Women were judged to be unfit for certain tasks, such as glass-cutting, because they were too clumsy and "unskilled," yet those same women made lace or silk thread, jobs which required an even higher level of dexterity than glass-cutting. Historians of the industrial period have pointed to the de-skilling of certain occupations, in which jobs that had traditionally been done by men were made more monotonous with the addition of machinery and so were redefined as unskilled and given to women, with a dramatic drop in status and pay. The opposite process can be seen in the early modern period in the transformation of stocking-knitting in some parts of Europe into a male-dominated occupation. During the sixteenth century, wherever the knitting frame was introduced, men began to argue that using it was so complicated that only men could possibly learn; the frame actually made knitting easier and much faster, but women were prohibited from using it anyway with the excuse that they were unskilled. They were relegated to knitting by hand, and had to sell their products more cheaply to compete with stockings made much more quickly by male frame-knitters.

Economic historians have viewed the early modern period as a time when the meaning of work changed because of the rise of capitalism from a medieval notion of work as all tasks that contributed to a family's sustenance, to work as participation in the market economy and particularly in production. Thus a woman's finding food for her children by begging or keeping her family solvent through efficient management of the family budget were no longer considered work. Economic explanations alone do not fully explain why the new meaning of work was so gender biased, however, why tasks for which women were paid, such as taking in sewing or boarders, came to be defined as housekeeping and therefore not work. To explain this fully, the process of professionalization, ideological changes brought by the Protestant Reformation, and

---

[1] Frankfurt guild records, 1663, quoted in Merry E. Wiesner, *Working Women in Renaissance Germany* (New Brunswick, Rutgers University Press, 1986), p. 160.

guild notions of honor discussed more fully below all have to be taken into account. Whatever its sources, the gendered notion of work meant that women's work was always valued less and generally paid less than men's. Because, as we saw in the last chapter, all women were thought of as "married or to be married," women were usually paid about half of what men were paid, even for the same tasks, with the reasoning that they were either single and had only themselves to support, or married and so were simply helping their husbands support the family. The large number of widows with dependent children, or women whose husbands had deserted them or could not work, did not affect the thinking of employers or the officials who set wage rates. All economies need both structure and flexibility, and during the early modern period these qualities became gender-identified: male labor provided the structure, so that it was regulated, tied to a training process, and lifelong; female labor provided the flexibility, so that it was discontinuous, alternately encouraged or suppressed, not linked to formal training, and generally badly paid. Women's work was thus both marginal and irreplaceable.

Women's work in the countryside

Despite enormous economic changes during the early modern period, the vast majority of people in almost all parts of Europe continued to live in the countryside, producing agricultural products for their own use and for the use of their landlords. Agricultural tasks were highly, though not completely, gender-specific, though exactly which tasks were regarded as female and which as male varied widely throughout Europe. These gender divisions were partly the result of physical differences, with men generally doing tasks that required a great deal of upper-body strength, such as cutting grain with a scythe; they were partly the result of women's greater responsibility for child care, so that women carried out tasks closer to the house which could be more easily interrupted for nursing or tending children; they were partly the result of cultural beliefs, so that women in parts of Norway, for example, sowed all grain because people felt this would ensure a bigger harvest. Whatever their source, gender divisions meant that the proper functioning of a rural household required at least one adult male and one adult female; remarriage after the death of a spouse was much faster in the countryside than in the cities, and the number of rural women who remained permanently widowed was much smaller than it was in the city. Those who could not find a husband were often forced into the city for work, because the opportunities for wage labor for women in the countryside were generally fewer than those in the cities, except at harvest time.

Rural women were largely responsible for tasks within or close to the house: they took care of poultry and small animals; prepared dairy products, beer, and bread; grew flax; made linen and wool cloth; did all cooking for the household's own consumption, generally over an open fire with perhaps a bread oven along its side. They also worked in the fields during harvest time, particularly in areas where grain harvesting was done with a sickle; a recent study of harvesting in seventeenth-century Yorkshire finds that women put in 38 percent of the time needed to bring in the grain. In areas where the harvesting was done with a scythe, women gathered and bound the grain and gleaned the fields, jobs that were actually physically more taxing than cutting because they involved constant stooping and bending. Women also transported rural products to market, particularly if this was done on foot, for driving teams was generally regarded as men's work. In parts of Europe where the adult men were away during the summer months, such as western Norway where the men fished or worked in shipping, agricultural production was completely the women's responsibility.

Women's labor changed as new types of crops and agricultural products were introduced and as agriculture became more specialized. During the seventeenth century, turnips and other root crops were increasingly grown in many parts of Europe, crops that were very labor-intensive and seen as women's responsibility because they were generally fed to animals. Raw materials for manufactured products, such as flax, hemp, and plants for dye, became important commodities in many parts of Europe, and were also cared for by women. Women in parts of Italy tended and harvested olive trees and grape vines, and carried out most of the tasks associated with the production of silk: gathering leaves from mulberry trees, raising the silk cocoons, and processing cocoons into raw silk by reeling and spinning. As certain areas intensified stock-raising, animals were fed all year in stables instead of being allowed to range freely in the summer – again creating more work for women. In fact, some historians would even see the late seventeenth and early eighteenth century as a period of the feminization of agriculture especially in central Europe, where the demand for female agricultural workers grew faster than that for male, and where the wives of artisans in many smaller towns were forced to raise food in nearby gardens or fields because the family's income from production was no longer able to support it. Demographic statistics support this view, with the significant increase in female life expectancy that began in the early nineteenth century attributed largely to the mechanization of agriculture, which lessened the physical demands on rural women somewhat.

In only a few parts of Europe were rural households still solely subsistence producers by the early modern period; most participated to some degree in a market economy, and some, such as serf households on the vast estates of eastern Europe, produced almost completely for an export market. Serf men and women in eastern Europe produced grain that was exported to western Europe, though they did not control or profit from this trade. In western Europe serfdom steadily declined in the early modern period, and rural women could make some choices as to what they would produce and sell. They made butter, cheese, and soap and sold these along with eggs, manure, small animals, and fruit in market towns, using the proceeds to buy manufactured products increasingly available from peddlers or to fulfill the household's rent and tax obligations. They traveled farther away to cities to sell nuts or herbs they had gathered, or made deals with urban middlemen (or middlewomen) to transport the produce to market for them. Unlike the sale of grain, which their husbands controlled, women's products were sold year-round, making such goods a particularly important part of the household economy. Women also peddled pins and needles, ribbons, candles, and other small items that they had obtained from other rural women or merchants in the cities. Women thus served as an important human link between the rural and urban economies, with rural women traveling to town to sell their products or their labor, and urban women going out to rural areas to buy products to sell or to work on parcels of land that were still owned by their families.

Besides selling products, rural women also sold their labor. Both women and men in poorer families hired themselves out to richer ones for agricultural tasks, with some landless families surviving solely by the labor of their members. Husbands and wives sometimes hired themselves out as a team, he cutting grain with a scythe while she bound it; they were generally paid according to how many bundles of grain they produced, one of the earliest examples of piecework. The sixteenth century was a period of inflation in most of Europe, and governments responded by attempting to limit wages and prices. From their maximum wage regulations, we can see that female agricultural laborers were to be paid about half of what men were, and were also to be given less and poorer quality food, which often formed the most important part of an agricultural worker's income. An ordinance from south Germany in 1550, for example, notes that male laborers were to be fed soup and wine for breakfast, beer, vegetables, and meat at midday, and vegetables and wine at night, while women were to receive only soup and vegetables in the morning, milk and bread at midday, and nothing in the evening; they thus received less food, decidedly less protein, and no alcohol. Despite these disparities, women were better off than in areas of Europe where payment for agricultural labor was completely in cash, for wages did not keep up with prices, and women's wages would often not have paid for enough food to keep them alive. Women's cash wages appear to have been determined more by custom than by the market, for they fluctuated much less than men's both over the life-cycle and with shifts in the economy; even during periods of rising wages, women's wages rose more slowly. In some parts of England, married women's wages were also less than those of widows for the same task, a wage structure based on the idea that married women needed less because they had a husband to support them, not on an evaluation of the quality of their work.

The inflation of the sixteenth century, which hit food prices particularly hard, and agricultural innovations in some parts of Europe which reduced the need for rural labor, led large numbers of landless agricultural workers of both sexes to drift continually in search of employment or better working conditions, in addition to those who migrated seasonally. It appeared to many contemporaries that poverty was increasing at an alarming rate, and that more of the poor were what they termed "sturdy beggars," that is, able-bodied people who could work if they chose rather than those who were poor through no fault of their own such as orphans, infirm elderly people, or the handicapped. Most cities in Europe began to pass laws forbidding healthy people to beg, ordering them to go back to their home area, or forcing them into workhouses. These laws were motivated both by increases in the actual numbers of the poor, and changes in attitudes toward them, as Protestant and Catholic authorities came to regard beggars not as opportunities to show one's Christian charity, but as dangerous vagrants to be expelled or locked up.

Rural women who migrated to cities in search of employment were particularly suspect, for any woman traveling on her own without a clear destination was thought to be dishonorable. In 1659, for example, the city of Dublin ordered that "a large cage [be] set up in the corn market to imprison all beggars, idle women and maids selling apples and oranges."[2] In many cities female migrants were placed in special women's workhouses along with orphans, prostitutes, and poor urban women, where they were supposed to be taught a trade like lace-making or glove-making so that they could escape poverty. In many of these institutions, the opportunities for actual training were minimal, although

---

[2] J. T. Gilbert and Lady Gilbert (eds.), *Calendar of the Ancient Records of Dublin* (Dublin, 1889), vol. 4, p. 157.

there were a few, such as the Presentation hospice in Grenoble, France, which did give women enough skills to allow them to at least support themselves. In Ireland, impoverished women were sometimes captured by press gangs and sent against their will to the English colonies of the New World, for English authorities saw this as a way to rid themselves of "dangerous rogues," and explicitly discussed the women's procreative role in increasing colonial populations.

The difference between male and female wages meant that in families with just a small plot of land, women often did all of the agricultural work on the family plot, while men worked for wages on other people's land or in fishing or forestry. Such families had little money to invest in new tools, so women continued to use old hand tools like the spade and hoe rather than horse-drawn plows; women also favored such tools because they could start and stop work with them easily, and so combine field work with care for children or animals.

Along with hiring women for specific agricultural tasks, rural households also hired them as permanent domestic servants. Ann Kussmaul has discovered that in England the proportion of women among farm servants was much higher than among full-time agricultural laborers; 66 percent of rural women between the ages of twenty and twenty-four were servants. Their period of service was rarely determined by a written contract, but instead by a verbal one sealed by a small sum of money. Servants were hired annually, often at local hiring fairs, and were supposed to stay with their employer for at least one year. Their tasks were similar to those of their mistresses – care of animals and production of animal products, particularly dairying, field work, and cooking. They received room, board, and some clothing from their employers, and, except for very young girls, also an annual salary. This salary was paid only at the end of the year, or even held until the servant left the household, so that servants actually lent their employers the use of their salary during their term of service. Young women generally regarded service as a time to save a dowry for later marriage, though they were also occasionally forced into service to pay off their parents' feudal dues, a practice that continued in Germany, Sweden, and Finland into the eighteenth century. In Muscovy (present-day Russia), where there was little wage labor, poor rural women sold themselves and occasionally their families (if they were heads of household) into slavery until the eighteenth century; about one-third of the slaves in Muscovy were women, with slaves making up about 10 percent of the population. Female slaves brought lower prices than male slaves, for male slaves were prized both for their managerial skills (i.e., running estates for absentee landlords) and for their physical strength. Female slaves generally worked at a variety of household tasks, and it appears that the Russian Orthodox prohibition of their being used for sexual purposes was generally effective.

Many parts of Europe began to specialize in certain crops as early as the fourteenth century, which often created greater opportunities for wage labor. In wine-growing areas, vast numbers of workers were needed during the harvest and at certain other times of the year, with workers frequently migrating seasonally from the cities. There was no clear division of labor along gender lines, though women were usually paid less for the same tasks, so that vineyard owners preferred them for all tasks other than those for which they regarded great physical strength as important. Silk growing also created paid employment, because women, or more accurately girls, were viewed as having greater dexterity and ability to concentrate than men, both necessary for the tedious task of unwinding silk cocoons. Girls were also probably the only ones willing to accept the extremely low wages paid for this task, though the lifelong damage to their eyes that could result from unwinding fine thread in low light made even poor girls think twice about steady work in silk-winding. Silk producers were often forced to hire whole orphanages (without the assent of the residents, of course) in order to have enough labor.

Women also found work in rural areas in non-agricultural tasks, particularly in mining. Though printed sources give very little information about the division of labor in mining, starting in the fifteenth century pictures and engravings show women carrying ore, wood, and salt, sorting and washing ore, and preparing charcoal briquets for use in smelting. Most of the work underground was carried out by adult men in the pre-industrial period, though the belief that women working underground brought bad luck was a consequence, and not a cause, of this division of labor, for it does not appear in any early modern sources. The development of large-scale capitalist mining operations which began in the late Middle Ages in some parts of Europe brought deeper tunnels, more use of machinery and more complex smelting processes, all of which led to a professionalization of mining as an occupation. Though women were not always specifically prohibited from beginning an apprenticeship in mining, almost all those who learned and practiced mining as a lifelong career were men. This did not mean that women disappeared from mining operations, but that their labor was more clearly identified as ancillary and assisting, and consequently badly paid. Their labor might, in fact, be completely invisible, because large firms hired adult men for certain tasks which could really only be performed through the work of a whole family; for example, men might be paid per basket for ore, but it was expected that this ore would be broken apart and washed, jobs that their wives, sisters, and children did. The records often do not indicate this, however, which led some middle-class officials in the eighteenth century to assume that women living in mining districts could easily improve their family's income by spinning during their otherwise "idle" days.

Large-scale capitalist investment was not limited to mining areas, but gradually began to have an impact on the economy in grain-growing areas as well beginning in the fifteenth century. Urban investors began to hire rural individuals or households to produce wool, linen, and later cotton thread or cloth (or cloth that was a mixture of these) paying the household or individual only for the labor and retaining ownership of the raw materials and in some cases the tools and machinery used. This is often termed domestic or cottage industry, because production went on in a household rather than a factory, or the "putting-out" system, as work was put out by capitalist investors, or proto-industrialization, as it was the earliest form of mass production. It is difficult to make generalizations about the impact of domestic industry on the labor of women which apply to all of Europe, because this impact varied depending on whether whole households or only individuals were hired.

In areas of Europe where whole households were hired, domestic industry often broke down gender divisions, for men, women, and children who were old enough all worked at the same tasks. This upset some observers, such as the German religious reformer Sebastian Franck, who commented after visiting the villages around Augsburg and Ulm in the early sixteenth century: "Not only women and maids, but also men and boys, spin. One sees contradictions; they work and gossip like women, yet are still vigorous, active, strong and quarrelsome people, the kind any area would want to have."[3] Domestic industry might also lead to role reversal, with women producing thread while, in the words of an eighteenth-century German observer, "men... cook, sweep and milk the cows, in order never to disturb the good, diligent wife in her work."[4] In other areas, men did not spin, for this was the occupation most clearly identified as female in the pre-industrial world, but they performed what were generally female household tasks so their wives and daughters could spin.

Whole households were generally hired in parts of Europe where the land was poorest and the agriculture was more or less subsistence. Some analysts find that in such areas the growth of proto-industrialization

[3] Gustav Schmoller, *Die Strassburger Tucher und Weberzünft: Urkunden und Darstellung* 2 vols. (Strasbourg, Karl J. Trübner, 1879), p. 519.
[4] Hans Medick, "The proto-industrial family economy: The structural function of household and family during the transition from peasant society to industrial capitalism," *Social History* 1 (1976), 312.

caused labor to become a more important economic commodity than property, which led to earlier marriage and weaker parental control over children. A woman's labor, rather than her father's occupation or wealth, determined her value as a marriage partner, giving her more power within the family and in the community at large. In other parts of Europe, however, proto-industrialization began in areas where there was a high level of seasonal unemployment, especially among women. In these areas, including parts of France, individual women, rather than whole households, were hired, with men continuing to work at agricultural tasks. In these areas there was no sharing of domestic duties or reversal of roles, for the men's tasks were more highly paid and generally away from the household, so the women continued to do most domestic labor. Proto-industrialization in these areas did not lead to great improvements in women's status, for, though the wages women earned gave the family some disposable income, it was the men of the family who decided when and how that income could be spent, and often gathered in taverns and by the eighteenth century in cafes to spend it.

Women's work in towns and cities

Domestic industry was just one of the ways in which the economies of city and countryside were linked in early modern Europe. As we have seen, in parts of Europe where serfdom did not restrict people's movements, rural residents traveled to urban areas to sell their products or to search for employment; poorer urban residents worked in the countryside during harvest and planting, and urban women in smaller cities and towns often tended family gardens and fields beyond the city walls. The work carried out by women was also more similar in urban and rural areas than that carried out by men; in both town and countryside, women's work was generally low status, frequently changing, dependent on family circumstances, and badly paid. We will therefore look first at the urban occupations that most closely paralleled those in the countryside, and then examine the opportunities for women in distinctly urban trades.

As in the countryside, domestic service was probably the largest employer of women in most cities throughout the period. Between 15 and 30 percent of the population of most cities was made up of domestic servants; the larger commercial and manufacturing centers had a higher percentage of servants than the smaller cities, whose economies were more dependent on agriculture. Cissie Fairchilds estimates that one out of every twelve people in Old Regime France were servants, two-thirds of them female, and Judith Brown finds that two-thirds of the servants identified in a 1631 census from Florence were female. Girls might begin service as young as seven or eight, traveling from their home village to a nearby town. They often depended on friends and relatives to find positions for them, or in some cities of Germany and France used the services of an employment agent. These employment agents were usually older women, the wives or widows of craftsmen or city officials who possessed a good knowledge of the households in their neighborhood. They were paid both by the servant and by the employer, and were licensed and regulated by the city. In other cities those in search of work simply gathered at certain spots, or talked to the people they met in hopes of a lead. A young woman had to be particularly careful, for the wrong employer could not only mean unpleasant duties or nonpayment of wages, but, as we saw in the last chapter, sexual advances that could result in an out-of-wedlock child and ruin her hopes of marriage. Some servants in Europe were, in fact, slaves, purchased from eastern Europe in Italian households or from northern and western Africa in Spanish and Portuguese ones. Occasionally such women accompanied their owners to the New World, for Spanish records mention both European and African slave women in the American colonies.

Most households that had servants could afford only one, a woman whose tasks were thus highly varied. She assisted in all aspects of running the household, and rarely received any official time off, as the poem by Mary Collier quoted at the beginning of this chapter so clearly expresses. In artisan homes the majority of her time was often spent in production, so that to call her a "domestic" is in some ways a misnomer. She generally ate and slept with the family, for there was rarely enough space for her to have separate quarters. Even in middle- or upper-class households that did have many rooms, servants were rarely separated from their employers the way they would be in the nineteenth century, but lived on quite intimate terms with them. Though they usually came from poor families, they identified in many ways with their employers, and tended to wear fancier clothing than other lower-class women. This upset bourgeois notions of the proper social order, and beginning in the sixteenth century many cities passed sumptuary laws, in essence urban dress codes that forbade servants to wear fine materials or jewels. Such laws were never very effective, for finer clothing was one of the ways in which servants tried to attract better marriage partners, a key aim of their deciding to go into service.

Sumptuary laws were only a small part of the regulations governing servants. No matter what their age, servants were legally considered dependents of their employers, and could be punished or dismissed by them with little recourse. Male heads of household in particular were expected to oversee the conduct of their servants at all times; employers in Frankfurt whose maids became pregnant were required to pay the costs of the delivery and care for the maid and her infant for three months no matter who the father was, because this would not have happened had they been fulfilling their duty. This dependent position meant that by law or custom servants were generally prohibited from marrying, and most women regarded service as a stage in life rather than a lifelong career. They hoped that the wages they earned would form a dowry large enough to attract a better husband than they could otherwise have done, and that their skills at running a household or experience in production would enable their new family to prosper. In Italian and German cities, being a servant was often seen as not entirely honorable, as it left a woman open to her master's sexual advances. City governments in some areas attempted to change this attitude once they realized domestic service was one way in which poor women could earn dowries and so marry rather than require public support, but in others they heightened such disdain by using very negative language in their regulations.

Servants were generally hired for a year at a time, and could regard their employment as somewhat stable. For unmarried women not able to find a position, or married women at all times, cities also offered other types of service employment on a daily or short-term basis. Many of these jobs were viewed as extensions of a woman's functions and tasks in the home – cleaning, cooking, laundering, caring for children and old people, nursing the sick, preparing bodies for burial, mourning the dead. They usually required no training beyond what a girl learned from her mother, and were poorly paid, with low status and no job security. Private account books tell us that households frequently hired women by the day for the heavy laundering and special cooking for weddings and funerals, and city expenditure records list women among those hired for heavy manual labor such as repairing city walls; what we don't know is exactly how these hirings were carried out, or whether such women received enough employment to support themselves and their families. The preponderence of women among those receiving public or religious charity in every city indicates that they probably did not.

Women not only received charity in early modern cities, but they also dispensed it. The hospitals, orphanages, and infirmaries run by the Catholic church were largely staffed by women, as were similar secular institutions that many cities set up beginning in the fifteenth century. These were not hospitals in the modern sense, but places where those with chronic, non-contagious diseases, poor expectant mothers, the handicapped, poor people recovering from injuries, foundling children, and mentally retarded or psychologically disturbed children or adults went for care. Those whose families could afford treatment or care in their own homes would not be found in such places, and conditions were often horrendous. There was never any attempt to shelter women from the danger or drudgery of working in these hospitals, however, and women cooked, cleaned, and cared for the patients, and also did administrative work and bookkeeping, led the patients in prayer, and carried out examinations for admission. In the Netherlands, for example, widows or married women often served as regentesses of almshouses, inspecting them daily, overseeing their operations, and contributing to the success of Dutch charity. In many cities throughout Europe women distributed poor relief to families in their own homes, with the city governments relying on the women's knowledge of their own neighborhoods to prevent fraud.

Though no one raised objections to women working in church or city hospitals, the early modern period saw increasing opposition to women caring for the sick outside of an institution. Women could not attend university medical schools, so could not call themselves "physicians" and were usually prohibited from performing diagnoses or prescribing treatment as a physician would. University medical training in the early modern period still largely depended on the teachings of Galen, however, so that most diagnoses were made by examining a patient's urine or eyes, and the most common treatment for any illness was bloodletting. Though because of this the treatments prescribed by physicians were at worst deadly and at best useless, their university training still gave physicians high social status and allowed them to charge high fees. Fortunately for their own health, most people in Europe could not afford the services of a physician, but instead relied on barber-surgeons for bloodletting and the treatment of external ailments, and on apothecaries for medications. Both barber-surgeons and apothecaries were trained through apprenticeship systems, with women increasingly forbidden to begin an apprenticeship or carry on a practice in which they had been serving as their husband's assistant after his death. Women who continued to practice medicine were often required to take no fees at all, or only treat children and women, despite their eloquent pleas, such as that of Elisabeth Heyssin at the beginning of this chapter, that care of the ill had been part of women's traditional role throughout European history. As those who practiced medicine for a fee were increasingly required to be licensed, women were lumped automatically with unlicensed "quacks and charlatans," no matter what the effectiveness of their treatments. Because most treatment of illness was still handled with home remedies, however, women continued to be the main practitioners of medical care, and all cookbooks, herbals, and household guides contained huge numbers of recipes for the treatment of everything from colds to the plague. As we saw in the last chapter, women also continued to dominate midwifery in most parts of Europe, the one female occupation whose practitioners developed a sense of work identity nearly as strong as that of men.

Domestic and other types of service occupations thus provided employment for both rural and urban women, and city women also joined those of the countryside in retail sales. The city marketplace, the economic as well as geographic center of most cities, was filled with women; more than three-quarters of the traders in the markets of early modern Polish cities were women. Along with rural women with their agricultural and animal products were city women with sausage, pretzels, meat pies, cookies, candles, soap, and wooden implements that they had made. Women sold fresh and salted fish that their husbands had caught or that they had purchased from fishermen, game and fowl they had bought from hunters, and imported food items such as oranges, and in the eighteenth century tea and coffee bought from international merchants. Pawnbrokers sold used clothing and household articles, and female money-changers exchanged travelers' money for the type of coinage that was accepted in the city. Because there was no way to preserve food easily, women or their female servants had to shop every day, and the marketplace was where they met their neighbors, exchanged information, and talked over recent events. Municipal market regulations were often very strict in terms of product purity, honest weights and measures, and fair prices, but they generally make no distinction between male and female traders, as long as the women were from the local area and not migrants. As we saw in Chapter 1, cities recognized that married women who carried out retail business needed to be able to buy and sell without their husbands' permission, so had the special category of *femme sole,* which allowed them much greater freedom. Records from many cities indicate that far more women were simply carrying on business anyway without any special legal approval.

Along with selling at the marketplace, women also ran small retail establishments throughout the city. They made beer, mead, and hard cider, and ran taverns and inns to dispense their beverages and provide sleeping quarters for those too poor to stay in the more established inns. These taverns also provided employment for serving-women, though there were perils with such a job; inn servants in France were the one group of women denied the right to sue their seducer if they became pregnant. Women's work as producers and distributors of alcohol changed somewhat during the period, for they often left or were pushed out of certain occupations, such as brewing beer, once these became larger-scale, requiring more capital investment but also producing more profit. Women pickled and smoked meat, made sauerkraut, and prepared tripe in their own kitchens and sold it directly from their houses. Although economic historians discussing the rise of the market economy in this period primarily focus on male capitalist investors, bankers, and wholesale merchants, these female retail traders were just as market-oriented. The market they served was largely one of women and poor people, for they provided goods of generally lower quality at a lower cost than those sold by guild masters and major merchants. Despite the small scale of their businesses, female retail traders were very quick to defend them against interlopers, calling people names in the street or hauling them into court; such market women often played a significant role in urban disturbances, from the iconoclastic riots associated with the Protestant Reformation to the political protests of the French Revolution.

Because retail trade was so clearly dominated by women, city governments in 1500 often appointed women to official positions as inspectors and overseers. Women served as grain inspectors, cloth measurers, toll collectors, weighers of merchandise at the city scales, and gatekeepers. Over the sixteenth and seventeenth centuries, women's names gradually disappeared from the records as the men who generally served in these positions tried to emulate higher officials like judges, city physicians, and lawyers. These higher positions all required university training, and so were closed to women; gradually the lower positions were closed to women as well, even though special training was still not required. Wives of male officals might still do most of the actual work – male gatekeepers, for example, often had another trade and so depended on their wives to "man" the gate many hours of the day – but they were not considered officials in their own right and no longer had to swear an oath of office.

Domestic industry provided employment for increasing numbers of urban, as well as rural women, particularly in spinning. Early modern techniques of cloth production necessitated up to twenty carders and spinners per weaver, so that cloth centers like Florence, Augsburg, or Antwerp could keep many people employed. As we have seen, in the rural areas both men and women might spin, but in the cities economic need appeared never to be strong enough to break down the association of spinning with women, and men beyond adolescence simply did not spin. The identification of women and spinning became stronger in the early modern period for several reasons. In many parts of Europe, bureaucrats and officials began to advise rulers to encourage cloth production in order to increase exports and provide jobs for the poor so that they would marry earlier and by so doing increase the population size. A healthy export trade and a growing population were prime aims of the most widespread school of economic theory in the early modern period, mercantalism, and to mercantalists the best way to achieve these was to have as much of the population as possible engaged in what they viewed as productive labor. Along with the rest of their contemporaries, mercantalists did not recognize much of what women did as productive, so saw them and children as a vast labor pool waiting to be tapped. They did recognize that spinning was the bottleneck in the production of cloth, and so suggested and implemented countless schemes to encourage more spinning. They attached spinning rooms to orphanages, awarded prizes to women who spun the most, made loans easier for those who agreed to spin, set up spinning schools for poor children. Poor law authorities in England opened spinstries for poor women, providing women too poor to own their wheels with the needed equipment. Women who were in the hospital or jail were expected to spin to defray part of the costs of their upkeep, and prostitutes in some cities were expected to produce a certain number of bobbins of yarn in their off hours.

Along with schemes or regulations that pulled women into spinning, there were also economic factors that pushed them into it. As we will see in more detail below, many occupations which had been open to women in the Middle Ages were closed to them by law or custom, so that spinning was often the only possible employment; only in the seventeenth century do unmarried women in England all come to be called "spinsters." So many women turned to spinning that wages were kept low, certainly too low to support a family and often too low to support the woman herself, which is why prizes and loans may have been necessary inducements; women identified as spinners often appealed to city councils for support, noting, "what little I make at spinning will not provide enough even for my own bread."[5]

Spinners' wages were also kept low for noneconomic reasons. The idea that all women were either "married or to be married" meant that both city authorities and the investors who set up domestic cloth production could choose to view spinning as simply a stopgap employment until women attained, or returned to, their "natural" married state, even though they knew that in reality many women supported themselves with spinning for decades. They also hoped that low wages would encourage women to live in the households of master-weavers or other male artisans rather than live on their own. As we noted in Chapter 2, the early modern period was a time of increasing suspicion of masterless

[5] Frankfurt guild records, 1615, quoted in Wiesner, *Working Women*, p. 184.

6   Geertruydt Roghman, *Woman Spinning*, before 1650. Harvey D. Parker Collection, Courtesy, Museum of Fine Arts, Boston. Roghman was one of the few women engravers active during the "golden age" of art in the seventeenth-century Netherlands. Her father and brothers were also engravers, but she concentrated more on the daily life of women; this is from a series of engravings of women's occupations.

persons, and unmarried women working and living on their own were the most mistrusted. Authorities at times even tried to prevent grown daughters from continuing to live with their parents, arguing that parents gave them too much freedom, which caused "nothing but shame, immodesty, wantonness, and immorality," with their idleness leading to "tearing hedges, robbing orchards, beggaring their fathers."[6] Low wages alone did not always succeed in forcing women into male-headed households, however. Spinners in Augsburg chose to pool their wages and live together, commenting in 1597 that they were not so dumb as to live with master-weavers who would deduct room and board from their wages at a rate higher than these were worth and so leave them with less than if they lived in rented rooms; the city responded by flatly forbidding all unmarried women to have their own households.

Religious and civic authorities also worried about what went on at spinning bees in both town and countryside, evening gatherings where young women brought their wheels or distaffs and spindles; they recognized that young men also gravitated to them, and that the spinning was accompanied by songs, jokes, and drinking. They often tried to prohibit spinning bees, though the mercantalists countered that such gatherings actually promoted marriage by allowing young men to compare the skill and industriousness of various marriage partners, and also promoted higher production levels because the young spinners competed with one another. Most authorities were more at ease when spinning bees were gradually replaced in urban areas by centralized locations at which women spun and wove under the direction of male overseers. Such centers, sometimes termed manufactories to distinguish them from the factories of the later Industrial Revolution, which used steam- or water-powered equipment, began to employ large numbers of young women in the early eighteenth century, paying them by the piece with frequent quality checks. Women were favored as workers because they would work for lower wages and were thought to have more delicate and nimble hands; the investors did not realize that these women also did rough housework and seasonal agricultural labor, so that their hands were swollen and scarred, which made their work uneven and led them to be fined for poor quality work. Conditions in these manufactories were often unpleasant and unhealthy, with cloth

---

[6] The first quotation is from a 1665 ordinance in Strasbourg, France, quoted in Wiesner, *Working Women*, p. 89; the second from an anonymous 1715 Scottish pamphlet, quoted in Jane Schneider, "Rumpelstiltskin's bargain: Folklore and the merchant capitalist intensification of linen manufacture in early modern Europe," in Annette B. Weiner and Jane Schneider, eds., *Cloth and Human Experience* (Washington, Smithsonian Institution Press, 1989), 191.

fibers filling the air and boiling vats causing them to be continually damp. Women's wages were much lower than those of men who worked in the same establishment, and they rarely achieved supervisory status, but young women sometimes preferred work in a manufactory over domestic service because it did allow a small amount of free time and a greater sense of independence.

Moral as well as economic considerations shaped urban women's employment in other types of domestic industry along with spinning. In Florence, for example, women made up about 40 percent of those employed in wool production, not counting spinners, and 84 percent of workers in the silk industry. They were concentrated in low-skill jobs, and only in those such as weaving that could be carried out in the home and did not require them to go out in public. This was not only because women were primarily responsible for domestic duties and child care along with their paid labor, but also because in Italy, more than in northern Europe, women were seen as the moral guardians of family honor whose reputations needed to be kept from any hint of scandal. Respectable women, even among the poor, were to avoid any jobs that put them in contact with men other than family members, so the range of paid employment open to them was even smaller than it was in northern Europe.

Along with occupations that paralleled those in the countryside, early modern cities also offered several distinctive types of employment for women. One of these was selling sex for money, or what later came to be called prostitution. During the late Middle Ages, most major cities in Europe and many of the smaller ones had an official brothel or an area of the city in which selling sex was permitted. Many cities in the fifteenth century set down rules for the women and their customers, and justified the existence of municipal brothels with the comment that such women protected honorable girls and women from the uncontrollable lust of young men, an argument at least as old as Augustine. In a few cities, such as Florence, authorities also noted that brothels might keep young men from homosexual relations, another far worse alternative in their eyes. Visiting brothels was associated with achieving manhood in the eyes of young men, though for the women themselves their activities were work. Indeed, in some cases the women had no choice, for they had been traded to the brothel manager by their parents or other people in payment for debt, or had quickly become indebted to him (or, more rarely, her) for the clothes and other finery regarded as essential to their occupation. Poor women – and men – also sold sex illegally outside of city brothels, combining this with other sorts of part-time work such as laundering or sewing.

Though selling sex for money was legal in the Middle Ages, the position of women who did so was always marginal, and in the late fifteenth century cities began to limit brothel residents' freedom of movement and choice of clothing, requiring them to wear distinctive head coverings or bands on their clothing so that they would not be mistaken for "honorable" women. They also began to impose harsher penalties on women who did not live in the designated house or section of town. Such restrictions increased dramatically after the Protestant Reformation, with most Protestant and then Catholic cities closing their municipal brothels, arguing that the possible benefits they provided did not outweigh their moral detriments. Selling sex was couched in moral rather than economic terms, as simply one type of "whoredom," a term that also included premarital sex, adultery, and other unacceptable sexual activities. As we have seen, religious reformers such as Luther described women who sold sex in very negative terms, and also regarded "whore" as the worst epithet they could hurl at their theological opponents. Closing the official brothels did not end the exchange of sex for money, of course, but simply reshaped it: smaller, illegal brothels were established; women moved to areas right outside city walls; police and other authorities were influenced or bribed to overlook it.

Government policy toward selling sex for money from the sixteenth century through the eighteenth varied throughout Europe, and in many places was typified by alternating periods of tolerance and suppression. In general, major Italian cities such as Florence and Venice were the most tolerant, favoring regulation over suppression and often viewing prostitutes as significant sources of municipal income. From 1559 until the mid-eighteenth century in Florence, for example, all women registered as prostitutes were required to contribute an annual tax based on their income, which went to support a convent for those women who wished to give up prostitution; payment of extra taxes would allow a woman to live where she wished in the city and wear whatever type of clothes she chose. In Amsterdam, houses termed *speelhuizen,* which combined dancing, nightlife, and the sale of sex, were opened during the seventeenth century; though officially prohibited and subject to prosecution, they were favorite haunts of the thousands of sailors from the East and West India Companies who came to Amsterdam every summer. (In the nineteenth century, most of continental Europe except for Spain permitted prostitution again, as long as the women registered and submitted themselves to weekly examinations for venereal disease.)

The official contempt of "whoredom" was not always internalized by women themselves, however, particularly in large cities like Rome where their number remained high despite all attempts at prohibition. Roman prostitutes often offered their customers music and poetry along with sexual services, and worked independently, living with other women or with their mothers or children; they often described their occupation in terms of the quality of their clients instead of simply monetary terms. Their neighbors did not shun them, but socialized with them and defended them against verbal and physical attacks. The clear distinction in the minds of Italian authorities between respectable and unrespectable women may have kept most women out of jobs that required regular contact with men, but it did not separate prostitutes and their neighbors on the streets of Florence or Rome.

In both Italian cities and the capitals of northern Europe such as Paris or London, there were always a few women who achieved great prominence, wealth, and near-respectability through their sexual connections with nobles, intellectuals, and officials, such as Ninon de Lenclos, who was friends with the playwright Molière, and Madame de Maintenon, the future wife of King Louis XIV. Such courtesans were often glamorized in plays and poetry, but it is important to remember that the lives of most women who sold sex were filled with violence, imprisonment, disease, and, by the seventeenth century, deportation. Their numbers went up, as one would expect, during times of war, famine, and economic depression, when many women could not find other types of work. Though authorities viewed such activities in moral terms, what few comments we have from women indicate they saw it as the only way not to "suffer from poverty, hunger, and need."[7]

Because many women who sold sex spent some time imprisoned, they generally came into contact with, and sometimes became part of, the criminal world that operated in all early modern cities. Women might also intentionally seek imprisonment during times of famine or economic depression, for prisoners often worked for pay, which could then be sent to their families outside. For a few women, crime became an occupation. As in contemporary societies, early modern women were far less likely to be involved in crimes of violence than men, but they were frequently arrested for theft or receiving stolen goods. Records from the west coast of Ireland, for example, mention a number of women arrested for plundering stranded ships or receiving goods from pirates, but only a few who actually sailed on pirate ships. Women were more likely to steal from households or shops than directly from persons, and often did so when short-term employment or domestic service gave them an opportunity. The number of women accused of theft increased during times of shortage, and city courts often gave women lighter sentences than men when they pleaded that they had stolen solely because of

---

[7] Woman's testimony from Stralsund, Germany in 1560, quoted in Beata Schuster, *Die freien Frauen: Dirnen und Frauenhäuser im 15. und 16. Jahrhundert* (Frankfurt, Campus, 1995), p. 200. My translation.

"unimaginable and incontestable poverty."[8] Simply being female did not lead to leniency, however, for women were regularly banished, mutilated by branding or having their nose or ears cut off, punished corporally, or executed for theft or other criminal activities. In fact, being female made one *more* likely to be accused of certain crimes, especially infanticide, witchcraft, and prostitution; far more women were punished for these three than for any other type of illegal activity.

If prostitution and crime represented the low end of the spectrum of urban female occupations in terms of respectability, honor, and what we might call status, the high end was represented by women who participated in craft guilds. Craft guilds were the most important way that production was organized in European cities in 1500, and continued to dominate the production and distribution of most products throughout the early modern period. There were a few all-female guilds in cities with highly specialized economies such as Cologne, Paris, and Rouen, but in general the guilds were male organizations and followed the male life-cycle. One became an apprentice at puberty, became a journeyman four to ten years later, traveled around learning from a number of masters, then settled down, married, opened one's own shop and worked at the same craft full-time until one died or got too old to work any longer. This process presupposed that one would be free to travel (something that was more difficult for women than men), that on marriage one would acquire a wife as an assistant, and that pregnancy, childbirth, or child-rearing would never interfere with one's labor. Transitions between these stages were marked by ceremonies, and master-craftsmen were formally inscribed in guild registers and took part in governing the guild.

Women fit into guilds much more informally. When urban economies were expanding in the High Middle Ages, the master's wife and daughters worked alongside him and the journeymen and apprentices, and female domestic servants also carried out productive tasks. When the demand for products was especially great, master-craftsmen hired female pieceworkers to assist and in some cities girls entered formal apprenticeships; women and girls thus served as a labor reservoir, to be utilized when guild needs required. Masters' widows ran shops after the death of their husbands, and were expected to pay all guild fees, though they could not participate in running the guild. Other than masters' widows and a small number of female apprentices, however, women's ability to work was never officially recognized and usually depended not on their own training, but on their relationship with a guild master.

---

[8] Munich city council minutes, 1544, quoted in Wiesner, *Working Women*, p. 109.

Even this informal participation began to change in the fifteenth century on the Continent, when explicit restrictions on women's work began. First masters' widows were limited in the amount of time they could keep operating a shop or prohibited from hiring journeymen, then female domestic servants were excluded from any productive tasks, then the number of his daughters a master-craftman could employ was limited. In extreme cases, such as watchmaking in Geneva, masters were flatly prohibited from teaching any daughters or even their wives the essential part of their craft. The timing of these restrictions varied from craft to craft, town to town, and country to country; they did not begin until the sixteenth century in Scandinavia. Girls in England were formally apprenticed and then practiced independently in some trades well into the eighteenth century; by the early nineteenth century, however, female apprenticeship in England had also become limited to certain needlework trades only. Whether restrictions occurred in the fifteenth century or the eighteenth, because women's participation in guild shops was generally not guaranteed by guild regulations and because widows had no political voice in running the guilds, women as a group were not able to protect their right to work. Individual women, especially widows, often requested that they be allowed to work despite the restrictions, appealing to the city council or other municipal or state authorities by stressing their poverty, old age, or number of dependent children and praising the mercy and "Christian charity" of the authorities. In a few cases, such as weavers in the Bologna area, women appealed to authorities in the name of a group of women, giving evidence of some type of organization, and emphasized their abilities rather than their need. Whatever the language of the women involved, however, the authorities to whom they appealed saw women's work as a substitute for charity, noting that it was "always better that one supports oneself than comes to the council for public charity," whereas men's work was their right.[9] They never allowed women as a group to continue working, however, but limited their permission to the woman or women making the request. As women were excluded from most guilds, state authorities sometimes set up separate guild-like structures especially for them, but still viewed these as charity. In Paris, Louis XIV and his economic adviser Colbert set up an all-female guild of dressmakers in 1675, noting that "this work was the only means that they had to earn their livelihood decently."[10]

---

[9] Strasbourg city council minutes, 1617, quoted in Wiesner, *Working Women*, p. 192.

[10] French royal statutes, 1675, quoted in Cynthia M. Truant, "The guildswomen of Paris: gender, power, and sociability in the old regime," *Proceedings of the Annual Meeting of the Western Society for French History* 15 (1988), 131.

A number of reasons have been suggested as to why women were excluded from craft guilds: the competition of rural and urban proto-industrial production; real or fabricated concerns over the quality of products; the increasingly political nature of guilds in some cities after the guild revolutions of the fourteenth century. These economic and political reasons played a part, but the most significant factor was an ideological one – guild honor. Jean Quataert has proposed that as proto-industrial domestic production increased and threatened the guilds' monopoly on market production, craft guilds devalued all occupations that were carried out in a household rather than a workshop. Though the line between household and workshop was sometimes hard to establish clearly, as small workshops might be simply part of one large room on the first floor of a house, guilds attempted to make a distinction, and claimed that all domestic work was inferior. Because women were identified with both the household and with proto-industrial production, guilds saw women's work as invariably domestic, and workshops that still employed women as tainted and dishonorable. This attitude among the guilds became reflected in official policy when women who spun or washed in their own homes were not considered workers (and thus, by the nineteenth century in some parts of Europe eligible for pensions), while male shoemakers and tailors were, though these crafts were not regarded as highly as those that had separate workshops.

Male bonding was another reason that guild work was increasingly seen as a "learned art and given to men alone."[11] Guild ceremonies and celebrations that did not include women grew more numerous and elaborate in the later Middle Ages, increasing the opportunity for the male members to bond with one another. The language of guild ordinances also became more exclusively male. For example, while medieval guild ordinances discuss the duty of masters to uphold decorum, an ordinance from the bakers of Linz, in Austria, in 1742 reads: "This ordinance is proclaimed for the preservation of unity and honorable male decorum among masters, journeymen and apprentices."[12]

Ironically, this championing of male unity came at a time when craft guilds were actually becoming more splintered, when journeymen were increasingly forming separate guilds as they came to define their interests as distinct from and often antithetical to those of the masters. In the Middle Ages, journeymen had generally simply been part of the craft

---

[11] Munich city council minutes, 1599, quoted in Wiesner, *Working Women*, p. 129.

[12] Quoted in Gerhard Danningen, *Das Linzer Handwerk und Gewerbe vom Verfall der Zunfthoheit über die Gewerbefreiheit bis zum Innungszwang*, Linzer Schriften zur Sozial und Wirtschaftsgeschichte, vol. IV (Linz, Rudolf Trauner, 1981), p. 75.

guild, and looked forward to the day when they, too, could marry, become masters, and open a shop. In a few trades they formed separate journeymen's associations, but these were generally only for religious and social purposes. This began to change in the late fifteenth century as craft guilds became more restrictive and limited membership to masters' sons or those who married a master's widow or daughter; many journeymen then began to work for a master all their lives, becoming essentially wage laborers. Their associations began to make economic demands, and new organizations were formed in trades that had previously not seen them. Often these organizations were secret, for public authorities and guild masters feared they would provoke social and political unrest and so prohibited them, but their secrecy made them even stronger. They met in taverns and inns, holding elaborate initiation ceremonies for new members and developing ever more complex rituals. Because journeymen traveled, they carried their organizations from town to town, and enforced their economic demands by boycotting a master and sometimes an entire town that refused to comply.

These journeymen's guilds were totally masculine in membership and even more male in their orientation than craft guilds; journeywomen in the guilds that remained open to women in France and England did not form similar associations. Journeymen's guilds came to be the most vocal opponents of women's work in guild shops, refusing to work not only in shops that still allowed women but also next to any journeyman who had once worked in such a shop. They also opposed women working in the new manufactories, smashing the looms in one instance in Berlin in 1794, and driving the women from the building. States such as Prussia and Austria attempted to break their power in the eighteeenth century in order to promote the free movement of labor, but their efforts often led to riots and strikes, or simply to total noncompliance. As their own working conditions became more like those of women (i.e., dependent on wages with little hope of advancement and under the control of someone else), journeymen viewed the maintenance of an all-male workplace as a key part of their honor.

Along with craft and journeymen's honor, another type of status consideration also increasingly kept women out of guild shops, what we might term bourgeois respectability. During the seventeenth and eighteenth centuries, the number of officials and professionals in most cities grew rapidly, men whose wives did not share in their occupation but concentrated on domestic tasks. Successful master-craftsmen and capitalist entrepeneurs often wanted to emulate these professionals, and increasingly regarded wives and daughters who did not engage in productive labor as a requisite of bourgeois status; the more elaborate meals, clothing, and household furnishings viewed as part of being bourgeois also meant that female household members would have little time for production, anyway. Poorer families did not have the luxury of pulling half their members out of the work force, but Keith Snell has discovered that even quite poor parents in eighteenth-century England chose to apprentice their daughters only to trades that were considered "genteel" such as mantua-making or millinery, whereas girls so poor that their apprenticeship fees had to be paid by the parish were apprenticed in a much wider range of trades. Though guild masters were still required to be married, this was no longer based on the notion that the wife's work was essential in running a shop, but on the idea that married men were more stable members of the community and more suitable heads of household. Occupations in which the married couple was still regarded as the unit of production, and "wife" was still regarded as an occupational label, were found only at the bottom of the social scale such as "fishwife." In 1500, by contrast, even "furrier's wife" would have been considered an occupational label as well as a designation of marital status.

Investment, management, and purchasing

Consideration of the ways in which ideas about status shaped the economy represents a relatively new direction of research within economic history. In their analyses of economic systems, historians have traditionally regarded production as the most important variable, with trade as a secondary factor, and consumption – the purchasing and use of the goods produced and traded – as a distant third. In part because consumption plays such an important role in today's post-industrial economy, historians are now paying greater attention to the role of the consumer in times past. Those who study the early modern period thus explore not only the rise of commercial and then proto-industrial capitalism, but also investigate changes in the consumption of goods and services that occurred during this period. As we have seen, the development of capitalism had both positive and negative effects on working women, on the one hand providing them with jobs that allowed them to contribute to a family income or to earn wages on their own, but on the other lessening the value of their unpaid domestic tasks and only rarely offering jobs that provided more than subsistence wages. What about women's other economic activities? Did capitalism expand or shrink their opportunities for active investment and management of property? How did capitalism shape their purchasing, and how, conversely, did gender differences in consumption shape trade and production?

The great merchant trading companies of Italy usually seen as the founders of commercial capitalism such as the Datini and the Medici were family firms, and female family members often invested money that they had inherited or acquired through marriage in business ventures. Widows were generally the most active in terms of independent investment, as they tried to increase the capital that they would hand on to their sons and daughters, or at least prevent its loss. As these and similar companies engaged in long-distance trade, banking, and large-scale moneylending opened themselves up to investment by non-family members, women generally formed at least a small share of the stockholders. Thirty-nine of the nearly 300 members of the Merchants' Society of Ravensberg, Germany, in the early sixteenth century were women, and women in the seventeenth and eighteenth centuries invested in the great overseas trading companies of northern Europe such as the Dutch and British East India Companies. Some of these women inherited their shares and probably had little say in managing them, though others bought and sold shares on their own, moving capital from one investment to another. Women did not act as representatives for these firms or carry out long-distance trade themselves, however, for their freedom to travel was generally limited by family responsibilities and by the lack of places for female travelers to stay. Unaccompanied female travelers were often suspected of being prostitutes or thieves and some cities specifically forbade inns to take them in.

We do find women actively directing commercial companies within individual cities, and a few were able to amass huge fortunes. These were almost all widows who did not have adult sons to compete with them, such as Elizabeth Baulacre of Geneva, widowed at twenty-eight in 1641, who transformed her husband's small dry-goods firm into the largest producer of gold thread and decorations in the city, employing hundreds of workers and leaving the second largest personal fortune in the city when she died. Widows in England ran coal mines, traded foodstuffs and wool wholesale, and made shipping contracts with the army and navy. Glickl bas Judah Leib (also known as Glückel of Hameln), a Jewish merchant's widow, inherited a business deep in debt, and through her own business acumen and constant work transformed it into a sizable fortune. She is one of the few women who traveled to fairs and markets herself, for in this her Judaism proved an advantage. Because Jews were prohibited from staying in most inns run by Christians, they often had networks of friends with whom women could stay safely; because Judaism prized the life of a scholar more than that of a merchant, Jewish women were often freer to run businesses than their Christian neigh-

bors, as long as they did not have any connections with religious requirements such as butchering.

Glickl is particularly unusual because she wrote her own memoirs,
which describe her family as well as business life. As we can see from the
quotation at the beginning of this chapter, she was proud of her achievements, but the memoirs also reveal the limitations placed on women
entrepreneurs. Despite her success while a widow, when she remarried
at fifty-four she turned her entire fortune over to her second husband,
who promptly went bankrupt; Glickl ended her life, widowed again, living in the household of her daughter. During the period before her second marriage, she gave large amounts of money to one of her sons for
his own business ventures, which all came to nothing and ended up cost-
ing her more when she paid off his creditors. Women's participation in
trade and commerce was not only dependent on their own energy and
skill, but on the abilities of male family members.

Women's participation in commerce was also restricted by their more
limited access to capital than that available to men of their class. The
capital available to female investors generally came to them through
inheritance or dowries, and in many parts of Europe there were increasing restrictions on women's ability to invest that capital in any way that
might threaten their children's inheritance. As we have seen in Chapter
1, married women were prohibited from borrowing money without the
assent of their husbands, and the women who were able to escape these
restrictions and have themselves declared *femme sole* were not borrowing at the level of a major investor. Such women, both rural and urban,
often served as small-scale moneylenders as well as borrowers; more
than half the loans made in Danzig and Warsaw in the seventeenth century were made by women. Thus women did facilitate the movement of
capital at the lowest level, but were unable to borrow money for major
investments.

Women were also increasingly limited in their access to the other
major form of wealth in the early modern economy – land. From the
thirteenth century on, most areas of Europe passed laws that either
established primogeniture (an inheritance system in which all landed
estates passed undivided to the eldest son, with younger sons and daughters inheriting much smaller portions of movable property and liquid
capital) or favored sons over daughters. Motives for this varied. In western Europe, aristocrats hoped this would maintain family power by
allowing them to retain an estate large enough to serve as a base of power
against growing centralized state authority. In Muscovy, the state itself
supported legislation in 1627 which prohibited childless widows from
inheriting family lands and limited daughters' access to land so that all

land would go to those capable of providing military service. Women were most likely to engage in the active management of landed property when they were widows with young sons, and records from many areas indicate that women's decline in access to land was not matched by a decline in their interest in or ability to administer that land for a profit. Women who were sole heirs also gained dispensations which enabled them to inherit land otherwise restricted to male heirs, but such cases often involved protracted legal battles and required the support of the woman's family in order to succeed.

Though land and liquid capital were the most important forms of wealth, most people had access to neither of these, and the property that they held or handed down to the next generation was solely in the form of movable goods; women from landed families might also have access only to movables once systems of primogeniture were established. Thus women's most important function in the transfer of property, and the function over which they had most independent control, was probably their disposal of movables through wills, marriage contracts arranged for their children, and grants made while living to the church or other individuals. An individual's ability to bequeath property as he or she wished was limited in many parts of Europe by laws that required heirs to be granted a minimum amount, although in England both women and men had relative testamentary freedom. Most legal systems limited a wife's ability to bequeath property without the express approval of her husband, but widows and unmarried women were not restricted in their disposition of movables, and women's wills include bequests not only of clothing and household goods, but also books, art objects, and in parts of Europe that still had slavery, slaves. (Women slaveholders were less common than women slaves, but they bought, sold, traded, inherited, and bequeathed slaves just as they did other forms of movable property.) Women were more likely than men to pass property to other women, and tended to specify a wider circle of relatives and friends for specific bequests than did men. They also generally included members of both their birth and marital families in their wills, and often contributed to the dowries of nieces from both birth and marital families with grants of property or cash while they were still alive.

Women made more and larger donations for religious purposes than did the men of their families, leading in at least one instance to laws that restricted their testamentary freedom. In 1501 the Strasbourg city council limited the amount of money a woman could donate to a convent or deed to a convent when she entered, claiming that this unfairly disinherited her relatives and decreased the city tax base. The preacher and moralist Geiler of Kaisersberg, normally no great friend of women, opposed this move, commenting that "widows who are responsible and sensible persons" should be able to handle their own financial affairs, and that "it is a mockery of God, a haughty service of the devil to forbid a pious person to give everything that she owns for the will of God."[13] Geiler's arguments were unsuccessful, the law stood, and the city council further declared that all widows and unmarried women should be assigned guardians for their financial affairs, a move that occurred in many other European cities later in the sixteenth or seventeenth centuries as well.

The picture that we get from looking at women's access to capital during this period is rather bleak, but turning our attention to consumption presents a more lively and colorful scene. The increases in production and trade of the early modern period provided Europeans, including many with moderate incomes, with cheaper and more diverse consumer goods of all types. From Europe's overseas colonies came new foodstuffs such as sugar, chocolate, tea, and coffee, new types of fabrics such as calico, and new types of household goods, such as lacquerware and the porcelain that came to be known as "china." Brewing and drinking tea became part of the lives of urban women in some countries, especially England, and even domestic servants bought their own teapots. Servants, and other relatively poor women, chose to spend their income on other "frivolous" consumer goods as well, such as parasols, fans, hats, hand mirrors, and lace. Middle-class women bought more and fancier clothing and home furnishings, paying attention not only to quality and price but also to changing styles, which they learned about through printed works and shop displays. A dramatic increase in the importation of sugar – and its production in tropical colonies – was perhaps the most obvious result of women's changing tastes, but their demands for certain types of decorative objects, garments, and foodstuffs – feathers, small tea tables, flowers, curtains, lace collars and cuffs, Chinese tea sets, lighter undergarments, sugared cakes – also shaped the development of trade both between Europe and the rest of the world and within Europe itself.

The early modern period has been viewed as a time of tremendous economic change, with the expansion of commercial capitalism, the beginning of proto-industrial production, and the creation of a world market

---

[13] Johannes Geiler von Kaisersberg, *Die aeltesten Schriften* (Freiberg in Breisgau, Herder'sche, 1877), p. 73.

system because of European colonization. When we evaluate women's economic role during this period, however, we find that continuities outweigh the changes. Women were increasingly pushed out of craft guilds, but they had only rarely been full members in the first place. They took over new types of agricultural tasks, but continued to be paid half of what men were paid no matter what types of work they did. They dominated the urban marketplace, but only rarely were able to amass much profit. Women's economic activities were increasingly restricted during the early modern period, but their legal dependence on father or husband, unequal access to family resources, and inability to receive formally acknowledged training had adversely affected their economic position in the Middle Ages and would continue to do so into the twentieth century. The vast majority of women's work continued for centuries to be low status, badly paid or unpaid, frequently shifting, and perceived as marginal, but essential to the operation of all rural and urban economies. These were also qualities that may be used to describe the work of many men in the early modern period, but they had the comfort of knowing that, however dismal their actual working conditions, their labor was valued higher than that of the women who worked beside them.

It is clear from the records, however, that restrictions did not mean women left the labor force entirely or had no impact on economic development. One recent study of the London labor market found that 72 percent of women in 1700 were doing full- or part-time paid work outside the home. Historians have suggested many reasons for the dramatic growth of the European economy and for European expansion around the world, including an "Industrious Revolution" in which Europeans reduced their leisure time and worked more in order to have money to purchase consumer goods. This Industrious Revolution not only involved women; it required their labor. It is also clear from the records that at least a few midwives, merchants, market-women, and medical practitioners took great pride in their work, seeing it as a vocation the way many men did their occupations. This same sense of a calling, of being destined to carry out certain tasks, also motivated some women and girls to learn to read and write, and to produce or support art, literature, music and science, topics we will take up in the following section.

Bibliography

In many ways, all studies of women's economic role during this period look back to the pioneering work of Alice Clark, *Working Life of Women in the Seventeenth Century* (London, Routledge & Kegan Paul, 1919), which has seen three mod-

ern reprints (in 1968, 1982, and 1992). Clark found women's participation in
the economy steadily decreasing, and attributed that decrease to the advent of
capitalism and the resulting end of domestic production. She gives detailed
accounts of the daily activities of all types of women from all social classes, so
that her work is still a mine of information; her recognition of the limits of her
own study, that there were "obscure actions and reactions between capitalism
and the position of women, worthy of more careful investigation" (p. 98) has
been the inspiration for much further research.

The most thoughtful criticisms of Clark's idea of a decline in women's economic role come from Judith M. Bennett, in a review of many recent studies of
women's work, "'History that stands still': women's work in the European past,"
Feminist Studies 14 (1988), 269–83, a wider-ranging essay, "Medieval women,
modern women: across the great divide" in David Aers (ed.), *Culture and History
1350–1699: Essays on English Communities, Identities and Writing* (London,
Harvester Wheatsheaf, 1992), and a debate, Bridget Hill and Judith Bennett
"Women's history: a study in change, continuity or standing still?" in *Women's
History Review* 2 (1993), 5–22 and 173–84. Chris Middleton, "Women's labour
and the transition to pre-industrial capitalism" in Lindsey Charles and Lorna
Duffin (eds.), *Women and Work in Pre-Industrial England* (London, Croom Helm,
1985), pp. 181–206 also critiques what he calls the "critical-pessimistic" view
that the transition to capitalism was detrimental to women's labor.

Much of the research on women's work has focused on cities, for they have left
more records and are also the place where economic change began. Studies that
investigate women in many sectors of the urban economy include: E. William
Monter, "Women in Calvinist Geneva," *Signs* 6 (1980), 189–209; Grethe
Jacobsen, "Women's work and women's role: ideology and reality in Danish
urban society," *Scandinavian Economic History Review* 31 (1983), 3–20; Mary
Prior, "Women and the urban economy: Oxford 1500–1800" in her *Women in
English Society 1500–1800* (London, Methuen, 1985), pp. 93–117; Diane Willen,
"Women in the public sphere in early modern England: The case of the urban
working poor," *Sixteenth Century Journal* 19 (1988), 559–73; Merry E. Wiesner,
Working Women in Renaissance Germany (New Brunswick, Rutgers University
Press, 1986); Peter Earle, "The female labour market in London in the late 17th
and early 18th centuries," *Economic History Review* 42 (1989), 328–53; Mary
Elizabeth Perry, *Gender and Disorder in Early Modern Seville* (Princeton,
Princeton University Press, 1990); Michael Roberts, "Women and work in sixteenth-century English towns," in Penelope J. Corfield and Derek Keene (eds.),
Work in Towns 850–1850 (Leicester, Leicester University Press, 1990). Studies
that focus more closely on women directly affected by the transition to capitalism, and nuance Clark's assertions, include: Martha Howell, *Women, Production
and Patriarchy in Late Medieval Cities* (Chicago, University of Chicago Press,
1986); Cynthia M. Truant, "The guildswomen of Paris: gender, power and sociability in the Old Regime," *Proceedings of the Annual Meeting of the Western Society
for French History* 15 (1988), 130–38; Daryl M. Hafter, "Gender formation from
a working class viewpoint: guildwomen in eighteenth-century Rouen,"
Proceedings of the Annual Meeting of the Western Society for French History 16
(1989), 415–22 and "Female masters in the ribbonmaking guild of eighteenth-
century Rouen," *French Historical Studies* 20 (1997), 1–14; Pamela Sharpe,

"Literally spinsters: a new interpretation of local economy and demography in Colyton in the seventeenth and eighteenth centuries," *Economic History Review* 44 (1991), 46–65 and *Adapting to Capitalism: Working Women in the English Economy 1700–1850* (New York, St. Martin's, 1996); Dora Dumont, "Women and guilds in Bologna: the ambiguities of 'marginality,'" *Radical History Review* 70 (1998), 4–25. Despite its title, Susan Cahn's *Industry of Devotion: The Transformation of Women's Work in England 1500–1660* (New York, Columbia University Press, 1987) concentrates on ideas about women's work held by educated men, not on work itself.

Studies that look at a slightly later period and the development of proto-industry, the putting out system, and early manufacturing, include: Maxine Berg, "Women's work, mechanization, and the early phases of industrialization," in R. E. Pahl (ed.), *On Work: Historical and Theoretical Approaches* (Oxford, Basil Blackwell, 1988) pp. 61–94 and *The Age of Manufactures, 1700–1820: Industry, Innovation and Work in Britain,* 2nd. ed. (London, Routledge, 1994); Sheilagh C. Ogilvie, "Women and proto-industrialisation in a corporate society: Württemberg woollen weaving, 1590–1760," in Pat Hudson and W. R. Lee (eds.), *Women's Work and the Family Economy in Historical Perspective* (Manchester: Manchester University Press, 1990), pp. 76–103; Sheilagh Ogilvie and Markus Cerman, *European Proto-industrialization* (Cambridge, Cambridge University Press, 1996); Deborah Simonton, *A History of European Women's Work, 1700 to the Present* (London, Routledge, 1998).

Works that address the rural world as well as the urban one are usually local, and include W. Thwaites, "Women in the marketplace: Oxfordshire c. 1690–1800," *Midland History* 9 (1984), 23–42; Carole Shammas, "The world women knew: women workers in the north of England during the late seventeenth century," in Richard S. Dunn and Mary Maples Dunn (eds.), *The World of William Penn* (Philadelphia, University of Pennsylvania Press, 1986), pp. 99–114; Judith Brown, "A woman's place was in the home: women's work in Renaissance Tuscany," in Margaret Ferguson, et al. (eds.), *Rewriting the Renaissance* (Chicago, University of Chicago Press, 1986), pp. 206–224; P.J.P. Goldberg, *Women, Work and Life Cycle in a Medieval Economy: Women in York and Yorkshire c. 1300–1520* (Oxford, Clarendon, 1992). The massive two-volume micro-history of one village by David Sabean, *Property, Production and Family in Neckarhausen, 1700–1870* (Cambridge: Cambridge University Press, 1990) and *Kinship in Neckarhausen, 1700–1870* (Cambridge: Cambridge University Press, 1998) addresses the division of labor and gender relations, and Rosalind K. Marshall, *Virgins and Viragos: A History of Women in Scotland from 1080 to 1980* (London, Collins, 1983) includes much information on women's economic role in that largely rural country.

There are now several good collections of essays on women's work, including that edited by Charles and Duffin cited above, Barbara Hanawalt (ed.), *Women and Work in Preindustrial Europe* (Bloomington, Indiana University Press, 1986); Daryl Hafter (ed.), *European Women and Preindustrial Craft* (Bloomington, Indiana University Press, 1995); Pamela Sharpe (ed.), *Women's Work: The English Experience 1600–1914* (Oxford, Oxford University Press, 1998). Another wide-ranging collection is a group of essays drawn from a conference on women's economic role in the 13th to the 18th centuries held in Prato, Italy, *La Donna nell'Economia Secc. XIII–XVIII* (Prato, Istituto Internazionale di Storia Economica "F. Datini," 1990). Though the book title is in Italian, over half the essays are in English, including those on eastern Europe which are often the only works available in English on women's economic role in those countries.

For those interested in the medieval period as well as the early modern, there are many studies. The notes in Maryanne Kowaleski and Judith M. Bennett, "Crafts, gilds and women in the Middle Ages: Fifty years after Marian K. Dale," *Signs* 14 (1989), 474–88 and the bibliography in David Herlihy, *Opera Muliebria: Women and Work in Medieval Europe* (New York, McGraw-Hill, 1990) are good places to begin.

In addition to studies that discuss women's work in a range of occupations, there are also more focused analyses of particular types of work, including: Sara Maza, *Servants and Masters in Eighteenth-century France* (Princeton, Princeton University Press, 1983); Cissie Fairchilds: *Domestic Enemies: Servants and their Masters in Old Regime France* (Baltimore, The Johns Hopkins University Press, 1984); Susan C. Karant-Nunn, "The women of the Saxon silver mines," in Sherrin Marshall (ed.), *Women in Reformation and Counter-Reformation Europe: Public and Private Worlds,* (Bloomington, Indiana University Press, 1989), pp. 29–46; Christina Vanja, "Mining women in early modern European society," in Thomas Max Safley and Leonard N. Rosenband (eds.), *The Workplace Before the Factory: Artisans and Proletarians, 1500–1800* (Ithaca, Cornell University Press, 1993); Judith Bennett, *Ale, Beer and Brewsters in England: Women's Work in a Changing World, 1300–1600* (New York: Oxford University Press, 1996); Daniel A. Rabuzzi, "Women as merchants in eighteenth-century northern Germany: the case of Stralsund, 1750–1830," *Central European History* 28 (1995), 435–56; Bridget Hill, *Servants: English Domestics in the Eighteenth Century* (New York, Clarendon Press, 1996); Raffaella Sarti, "Notes on the feminization of domestic service: Bologna as a case study," *Acta Demographica* 13 (1997), 125–63.

Prostitution has been explored for many European areas: Kathryn Norberg, "Prostitutes," in Natalie Zemon Davis and Arlette Farge (eds.), *History of Women in the West, III: Renaissance and Enlightenment Paradoxes* (Cambridge, Mass.: Harvard University Press, 1993), pp. 458–74; John Brackett, "The Florentine *onestà* and the control of prostitution, 1403–1680," *Sixteenth Century Journal* 24 (1993), 273–300; Ruth Karras, *Common Women: Prostitution and Sexuality in Medieval England* (Oxford, Oxford University Press, 1996) and "Prostitution and the question of sexual identity in Europe," *Journal of Women's History* 11 (1999), 159–77 (with replies by Theo van der Meer and Carla Freccero); Stanley D. Nash, *Prostitution in Great Britain, 1485–1901* (Metucken, N.J., Scarecrow Press, 1994); Elizabeth S. Cohen, "Seen and known: prostitutes in the cityscape of late sixteenth-century Rome," *Renaissance Studies* 12 (1998), 392–409. Margaret F. Rosenthal, *The Honest Courtesan: Veronica Franco, Citizen, and Writer in Sixteenth Century Venice* (Chicago: University of Chicago Press, 1992) explores the life of one particularly well-known and gifted courtesan. An English translation of Lotte van de Pol's study of prostitution in early modern Amsterdam is forthcoming from Macmillan.

The interplay between women's work patterns and opportunities and the structure of the family has received a great deal of attention. Two of the most important studies in this area, though they focus on a slightly later period, are

Louise A. Tilly and Joan W. Scott, *Women, Work, and Family* (New York and London, Methuen, 1978, rpt. 1987) and Bridget Hill, *Women, Work and Sexual Politics in Eighteenth-century England* (Oxford, Basil Blackwell, 1989). Other useful discussions are those by Olwen Hufton, such as "Women and the family economy in eighteenth-century France," *French Historical Studies* 9 (1975), 1–22 and "Women, work, and family," in Natalie Zemon Davis and Arlette Farge (eds.), *A History of Women in the West. Volume III: Renaissance and Enlightenment Paradoxes* (Cambridge, Harvard University Press, 1993), pp. 15–45 and the essay by Hans Medick cited in the notes for this chapter.

Though Clark and other early historians of women's work such as Ivy Pinchbeck (*Women Workers and the Industrial Revolution, 1750–1850* [New York, Routledge, 1930]) were mainly concerned with economic and material issues, many recent studies have shifted the focus to non-economic determinants of women's work. Jean H. Quataert looks at the way in which being associated with the household and women had a negative effect on many occupations in "The shaping of women's work in manufacturing: guilds, households, and the state in central Europe, 1648–1870," *American History Review* 90 (1985), 1122–48. Michael Roberts analyzes the way in which popular ideas about the nature of work affected women's employment in "'Words they are women, and deeds they are men': images of work and gender in early modern England' in Charles and Duffin (eds.), *Women and Work*, cited above, pp. 122–81. Judith M. Bennett traces how misogynist attitudes affected female brewers in England in "Misogyny, popular culture and women's work," *History Workshop Journal* 31 (1991), 166–88. Merry E. Wiesner analyzes the way in which guild notions of honor limited women's work as artisans in: "Guilds, male bonding and women's work in early modern Germany," *Gender and History* 1 (1989), 125–37 and "*Wandervogels* and women: journeymen's concepts of masculinity in early modern Germany," *Journal of Social History* 24 (1991), 767–82. More general collections of essays on non-economic determinants of work that contain information on women include Steven Laurence Kaplan and Cynthia J. Koepp, *Work in France: Representations, Meaning, Organization, Practice* (Ithaca, Cornell University Press, 1986); Patrick Joyce (ed.), *The Historical Meanings of Work* (Cambridge, Cambridge University Press, 1987); Philippe Desan (ed.) "Work in the Renaissance," special issue of *Journal of Medieval and Renaissance Studies* 25/1 (1995). Two studies that highlight gender differences in exploring the problems of poverty are Kathryn Norberg, *Rich and Poor in Grenoble, 1600–1814* (Berkeley, University of California Press, 1985) and Robert Jütte, *Poverty and Deviance in Early Modern Europe* (Cambridge, Cambridge University Press, 1994).

As you can see, many of the discussions of non-economic determinants of women's work also include analyses of men's work patterns. This broadening of focus is also evident in several recent studies of rural work, including: Michael Roberts, "Sickles and scythes: women's work and men's work at harvest time," *History Workshop Journal* 7 (1979), 3–29: Ann Kussmaul, *Servants in Husbandry in Early Modern England* (Cambridge, Cambridge University Press, 1981); Brit Berggren, "The female peasant and the male peasant: division of labour in traditional Norway," *Ethnologia Scandinavica* (1984), 66–78; Gay L. Gullickson, *Spinners and Weavers of Auffay: Rural Industries and the Sexual Division of Labor in a French Village, 1750–1850* (Cambridge, Cambridge University Press, 1986); Keith Snell, *Annals of the Labouring Poor* (Cambridge, Cambridge University Press, 1987); Chris Middleton, "The familiar fate of the *famulae:* gender divisions in the history of wage labour," in R. E. Pahl (ed.), *On Work,* (Oxford, Basil Blackwell, 1988), pp. 21–46. Gender divisions in both rural and urban areas have been discussed in: Katrina Honeyman and Jordan Goodman, "Women's work, gender conflict and labour markets in Europe, 1500–1900," *The Economic History Review* 44 (1991), 608–628; Merry E. Wiesner, "Gender and the worlds of work," in Sheilagh Ogilvie and Robert Scribner (eds.), *Germany: A Social and Economic History* (London, Edward Arnold, 1992); Jordan Goodman, "Cloth, gender and industrial organization: towards an anthropology of silkworkers in early modern Europe," in Simonetta Cavaciocchi (ed.), *La seta in Europa secx. XII–XX: Atti della 24esima Settimana di Studi, Istituto Internazionale di Storia Economica "F. Datini," 4–9 May 1992* (Florence, Le Monnier, 1993).

Women's roles as owners and managers of property have been investigated in Sandra Levy, "Women and the control of property in sixteenth-century Muscovy," *Russian History* 10 (1983), 201–12; Richard Helle, "Women and slavery in Muscovy," *Russian History* 10 (1983), 213–29; B. A. Holderness, "Widows in pre-industrial society: an essay upon their economic function," in Richard M. Smith (ed.), *Land, Kinship and Life-Cycle* (Cambridge, Cambridge University Press, 1984), pp. 412–56; James Collins, "The economic role of women in seventeenth-century France," *French Historical Studies* 16 (Fall 1989), 436–70; Susan Staves, *Married Women's Separate Property in England, 1660–1833* (Cambridge, Mass., Harvard University Press, 1990); Marc A. van Alphen, "The female side of Dutch shipping: financial bonds of seamen ashore in the seventeenth and eighteenth centuries," in J. R. Bruyn and W.F.J. Mörzer Bruyns (eds.), *Anglo-Dutch Mercantile Marine Relations, 1700–1850* (Leiden, Rijksuniversiteit, 1991), 125–32; Robert J. Kalas "The noble widow's place in the patriarchal household: the life and career of Jeanne de Contault," *Sixteenth Century Journal* 24 (1993) 519–40; William C. Jordan, *Women and Credit in Pre-industrial and Developing Societies* (Philadelphia: University of Pennsylvania Press, 1993); Amy Louise Erickson, *Women and Property in Early Modern England* (London, Routledge, 1995) and in many of the essays in Prato book noted above. Natalie Davis provides an in-depth look at the activities of Glickl bas Judah Leib in *Women on the Margins: Three Seventeenth-Century Lives* (Cambridge, Mass., Harvard University Press, 1995), pp. 5–62.

The study of consumers and patterns of consumption in early modern Europe is growing quickly, and much of the literature includes discussions of women's role as consumers. See Carole Shammas, *The Pre-industrial Consumer in England and America* (Clarendon, Oxford, 1990); J. Brewer and Roy Porter (eds.), *Consumption and the World of Goods* (London, Routledge, 1993); John Brewer and Susan Staves (eds.), *Early Modern Conceptions of Property* (London, Routledge 1995); Maxine Berg, "Women's consumption and the industrial classes of eighteenth-century England," *Journal of Social History* 30 (1996), 415–34. Marcia Pointon, *Strategies for Showing: Women, Possession, and Representation in English Visual Culture 1665–1800* (Oxford, Oxford University Press, 1998) includes an extensive analysis of the relations between ideas of gender and "luxury," and a useful appendix of women's wills relating to property.

In addition to sources that specifically discuss women's economic role in the early modern period, there are many more theoretical studies stemming from the feminist critique of Marxist analysis which have relevance for many of the issues discussed here. Some of the more useful of these that explore the relations between gender and class hierarchies in economic matters include: Roberta Hamilton, *The Liberation of Women: A Study of Patriarchy and Capitalism* (London, George Allen and Unwin, 1978); Heide Hartmann, "The unhappy marriage of Marxism and feminism: towards a more progressive union," *Capital and Class* 8 (1979), 1–33 and "The family as the locus of gender, class and political struggle: the example of housework," *Signs* 6 (1981), 366–94; Joan Kelly, "The doubled vision of feminist theory" in her *Women, History and Theory* (Chicago, University of Chicago Press, 1984), pp. 51–64; Marilyn Waring, *If Women Counted: A New Feminist Economics* (San Francisco, Harper & Row, 1988); Wally Seccombe, *A Millennium of Family Change: Feudalism to Capitalism in Northwestern Europe* (London, Verso, 1992); Mary Murray, *The Law of the Father: Patriarchy in the Transition from Feudalism to Capitalism* (London: Routledge, 1995); Carol Johnson, "Does capitalism really need patriarchy? Some old issues reconsidered," *Women's Studies International Forum* 19 (1996), 193–202.

Part II

Mind

4 Literacy and learning

And if any woman becomes so proficient as to be able to write down her thoughts, let her do so, and not despise the honor but rather flaunt it instead of fine clothes, necklaces, and rings. For these may be considered ours only by use, whereas the honor of being educated is ours entirely. . . Apart from the good name our sex will acquire thereby, we shall have caused men to devote more time and effort in the public good to virtuous studies for fear of seeing themselves left behind by those over whom they have always claimed superiority in practically everything. . .

> Louise Labé, 1555, quoted and translated in Julia O'Faolain and Lauro Martines (eds.), *Not in God's Image: Women in History from the Greeks to the Victorians* (New York: Harper Torchbooks, 1973), pp. 184–5

My deep regard for learning, my conviction that equal justice is the right of all, impel me to protest against the theory which would allow only a minority of my sex to attain to what is, in the opinion of all men, most worth having. For since wisdom is admitted to be the crown of human achievement, and is within every man's right to aim at in proportion to his opportunities, I cannot see why a young girl in whom we admit a desire for self-improvement should not be encouraged to acquire the best that life affords.

> Anna Maria van Schurman, *The Learned Maid or Whether a Maid May Be Called A Scholar?* (London, 1659), p. 55

For since GOD has given Women as well as Men intelligent Souls, why should they be forbidden to improve them? Since he has not denied to us the faculty of Thinking, why shou'd we not (at least in gratitude to him) employ our Thoughts on himself their noblest Object, and not unworthily bestow them on Trifles and Gaieties and secular Affairs?

> Mary Astell, *A Serious Proposal to the Ladies* (London, 1694)

Advocates of women's rights in both the nineteenth and twentieth centuries have made equal access for women to educational institutions one of their key demands. Only through education, they have argued, could women become knowledgeable citizens or enter careers in which they would be economically independent; they have seen education as inseparable from political and economic rights. Nineteenth-century feminists called for the opening of universities and professional schools to middle-class women who could afford to attend them, and many twentieth-century feminists have demanded greater public funding of higher education to make it more accessible to lower-class women and men.

The early modern period also saw numerous calls for the improvement of women's education, particularly from women who had gained access to learning themselves, but the lines of argument were very different. Learning, by which its advocates meant training in classical languages, philosophy, the sciences, theology, and history, was primarily for a woman's individual fulfillment or to make her a better Christian; it was not linked with political or vocational aims. Anna Maria van Schurman, quoted above and widely regarded as the most highly educated woman in Europe, stated plainly that "the pursuit of letters does not involve any interference with public affairs."[1] Only rarely was the suggestion made that formal educational institutions, such as humanist academies, universities, or professional schools, be opened to women, but simply that women should be able to hire private tutors or perhaps that separate academies for women should be established. Early modern advocates of learning for women were even more class-biased than their nineteenth-century successors; learning was only for women (quoting Schurman again) who are "provided with necessaries and not oppressed with want. . . [who] have spare hours from [their] general and special calling, that is, from the Exercises of Piety and household affairs."[2] She is not complaining about this here, as Virginia Woolf later so eloquently did, but advocating it.

Early modern supporters of women's learning felt it necessary to stress that their demands would not lead to social or political upheaval because what they were advocating, though it seems modest to us, was regarded as radical by most of society. For a number of reasons, formal educational opportunities for boys and men grew steadily during the early modern period. With the development of the printing press, written instructional manuals could supplement personal training by a master-craftsman, so that artisan parents felt it important that their sons learn to read; by the end of the sixteenth century, nearly all male workers in certain trades, such as printing and goldsmithing, could read. Protestant reformers in many areas supported the opening of vernacular-language schools to allow individuals to read the Bible and other reli-

---

[1] Anna Maria von Schurman, "Letter to Dr. Rivet" quoted in Una Birch, *Anna van Schurman: Artist, Scholar, Saint* (London, Longman, 1909), p. 70.
[2] Anna Maria van Schurman, *The Learned Maid or Whether a Maid May Be a Scholar* (London, Redmayne, 1659), p. 3.

gious literature, and the vast majority of these were for boys only. For middle- and upper-class boys, training in Latin began at seven or eight, preparing them for later attendance at a university and an eventual professional career as a physician, lawyer, university professor, or government or church official. The suggestion that women should share in these advances was viewed as at best impractical and at worst dangerous. Why should parents forgo the help of their daughters in the household while they learned things they would never use in later life? Why should women learn Latin, when they were forbidden to attend universities and none of the professions that required it were open to women? Why did women need to read the Bible themselves, when they could listen to their fathers, brothers, or husbands read from it? Why couldn't women be content with education that was primarily training in the type of domestic skills they would use as married women, whether milking cows or hiring servants? Wouldn't a woman's reading or writing distract her from caring for her children and household? The supporters of female education had to answer questions like these continually, and the concerns such questions express meant that the gap between levels of literacy and learning for men and women of the same social class grew larger, not smaller, during the period. It is clear, from the vehemence of the opposition, that though the advocates of women's education chose to downplay the connections between learning and social change, the opponents recognized that learning to read and write could radically alter a woman's view of the world and her place in it.

In this chapter we will investigate the ways in which, despite opposition and hostility, early modern women became literate, and note what reading material was available to them once they had learned to read. We will then examine the small group of women who went beyond basic literacy to gain a humanist education, and discuss several women's plans for formal institutions of learning. The chapter ends with a look at two sites of political and social, as well as intellectual, training for an even smaller group of women – the court and the salon – and the ways in which learned women in these milieus supported the careers of learned and talented men through social and financial patronage.

Basic training in reading and writing

Before we go any further in this chapter, it is important to remind ourselves that even basic literacy was never achieved by the vast majority of women in Europe during the early modern period. They were not necessarily uneducated, for they may have been very highly skilled in a trade and astute about the world around them, but this education came through oral tradition and training in a workshop, not through books. As we saw in the last chapter, even their oral training was generally less formal than that of men, learned from their fathers and mothers or when an employer chose to teach them, rather than through a structured apprenticeship program.

A girl's parents were often her first teachers in reading as well. The words of Thomas Aquinas were frequently cited by Catholic authorities to urge fathers to take a greater interest in their young children's education: "For this the activity of the wife alone is not sufficient, but the intervention of the husband is better suited, whose reason is better suited for intellectual instruction and whose strength for the necessary discipline."[3] Protestant reformers urged both fathers and mothers who could themselves read to pass this knowledge on to their children, or to send their small children to friends or neighbors who could. Older women in many towns and cities ran small "cranny schools" which combined child care with teaching young children their letters and the recitation of Bible verses or psalms. Often these women were barely literate themselves, only being able to read but not write, so that they escaped the attention of authorities who were responsible for licensing and regulating teachers. If a woman became too successful, however, the official city schoolmasters often complained to the city council that she was drawing pupils away from them, and the council responded by ordering her to limit herself to basic reading only, and only to take in girls. Jewish women in Italy taught children the Hebrew letters and the correct reading of scripture in Hebrew, though translation and commentary were reserved for male teachers.

First in Protestant areas and then in Catholic, learning to read was viewed as a part of religious instruction, and political and religious authorities encouraged the opening of girls' elementary schools to teach girls who could not learn at home. In the sixteenth century, about forty Protestant church ordinances in Germany called for the establishment of girls' schools, though it is difficult to tell how many schools were actually opened, for many areas do not have good records. One that does is the province of Electoral Saxony in central Germany, whose records indicate that by 1580, 50 percent of the parishes had licensed German-language schools for boys, and 10 percent for girls; by 1675 those numbers had increased to 94 and 40 percent. By 1600 there were also a number of girls' schools in southwestern Germany and in the province of Brandenburg, although many of these disappeared in the turmoil of

---

[3] Thomas Aquinas, *Summa contra gentiles*, III, c. 123.

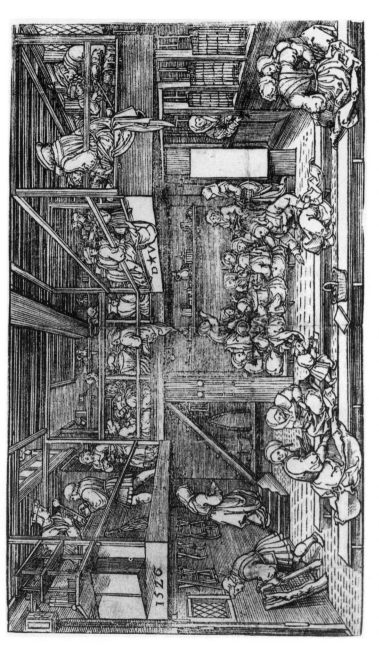

7 Dirk Vellert, *The School Room*, 1526. In this woodcut, Vellert portrays not the reality of sixteenth-centruy schools, but a scene which depicts the importance of education in bringing about order to the community, an idea which Protestant reformers felt needed frequent repetition. Here men and boys in secular dress study above and respectable women work, read, chat, and oversee the learning of children below; the vertical fold down the middle indicates that the woodcut may have originally been bound or pressed into a book, perhaps a Protestant pamphlet on education. Probably no actual early modern school ever looked like this, for boys and girls were separated except in their earliest years, and adult women in Protestant areas had no place to gather other than a private home.

the Thirty Years' War. Because of these girls' schools, it was long held that the Protestant Reformation increased opportunities for female education. More recent historians, especially Susan Karant-Nunn, have noted the continuation of a large gap between boys' and girls' opportunities for learning in even the most enlightened German states. She points out that the opening of girls' schools must be balanced against the closing of convent schools which had served noble and upper middle-class girls, and the prohibition of unlicensed "cranny schools' which had been places not only for poorer girls to learn, but women to teach.

Even where schools were established, the education they offered was meager. Girls attended for an hour or so a day, for one to two years, and were to learn, "reading and writing, and if both of these can't be mastered, at least some writing, the catechism learned by heart, a little figuring, a few psalms to sing."[4] What did Protestant authorities see as the aim of girls' education? "[To habituate girls to the catechism, to the psalms, to honorable behavior and Christian virtue, and especially to prayer, and make them memorize verses from Holy Scripture so that they may grow up to be Christian and praiseworthy matrons and house-keepers."[5] While boys were engaged in competitions in Latin rhetoric, the best student in the Memmingen girls' school in 1587 was chosen on the basis of her "great diligence and application in learning her catechism, modesty, obedience, and excellent penmanship."[6] Along with reading, writing, and religion, sewing and other domestic skills were also often part of the curriculum at these schools, which worked to the advantage of female teachers, who were also hired in preference to male because they could be paid less; scholarships set up for poor girls read: "To be sent to school, and especially to learn to sew."[7] A potential teacher's intellectual abilities often came third in the minds of city councils establishing girls' schools, after her "honorable lifestyle" and ability to teach domestic skills.

Along with urban schools specifically for girls, in some parts of Protestant Germany village schools for children of both sexes were established in the late sixteenth and seventeenth centuries. In these rural areas, the percentage of girls attending school was much closer to that of

---

[4] A 1533 ordinance of the girls' school in Wittenberg, Germany, translated and quoted in Gerald Strauss, "The social function of schools in the Lutheran Reformation in Germany," *History of Education Quarterly* 28 (1988), 197.

[5] A 1552 school ordinance from Mecklenburg, Germany, quoted in ibid., 198.

[6] A 1587 ordinance of the girls' school in Memmingen, Germany, quoted in Merry E. Wiesner, *Working Women in Renaissance Germany* (New Brunswick, Rutgers University Press, 1987), p. 81.

[7] Ibid., p. 82.

boys than in urban areas, though neither sex attended school as long nor as regularly as boys in the city. The curriculum for both sexes was identical, with no Latin or the advanced subjects offered to boys in the cities, so that rural girls' classroom experience was much closer to that of their brothers than that of urban girls, and the gender gap in education was not as pronounced.

During the sixteenth century instruction for girls in Catholic areas, other than in convents, which were largely limited to the nobility and wealthy, lagged behind even the meager offerings of Protestant areas. A survey of schools in Venice in 1587–88 found about 4,600 male pupils, or about one-forth of the school-age boys in the city, and only 30 girls. There were some informal catechism schools in Italy and Spain (those for boys taught by men and for girls by women) that did teach reading, but these only met for about two hours on Sundays and religious holidays so that the level of literacy achieved was not very high. Opportunities for girls increased in the seventeenth century in some parts of Catholic Europe with the spread of the female teaching orders such as the Ursulines, who opened more convent boarding schools for upper-class girls and day schools for poorer ones. Convent education emphasized piety and morals more than academic subjects, with everything taught by means of rote memorization. Even this limited curriculum was beyond the reach of most girls, however, for though religious orders and private individuals did open some charity day schools for girls, these were still far fewer than those opened for boys. A survey of school-age children in southern France in the late eighteenth century found about two-thirds of boys receiving some schooling, compared to only one girl in fifty.

Where girls' schools did exist, girls attended for a much briefer period than their brothers, which often meant they learned to read but not to write because the two were not taught simultaneously. Writing was also more expensive to learn, as pupils had to have some material on which to write, which parents were often unwilling to provide for their daughters. Parish registers, marriage contracts, and wills throughout the early modern period generally reveal that about twice as many men as women from similar social classes could sign their names, and that the women's signatures are more poorly written than the men's, so that their name might have been the only thing these women ever wrote. Women who were technically literate thus could not take jobs in which writing or figuring was required, which did not dramatically shape their employment opportunities in 1500 when few artisans could read, but did by 1750 or even 1650 when in many cities of Europe the majority of male artisans could both read and write. Teaching women to read but not write was the result not only of an economic decision on the part of parents, but also of contemporary notions about the ideal woman. Learning to read would allow a woman to discover classical and Christian examples of proper female behavior and to absorb the ideas of great (male) authors. Learning to write, on the other hand, would enable her to express her own ideas, an ability that few thinkers regarded as important and some saw as threatening.

The fact that women learned to read but not write makes measuring levels of female literacy very difficult, for the ability to sign one's name is often taken as the basic indication of literacy. David Cressy's study of illiteracy in England, for example, finds 95 percent of women in Norfolk and Suffolk between 1580 and 1640 could not sign their names, a proportion that had only dropped to 82 percent between 1660 and 1700. From other types of sources, such as women's wills and the inventories taken at death, we know that the proportion of women who could not read, at least among the nobility and the upper bourgeoisie, was much lower, but there is no way of arriving at exact figures. The safest generalization is that literacy levels for women, as for men, were highest among the urban upper classes of northwestern Europe, and lowest among the rural peasantry of south and east Europe, and that they slowly increased from 1500 to 1750, though much more slowly than literacy levels for men. The greatest gap between male and female literacy was in the middle of the social scale, for by 1750 almost all upper-class men and women could read, and only a small minority of male or female peasants could.

Once a girl or woman learned to read, what reading material was available? This, too, was highly class specific, for though the development of the printing press in the fifteenth century had reduced the cost of books dramatically, not until the early eighteenth century had improvements in the printing process made books cheap enough so that most artisan households could afford more than a few small books. During the sixteenth century, the vast majority of reading material produced was religious, ranging from expensive illustrated Bibles to small collections of psalms or devotional verses to even less expensive pamphlets of religious controversy or saints' lives. From wills and inventories, it appears that women were slightly more likely than men to limit their book ownership to religious works in the sixteenth century, and to works of a pious and devotional nature rather than those of religious controversy; when parents divided their books among their children, daughters usually received fewer and smaller books, and only rarely any that were not religious. The proportion of non-religious books produced increased steadily throughout the seventeenth and eighteenth centuries, so that women were reading a wider variety of materials in 1750 than they were in 1500. How-to manuals and household guides were popular, as were letter-writing manuals, travel reports, translations of classical Greek and Roman authors, and increasingly chivalric romances and books of stories, often produced as small chapbooks with paper covers which made them affordable.

Because male readers vastly outnumbered female, most books were produced with both sexes in mind, but beginning as early as the sixteenth century there were also books published specifically for girls and women. The first books written solely for girls were Protestant religious works, especially prayer books and books about virtuous young women in the Bible, whose authors often dedicated them to their daughters and envisioned the girls reading them aloud to their friends and servants who could not read. They differed from religious books for adults both in language and tone, with shorter, easier sentences, and a milder tone, rarely mentioning hell and damnation. The prayer books often include special prayers for girls in special circumstances, such as orphans or the chronically ill, and reflections on the relative value of different types of suitors and on marriage in general. By the late seventeenth century, a few secular books were written specifically for girls, such as guides to conversation and manners, and even romances, though they continued to be strongly moral in tone and concentrated on chastity.

Books addressed to adult women readers were also largely devotional and published in small format so that they would be relatively cheap. There were books on marriage and general guides for how to be a Christian wife and mother written by men, though not nearly as many as similar guides directed to male heads of household. There were small books of devotions and consolation specifically designed for pregnant women, although it is doubtful how much solace a prayer thanking God for providing the opportunity of Christian service through dying in childbirth or gruesome stories about women who carried dead fetuses around for years would actually offer. Several cookbooks were addressed specifically to women and a few written by women, such as the nearly 1,000-page *The Excellent [Female] Cook Descended from Parnassus* published by Susanna Endter in 1691. Such works were designed primarily for the noble or upper-bourgeois household, and also included recipes for home remedies, as the title of Anna Wecker's 1597 cookbook makes clear: *A delicious new Cookbook, not only for the healthy, but also and primarily for those sick with all types of illnesses and infirmities and also pregnant women, newly-delivered mothers and old weak people.* As literacy became more common among midwives, midwives' manuals were frequently reprinted and translated, for they provided printers with a steady market.

The vast majority of books for women, even midwives' guides and those discussing needlework, were written by men, and probably purchased by men for their wives and daughters. The message they convey is, not surprisingly, not one promoting greater egalitarianism, but one in which gender and class distinctions are paramount. Through all types of books, women were instructed to be chaste, silent, and obedient, as Suzanne Hull has summarized in a study of English books for women published between 1475 and 1640. Though we cannot know if women received the message that was intended (or even that they actually read the books purchased for them) we do know that male authorities and authors worried about the possible effects of even the most pious material. The most extreme example of this was an act of Henry VIII of England in 1543, which forbade women to read the Bible except for "noblewomen and gentlewomen [who] might read it privately, but not to others."[8] Thomas Bentley simply altered the Bible to suit his purposes; in his *Monument of Matrones* (London, 1582) a guide for married women, he included all verses from Paul's letters to the Corinthians which stress female subservience, but omitted without noting it those that suggest the interdependence of men and women. In the eighteenth century, German authors warned even upper-class women against letting their reading interfere with their household tasks; one designed a special reading platform for women so that they could spin, sew, or knit while they read. Such suggestions indicate that both female reading and female productive tasks were regarded as qualitatively different from male – neither required a woman's full attention, so that neither would be up to male standards.

Humanist education

The most important change in education during the early modern period is often seen as the spread of Renaissance humanism northward from its Italian birthplace. Humanism was an intellectual movement that admired the works of ancient Greeks and Romans for both their content and style, and so advocated the study of classical literature as the best type of learning. Humanist teachers in Italian cities and courts established schools in which pupils began with Latin grammar and rhetoric, went on to study Roman history and political philosophy, and then

---

[6] Quoted in Suzanne Hull, *Chaste, Silent and Obedient: English Books for Women 1475–1640* (San Marino, Calif., Huntington Library, 1982), p. xii.

learned Greek in order to study Greek literature and philosophy. Humanists viewed an education in the classics as the best preparation for a political career as either a ruler or adviser, for it taught one how to argue persuasively, base decisions on historical examples, write effectively, and speak eloquently. Conversely, they taught that a public political career or the creation of a public reputation through writing should be the aim of all educated individuals, for the best life was not a contemplative one, but a life of action. In this they disagreed with medieval scholars, who had viewed the best use of an education to be the glorification of God through prayer, manuscript copying, writing, or teaching. Education, humanists taught, was not simply for individual or religious purposes, but directly benefitted the public good by providing knowledgeable public servants.

This emphasis on the public role and reputation of the educated individual made humanists ambivalent in their attitudes toward education for women. If the best models of moral behavior and clear thought were to be found in classical authors, why should women be denied access to these? But was a program of study that emphasized eloquence and action ever proper for a woman, because, in the words of one fifteenth-century Italian humanist, "an eloquent woman is never chaste"?[9] If simply learning to read was questioned because it might draw women away from their family responsibilities, how were women to have the time for an extended education in the classics?

Male humanists resolved these ambiguities in several ways. Some, such as Juan Luis Vives, restricted the class of women for whom a humanist education was proper to those who might be forced into public service, such as Princess Mary Tudor, for whom he wrote *Instruction of a Christian Woman* in 1523. Even princesses were not to participate fully in humanist training, however, for Vives advocated omitting rhetoric from any program of study for girls: "As for eloquence, I have no great care, for woman needeth it not, but she needeth goodness and wisdom. . . if she be good, it were better to be at home and unknown to other folks, and in company to hold her tongue demurely, and let few see her, and none at all hear her."[10] Jean Marot, a French humanist, commented in *Doctrinal des princesses et nobles dames* (Paris, 1537) that all women, including rulers, must be taught to speak the plain truth at all times, though he recognized the importance for effective governing of

---

[9] Translated and quoted in Margaret King, "Thwarted ambitions: six learned women of the early Italian Renaissance," *Soundings* 76 (1976), 284.

[10] Juan Luis Vives, *Instruction of a Christian Woman*, trans. Richard Hyrd (London, 1540), pp. 54, 55.

evasive speech and concealing one's motives. Italian humanists also forbade women to study rhetoric and suggested that all study stop when a woman married; if she wished to continue her studies, a convent or a life of seclusion were the only avenues. All humanists – even Thomas More whose daughters were viewed as the most highly educated women in Europe in the sixteenth century – emphasized Christian reading material for women in preference to pagan classics, and totally omitted satires and comedies, which they felt contained immoral allusions.

Despite reservations on the part of male humanists, there were women who were excited by the new style of learning, and who through their fathers, tutors, and programs of self study (none of the humanist academies were open to them) became extremely well educated. The first of these women, such as Laura Cereta, lived in Italian cities during the fourteenth and fifteenth centuries, where they wrote and recited public orations, and corresponded with leading male scholars. The most learned among these, such as Cassandra Fedele and Isotta Nogarola, received the highest praise possible from their male colleagues: they were judged to have overcome their sex. The scholar Angelo Politian wrote of Fedele: "For this we know indeed, this we know, that she was not damned along with her sex to dullness and stupidity"; and Lauro Querini wrote of Nogarola: "The greatest praise is justly bestowed upon you, illustrious Isotta, since you have. . . overcome your own nature. For that true virtue, which is essentially male, you have sought with singular zeal. . . such as befits the whole and perfect virtue that men attain."[11] Many humanist women internalized such values, regretting having been born women because of "the boundaries of my sex and mental powers," and sought to distance themselves from other "babbling and chattering women."[12] They also recognized that they could not combine learning with marriage and family responsibilities, so chose to retreat into what Isotta Nogarola termed her "book-lined cell" and live as solitary scholars.

During the sixteenth century, male scholars brought humanist ideas to England, and a small cluster of women gained a humanist education. These were almost all from high noble families, such as Lady Jane Grey, the daughters of Anthony Cooke, and Mary and Elizabeth Tudor. The most celebrated of these was Thomas More's oldest daughter Margaret Roper. Through his own teaching and that of tutors, More educated his children, their spouses, and other relatives in Latin and Greek, studying

---

[11] Translated and quoted in Margaret King, "Book-lined cells: women and humanism in the early Italian Renaissance," in Patricia H. Labalme (ed.), *Beyond Their Sex: Learned Women of the European Past* (New York, New York University Press, 1980), p. 76.

[12] Cassandra Fedele and Laura Cereta, translated and quoted in ibid., pp. 71, 73.

works of philosophy, poetry, science, and theology. His pupils prepared translations, gave oral disputations and dramatic performances, and came into contact with the leading humanist scholars of Europe. Margaret Roper also wrote a number of original Latin orations, poems, and treatises, though the only work of hers that was published, other than letters, is her English translation of Erasmus's *A devout treatise on the Pater Noster,* published in 1524. This is exactly the type of work by a learned woman that gained her praise instead of censure: it is a translation of a work written by a family friend, on a pious subject, and was originally published anonymously, though anyone with contacts with the More family would have known who the translator was. It therefore gained Roper a public reputation, but one that demonstrated qualities regarded as admirable in women: piety, family loyalty, reticence. It is not simply derivative, however, but shows an independence of expression which places greater stress on human unworthiness and God's kindness than Erasmus's Latin original did; it is also written in a graceful, flowing, and straightforward style at a time when much English prose was very awkward and stilted. Roper was clearly very talented, although it is difficult to arrive at an objective assessment of her abilities as the contemporaries who described them generally saw them primarily as a reflection of Thomas More's own learning and moral character. She was praised already in the sixteenth century by More's biographers, who depicted her as the perfect woman: "The good, loving, and tender daughter. . . excellent, learned and vertuous matrone. . . so good, so debonaire, and so gentle a wife."[13] Over the next two centuries her life was frequently used as an example by those who argued that education could augment rather than harm a woman's virtue. It is clear from More's own letters, however, particularly those relating to Roper's arguments with him over his defiance of King Henry VIII (which led to his execution), that she could also use her humanist education to oppose her father. She never used it to reflect on her own condition or that of women in general, however, for, unlike many of the humanist men with whom she was well acquainted, Roper made no public statements about women's education nor did she publish any of her own original works; this is also the case with the other women who received a humanist education in sixteenth-century England.

Sixteenth-century French humanist women were more willing to show their learning in public than their English or Italian counterparts, and to use it to suggest reforms or to question commonly accepted notions.

---

[13] Nicholas Harpsfield, *The Life and Death of Sr. Thomas Moore,* ed. Elsie V. Hitchcock and R. W. Chambers. Early English Text Society Original Series 186 (London, Early English Text Society, 1932), pp. 199, 5, 80.

Marguerite of Navarre, the sister of one French king (Francis I) and the grandmother of another (Henry IV), supported religious reform in her own writings and by protecting reformers at her court. She encouraged the education of the women at her court, including not only prominent French noblewomen, but Mary and Anne Boleyn, the future mistress and wife of Henry VIII of England, and Catherine de Medici, the Italian future queen of France. Through the *Heptameron,* a group of seventy-three stories that she wrote and that were published shortly after her death, her influence extended far beyond her court. The book was extremely popular in France, was translated quickly into English, and many of the stories were lifted by other authors and published in their own story collections; English humanists complained that her stories were the favorite reading of literate women. Though they do not explicitly advocate women's education or improved social status, the stories do provide examples of assertive daughters and wives and criticize traditional views of marriage; they give female readers alternative models to the patient wives and daughters found in the Bible or early Christian writers.

Marguerite's willingness to break with both religious tradition and injunctions to female silence stemmed largely from her class position, as was also the case for other French noblewomen educated as humanists, such as Marguerite's daughter Jeanne d'Albret, her nieces Renée de France and Marguerite de France, and Jacqueline Longwy, the Duchesse de Montpensier. More unusual are the writings of several middle-class French women, which explicitly state that male restrictions rather than female inferiority are responsible for women's lesser levels of learning. Louise Labé, quoted at the beginning of this chapter, urged women to show off their learning and not restrict themselves to a domestic setting: "It seems to me that those of us who can should use this long-craved freedom to study and to let men see how greatly they wronged us when depriving us of its honor and advantages."[14] She took her own advice, publishing a collection of her writings and sonnets written by men in her honor in Lyons in 1555; this work received praise in some circles, but was also severely criticized, particularly because Labé primarily concerned herself with romantic love, which was viewed as a highly inappropriate topic for women. Using the type of criticism frequently directed against eloquent women, John Calvin, the religious reformer of Geneva, accused her of gaining popularity by providing sexual services to local nobles and clergy. Her work shows great familiarity with classical literature and skill at the conventions of

[14] Louise Labé, quoted and translated in Julia O'Faolain and Lauro Martines (eds.), *Not in God's Image: Women in History from the Greeks to the Victorians* (New York, Harper Torchbooks, 1973), p. 185.

classical rhetoric, and treats the issue of unrequited love both tragically and humorously.

Labé solved the problem of how to reconcile humanist demands for public honor with restrictions on women's public actions and speech by simply ignoring the restrictions, and recommending all women who could get an education do the same. For Madeleine and Catherine des Roches, a mother and daughter who also published their own work and were the center of a humanist circle in Poitiers, the issue was more complex. On the one hand, Madeleine deplored the poverty of women's education:

> Our parents have the laudable custom,
> In order to deprive us of the use of our wits,
> Of keeping us locked up at home
> And of handing us the spindle instead of the pen.
>
> A woman who is smart enough
> To spin and keep house,
> That is really more profitable. . .
>
> Men have all the authority
> Against reason and against fairness
> It is enough if I can make men see
> To what point their laws commit violence upon us.[15]

Yet Catherine also expressed ambivalence about whether she wanted to leave the domestic world of women completely and try to gain public recognition through her writing:

> To my spindle
> My spindle and my care, I promise you and swear,
> To love you forever, and never to exchange
> Your domestic honor for a good which is strange,
> Which, inconstant, wanders, and tends its foolish snare.
> With you at my side, dear, I feel much more secure
> Than with paper and ink arrayed all around me
> For, if I needed defending, there you would be
> To rebuff any danger, to help me endure.
> But spindle, my dearest, I do not believe
> That, much as I love you, I will come to grief
> If I do not quite let that good practice dwindle
> Of writing sometimes, if I give you fair share,
> If I write of your merit, my friend and my care,
> And hold in my hand both my pen and my spindle.[16]

---

[15] Quoted and translated in Tilde Sankovitch, "Inventing authority of origin: the difficult enterprise," in Mary Beth Rose (ed.), *Women in the Middle Ages and the Renaissance: Literary and Historical Perspectives* (Syracuse: Syracuse University Press, 1986), pp. 231–32.

[16] Ibid., p. 240.

Like Isotta Nogarola, Catherine decided that despite her desire to have both "pen and spindle" she could not balance private domestic responsibilities with learning and writing, so she never married, but continued to publish original works and translations to the end of her life. She and her mother did not feel compelled to retreat from the world as Italian humanist women had, however, but remained the center of a group of French humanist writers and thinkers. They shared with their male colleagues a new sense of pride in French culture and devotion to the French monarchy, which perhaps explains why they were praised rather than criticized for publishing their writings.

Though the Mesdames des Roches were unusual among humanist women in receiving praise for public demonstrations of their learning and talent, they fit a more general pattern in another way. Like Margaret Roper and Isotta Nogarola, they were celebrated as exceptions to the rule; their achievements and writings never led male humanists, or most women in the sixteenth century educated in the humanist tradition, to question the exclusion of women as a group from advanced learning.

Humanism began as an elite movement, but gradually the classical learning which it advocated became the basis for intermediate and advanced education for a large share of the male middle- and upper-class population in Italy, France, England, and Germany, particularly when private, municipal, and princely schools adopted humanist curricula. Among women, humanism never spread beyond a tiny elite. This was partly the result of the lack of formal institutions of learning for women, but also stemmed from a recognition that humanist ideas about the public duties of educated individuals directly contradicted society's expectations for women. The combination of the spread of humanism and the Protestant rejection of celibacy meant that men no longer had to choose between marriage and the life of a scholar as they had had to in the Middle Ages; indeed, both humanism and Protestantism argued that the best life for any man was that of husband, father, and head of household. Those few women with access to humanist training still had to choose, however, and their choice of a life of learning often cut them off from the concerns of most women in a way a similar choice no longer did for men. Not surprisingly, most humanist women stopped studying and writing once they married, so that their reputations are those of youthful prodigies rather than mature scholars. Thus not only in the realm of basic literacy did the gap between male and female education grow in the sixteenth century, but at the level of higher education, particularly literacy in Latin and familiarity with the classics, it became a chasm.

Learned women, 1600–1750

During the seventeenth century, some women and men recognized the limitations inherent in humanist programs for women's education, and adjusted those programs both philosophically and institutionally. They built on the humanist idea that education was important for the public good, but rejected the notion that the public good was only served by men in political careers. Women, too, could serve the public good through their influence on children and their management of households in their husband's absence or as widows. By being more interesting companions to their husbands through education, women could keep their husbands from prostitutes or other vices that harmed the public welfare. Some writers recognized that not only female rulers, but other types of women might also be thrust into more "masculine" types of public service during times of war or revolt, which occurred in many parts of Europe during the seventeenth century. A few also realized that education would never be available for most women if it was left up to fathers and tutors, and called for setting up schools and academies for women.

Advocates of serious learning for women were generally not pleased with the type of education offered by the few schools for girls which were beginning to be established in the seventeenth century. In English, French, and German cities, a few boarding schools for upper- and middle-class girls were opened, which offered subjects judged to make their pupils more attractive marriage partners. These were usually termed "accomplishments," and included needlework, dancing, calligraphy, drawing and painting, moral instruction, domestic skills appropriate to their class such as planning meals, and in England, the Low Countries, and Germany, some instruction in French. Toward the end of the century women also began to offer courses in similar subjects in their own homes to enterprising lower-class girls, to make them more attractive not to prospective husbands but to prospective female employers, who wanted such "genteel" skills in their personal maids. Critics of such schools decried their shallowness, arguing that by not teaching Latin they cut women off from classical culture and instead taught them frivolous ways to fill their time rather than things that were morally, spiritually, or socially useful.

Most supporters of more serious education for women, male or female, had themselves received classical training, in which the most effective way to argue was held to be by example. They thus published entire books which are essentially lists of learned and talented women with short biographies describing their achievements, often ranging from mythological figures such as the muses or the goddess Athena, through classical queens and writers, medieval abbesses and humanist women, to poets, translators, writers of hymns and prayers and women simply reputed to be well-learned who were their contemporaries. Such works include Gilles Ménage's *Historia Mulierum Philosopharum* (The History of Women Philosophers – Paris, 1690), C. F. Paullini's *Hoch- und Wohlgelahrtes Teutsches Frauenzimmer* (The Highly-and Well-educated German Lady – Frankfurt and Leipzig, 1712), and the two-volume *The Female Worthies* (London, 1766), all of which went through several editions and were frequently plagiarized by other writers. The authors generally regard quantity as a more effective argument than quality, and so include any woman they have heard or read about, which is fortunate for modern scholars of women's learning and writing as they often mention women whose works are now lost or were never published. Though by terming such women "illustrious" and "extraordinarily accomplished" the authors appear to have accepted the argument that the capacity for learning in women is highly unusual, they viewed their lists instead as proof that large numbers of women could reach such heights if given the opportunity, and that female learning was neither new nor dangerous.

Among the contemporary women included in such lists, Anna Maria van Schurman (1607–78) was often described as the ultimate learned woman; Paullini spends eight pages discussing her while most other women receive a paragraph or two, and Johann van Beverwijck, a Dutch writer, calls her a sun whose "bright splendor dulls the sparkling starlight. . . of these other [learned] ladies."[17] Born in Utrecht, the Netherlands, she was educated at her father's command alongside her two brothers. She first concentrated on painting, engraving, and other forms of art, then became friends with several well-educated noblewomen and male scholars and began to learn ancient languages, including Hebrew, Chaldean, Arabic, and Syriac. She wrote an Ethiopian grammar, and was granted the rare privilege of attending lectures at the University of Utrecht, though she had to stand behind a curtain. She became widely known for her learning throughout Europe and was visited by male scholars, but she also attracted criticism. In answer to her critics, she wrote a brief treatise in Latin debating the question "whether the study of letters is fitting to a Christian woman" which was first published in Paris in 1638, and translated into English in 1659 as *The Learned Maid or Whether a Maid may be called a Scholar*. As we noted at the beginning of this chapter, Schurman answers her own question with a clear "yes," but only for unmarried middle- or upper-class women who

---

[17] Translated and quoted in Joyce Irwin, "Anna Maria van Schurman: from feminism to pietism," *Church History* 46 (1977), 48.

8   Anna maria van Schurman, self-portrait, 1633, engraving on copper. Note her fashionably curled hair and very elegant dress, styles she later rejected when she became more interested in religion.

desired to serve God through study. For such women, education in subjects such as science and languages would lead to stronger faith, moral improvement, and "a more tranquil and free life." By stressing this last result and seeing education as an end in itself, Schurman opposed the humanist contention that all education must have some further purpose, and argued that women's lack of opportunity for public careers was no reason to deny them classical learning. Schurman in fact goes further than this, commenting that educating women would not cause them to upset the political or social status quo but would lead them to support it: "Nor is there any reason why the Republic should fear such a change of this kind for itself, since the glory of the literary order in no way obstructs the light of the rulers. On the contrary, all agree that that state at length will flourish most which is inhabited by many subjects obedient not so much to laws as to wisdom."[18] Her call for women's education was thus a very conservative one, and it is perhaps not surprising that during her later life she rejected her earlier learning and argued that reading the Scriptures while guided by the Holy Spirit was all the education any Christian, male or female, needed.

Though she herself rejected them, Schurman's reasons for supporting serious education for women were picked up by other writers, particularly in England, where they led in the late seventeenth century to several specific proposals for women's academies. In 1673, Bathsua Makin, who had admired and corresponded with Schurman, published *An Essay to Revive the Antient Education of Gentlewomen, in Religion, Manners, Arts and Tongues,* to which was appended a propectus for her school near London. She argues that education will give women "something to exercise their thoughts about," be a "Hedge against Heresies" and in a more practical vein than Schurman, allow widows to "be able to understand and manage their own Affairs," wives to "be very useful to their Husbands in their Trades," and mothers to assist "their Children by timely instructing them."[19] She states clearly that educating women whose families are wealthy enough to allow it will benefit the public good, but also that she does not see this as leading to greater calls for equality:

Women thus instructed will be beneficial to the Nation. Look into all History, those Nations ever were, now are, and always shall be, the worst of Nations, where Women are most undervalued; as in Russia, Ethiopia, and all the Barbarous Nations of the World. One great Reason why our Neighbors the Dutch have thriven to admiration, is the great care they take in the education of their Women, from whence they are to be accounted more vertuous, and to be sure more useful than any Women in the World. We cannot expect otherwise to prevail against the Ignorence, Atheism, Prophaneness, Superstition, Idolatry, Lust, that reigns in our Nation, than by a Prudent, Sober, Pious, Vertuous Education of our Daughters. Their Learning would stir up our Sons, whom God

---

[18] Anna Maria van Schurman, *Opuscula,* translated and quoted in ibid., p. 55.

[19] Bathsua Makin, *An Essay to Revive the Antient Education of Gentlewomen* (London, 1673), reprinted in Moira Ferguson, *First Feminists: British Women Writers 1578–1799* (Bloomington: Indiana University Press, 1985), pp. 136–38.

and Nature hath made superior, to a just emulation. . . My intention is not to Equalize Women to Men, much less to make them superior. They are the weaker Sex, yet capable to impressions of great things, something like to the best of Men.[20]

During the 1640s, Makin had been a tutor to the daughters of King Charles I, and though we have little specific evidence about her school, we know that several writers and other women later known for their learning are said to have been educated there.

If Makin emphasized the practical benefits to their families and society at large of women's education, Mary Astell (1666–1731) returned to Schurman's idea that at least some women could claim an education solely for their own benefit. In *A Serious Proposal to the Ladies. . . By a Lover of Her Sex* (London, 1694 and 1697) she called for the establishment of a spiritual and intellectual retreat for unmarried women and widows which would give them freedom to study away from male society. Her emphasis on the religious as well as educational purposes of such an institution, and her sharp critiques of marriage and male treatment of women – for example, "the deceitful Flatteries of those who under pretence of loving and admiring you, really served their own base ends" – led her proposal to be ridiculed and attacked as a "Protestant nunnery."[21] Though she denies this by noting that there would be no vows, Astell was not alone among Protestant women, especially in England, who regretted the closing of the convents as an option for single women. Hostility to institutions that both looked Catholic and offered women a chance to be independent from men was so strong that Astell's proposal was never followed until the nineteenth century when orders of Protestant deaconesses in England and Germany, and women's colleges attached to Oxford and Cambridge began to offer serious spiritual and intellectual education for unmarried women. Expansion of the curriculum in most girls' schools to include the classical and practical training advocated by Schurman, Makin, and Astell did not begin until the late eighteenth century in northern Europe, and until the mid-nineteenth century in southern and eastern Europe.

Courts and salons

Though most schools for girls in early modern Europe taught little besides basic literacy and genteel accomplishments, there were two other

[20] Ibid., pp. 138–39.
[21] Mary Astell, *A serious Proposal to the Ladies. . . By a Lover of her Sex,* reprinted in Ferguson, *First Feminists,* p. 186.

types of places where upper-class girls and women could gain training in practical politics and intellectual subjects, and where they could make the types of connections that would allow them to further their own interests and those of their families that men could in academies and universities. If we think of education as a lifelong process of acquiring skills and deepening one's understanding of the world, courts and salons were probably more important than schools in educating women from Europe's elite and allowing them to gain intellectual influence.

Upper-class families generally attempted to arrange a period of service for their daughters in the household of a family of higher status or at the court of their territorial ruler if their own status was high and the daughter physically attractive, especially intelligent, or unusually talented in things like music. During the period from the Reformation to the French Revolution, Europe's courts were not only sites of political and economic power, but also cultural centers. Under the influence of humanists, who created a new ideal for rulers often termed the "Renaissance monarch," rulers began to support writers, artists, thinkers, and musicians in order to demonstrate their own learning and cultural interests. Thus young women serving as ladies-in-waiting at a court could often come into contact with an area's leading intellectuals, and expand their own learning through informal discussions or more formally arranged classes. At the English court, for example, young women from the most prominent noble families not only learned to play musical instruments, dance, and recite poetry, but also joined the monarch's daughters and nieces for lessons in Latin, French, and history. Scottish noble daughters, by contrast, were rarely sent to London once Scotland had been joined to England, so that their level of education and sophistication lagged far behind that of their brothers who felt it important to spend time at court.

In France, Spain, and Portugal beginning in the sixteenth century, and then later in central and eastern Europe, territorial rulers claimed greater personal political power, gradually building up absolutist states. Noble families who had long held power independently became more dependent on the wishes and whims of the ruler, and were forced to be more deferential if they wished to gain or hold political office, or receive economic benefits. Noblemen had to learn their new roles as courtiers, for which the best guide was the Italian courtier Baldassar Castiglione's handbook *The Book of the Courtier*. In many ways Castiglione's advice to men was that they act more like women were supposed to – pay attention to their appearance, flatter those with power, never speak too forcefully, never appear too skilled at any one thing but show interest in whatever those with power are interested in, be discreet in all matters, and pay careful attention to their reputations.

Castiglione's advice to female courtiers was largely the same, and women who were able to learn the new role well could gain great influence over a ruler, which resulted in financial benefits and political offices for the male members of their families. In early modern monarchies, great attention was paid to ceremonies, rituals, and the physical and emotional needs of the the monarch. Female courtiers spent long hours dressing and preparing their hair to take part in processions, play cards or games with the monarch (and lose if they were smart), observe or serve at royal meals, or simply, as the name "lady-in-waiting" implies, wait until the monarch called for them as well as wait on the monarch in whatever way he or she chose. The most prestigious tasks were those associated with the physical needs of the monarch – bringing in breakfast, handing napkins, emptying the royal chamber pot. Though we may view these activities as demeaning or disgusting, they offered great opportunities for personal access to the ruler. The woman who had learned her skills well, who was pleasant, charming, patient, and attentive, could gain a lucrative living allowance, high political positions for her father and brothers, and a prestigious marriage.

Though Castiglione emphasized the importance for court ladies of both chastity and the reputation for chastity, at many courts young women quickly learned that sexual favors were one of their most powerful tools, and the women who achieved the most personal and familial power were often royal mistresses. The presence of royal mistresses was accepted without question at most courts, with French kings such as Louis XIV even raising one woman at a time to the position of official mistress, *maîtresse-en-titre*. The most influential of these women was Madame de Pompadour, *maîtresse-en-titre* for nearly twenty years to Louis XV, who read voraciously, patronized writers, composers, and architects, and reorganized several royal porcelain factories. Though Mme. de Pompadour was the antithesis of Mary Astell's learned woman, with an education geared almost completely to making her more appealing to the king, she fulfilled the humanist goal of education as training for public service in one of the few ways possible for early modern women.

Along with royal mistresses, the other type of woman who could demonstrate her knowledge and skills in a public forum without automatically inviting criticism was a queen. The early modern period saw a large number of queens and other types of female rulers throughout Europe, some ruling in their own names such as Mary and Elizabeth Tudor in England and Christina in Sweden, some as advisers to minor or incompetent sons such as Catherine de' Medici in France, and some as regents for part of a dynasty's holdings such as Margaret of Parma, a

Hapsburg who ruled the Low Countries. Fortunately for their subjects, many of these women had not been limited to "accomplishments" in their education, but had been given training in Latin and modern languages, which allowed them to communicate effectively with diplomats, courtiers, and other monarchs, lessons in history and the natural sciences, which aided them in military and economic decisions, and practical training in political skills, which strengthened their diplomacy and choice of advisers. Their sense of the privileges that came with rank made none of them strong advocates of better education for most women, although those with children generally took a keen interest in the education of their own offspring, and they appear to have been slightly more concerned about the training of their daughters than male monarchs were.

During the middle of the seventeenth century, several women in Paris created another institution that would allow them to gain access to the world of learning and "letters" (as literature and philosophy were often termed) – the salon. Salons were gatherings of men and women for formal and informal discussion of topics decided upon by the women who ran them, held in the drawing rooms (*salon* in French) of their own homes. They were in many ways outgrowths of literary circles such as those the Mesdames des Roches participated in, but differed from these in being organized by women. The salon hostess selected the guests, determined whether the conversation on any particular night would be serious or light, and decided whether additional activities such as singing, poetry readings, or dramatic productions would be part of the evening's offerings. The first real salon is often regarded as that of Madame Rambouillet (1588–1666), and by the last quarter of the seventeenth century a number of other Parisian women had followed her example.

The women who ran and attended salons in the seventeenth and early eighteenth centuries were generally from noble families, but families who had been ennobled relatively recently. Often these women married into families of higher standing and prestige, and the salons themselves mixed old and new nobles and wealthier non-nobles. They were not democratic institutions, but did allow the old and new elite to mix, and, as Carolyn Lougee has commented, probably preserved the aristocratic structure of society by defusing the threat of the new elites to the traditional aristocracy. The women who founded and attended salons had generally been educated at convent schools, with their emphasis on piety and morals. The women recognized the deficiencies in their own education, and explicitly viewed the salon as a place to improve their understanding of the world. They took what they did seriously, preparing themselves for their gatherings by reading and practicing letter-writing and conversational skills. Saloniéres were mocked by writers like Moliére as intellectually pretentious and more interested in style than substance, but recent research has demonstrated that some were extremely powerful, which may be why Moliére chose to satirize them. They did not have any official public or academic role, but the approval of certain salon hostesses was often an unoffical requirement for a man to gain election to the French Academy, the highest honor for a French intellectual or writer.

Women generally learned how to be salon hostesses by attending one of an older woman for years; running a salon may best be seen as a type of career for educated women, with a period of apprenticeship and mastership, though with no monetary income. Besides their protégées, saloniéres often raised their own daughters to be highly educated, though the intellectual independence that resulted from this education often led daughters to open salons with pointedly different emphases than those of their mothers. Salons are only beginning to receive serious attention from historians, with those of the later eighteenth century now recognized as important institutions in the development and dissemination of Enlightenment ideas. During the second half of the eighteenth century, salons were also created by women in England, where they supported women writers, and in Germany, where they were one of the few places where Christians and Jews could mix. Though particularly in France salons were still centered on male intellectuals and writers, with women acting more as facilitators, they did give a few women in Europe's largest cities access to learning that was otherwise completely unobtainable. They also allowed some women to play a quasi-public role, leading conservatives particularly in France to warn of the resultant "feminization" of culture and weakening of the country's military and work ethic. The true influence of the salons on French society no doubt falls somewhere between these dire warnings and Moliére's dismissal, but in terms of women's education they were unique, the only place in the seventeenth and early eighteenth centuries where women were actually encouraged to be in the company of other educated women and men.

Patronage

Women serving at royal courts in early modern Europe not only used their influence to further the careers of male family members, but also to assist writers, composers, and artists. This was a period in which patronage was the most important factor in a literary or artistic career.

Though some writers, composers, and artists simply produced works and then tried to sell them, more attempted to gain the attention of rulers or wealthy individuals, who then paid them to write, compose, sculpt, or paint. Many patrons were very particular in their demands, suggesting themes and styles, ordering specific types of work, and requiring changes while a work was in progress. As certain artists, writers, and composers became popular and well known, they could assert their own artistic style and pay less attention to the wishes of a patron, although even major artists like Raphael or Rubens generally worked according to a patron's specific guidelines.

The patronage system was not new in early modern Europe, nor were women's activities as patrons. Throughout the Middle Ages, queens and noblewomen had supported artists, musicians, writers, and poets, for artistic and literary matters were considered part of women's sphere; their influence was certainly felt in the development of courtly love literature, and some art historians have argued that women's tastes shaped styles of painting and sculpture. The new ideal for rulers created by humanists in the sixteenth century made the arts and literature a male concern as well, for Renaissance monarchs were expected to support cultural activities as part of proving themselves well-rounded individuals. Large public buildings, musical compositions, and literary works began to reflect more of the tastes and character of male patrons; Louis XIV's palace at Versailles, for example, captures his personality and concepts of society exquisitely.

Patronage by noblewomen and female rulers also remained important, however. Noblewomen hired architects and sculptors to transform castles designed for defense into châteaux and palaces where they could live comfortably, and to construct elaborate tombs for themselves and their husbands. They arranged for the building and decoration of convents, churches, hospitals, and orphanages, choosing the architect and often approving the plans down to the smallest detail. Female rulers and the wives of rulers also established permanent positions at their courts, hiring court composers and musicians, official portrait artists, and by the very late seventeenth century, scientists and philosophers. Sophie Charlotte of Prussia, for example, founded the Berlin Academy of Sciences, setting it up under the direction of Gottfried Leibniz, who had been her tutor from an early age. Noblewomen such as Anna Maria Luisa de'Medici, the last in the line of the Grand Dukes of Tuscany, recognized the importance of preserving as well as creating artistic products. She could not inherit the throne of her father because of her gender, and it passed to the royal house of Lorraine in 1737, but in the agreement arranging the transfer of power, called the Family Pact, she forbade the exportation out of Florence of any of the artistic works held by the Medici family, stating that these were for "the use of the Public and for the attraction of the curiousity of Foreigners."[22] The works that she held together form the core of the major art museums in Florence to this day.

Though a small commercial market in art and literature developed during the early modern period, most writers and artists still sought individuals who would provide them monetary support in return for being depicted as classical figures or pious onlookers in religious scenes, or in return for having a book dedicated to them. Writers who felt that their work might not be acceptable for some reason took special care to find a powerful dedicatee, hoping that this individual would be flattered enough not only to provide a financial grant but also to push for the work's publication and sale. Women authors in particular, or those who wrote works directed to women or favorable works about women, often chose one or more powerful upper-class women, hoping that this would forestall or lessen criticism.

With the expansion of literacy, wealthier middle-class women also became more significant as patrons of culture after 1500. They paid composers for their work, bought books of musical compositions, scientific treatises, and all types of literature. Women's reading often brought them into contact with the world of palaces and courtly life, and middle-class women responded by making their own homes more elaborate and their clothing more decorative. Though rulers and church officials (mostly male) set the style for large public buildings, women frequently decided how private homes were to be decorated, as we can tell from letters between husbands and wives and family account books. They ordered more furniture, small paintings of still life and domestic scenes, and silver table pieces. They also wore more jewelry, patronizing certain silver- and goldsmiths, and more lace and other costly fabrics.

We might wonder how much women's role as patrons or consumers actually influenced literary or cultural developments, however, particularly because in the twentieth century styles in clothing, home furnishings, and music are so often determined by a few designers and promoters and then marketed through mass advertising. Patrons in the early modern period were sometimes similarly passive, but, as we have seen, were often very active; there is some evidence that middle-class

---

[22] Translated and quoted in Elena Ciletti, "The extinction and survival of the Medici: Anna Maria Luisa de Medici and the Family Pact," in Cynthia Lawrence (ed.), *Women and Art in Early Modern Europe: Patrons, Collectors, and Connoisseurs* (University Park, Pennsylvania State University Press, 1997), p. 223.

women were just as specific in their orders for paintings or silverware as Louis XIV was in his for the decoration of Versailles.

Are there any significant differences between male and female patronage? This is a question that must be answered very carefully. In realms other than culture, women's patronage does appear at times to be different from that of men. Because they were often not rulers themselves, but the wives or female relatives of rulers, women were slightly freer than men to support religious thinkers who were regarded as questionable or suspect. Advocates of church reform in sixteenth-century France, for example, were protected and supported by a group of royal women, though discussion of reform was officially unacceptable. Evidence from Venice and Florence indicates that women's charitable patronage was generally directed toward poorer families in their own neighborhoods, whereas men's gifts went to support city-wide projects such as the building of churches and hospitals.

In terms of literary and cultural patronage, it does appear that in the sixteenth century women were more likely to support projects with religious themes and purposes than were the men of their families, a finding not terribly surprising. During the seventeenth century in the visual arts, class appears to be as important as gender, for queens such as Maria de Medici favored large history pieces (in which they were prominently displayed) while middle-class Dutch women purchased still lifes. In terms of literature, philosophy, and music, however, there are a few tantalizing hints that some female patrons showed a consciousness of gender distinctions. As we have seen, the women who ran salons regarded themselves as better arbiters of grace and style in writing than the men they supported, and specifically favored language they thought more refined, delicate, and "feminine." The subject of *La Liberazione di Ruggiero,* a musical piece that retold a familiar story from a woman's point of view and which we will discuss at greater length in Chapter 5, was suggested to its female composer by the female ruler of Florence, the Archduchess Maria Maddalena d'Austria. Elizabeth of Bohemia and Christina of Sweden, Descartes's noble patrons, were both especially concerned with the duality of matter and spirit, a philosophical issue generally connected to ideas about gender differences in the early modern period, when women were thought to be dominated more by matter and men by spirit. Because letters to and from patrons have often survived, this is an area of research that may yield many more examples in the future.

The early modern period has often been described as a time of one educational advance after another: humanism, with its emphasis on practical training in writing and speaking; the Protestant Reformation, with its emphasis on basic literacy; the beginnings of publicly funded schooling, with the goal of mass literacy. According to some commentators, it was during this period that Europe was transformed from an oral to a written culture. As we have seen in this chapter, however, women did not share equally in these educational advances. From basic literacy to advanced schooling, their educational opportunities were much more resticted than those of the boys and men of their social class, and even the most "learned lady" or sophisticated salon hostess recognized the limits of her training. These unequal opportunities affected women's abilities not only able to absorb information and provide patronage, but also to use what they had learned to create literature, art, music, and science, a topic we will explore in the next chapter.

Bibliography

Because the opportunities for girls to gain basic schooling in reading and writing were so much less than those for boys, discussions of girls' education are often found as brief sections within works focusing on boys. These include: Rosemary O'Day, *Education and Society 1500–1800: The Social Foundations of Education in Early Modern Britain* (London and New York, Longman, 1982); George Huppert, *Public Schools in Renaissance France* (Urbana and Chicago, University of Illinois Press, 1984); JoAnn Hoeppner Moran, *The Growth of English Schooling, 1340–1548: Learning, Literacy and Laicization in Pre-Reformation York Diocese* (Princeton, Princeton University Press, 1985); Anthony Grafton and Lisa Jardine, *From Humanism to the Humanities: Education and the Liberal Arts in Fifteenth- and Sixteenth-Century Europe* (Cambridge, Mass., Harvard University Press, 1986); Paul F. Grendler, *Schooling in Renaissance Italy: Literacy and Learning, 1300–1600* (Baltimore and London, The Johns Hopkins University Press, 1989); Paul F. Grendler, "Education in the Renaissance and Reformation," *Renaissance Quarterly* 43 (1990), 774–824, which also includes an extensive bibliography of recent works; Pavla Miller, *Transformations of Patriarchy in the West, 1500–1900* (Bloomington, Indiana University Press, 1998). The general survey that best integrates the experiences of girls and women is R. A. Houston, *Literacy in Early Modern England: Culture and Education 1500–1800* (London and New York, Longman, 1988; 2nd ed. 2001). Differences between male and female literacy rates have been discussed in David Cressy, "Levels of illiteracy in England, 1530–1730," in Harvey J. Graff (ed.), *Literacy and Social Development in the West: A Reader* (Cambridge, Cambridge University Press, 1981), pp. 105–21. One of the few books that focuses only on women is Phyllis Stock, *Better Than Rubies: A History of Women's Education* (New York, G. P. Putnam's Sons, 1978), which is primarily a survey of girls' and women's opportunities for formal schooling across the centuries and does not really consider the changing social context of education. Less formal educational settings have been analyzed in Kenneth Charlton, "'Not publike only but also private and domesticall': mothers and familial education in pre-industrial England," *History of Education* 17 (1988), 1–20. Gerda Lerner, *The Creation of Feminist Consciousness: From the Middle Ages to Eighteen-seventy* (Oxford, Oxford University Press, 1993) includes discussion of literate women in the early modern period in several chapters.

Divergent ideas about the effects of the Protestant Reformation on women's education may be found in Lowell Green, "The education of women in the Reformation," *History of Education Quarterly* 19 (1979), 93–116, which takes a positive view, while Gerald Strauss, *Luther's House of Learning: Indoctrination of the Young in Luther's Germany* (Baltimore and London, The Johns Hopkins University Press, 1978) and Susan Karant-Nunn, "The reality of early Lutheran education: The Electoral district of Saxony – a case study," in *Responsibility for the World: Luther's Intentions and their Effects,* Sonderdruck aus *Lutherjahrbuch* (Göttingen, Vandenhoeck and Ruprecht, 1990), pp. 128–46 take a more negative view. Kenneth Charlton, *Women, Religion and Education in Early Modern England* (London, Routledge, 1999) discusses both the opportunities for greater control and for greater freedom that Catholics and Protestants offered women through education, while Judith R. Baskin "Some parallels in the education of medieval Jewish and Christian women," *Jewish History* 5 (1991), 41–51 compares Jewish and Christian women.

Peter Petschauer has published several articles on women's education in Germany: "Improving educational opportunites for girls in eighteenth-century Germany," *Eighteenth-century Life* 3 (1976): 56–62; Christina Dorothea Leporin (Erxleben), Sophia (Gutermann) von la Roche, and Angelika Kauffmann: background and dilemmas of independence," *Studies in Eighteenth-Century Culture* 15 (1986), 127–44; "Eighteenth-century German opinions about education for women," *Central European History* 19 (1986), 262–92. Caroline Bowden has addressed several issues regarding women's learning in England: "Women as intermediaries: an example of the use of literacy in the late sixteenth and early seventeenth centuries," *History of Education* 22 (1993); "Parental attitudes towards the education of girls in late sixteenth and early seventeenth century England," in Jeroen Dekker, et al. (eds.), *Education and Cultural Transmission: Developments in Europe and International Trends Since Early Modern Times,* Paedagogica Historica, Supplementary Series vol. 2 (Ghent, 1996).

Books that address the issue of reading material for girls and women include Margaret Spufford, *Small Books and Pleasant Histories: Popular Fiction and its Readership in Seventeenth-Century England* (London, Methuen, 1981); Suzanne Hull, *Chaste, Silent and Obedient: English Books for Women 1475–1640* (San Marino, Calif., Huntington Library, 1982) and Cornelia Niekus Moore, *The Maiden's Mirror: Reading Material for German Girls in the 16th and 17th Centuries.* Wolfenbütteler Forschungen, 36 (Wiesbaden, Harrasowitz, 1987). Juliet Fleming provides a fascinating discussion of early dictionaries for women in "Dictionary English and the female tongue" (pp. 175–204) and Mary Erler of female book ownership in "The books and lives of three Tudor women," (pp. 5–18), both in Jean R. Brink (ed.), *Privileging Gender in Early Modern England,* Sixteenth Century Essays and Studies, vol. 23 (Kirksville, MO., Sixteenth Century Journal Publishers, 1993). Cornelia Niekus-Moore looks at women's independent reading in "The quest for consolation and amusement: reading habits of German women in the seventeenth century," in Lynne Tatlock (ed.),

The Graph of Sex and the German Text: Gendered Culture in Early Modern Germany (Amsterdam, Rodopi, 1994).

Margaret King has provided the most thought-provoking analyses of the ambiguous position of Italian humanist women in the two articles mentioned in the notes for this chapter and in *Women of the Renaissance* (Chicago, University of Chicago Press, 1991). She and Albert Rabil have also edited a collection of original sources, *Her Immaculate Hand: Selected Works by and about the Women Humanists of Quattrocento Italy* (Binghamton, Center for Medieval and Early Renaissance Studies, SUNY at Binghamton, 1983). Other discussions of humanist women include: Norma McMullen, "The education of English gentlewomen 1540–1640," *History of Education* 6 (1977), 87–101; Alice T. Friedman, "The influence of humanism on the education of girls and boys in Tudor England," *History of Education Quarterly* 25 (1985), 57–70; Joan Gibson, "Educating for silence: Renaissance women and the language arts," *Hypatia* 4 (1989), 9–27; Nancy Virtue, *"Le Sainct Esperit. . . parlast par sa bouche:* Maguerite de Navarre's evangelical revision of the *Chastelaine de Vergi,"* *Sixteenth Century Journal* 28 (1997), 811–24.

A new series from the University of Chicago Press, The Other Voice in Early Modern Europe, edited by Margaret King and Albert Rabil, Jr., has begun to publish translations of works by many continental women writers, particularly Italians. Included among these are works by several learned women discussed in this chapter: Laura Cereta, *Collected Letters of a Renaissance Feminist,* ed. and trans. Diana Robin (1997); Cassandra Fedele, *Letters and Orations,* ed. and trans. Diana Robin (1997); Anna Maria van Schurman, *Whether a Christian Woman Should Be Educated and Other Writing from Her Intellectual Circle,* ed. and trans. Joyce L. Irwin. (1998). Future volumes in the series include Isotta Nogarola, *Selected Letters* and Giuseppa Eleonora Barbapiccola and Diamante Medaglia Faini, *The Education of Women;* references to other books in the series may be found in the bibliographies of Chapters 5, 6, and 8.

Learned women have been the focus of several essay collections, including that of Labalme, noted above, and Jean R. Brink, *Female Scholars: A Tradition of Learned Women before 1800* (Montreal, Eden University Women's Publications, 1980). Una Birch, *Anna van Schurman: Artist, Scholar, Saint* (London, Longman, 1909), Joyce Irwin, "Anna Maria van Schurman: from feminism to pietism," *Church History* 46 (1977), 48–62, and Mirjam de Baar, et al. (eds.), *Choosing the Better Part: Anna Maria van Schurman (1607–1678)* (Dordrecht, Kluwer Academic Publishers, 1996) discuss the life and ideas of this most unusual woman.

Women's proposals for institutions of higher education have been discussed in Bridget Hill, "A refuge from men: The idea of a Protestant nunnery," *Past and Present* 117 (1987), 107–30 and Moira Ferguson, *First Feminists: British Women Writers 1578–1799* (Bloomington, Indiana University Press, 1985). The bibliography following Chapter 5 includes further sources about learned women, especially women writers.

Women and the salons have been discussed in: Katherine Clinton, "Femme et philosophe: Enlightenment origins of feminism," *Eighteenth Century Studies* 8 (1975), 283–99; Evelyn Gordon Bodek, "Salonières and bluestockings: educated obsolesence and germinating feminism," *Feminist Studies* 3 (1976), 185–99;

Dena Goodman, "Enlightened salons: the convergence of female and philosophic ambitions," *Eighteenth Century Studies* 22 (1989), 329–50 and "Filial rebellion in the salon: Madame Geoffrin and her daughter," *French Historical Studies* 16 (1989), 28–47. Caroline Lougee, *Les Paradis des Femmes: Women, Salons and Social Stratification in Seventeenth-century France* (Princeton, Princeton University Press, 1976) remains the most important longer study of the issue.

Women's patronage, like their schooling, is often mentioned briefly in general discussions of mostly male patrons, and is also beginning to get more comprehensive treatment. The most detailed treatment is Catherine King, *Renaissance Women Patrons: Wives and Widows in Italy c. 1300–1550* (Manchester, Manchester University Press, 1998) and the essays in Cynthia Lawrence (ed.), *Women and Art in Early Modern Europe: Patrons, Collectors, and Connoisseurs* (University Park, Pennsylvania State University Press, 1997). More specialized studies include: D. Marrow, *The Art Patronage of Maria de'Medici*. Studies in Baroque Art History, 4 (Ann Arbor: UMI Research Press, 1982); Sharon Kettering, "The patronage power of early modern French noblewomen," *Historical Journal* 32 (1989), 817–41; Carolyn Valone, "Roman matrons as patrons: various views of the cloister wall," in Craig Monson (ed.), *The Crannied Wall: Women, Religion and the Arts in Early Modern Europe* (Ann Arbor, University of Michigan Press, 1992), pp. 49–72 and "Piety and patronage: women and the early Jesuits," in Ann Matter and John Coakley, *Creative Women in Medieval and Early Modern Italy* (Philadelphia, University of Pennsylvania Press, 1997); Sheila ffolliott, "A queen's garden of power: Catherine de Medici and the locus of female rule," in Mario Di Cesare (ed.), *Reconsidering the Renaissance* (Binghamton, State University of New York Press, 1992), pp. 245–55; M. Dunn, "Piety and patronage in Seicento Rome: two noblewomen and their convents," *Art Bulletin* 76 (1994), 644–63. For medieval women patrons, see June Hall McCash (ed.), *The Cultural Patronage of Medieval Women* (Athens, University of Georgia Press, 1996).

5 Women and the creation of culture

You will find the spirit of Caesar in the soul of this woman.
Artemisia Gentileschi, describing herself in a letter to her patron Don
Antonio Ruffo, 1649, quoted in Ann Sutherland Harris and Linda Nochlin,
Women Artists: 1550–1950 (New York, Alfred A. Knopf, 1976), p. 120.

But I hope my readers will not think me vain for writing my life, since
there have been many that have done the like, as Caesar, Ovid and
many more, both men and women, and I know of no reason I may not
do it as well as they. But I verily believe some censuring readers will
scornfully say, why hath this lady writ her own life? Since none care to
know whose daughter she was, or whose wife she is, or how she was
bred, or what fortunes she had, or how she lived, or what humour or
disposition she was of? I answer that it is true, that 'tis no purpose to
the readers, but it is to the authoress, because I write it for my own
sake, not theirs. Neither did I intend this piece for to delight, but to
divulge; not to please the fancy, but to tell the truth. Lest after-ages
should mistake, in not knowing I was daughter to one Master Lucas of
St. John's near Colchester in Essex, second wife to the Lord Marquis
of Newcastle; for, my lord having had two wives, I might easily have
been mistaken, especially if I should die and my lord marry again.
Margaret Cavendish, *A True Relation of my Birth, Breeding, and Life*
(London, 1656), p. 391.

During the Middle Ages, culture was largely the province of the church.
Most art, music, and drama had religious themes and was displayed or
performed in church buildings, the majority of literature was written and
copied by clerics and concerned religious topics, most philosophers and
scientists were members of the clergy and viewed these topics as intimately
related to theology, most musicians were clerics. This began to change in
Italy during the fourteenth century with the Renaissance, when secular
subjects and secular purposes also became acceptable. Though church
officials remained important supporters of art, music, and literature, and
religious themes continued, the bulk of cultural creation in the early modern period was no longer tied to the church. Scientists and philosophers
in particular divorced themselves from religious institutions, and
approached their subjects in a more secular manner.

175

A new attitude toward artists, writers, composers, and other creators of culture also developed during the Renaissance. During the Middle Ages, such individuals had been viewed as artisans just like shoemakers or bakers, and their products the creation of a workshop, not an individual; this is the reason we know the names of so few medieval artists. During the Renaissance, the notion of the artist or writer as creative genius began to develop; artists started to sign their works, and certain branches of art – in particular painting, sculpture, and architecture – were deemed more significant than other types of art, such as needlework, porcelain manufacture, goldsmithing, and furniture making. This division hardened in the sixteenth century, particularly through the influence of Giorgio Vasari, who is often described as the first art historian. Painting, sculpture, and architecture were termed the "major" arts and everything else the "minor" or "decorative" arts. A similar split occurred in literature, with certain types of writing, such as poetry, history, and epics, now defined as "literature" and other types of writing, such as letters and diaries, excluded from this category.

New institutions for the creation of culture also developed during the early modern period. Though many visual artists and musicians still trained through apprenticeships, rulers also set up court-supported schools and hired large numbers of painters, sculptors, musicians, and composers. After the development of the printing press, journals that included and promoted the work of poets and other writers began to be published at regular intervals. Regional and national academies and societies that rewarded and supported creativity in science, literature, and the visual arts were established, usually with a very limited number of members. These journals, academies, and societies increasingly determined which artistic and literary genres and styles and which scientific theories would be judged praiseworthy, and thus which artists, writers, and scientists would get commissions or support from patrons.

All of these developments led to a growing split between learned and popular culture in early modern Europe, and between professional and amateur. They also had dramatic effects on women's ability to participate in the creation of culture, particularly in those areas and genres judged most important. Women were often by regulation or practice excluded from schools and academies, and their writings were rarely accepted by literary journals. The self-promotion required by an artist, writer, composer, or thinker attempting to gain the support of a patron was judged unacceptable behavior when done by a woman. Europe's intellectuals debated whether women were capable of true creative genius, or had the rational capacity for scientific or philosophical

insights. The major arts, the most celebrated forms of music and literature, and the most noted philosophical ideas were all regarded as tied to
characteristics deemed masculine – forcefulness, strength, power, logic,
singularity of purpose. The work that women artists, writers, and scientists did produce was often judged to be the result not of genius, but of
nimble fingers, diligence in observation, skill at following the example of
a male teacher, or bee-like industriousness, in other words, "craft," not
"art" or "science." If her work could not be dismissed in this way, the
woman was said to have "overcome the limitations of her sex" and set
herself apart from all other women, or she was judged a hermaphrodite,
or the work was attributed to her male teacher or a male member of her
family.

Thus to evaluate women's artistic creations, musical compositions,
and literary works, their participation in scientific and philosophical
debates, and their theatrical and musical compositions and performances, we cannot ignore the social and intellectual setting. Restrictions
on women's ability to participate in the creation of culture varied across
time and from one geographic area to another, and varied even more
sharply from one artistic or literary genre and one scientific field to
another, but at no time or place was women's access to cultural institutions the same as men's and at no time was the gender of the creator not
a factor in how a work was judged.

Visual artists

The gender bias inherent in the Renaissance division of the visual arts
into "art" and "craft," and "major" and "minor" meant that new genres
which women created would never achieve the status of major arts, and
genres in which substantial numbers of women continued to work would
decrease in status. Two examples of the former are miniature portraits
painted on ivory, invented by Rosalba Carriera (1675–1757) and paper
collage, invented by Mary Delany (1700–88). One example of the latter
is flower painting, which in the seventeenth century was an important
branch of still life in Holland, but has been demoted in the eyes of more
recent art historians. According to one commentator writing in the
1970s, flower painting, "demands no genius of a mental and spiritual
kind, but only the genius of taking pains and specific craftsmanship"; the
best proof of this, in his eyes, is that of all known flower painters "at least
half of them are women."[1]

---

[1] Michael Grant, *Flower Painting Through Four Centuries* (Leigh-on-Sea, Lewis, 1972), p.
21.

The best example of loss of status in an art form is embroidery, which in the Middle Ages was practiced by both women and men often organized into male-directed craft guilds and paid on a scale equivalent to painting, but which throughout the early modern period became increasingly identified as feminine. Middle- and upper-class girls were taught to embroider because embroidered clothing and household objects became signs of class status, and because embroidery was seen as the best way to inculcate the traits most admired in a woman – passivity, chastity, attention to detail, domesticity. As more embroidery was produced in the home for domestic consumption, it was increasingly considered an "accomplishment" rather than an art, and those who embroidered for pay received lower wages, except for the male designers of embroidery patterns and the few men employed as court embroiderers by Europe's monarchs.

Though most early modern women accepted the prevailing view of their needlework and would not have termed it "art," our recognition of the historically determined nature of artistic hierarchies allows us to view embroidery and other types of needlework as one of the visual arts, in the same way that quilts are now discussed as a standard part of American art history. In many ways, early modern embroidery parallels early modern painting. During the sixteenth century, the embroidery of plants, flowers, birds, and animals grew increasingly naturalistic, though embroiderers were also conscious of the symbolic meaning of these motifs. Both painted and embroidered emblems, designs that linked an image and a saying or motto, were very popular. Embroiderers experimented with perspective, paid greater attention to proportion and shadowing, and took their subjects from antiquity just as Renaissance painters did. In the seventeenth century embroiderers dressed their subjects in elaborate clothing and filled their work with details from the natural world, in the same way as baroque painters did, and in the eighteenth they portrayed Arcadian scenes of shepherdesses and milkmaids just as painters were doing. The lines of influence between painting and embroidery ran both ways, with embroiderers often copying paintings or taking their motifs from them, and painters in turn attempting to portray embroidered brocades and laces or using scenes of women embroidering to represent domestic virtues.

Because embroidery was a visual art created primarily by women, however, it also differs from painting in major respects. Embroiderers were not trained to view their work as a product of individual genius, so they rarely included their names on their work, other than on samplers that were meant to demonstrate a girl's growing proficiency with a needle. The subjects embroiderers chose often reflected general cultural changes in women's role and position. Images of Mary and female saints became younger and gentler than they had been in the High Middle Ages, stressing their dependence on the power of God the Father rather than their independent authority. In Protestant areas, girls portrayed images of happily married couples from the Bible and stitched verses stressing daughterly and wifely obedience. Adult women in the seventeenth century, on the other hand, often chose to depict images of women who acted heroically, sometimes with men and sometimes against them, or who ruled virtuously. As we discussed in Chapter 1, this was the period of a great debate in many parts of Europe about the proper roles of men and women and the proper balance of power between them, and the art historian Rozsika Parker has noted that women's choosing such images in the very medium intended to teach passivity and obedience reflects this debate. By the eighteenth century, heroic women were replaced by domestic scenes and farmyards, as women's links with the home and natural world were accepted as givens rather than open to dispute.

Though architecture and sculpture remained male preserves in the early modern period – the sculptor Properzia de' Rossi (1490–1530) is the only exception that has been identified so far – and many more women produced art with the needle than the brush, there were women who did not accept the general view that only men could paint professionally. During the sixteenth century, several women became prominent painters in Italy, and a number of others are known to have painted regularly, though all or most of their works are now lost; during the seventeenth century the best opportunities for women painters were in the Netherlands, and by the mid-eighteenth in France. Though stylistically their work is very different, the careers of female painters show many similarities. The majority of female painters were the daughters of painters; one of the earliest identifiable female painters, Caterina van Hemessen (1528–after 1587), even signed her work "Caterina, daughter of Jan van Hemessen" indicating she recognized the importance of this relationship. Those who were not the daughters of painters were often the daughters of intellectuals or minor noblemen with ties to intellectual or artistic circles. Many were eldest daughters or came from families in which there were no sons, so their fathers took unusual interest in their careers. A significant number came from aristocratic families, whereas most male painters had an artisanal background. Many women began their careers before they were twenty, and produced far fewer paintings after they married, or stopped painting entirely. Of those who married, many married painters.

Women were not allowed to study the male nude, which was viewed as essential if one wanted to paint large history paintings with many figures, so they generally painted portraits, smaller paintings with only a

9 Sofonisba Anguissola, *Lucia, Minerva, and Europa Anguissola Playing Chess,* 1555. This painting of the artist's three younger sisters shows each of them looking at the sister immediately her elder, with the oldest (who has just won the game) looking directly at the painter herself. Chess playing became more popular with women and a wider group of people in general in the sixteenth century when the rules were changed to make the queen and several other pieces more powerful so that the game could go faster.

few subjects, or, by the seventeenth century, still lifes and interior scenes. Though we might consider such subjects more appealing than large history paintings, the national academies of art from the seventeenth through the nineteenth centuries ranked them much lower in importance, which meant female painters could never gain the highest level of official recognition. Women could also not learn the technique of fresco, in which colors are applied directly to wet plaster walls, because such works had to be done out in public, which was judged inappropriate for women. They were thus limited in the media they could use as well as their subject matter.

The number of women recorded as active painters steadily increased throughout the early modern period, but this resulted more from better recording of the names of all painters than from continually expanding opportunities for women. Women's ability to gain recognition through painting followed a more circuitous path. They were generally more successful when there were only a very few, for they could then be viewed as novelties. This was the case with Sofonisba Anguissola (1532/35–1625), the first Italian woman to gain international recognition for her art. Anguissola spent ten years as a court painter to Philip II of Spain, and was extremely popular as a portrait painter. The women who took her as a model, such as Lavinia Fontana (1552–1614) and Fede Galizia (1578–1630), never received the same level of praise, and were openly resented for their success at winning public commissions. Seventeenth-century Italian women artists were fortunate in that they could at least gain commissions, unlike their French counterparts; the majority of commissions in seventeenth-century France came from the king, who wanted only large-scale history paintings and hired only artists who were members of the Académie Royale, thus categorically excluding women painters. (A very few women were elected to the French Académie Royale in its early years, but after 1682 admission was limited to men, with a handful of exceptions, most of them foreigners.) In general, an open market for art, such as existed in the seventeenth-century Netherlands, was more favorable for women's work than one that was totally linked to commissions. Not only was it difficult for women to gain the type of training usually regarded as necessary for large public works, but they also had difficulties traveling to establish a reputation with private patrons or determining a way to advertise their skills which would not jeopardize their reputation for respectability.

Women painters were also more successful when the genres in which they excelled were popular. The seventeenth-century Netherlands was advantageous in this regard as well, for wealthy middle-class families wanted still lifes, flower paintings, and small-scale portraits for the walls of their increasingly luxurious homes, paying for them with profits from the contemporary economic boom in their country. Clara Peeters (1594–c. 1657), and Rachel Ruysch (1666–1750) established many of the stylistic and iconographical conventions that later still-life and flower painters would follow, and their work is still widely appreciated for its compositional sophistication, treatment of differently textured surfaces, technical virtuosity, and sheer beauty. In the early eighteenth century, pastel portraits grew very popular, and Rosalba Carriera, who had earlier developed miniatures on ivory, became one of the most highly regarded artists in Europe in this medium. Pastel is worked with dry colored chalks rather than liquid paints, and Carriera used it brilliantly to capture the elegant fabrics and powdered hair prized by her contemporaries; her self-portrait in pastel, holding a portrait of her sister, appears on the cover of this book.

The sex of early modern female painters thus clearly affected the media and genres that they chose, but did it also shape their treatment of subject matter or their techniques? This is a very difficult question, in part because art critics and historians since the sixteenth century have used "feminine" – by which they mean delicate, decorative, intimate, domestic – as a code word for "less worthy," and because it risks introducing biological essentialism into aesthetic judgments. It has been asked recently, however, by feminist art historians about the work of two of the most important early modern female painters, Artemisia Gentileschi (1593–1652/3) and Judith Leyster (1609–61), particularly because their work was judged in their own time and ours to be almost disturbingly "masculine" – vigorous and exuberant in the case of Leyster and violent and dramatic in the case of Gentileschi. Leyster's work is probably the best argument against seeing something distinctly "feminine" in the technique of female painters, for her existence was unknown from some time after her death until 1893, during which time all of her paintings were unquestioningly attributed to Franz Hals or his male followers. In terms of her treatment of subject matter, we can see a few differences. Many of her works show greater sympathy for the lives of women than those of her male contemporaries, especially those that depict women working at household tasks. Her most celebrated painting is *The Proposition* (1631), which shows a modestly dressed woman bent over her sewing while a man touches her arm and offers her a handful of coins. It contrasts dramatically with seduction and brothel scenes painted by her male contemporaries, in which the women are always clearly willing participants, and, as Ann Harris and Linda Nochlin have commented, "will instantly engage the sympathy of any woman who has ever been similarly approached by a man who stubbornly refused to believe that his attentions were unwelcome."[2]

Leyster's painting would have been well understood by Artemisia Gentileschi, who until recently gained greater notice from many art historians for the fact that she was raped by one of her teachers than for her paintings or her role in spreading the dramatic style of Caravaggio, which she learned from her father. The rape was viewed as the reason so many of her paintings depict strong women in acts of violence against men and conversely (often by the same author) as the reason for her allegedly numerous illegitimate children. Gentileschi does concentrate

[2] Ann Sutherland Harris and Linda Nochlin, *Women Artists: 1550–1950* (New York, Alfred A. Knopf, 1976), p. 140.

10   Judith Leyster, *The Proposition.*

on women in most of her works, no doubt because she was so skilled at portraying the female nude and biblical and mythological heroines were extremely popular subjects. The art historian Mary Garrard's careful analysis of her paintings, especially her numerous depictions of the Old Testament heroine Judith, who cut off the head of the tyrant Holofernes during his war with the Israelites, shows that she does portray Judith as more powerful and the relationship between her and the maidservant

11   Artemesia Gentileschi, self-portrait.

who assists her as more personal and companionate than do male artists. Gentileschi appears to have recognized some of the ambiguities of her position as a female painter in a culture where women were more accepted as the inspiration for art than as artists. In a self-portrait, she depicts herself as an allegory of Painting itself, something that was impossible for male artists because Painting ("La Pittura") was always portrayed allegorically as female. In a letter to one of her patrons she makes the comment that opens this chapter, a clear assertion that she recognized the limitations on female painters but chose to ignore them as much as possible.

Musicians, composers, and actresses

The same question posed by art historians, whether and how a woman's gender influenced her painting, has also been asked recently by historians of music as they are slowly discovering the role played by women in musical composition and performance. Many of the factors that shaped women's production of visual art also shaped their production of music. Though sixteenth-century writers worried about women using music to lure men into the dangers of love, by the seventeenth century singing and playing an instrument became suitable "accomplishments" for middle- and upper-class young women. As the author of *The Young Ladies Conduct* wrote, "Music refines the Taste, polishes the Mind; and is an Entertainment, without other views, that preserves them [young women] from the Rust of Idleness, that most pernicious Enemy to Virtue."[3] Writers such as Mary Astell who favored a serious education for women were critical of the amount of time young women were expected to devote to their musical lessons, and other writers criticized or satirized lower-class families who tried to give their daughters "accomplishments" rather than training them in more marketable skills.

For most middle- and upper-class women, there was no acceptable public outlet for their years of musical training. They were to perform only for their own families, and not even in the semi-public performances which typically brought together professionals and amateurs in the seventeenth and eighteenth centuries. One upper-class father even had his daughter arrested for playing in public. Ironically, cartoonists and satirists frequently bemoaned the low level of skill of the amateur men who sang or played instruments – training in music was not a standard part of the education of an upper- or middle-class man – without recognizing that the female audience would have been much more competent had they been able to perform. Not surprisingly, many women gave up their music when they married, though music was often used as a symbol of marital bliss, its harmony a parallel to marital harmony. We have very few comments on the reasons for this from women themselves, so we cannot judge whether they lost interest in an "accomplishment"

---

[3] John Essex, *The Young Ladies' Conduct: Or Rules for Education* (London, 1722), p. 85.

that was specifically promoted as a way to win a husband, or simply had no time for music because of domestic responsibilities.

We also have great difficulty in assessing precisely the involvement of women in the composition and performance of folk ballads, songs, lullabies, and other types of popular music. Many of these were never published or even written down, or else published only long after they were composed. Most were published anonymously or attributed to a composer whose authorship was as much a matter of myth as the events they describe. There is no reason to assume that women did not write any of them – as one historian has put it "anonymous was a woman" – especially because many of them were songs that accompanied traditionally women's work such as child care or weaving. Some scholars have identified certain attributes as typical in songs they suspect were written by women – women are described as whole persons rather than according to their physical attributes, relations between men and women are marked by mutuality rather than dominance, mother/child relationships involve both joy and sadness, or the song was traditionally sung only by women. Women were often the most well-known singers of all types of songs, adding verses, changing content, and altering tunes as they sang them. When folklorists began to be interested in these songs and ballads in the nineteenth century, first writing them down and then recording them, they turned to female singers.

The composition and performance of ballads and other songs relating heroic exploits were very much part of high culture during the Middle Ages – the best-known medieval poets are the male and female troubadours who sang and played at noble courts – but during the Renaissance and early modern period more elaborate forms of music developed which usually required years of training to compose or perform. Though amateur or mixed amateur and professional performances continued, church officials and nobles increasingly hired permanent professional composers and musicians. Until 1500 these were almost all men, but gradually singing became one of the duties expected of court ladies at many northern Italian courts. Women were taken on specifically for their singing abilities, more music was written that required trained women's voices, and in 1580 the Duke of Ferrara established a separate group of singing women, the *concerto di donna*. This practice was copied by other Italian courts in the 1580s and 1590s, with female instrumentalists often added as well, and by the seventeenth century, some of these women composed much of their own music.

Like female painters, many female musicians were the daughters of musicians or came from musical families, and their fathers not only trained them but helped them to get their music published. The best known of these singer-composers in seventeenth-century Italy, Francesca Caccini (1587–?), at one point the highest-paid performer at the Medici court in Florence, and Barbara Strozzi (1619–?), who wrote and sang arias and cantatas and ran a musical salon in Venice, both fit this pattern. Their careers also parallel those of female painters in other ways. Both disappeared from the records at mid-life, and composed in a more limited number of genres than their male contemporaries; Strozzi, for example, composed only small private pieces, most with the theme of unrequited love, at a time when opera was at its peak in Venice. Strozzi was accused of being a courtesan, a charge leveled at other female musicians as well, particularly those who had ties to the theater. Despite these limitations, Caccini and Strozzi set a pattern for other female composers both in Italy and the rest of Europe. By 1700, twenty-three women in Italy had had their music published, and during the early part of the next century women began to compose larger pieces as well. Elisabeth-Claude Jacquet de la Guerre (1664?–1727) wrote an opera and major instrumental pieces, and Camilla di Rossi and several other women composed oratorios at the command of the Emperor in Vienna.

Along with the courts, convents also provided opportunities for female musicians and composers; more than half of the women whose music was published before 1700 were nuns who wrote both secular and sacred music. In the early sixteenth century, convents began to perform polyphonic music, with nuns playing all types of instruments, and many nuns composed as well. In some places this was encouraged, most notably in Venice, where the city government even established special musical training schools for girls at four of the city's orphanages. The choirs these schools produced became so renowned that girls who were not orphans were taken on as day students, including some daughters of Venice's elite. These Ospedali grandi were not strictly convents, but the girls vowed to sing or play for ten years after they were trained, so could not leave until they were about thirty. They gave frequent public performances, which the city used as a source of income, and it also encouraged the girls and women to develop their talents by sending them to study with distinguished teachers and commissioning special works for them.

After the Council of Trent in 1563, the Venetian Ospedali and women's convents throughout Italy were ordered by the Catholic hierarchy to stop their performances of polyphonic music and the playing of any instrument except the organ. The Venetian city government was strong enough to ignore this order, and some convents were as well, especially those in Milan and Bologna, but in general the opportunities for convent residents to perform and create music began to decrease. In

1686 Pope Innocent XI extended this prohibition, forbidding all women – single, married, or widowed as well as nuns – to learn music for any reason from any man, including their fathers or husbands, or to play any musical instrument, "because music is completely injurious to the modesty that is proper for the [female] sex."[4] This edict was renewed in 1703, and, though it was certainly not enforced everywhere, it does reflect a negative attitude toward women's musical creativity, which the women who did publish their compositions also noted by commenting that they expected to be criticized for their lack of modesty.

Many of the women who became noted as singers were also actresses, both in opera and spoken theater. From the middle of the seventeenth century opera began to use women instead of castrati for female parts, and starting in the late sixteenth century, female actresses began to appear in French and Italian court performances and in wandering troupes of players who performed comedy for popular audiences. Previously all parts had been taken by men and boys, a tradition that continued in school and religious drama throughout the early modern period and in England until the restoration of the monarchy after the civil war in 1660. A few women took over the leadership of traveling companies, such as Madeleine Bejart in France and Caroline Neuber in Germany; one of these actress-directors, Catherina Elisabeth Velten, also published a pamphlet defending the honor of popular comedy and the women involved in it. In general, however, actresses, opera singers, and ballerinas were not regarded as honorable women, and many were able to support themselves only by also being the mistress of an artistically inclined male patron.

As with female painters, a woman's sex thus shaped her opportunities for singing, playing music, or acting, and determined what genre of music she would be most likely to compose. It may have also shaped the content of her compositions to some degree, as, for example, Francesca Caccini's theatrical piece, *La Liberazione di Ruggiero dall-isola d'Alcina* (1625), which took a story familiar to Italian audiences, the liberation of the knight Ruggiero from the love magic of the wicked sorceress Alcina, but told it from Alcina's point of view and portrayed her sympathetically as abandoned and betrayed. Caccini composed this at a court that was, as we saw in the last chapter, ruled by a woman, and that was engaged in a debate about the merits and faults of women, where the writer Cristoforo Bronzini was in the middle of publishing an eight-volume

---

[4] Translated and quoted in Jane Bowers, "The emergence of women composers in Italy, 1566–1700," in Bowers and Judith Tick (eds.), *Women Making Music: The Western Art Tradition, 1150–1950* (Urbana, University of Illinois Press, 1986), p. 139.

work *On the Nobility and Dignity of Women* (Florence, 1622–30). Caccini's composition reflects this debate, conveying the ambiguous position of any powerful woman in a world where the rules of conduct are made by men.

Writers

When analyzing the art and music produced by women during the early modern period, it is fairly easy to make distinctions between that done for private use or enjoyment and that intended for public consumption. At first glance, women's writings seem similarly divided between unpublished works such as letters, diaries, and personal collections of quotes and reflections, and works that were published. On closer analysis, it is very difficult to draw a sharp line between the two. On one hand, writing that we regard as private, such as letters, was not regarded in the same way in the early modern period. Letters often contained political news as well as personal matters, and their writers knew that they would be circulated among a group of people, for this was a period before regular newspapers. Most of the letters that have survived were written by members of Europe's elite, who tended to regard letter-writing as more of a literary activity than we do today; they took great care with language and loaded their letters with classical allusions. Women in particular realized that letters might be the best or only place they could demonstrate their learning and creativity with language, and so used letters to develop a personal literary style. Their addressees recognized this, and saved them; for Madame de Sévigné, for example, often described as the greatest letter-writer in French literature, more than 1,300 letters survive. Many historians of literature view the letter as one of the ancestors of the novel, a literary form that was also developed to a great extent by women in the eighteenth century. Many early novels were, in fact, written in epistolary form, that is, as an exchange of letters. Handwritten journals, diaries, and collections of quotes were also often written to be handed down to future generations, with the writer careful about how she portrayed herself and intent on teaching a lesson to others through her writings.

"Private" writing thus often had a public audience in mind, and on the other hand, the injunction to female silence was so strong that the majority of women who did publish felt the need to justify their boldness. Women's public speech was often linked with sexual dishonor in many people's minds; a "loose" tongue implied other sorts of loose behavior, and a woman who wanted her thoughts known by others was suspected of wanting to make her body available as well. Women who did publish thus claimed that their works were really private, but that some external force had compelled them to be published. For writers of religious works it was divine inspiration, of advice manuals their duty as mothers, of political pieces the special gravity of the situation. Poets and playwrights stressed the pressures by male friends or the desire to stop pirated versions of their work that had been published without their knowledge. Katherine Philips (1632–62), one of the most widely acclaimed seventeenth-century female English poets, staunchly maintained:

> [I] never writ any line in my life with an intention to have it printed. . . but only for my own amusement in a retir'd life. . . I am so innocent of that wretched Artifice of a secret consent (of which I am, I fear suspected) that whoever would have brought me those copies [of my poems] corrected and amended, and a thousand pounds to have bought my permission for their being printed, should not have obtained it.[5]

Even those who published women's works posthumously, often their husbands or other male relatives, included such justifications, noting that the author had been a paragon of female modesty whose writing had been done only out of duty to God or her children and had never interfered with her household or marital duties.

It is difficult to know exactly how to interpret these justifications. Did the authors include them in order to escape censure and the suspicion of immorality, or to get their work published more easily? (Male authors, too, often mention divine inspiration and their own unworthiness.) Or do they reflect the author's internalization of the command to silence? Or simply ambiguous feelings about letting other people read her work? Any interpetation is complicated by the fact that many authors also apologized for their lack of skill, noting that as women they could never meet the standards set by male authors; the tone of these explanations varies widely, from anger at not being accorded the same educational opportunities as men to subservient deference. Whatever the reasons for these justifications and apologies, and they probably vary with each author, even the most bitter and self-assertive ones reinforced the idea that women's writing was highly unusual and needed to be excused. By 1750, as more women began to publish, such explanations are slightly less frequent and less abject, but they are still there.

Along with directly apologizing, women writers also found other ways to conform to the cultural convention of silence and yet still publish. They published anonymously, but then let their friends and acquain-

---

[5] Katherine Philips, *Poems* (London, 1667).

tances know the true author. They used male or female pseudonyms, but did not completely hide their identity. They published translations or editions of male works, but, as Margaret Hannay has shown in her study of women's writings in Tudor England, subverted the text by their choice of words in order to insert personal and political statements. Mary Sidney, for example, only published works that were translations or revisions of works by male authors, though her alterations and revisions are so extensive that they are usually considered original pieces. She did not claim them as original, however; despite the fact that she was a member of the most prominent literary family in England and an important patron of humanists and writers, she still felt obliged to deflect criticism by calling her writing translations.

Because the line between public and private writing is fuzzy, then, it is best not to pay too much attention to whether a piece was published or not, and simply examine the work of women writers by genre. (Nevertheless, we have to recognize that our analysis will be skewed by the fact that a much greater share of women's published writings survive than their unpublished ones, and that we have very few unpublished writings by non-elite women.) Throughout the period, publications by women represent a tiny share of the total amount of printed material; Patricia Crawford has determined that women's works comprise only 1.2 percent of the publications in England from 1640 to 1700, though even this figure represents a doubling of their pre-Civil War rate. It is more difficult to make statistical comparisons for other countries, but publications by women probably accounted for less than 1 percent of the total, though their share elsewhere also increased during the early modern period.

In addition to the cultural admonitions advocating female silence and to women's relative lack of educational opportunities, economic factors also kept women from publishing. Authors who could not pay for a work to be published themselves had to find a patron who would, or convince a publisher that a work would sell enough to earn back the investment. This was much more difficult for women than men, so that the most prolific female authors were those who paid for the publication themselves, such as Lady Eleanor Douglas, whose thirty-seven works of prophecy were all printed at her own expense. Almost all of the published works by women which appeared in seventeenth-century Germany were by members of the nobility, a result of both their ability to absorb the costs of printing, and the fact that their class position at least partially deflected any criticism that resulted from their gender.

The majority of women's published works were religious, particularly in the sixteenth and early seventeenth centuries when the vast majority of all publications were religious. As we will see in greater detail in Chapter 6, the Reformation inspired women to publish polemical works, the Puritan and Quaker movements led them to publish conversion narratives detailing their own religious convictions, and the wars of the seventeenth century provoked them to publish religious prophecies and warnings to repent. Most women authors did not write such dramatic or doctrinal works, however, but chose forms that were considered more acceptable for women – prayers, meditations, poems based on the psalms or epistles, spiritual and moral advice to children, reflections on death, or translations of works by men. Many of these express very traditional pious sentiments or support existing religious institutions, but the mere fact that they were written by a woman made many male contemporaries uneasy. They also use female metaphors more often and in a different way than similar works by men; women use female metaphors for religious experiences in a way that stresses how faith and devotion can overcome differences between people and between the believer and God, while men use female metaphors more often to stress the distinction between the human and the divine. Women's religious writings occasionally reveal very unusual aims. Anna von Medum, for example, published *Geistlicher Judischer Wunderbalsam* in 1646, trying to convince Jews to convert to Christianity and her fellow Christians to give up non-Biblical practices so the Jews would convert. Like most women writers of religious works, she emphasizes God's command to take up this task, but expresses this in very female terms; once she was a widow, she notes, God became her husband, impregnated her with spiritual seed and then sustained her during the delivery as any good husband would.

Many women who wrote religious works, and the majority of women who wrote about non-religious topics, chose poetry as their preferred mode of expression. Most female poets, in fact, wrote both religious and secular poetry, and even their secular poetry includes moral advice or overtones of divine love; they were less likely than their male counterparts to use literary forms such as the pastoral, elegy, or love sonnet without in some way Christianizing or moralizing them, although a few women did write purely secular love lyrics. Male poets in Italy and Germany in the seventeenth century formed themselves into literary societies and academies to provide themselves with a regular audience for their poetry and to support its publication. These societies generally accepted no women or only those with family connections to male members, leading a few women to found all-female literary societies, such as the Academie des Loyales and the Tugendliche Gesellschaft. Like male societies, these groups encouraged their members to correspond with one another, study, and write, though they emphasized the importance of moral virtues and religious conviction as well as poetic talents. The motto of one of them was distinctly non-literary – "Virtue Brings Honor."

As feminist literary critics have pointed out, one of the most difficult tasks facing a female poet was adapting literary conventions that had been created by men to a female voice. Veronica Gambara (1485–1550), Vittoria Colonna (1492–1547), Gaspara Stampa (1524–54), and Louise Labé (1515/1524?–66) all worked within the tradition of Petrarchan love poetry, but adapted it so that women could be active lovers and not simply passive objects of male desire. They asserted that love could be a legitimate inspiration for their poetry, just as it was for male poets. Gaspara Stampa wrote:

> Love, Having Elevated Her to Him, Inspires Her Verses
>
> If, being a woman so abject and vile,
> I nonetheless can bear so high a flame,
> Why should I not give to the world the same,
> At least in part, in proper wealth and style?
>
> If Love, with a new unprecedented spark,
> Could raise me to a place I could not reach,
> Why cannot pain and pen combine to teach
> Such arts as, never known, shall find their mark?[6]

Sibylle Schwarz (1621–38) went even further, describing the love of writing poetry as one that would enable women to rise above the need for any mere physical love. Pernette du Guillet (1520–45), Catherine des Roches (1542–87), and Anna Owen Hoyer (1584–1655) and all claimed the right to fame, although in more indirect ways than male poets. Katherine Philips wrote numerous poems celebrating her friendships with both women and men, asserting that women could be friends and not just lovers, seductresses, rivals, or accomplices.

Along with poetry, women also wrote long and short fictional pieces and plays, some of which were published during the author's lifetime. In Italy, Beatrice del Sera and other nuns wrote plays that were performed in convents, with nuns playing all parts; they were spiritual in message, but included profane themes in their serious and comic episodes and occasionally won their authors a reputation beyond the convent. As we will see in Chapter 6, nuns also wrote autobiographies, often at the request or demand of their male spiritual advisers, but portraying their

---

[6] Translated and quoted in Frank J. Warnke, "Gaspara Stampa: Aphrodite's priestess, love's martyr," in Katherina M. Wilson (ed.), *Women Writers of the Renaissance and Reformation* (Athens, University of Georgia Press, 1987), p. 12.

own personal and spiritual development. In France, Madeleine de Scudéry published *Grand Cyrus* in 1649, beginning a period of female dominance in the writing of romantic fiction; such works were generally set in a remote time and place, and always included moral advice. In England, the most prolific writer was Aphra Behn (1640?–1689), who is usually described as the first British woman (and sometimes as the first woman anywhere) to earn her living by selling her writing. She wrote almost sixty works, nearly one-tenth of the works published by women during her lifetime, including at least eighteen plays that appear to have been performed frequently. Her success resulted in vitriolic criticism, accusations of plagiarism, and charges of immodesty and lewdness, particularly because her plays were the bawdy comic romances popular with contemporary English audiences. Behn defended herself (often in her next play) against these charges, stating clearly that such criticism was largely the result of her sex:

The play had no other misfortune but that of coming out for [i.e., being written by] a woman: had it been owned by a man, though the most dull unthinking rascally scribbler in town, it had been an admirable play. [They said] *that is was bawdy,* the least and most excusable fault in the men writers, *but from a woman it was unnatural.*[7]

Like women painters, women writers who wished their works to be a commercial success followed popular styles, which Behn comments is no grounds for criticism; she describes herself as, "[one] who is forced to write for bread and not ashamed to own it, and consequently ought to write to please (if she can)."[8] Women playwrights were more likely than their male counterparts to give more and larger parts to women than their male contemporaries, and there are some themes that female authors tend to emphasize more than male authors. Many women, including Behn and her fellow English playwrights Margaret Cavendish, the Duchess of Newcastle (1623–1673), Frances Boothby (fl. 1670), and Elizabeth Polwhele (fl. 1670) all regard marriage, whether arranged or for love, as problematic for women. As one female character in Cavendish's *Love's Adventures,* refusing a public celebration of her wedding, states bluntly: "Do you call that a triumphant day, that enslaves a woman all her life after? No, I will make no triumph on that day."[9] In her collections of short stories published in Madrid, Maria de Zayas y Sotomayor (1590–1661 or 1669) describes husbands who lock up,

---

[7] Aphra Behn, *Sir Patient Fancy,* (London, 1678) sig. A.
[8] Ibid.
[9] Margaret Cavendish, *Love's Adventures* (London, 1662), p. 66.

starve or beat their wives; many of her female characters decide to go into the convent, which she describes for one character as "not a tragic end, but the happiest that could be, since coveted and desired by many, she subjected herself to none."[10] Despite her harsh denunciation of marriage, Zayas y Sotomayor's works were frequently reprinted into the eighteenth century. Along with revealing a more negative view of the effects of marriage on women, women also create heroic female characters more often than do male authors. Their female heroes do not necessarily challenge convention, however, for the virtues for which they are most praised are those that are culturally approved: constancy, modesty, patience, chastity. Mariam in Elizabeth Cary's *The Tragedie of Mariam*, the Jewish queen executed by her tyrant husband through no fault of her own, all the while worrying whether she is guilty of wifely disobedience, Pamphilia in Lady Mary Wroth's *Urania*, who remains true to her beloved despite his inconstancy, and Mandane in Madeleine de Scudéry's *Grand Cyrus*, who survives a series of abductions with her honor intact, are prime examples of this conventional, though heroic, behavior.

Female authors were more likely than male to include moral advice in their poetry, drama, and fiction, and also, like men, wrote and published pure advice books. These include cookbooks, almanacs, midwives' manuals, practical medical guides, and housekeeping manuals. In the early eighteenth century in England, several women's advice journals such as *The Female Tatler* (1709–10) and *The Female Spectator* (1744–46) had short runs of publication and contained articles by women as well as men. Advice manuals by women also include a number of books written by mothers for their children, often when the women were dying or suspected they were. Most advice books written in Germany were by reigning noblewomen instructing their sons on how to govern, but those written in England, more than ten in the seventeenth century, were largely by members of the gentry or middle class. One would think that a mother's duty to her children would alone provide enough justification for a woman to write, but many of the authors also included elaborate apologia describing their spiritual as well as maternal calling. Dorothy Leigh, the author of *The Mother's Blessing* (London, 1627) which went through fifteen editions in the seventeenth century, specifically says that through showing their religious devotion in writing, women could rid

---

[10] Maria de Zayas y Sotomayor, *Desengaños amorosos*, translated and quoted in Sandra M. Fox, "Maria de Zayas y Sotomayor: Sibyl of Madrid (1590?–1661?)," in J. R. Brink (ed.), *Female Scholars: A Tradition of Learned Women before 1800* (Montreal: Edens Press, 1980), p. 59.

themselves of the sin of Eve: "because wee must needes confesse that sinne entred by us into our posterity; let us shew how carefull we are to seeke to Christ, to cast it out of us and our posterity" (p. 17).

Women also saw writing autobiographies and memoirs as a way of providing spiritual guidance and moral lessons to others, sometimes through the bad example of their own lives. Up to the middle of the seventeenth century, most autobiographies by both women and men were spiritual, detailing the author's religious conversion and spiritual progress; we will discuss these more fully in the next chapter. After that point, men began to write autobiographical works generally describing their public careers, and women ones that delved more deeply into emotional matters. These personal autobiographies are viewed, like letters, as a genre that contributed to the development of the novel, for they introduced the idea that one's emotions were appropriate subject matter for published works. Though women's autobiographical writings differ widely in form, style, and intent, and the authors emphasize their own uniqueness as they try to arrive at some kind of self-definition, the works do show certain common features. The authors all compare themselves with the accepted standards for female behavior, and often discuss some kind of oppression they have experienced; they are very conscious of the actual writing process and frequently discuss their problems in achieving objectivity and "truth." All of these features appear in the quotation from Margaret Cavendish which opens this chapter; she also recognizes that women's individual identities were more easily lost than men's because they changed their names on marriage.

Women charged with criminal acts also often wrote their life histories which were peddled as small pamphlets; sensational or scandalous cases could become best-sellers. Such authors did not show the same level of introspection as those who wrote longer autobiographies, but they did hope to vindicate themselves by publishing their side of the story and make enough money to support themselves while in prison. They manipulated feminine stereotypes to make themselves appear less culpable, a tendency that also emerges in women's written requests to political authorities for pardons.

A concern for "truth" also emerges in memoirs written by female courtiers in the late seventeenth century. Especially at the French court, Madame de Lafayette, the Comtesse de Murat, and a number of other noblewomen wrote memoirs of court life explicitly to defend their names against gossip and rumor and tell the true stories of their actions; they had clearly internalized the concern with reputation that we saw in the last chapter was so important for female courtiers. Like letters, such memoirs can be seen as precursors to the novel, for their authors were much more concerned with relationships between people and with individual life stories than the male memoirists of the time who concentrated on military and political matters. Natalie Davis has suggested that we can also view such memoirs as precursors to modern social history, which also explores personal stories and relationships and does not simply focus on public political events.

Women's writing of history in the early modern period was not limited to court memoirs, however, for the sense of self and of having something valuable to say which inspired some women to write autobiographies inspired others to write and publish other types of nonfiction. In the seventeenth century, Charlotte Arbaleste, Lucy Hutchinson, and Margaret Cavendish all wrote biographies of their husbands which included analyses of political events. By the middle of the eighteenth century, several French women such as Marguerite de Lussan were writing local and national histories based on chronicles and manuscripts, and Catherine Macaulay published her widely respected eight-volume history of England. The English Civil War saw a dramatic upsurge in women's political writings – from six in the entire period 1600–1640 to seventy-seven in the decade 1641–1650 alone – ranging from political prophecy to women's petitions to Parliament to pamphlets arguing every political position from staunch royalist to radical Leveller. There was no similar expansion anywhere on the Continent, although the horrors of the Thirty Years' War did lead a few women, such as Martha Salome von Belta, to publish their own views of the war's causes and probable consequences.

Scientists and philosophers

Just as what any society judges to be art and literature is culturally determined, so is what it judges to be philosophy and science, and who merits the label "philosopher" or "scientist." In the ancient world, philosophy and science were intimately related, with what we would call "science" considered part of philosophy and called "natural philosophy"; this term continued to be used until the eighteenth century. The medieval world connected philosophy with religion as well; philosophical and scientific speculation were couched in Christian terms and most philosophers and scientists were members of the clergy. During the seventeenth century, the period of the Scientific Revolution, the most highly respected philosophers and scientists were no longer clerics, but men trained in the new secular scientific academies. Though no major seventeenth-century scientist openly broke his ties with the Christian church, and religion remained an important justification for the pursuit of science, greater emphasis was placed on secular interpretations and natural explanations. The link between science and philosophy remained, however, and may have even been strengthened during this period, for many philosophers, particularly those eager to show their modernity, used mathematical language to express their ideas and took their examples and models from the natural world.

This new more secular science and philosophy had immense popular appeal during the seventeenth century. Informal groups for the discussion of scientific ideas were established in many European cities, public lectures and classes in anatomy, astronomy, physics, and chemistry drew large audiences, and books that explained complex scientific ideas to the layperson were published in England, France, Germany, and Italy. Science, or, to use the terminology of the period, natural philosophy, became a topic about which every educated person was expected to know at least a bit in order to be able to converse intelligently. To be regarded as modern and sophisticated, one's library should contain some scientific works, a requirement made easier by the decreasing price of books relative to other commodities in the seventeenth century.

Women formed a significant share of the audience for all of these activities, and some books and lectures were directed specifically to them. Many of the popular scientific works, such as Baron de Fontenelle's *The Plurality of Worlds,* which discusses Descartes's cosmology, were written as dialogues between a woman and a man, and others bore titles such as *Newtonism for the Ladies.* We can tell that women read or at least purchased these books by the fact that they show up in women's personal libraries, and women's names appear on publishers' subscription lists. (Publishers often sold books in advance, by subscription, to be sure they would get an adequate return on their investment.) A popular imitator of the Royal Society of England, the Athenian Society, described its role specifically as the communication of the "Sciences to all men, as well as to both Sexes."[11] In 1704, the first women's almanac containing scientific information, *The Ladies Diary,* began to be published in England; John Tipper, the editor, originally included recipes and household hints, but his female readers requested that he stick to science and mathematics, so that after 1709 the almanac devoted itself exclusively to science. Directing scientific information to

---

[11] Quoted in Hilda Smith, "'All men and both sexes': concepts of men's development, women's education and feminism in the seventeenth century," in Donald C. Mell, Jr., et al. (eds.), *Man, God, and Nature in the Enlightenment* (East Lansing, Mich., Colleagues Press, 1988), p. 75.

women demonstrated that it was no longer to be the province of (male) clergy alone, but available to all educated lay people.

Women were not only an audience for the new science, however, but also active participants. A number of women contributed articles and brainteaser puzzles to *The Ladies Dairy* and translated both popular and learned scientific works; the most important and difficult of these was Madame du Châtelet's (1706–49) translation of Newton's *Principia* from Latin into French, which remains the sole French translation. She also published an original work explaining Newton and Leibniz to a French audience, and was probably the best-known woman scientist in the eighteenth century. Though unusual in her talents, du Châtelet was also typical of many women known to have scientific or philosophical interests in the early modern period: she was a member of the nobility who learned her science through personal contacts; created a scientific circle in her household which drew learned men to her; published only translations or derivative works while keeping her original work unpublished. Anne Finch, the Viscountess Conway (1631–79), who has recently been recognized as one of the sources of some of Leibniz' ideas, and Baroness Martine de Beausoleil, a geologist, both fit this pattern as well. The most prolific female scientific author of the period, Margaret Cavendish, the Duchess of Newscastle, was also a noblewoman, but otherwise she was absolutely unique. Along with the plays and biographies we have already discussed, she wrote seven works of philosophy and science, giving her opinions on current topics of interest including matter and motion, the vacuum, atoms, sense perception, truth, perfection, and the mind. She based her first works solely on her own perceptions, arguing, like Hobbes, that one's own rational capacity was more valuable than outside authority, but by her later works she was also incorporating ideas from Locke, Descartes, and van Helmont.

Not all women scientists were members of the nobility, however. A few, particularly in Italy, were the daughters of university professors and went on to receive university degrees themselves. Most of these women never taught in a public capacity, but Laura Bassi apparently taught physics at the University of Bologna from 1732 to 1778 after receiving her doctorate in physics at that university; it is not certain that any of these women actually *attended* classes at a university, however. Several women in France and Germany, usually trained by their fathers, became well known for their botanical and anatomical illustrations, or their mapmaking. Maria Sibylla Merian, for example, depicted plants and insects in *Wonderful Metamorphosis and Special Nourishment of Caterpillars* (1679) and later in life traveled to the Dutch colony of Surinam with her daughter where she gathered and drew insects and plants in preparation for her major scientific work, a study of the life-cycle of Surinam insects. Astronomy was another science initially open to the work of women. Most astronomical observatories in seventeenth-century Germany, for example, were in private homes rather than public buildings or universities, and the daughters and wives of male astronomers peered through telescopes and calculated the movement of heavenly bodies along with their fathers and husbands. These women were not simply assistants, however, but made observations and sometimes published findings on their own.

Though in the nineteenth and twentieth centuries science and mathematics have become fields of study clearly identified as masculine, in the early modern period experimental science, especially on the Continent, was sometimes regarded as feminine. Those who had a negative view of women's intellectual capacities saw laboratory experiments as not too different from cooking, and observation of the natural world, especially botany, as likely to induce greater religious reverence. Science was also something women could do in their own homes, for even the most advanced scientific equipment, such as the microscope, was within the budgets of many upper-middle class and noble households and mathematics required no equipment at all. Classics, on the other hand, was regarded as masculine, for only the stronger male mind was up to the rigors of learning Latin and Greek, a requirement for all fields of university study until the late eighteenth century. Those who had a positive view of women's intellect also saw science and women as made for each other, for women's lack of a classical education would enable them to carry out more objective and original research, not influenced by the mistaken ideas of the past. Women, or better said, ladies, also had more time to speculate on scientific matters, as they were unable to participate in politics and generally did not have to concern themselves with economic matters.

In some ways, then, an interest in science was yet another "accomplishment" welcomed in middle- and upper-class women, but never to be used professionally. Like other accomplishments, it was satirized as amateurish dilettantism, as a feminine fad first by the French playwright Molière in *Les Femmes Savantes (The Learned Ladies)* and then by other French and English playwrights who copied him. A more serious type of criticism came from Francis Bacon and other English scientists, who regarded continental scientists with their frequent ties to noblewomen as "effeminate," and called for a "masculine" science. The explicit goals of the Royal Society of London were "to raise a Masculine Philosophy" and to promote the "Masculine Arts of Knowledge."[12] What they meant by

---

[12] Francis Bacon, quoted in Londa Schiebinger, *The Mind Has No Sex? Women in the Origins of Modern Science* (Cambridge, Mass., Harvard University Press, 1989), p. 138.

this was a science that was active, strong, and not tied to the past, all qualities that female scientists prized in their own work, but which the Royal Society viewed as intrinsically male as well as masculine. Other than a single visit to the Royal Society by the Duchess of Newcastle in 1667, a visit described satirically in a ballad by one of the Society's members, no women had any contact with England's leading scientific society throughout the period. Not until 1945, in fact, was a woman admitted as a full member.

This exclusion from the Royal Society was not peculiarly English, however, and points to what became more serious limitations on women's participation in science than satirical plays or Baconian ideas. Though women were part of the informal scientific circles that were the precursors to formal scientific and philosophical societies, and though popular societies like the Athenian Society in England saw part of their mission as communicating scientific information to women, no woman was ever admitted as a member to a scientific academy or society, except for a very few women in several of the less prestigious Italian academies. No academy had formal statutes that barred women as a group, but when female scientists and philosophers applied they were excluded explicitly on the basis of their sex. By the end of the eighteenth century, there were academies in every country of Europe, and much of the publication and communication of ideas was carried out at their meetings and through their journals; the exclusion of women meant female scientists and philosophers would always remain at the peripheries. The addition of courses in science to the university curricula at many European universities also created another avenue of scientific education which was blocked to women.

Anatomy and astronomy also became more closely tied to institutions that excluded women during the early modern period. Lectures and demonstrations in anatomy were added to university medical training for physicians, and to the training of barber-surgeons and male midwives; proposals by female midwives for similar training, such as that of Elizabeth Cellier to James II of England in 1687, were never granted, except in Italy, where male midwives remained completely unacceptable to all social classes. Scientific academies opened astronomical observatories, where official positions were reserved for men. This was not because women had no access to training, for much astronomical training was still carried out privately, or because they were not skilled, but because such positions were public ones and therefore closed to women. Maria Winkelmann was told this explicitly when she applied for an appointment as an assistant astronomer with the Academy of Sciences in Berlin. She had assisted her husband, the academy's official astronomer, for ten years and had published observations both with him and on her own; the two of them together prepared astronomical and astrological calendars, which the Academy sold to support its projects. When her husband died, Winkelmann asked that she and her son be appointed assistant astronomers for the making of calendars, because she clearly had the skills and because widows in many crafts often carried on their husbands' businesses. Her request was flatly rejected, not on the grounds of her lack of talent or training (she was later asked to assist the man who was appointed), but because, as the secretary of the Academy wrote: "Already during her husband's lifetime the society was burdened with ridicule because its calendar was prepared by a woman. If she were now to be kept on in such a capacity, mouths would gape even wider."[13]

Thus in science and philosophy, as in art and music, the early modern period saw increasing division between professional and amateur, between formally trained and privately taught, between high culture and popular. As we noted in the case of women's work identity, both society's and women's own concepts of their role in the creation of culture changed. Women might call their embroidery "art" (although usually downplaying it with the term "domestic arts") but did not call themselves artists. They played the harpsichord or sang, but were not musicians, or only "lady musicians," a term that became popular in the eighteenth century; they observed the stars but were not scientists. In the realm of the mind, that is, in both education and culture, gender became an increasingly important factor during the early modern period. When they objected to their fewer opportunities, women were often consoled with the comment that at least in the realm of the spirit they were men's equals, a statement we will assess in the following section.

Bibliography

Feminist art criticism has in many ways led the way in understanding the gendered nature of the value placed on certain genres. The most important early theoretical essay is Linda Nochlin, "Why are there no great women artists?," in Elizabeth C. Baker and Thomas B. Hess (eds.), *Art and Sexual Politics: Women's Liberation, Women Artists and Art History* (New York, MacMillan, 1973), pp. 1–43 which analyzes why there have always been a smaller absolute number of women artists and why their work has been slighted; the book also contains replies to Nochlin by ten contemporary women artists. Fredrika H. Jacobs, *Defining the Renaissance Virtuosa: Women Artists and the Language of Art History and Criticism* (Cambridge, Cambridge University Press, 1997) provides a longer discussion of

[13] Translated and quoted in ibid., p. 92.

the ways in which ideas about gender shaped perceptions of art and the artist in Renaissance Italy. Several good surveys of women and art that include consideration of the early modern period are: Eleanor Tufts, *Our Hidden Heritage: Five Centuries of Women Artists* (New York, Paddington Press, 1974); Ann Sutherland Harris and Linda Nochlin, *Women Artists: 1550–1950* (New York, Alfred A. Knopf, 1976); Germaine Greer, *The Obstacle Race: The Fortunes of Women Painters and their Work* (New York, Farrar, Strauss, Giroux, 1979); Rozsika Parker and Griselda Pollock, *Old Mistresses: Women, Art and Ideology* (New York, Pantheon Books, 1981); Wendy Slatkin, *Women Artists in History from Antiquity to the 20th Century*, 2nd ed. (Englewood Cliffs, N. J., Prentice-Hall, 1990); Whitney Chadwick, *Women, Art, and Society* (London, Thames and Hudson, 1990); Nancy G. Heller and Nancy Grubb (eds.), *Women Artists: An Illustrated History* (New York, Abbeville Press, 1997); Liana De Girolami Cheney, et al. (eds.), *Self Portraits by Women Painters* (London, Gower Technical, 1999). Rozsika Parker, *The Subversive Stitch: Embroidery and the Making of the Feminine* (London, The Woman's Press, 1984) places women's embroidery over many centuries within its ideological and social context.

Within the last ten years there have been many studies of early modern women artists, art produced for women, visual depictions of women and gender, and the relationships among all of these topics. These include: Frima Fox Hofrichter, *Judith Leyster: A Woman Painter in Holland's Golden Age* (Doornspijk: Davaco Publishers, 1989); Yael Even, "The Loggia dei Lanzi: a showcase of female subjugation," in Norma Broude and Mary D. Garrard (eds.), *Expanding Discourse: Feminism and Art History* (New York, HarperCollins, 1992), 127–37; Frederika H. Jacobs, "Woman's capacity to create: the unusual case of Sofonisba Anguissola," *Renaissance Quarterly* 47 (1994), 74–101. Mary D. Garrard, "Here's looking at me: Sofonisba Anguissola and the problem of the woman artist," *Renaissance Quarterly* 47 (1994), 556–621; Cristelle Baskins, *Cassone Painting, Humanism and Gender in Early Modern Italy* (Cambridge, Cambridge University Press, 1998) and "Gender trouble in Italian Renaissance art history: two case studies," *Studies in Iconography* 16 (1994), 1–36; Geraldine A. Johnson and Sara F. Matthews Grieco (eds.), *Picturing Women in Renaissance and Baroque Italy* (Cambridge, Cambridge University Press, 1997); Paola Tinagli, *Women in Italian Renaissance Art: Gender, Representation and Identity* (Manchester, Manchester University Press, 1997); Letitia Panizza (ed.), *Women in Italian Renaissance Culture and Society* (Oxford, European Humanities Research Center, 1997); Katherine A. McIver, "Lavinia Fontana's self-portrait making music," *Woman's Art Journal* 19 (1998), 3–8; Jeffrey Hamburger, *The Visual and the Visionary: Art and Female Spirituality in Late Medieval Germany* (New York, Zone Books, 1998). Of all female artists, Artemisia Gentileschi has received the most attention. See: Mary Garrard, *Artemisia Gentileschi: The Image of the Female Hero in Italian Baroque Art* (Princeton, Princeton University Press, 1989); R. Ward Bissel, *Artemisia Gentileschi and the Authority of Art: Cricial Reading and Catalogue Raisonne* (University Park, Pa., Pennsylvania State University Press, 1999); Elizabeth S. Cohen, "The trials of Artemisia Gentileschi: a rape as history," *Sixteenth Century Journal* (2000). Anne Schutte, "Irene di Spilimbergo: the image of a creative woman in late Renaissance Italy," *Renaissance Quarterly* 44 (1991), 42–61 discusses the way in which humanists paid tribute to a talented painter who died very young, and David Wilkins, "Woman as artist and patron in the Middle Ages and the Renaissance," in Douglas Radcliffe-Umstead (ed.), *The Roles and Images of Women in the Middle Ages and Renaissance* (Pittsburgh, Center for Medieval and Renaissance Studies at the University of Pittsburgh, 1975), pp. 107–31 includes information on the relationship between female painters and their families. Natalie Davis includes study of the illustrator Maria Sibylla Merian in *Women on the Margins: Three Seventeenth-Century Lives* (Cambridge, Mass., Harvard University Press, 1995).

Women's role in music has received much less study. The only collection of articles available in English is Jane Bowers and Judith Tick (eds.), *Women Making Music: The Western Art Tradition, 1150–1950* (Urbana, University of Illinois Press, 1986), which fortunately contains many excellent essays. Carol Neuls-Bates, *Women in Music: An Anthology of Source Readings from the Middle Ages to the Present* (New York, Harper & Row, 1982) has some interesting original sources. Craig Monson (ed.), *The Crannied Wall: Women, Religion and the Arts in Early Modern Europe* (Ann Arbor, University of Michigan Press, 1992) and Ann Matter and John Coakley, *Creative Women in Medieval and Early Modern Italy* (Philadelphia, University of Pennsylvania Press, 1997) contains several essays on the composition and performance of music in Italian convents. The music of Italian nuns has received further study in: Robert Kendrick, *Celestial Sirens: Nuns and Their Music in Early Modern Italy* (Oxford, Clarendon, 1996); Jane Baldauf-Berdes, *Women Musicians of Venice: Musical Foundations, 1525–1855* (Oxford, Oxford University Press, 1993) and "The women musicians of Venice," in Frederick M. Keener and Susan E. Lorsch (eds.), *Eighteenth-century Women and the Arts* (New York, Greenwood, 1988), pp. 153–62; Craig Monson, "Elena Malvezzi's keyboard manuscript: a new sixteenth-century source," *Early Music History* 9 (1989), 73–128 and *Disembodied Voices: Music and Culture in an Early Modern Italian Convent* (Berkeley, University of California Press, 1995); Barbara Garvey Jackson, "Oratorios by command of the Emperor: the music of Camilla de Rossi," *Current Musicology* 42 (1986), 7–19. Richard D. Leppert, "Men, women and music at home: the influence of cultural values on musical life in 18th-century England," *Imago Musical: International Yearbook of Musical Iconography* 3 (1985), 51–133, is one of the few studies of women's music outside of Italy. For actresses and women's stage roles, see Elizabeth Howe, *The First English Actresses: Women and Drama, 1660–1700* (Cambridge, Cambridge University Press, 1992) and Viviana Comensoli and Anne Russell (eds.), *Enacting Gender on the Reniassance Stage* (Champaign/Urbana, University of Illinois Press, 1999).

While women's music has only recently begun to be studied, women's writings have received a great deal of attention. This is particularly the case for English women writers during this period, for whom there are nearly 100 analyses or text editions, and countless articles. The following is thus just a sample; for further references, see Betty S. Travitsky and Josephine A. Roberts, *English Women Writers, 1500–1640: A Reference Guide (1750–1996)* (New York, G. K. Hall, 1997). For the Tudor period, see: Margaret Hannay, *Silent But for the Word: Tudor Women as Patrons, Translators, and Writers of Religious Works* (Kent, Ohio, Kent State University Press, 1985); Elaine Beilin, *Redeeming Eve: Women Writers of the English Renaissance* (Princeton, Princeton University Press,

1987); Anne M. Haselkorn and Betty S. Travitsky, *Renaissance Englishwomen in Print: Counterbalancing the Canon* (Amherst, University of Massachusetts Press, 1989); Tina Krontiris, *Oppositional Voices: Women as Writers and Translators of Literature in the English Renaissance* (London, Routledge, 1992); Louise Schleiner, *Tudor and Stuart Women Writers* (Bloomington, Indiana University Press, 1994); Helen Wilcox (ed.), *Women and Literature in Britain, 1500–1700* (Cambridge, Cambridge University Press, 1996). For the seventeenth and early eighteenth century, see Fidelis Morgan, *The Female Wits: Women Playwrights on the London Stage 1660–1720* (London, Virago, 1981); Jane Spencer, *The Rise of the Woman Novelist: From Aphra Behn to Jane Austen* (Oxford, Basil Blackwell, 1986); Mary Anne Schofield and Cecilia Macheski, *Fettered or Free: British Women Novelists 1670–1815* (Athens, Ohio University Press, 1986); Sara Heller Mendelson, *The Mental World of Stuart Women: Three Studies* (London, Harvester Press, 1987); Elaine Hobby, *Virtue of Necessity: English Women's Writing 1649–88* (Ann Arbor, University of Michigan Press, 1988); Isobel Grundy and Susan Wiseman (eds.), *Women, Writing, History: 1640–1740* (Athens, University of Georgia Press, 1992); Barbara Kiefer Lewalski, *Writing Women in Jacobean England* (Cambridge, Mass., Harvard University Press, 1993); Anita Pacheco (ed.), *Early Women Writers: 1600–1720* (London, Longman, 1996); Jonathan Goldberg, *Desiring Women Writing: English Renaissance Examples* (Stanford, Stanford University Press, 1997); Kate Chedgzoy, et al. (eds.), *Voicing Women: Gender and Sexuality in Early Modern Writing* (Keele, Keele University Press, 1996); Margarete Rubik, *Early Women Dramatists, 1550–1800* (Boston, Bedford, 1998); Susan P. Cerasano and Marion Wynne-Davies (eds.), *Readings in Renaissance Women's Drama* (London, Routledge, 1998); Gwynne Kennedy, *Just Anger: Representing Women's Anger in Early Modern England* (Carbondale, Southern Illinois University Press, 2000) and several of the essays in "Women in the Renaissance: An Interdisciplinary Forum (MLA 1989)" *Women's Studies* 19 (1991). Two studies that address the issue of women's authorship are: Wendy Wall, *The Imprint of Gender: Authorship and Publication in the English Renaissance* (Ithaca, N.Y., Cornell University Press, 1993) and Laura J. Rosenthal, *Playwrights and Plagiarists in Early Modern England: Gender, Authorship, Literary Property* (Ithaca, N.Y., Cornell University Press, 1996) For studies of English writers that contain long selections from their works, see: Moira Ferguson (ed.), *First Feminists: British Women Writers, 1578–1799* (Bloomington, Indiana University Press, 1985); Margaret Hannay (ed.), *The Collected Works of Mary Sidney Herbert, Vols. I and II* (Oxford, Oxford University Press, 1996); Susan Cerasano and Marion Wynne-Davies, *Renaissance Drama by Women* (London, Routledge, 1996); James Fitzmaurice, et al. (eds.), *Major Women Writers of Seventeenth-Century England* (Ann Arbor, University of Michigan Press, 1996); Randall Martin (ed.), *Women Writers in Renaissance England* (London, Longman, 1997); Marion Wynne-Davies, *Women Poets of the Renaissance* (London, Routledge, 1999). An invaluable resource for any study of seventeenth-century writers is Hilda L. Smith and Susan Cardinale, *Women and the Literature of the Seventeenth Century* (New York, Greenwood, 1990), a 300-page annotated bibliography of all the books by, for, and about women published in English throughout the world 1641–1700. Margaret Hannay and Susanne Woods (eds.), *Teaching Tudor and*

Stuart Women Writers (New York, Modern Language Association, 2000) provides useful approaches to a number of different authors. A new series published by Ashgate, Women and Gender in Early Modern England, 1500–1750, edited by Betty S. Travitsky and Patrick Cullen, has a number of additional monographs and collections forthcoming.

Along with analyses of the writings of Englishwomen, there are now three series devoted to the reprinting or electronic dissemination of their works: The Early Modern Englishwoman: A Facsimile Library of Essential Works, published by Ashgate and edited by Betty S. Travitsky and Patrick Cullen; Women Writers in English 1350–1850, published by Oxford University Press and edited by Susanne Woords and Elizabeth H. Hageman; the Brown University Women Writers Project, which offers more than 200 texts from 1450–1830, and is available on-line (with some parts free and some by license) at www.wwp.brown.edu.

Writings by English women which were not strictly literary have been collected and analyzed in: Marilyn L. Williamson, *Raising Their Voice: British Women Writers, 1650–1750* (Detroit, Wayne State University Press, 1990); Charlotte Otten, *English Women's Voices: 1540–1700* (Miami, Florida International University, 1992); Valerie Frith (ed.), *Women and History: Voices from Early Modern England* (London, Coach House, 1995); Clare Brant and Diane Purkiss (eds.), *Women, Texts and Histories 1575–1760* (London, Routledge, 1992); Sylvia Brown, *Women's Writing in Stuart England: The Mother's Legacies of Elizabeth Joscelin, Elizabeth Richardson and Dorothy Leigh* (London, Sutton, 1999). Two recent editions of English women's diaries are D.J.H. Clifford (ed.), *The Diaries of Lady Anne Clifford* (London, Sutton, 1991) and Joanna Moody (ed.), *The Private Life of an Elizabethan Lady: The Diary of Lady Margaret Hoby 1599–1605* (London, Sutton, 1998).

English women's writings, along with those from women living in other parts of Europe, are also contained in three collections edited by Katharina M. Wilson, *Medieval Women Writers, Women Writers of the Renaissance and Reformation, Women Writers of the Seventeenth Century* (Athens, University of Georgia Press, 1984, 1987, 1989). These contain selections from the work and discussions of the writings and lives of about twenty women each, providing some of the few translations easily available in English of the works of not only French, German, Spanish, and Italian women, but also several from Hungary, the Netherlands, and Scandinavia. If you are seeking to gain a broad overview of women's writings over the centuries, these three books are the best place to start. Another good series that reprints women's writings from the period and provides parallel texts of the original language and English is: Domna Stanton (ed.), *The Defiant Muse: French Feminist Poems from the Middle Ages to the Present;* Beverly Allen, Muriel Kittel, and Keale Jane Jewell (eds.), *The Defiant Muse: Italian Feminist Poems from the Middle Ages to the Present;* Susan L. Cocalis (ed.), *The Defiant Muse: German Feminist Poems from the Middle Ages to the Present;* Angel Flores and Kate Flores (eds.), *The Defiant Muse: Hispanic Feminist Poems from the Middle Ages to the Present* (New York, Feminist Press, 1986). A large microfilm series, Women Advising Women, Part 5: Women's Writing and Advice, 1450–1700, produced by Adam Matthew Publications, includes English and French sources from the Bodleian Library, Oxford, and is available at some research libraries.

Over the last five years, the works of primarily Italian and French women have received excellent editions and translations in the series The Other Voice in Early Modern Europe, edited by Margaret King and Albert Rabil, Jr., and published by the University of Chicago Press. Along with the works mentioned in the bibliographies of Chapters 4, 6, and 8, these include or will soon include works by Tullia d'Aragona, Veronica Franco, Antonia Pulci, Isabella d'Este, Olympia Morata, Marie de Gournay, Madeleine de Scudry, Oliva Sabuco, Sara Copio Sullam, and Cassandra Fedele. For further translations and analyses of French and Italian works, see: Ann Rosalind Jones, "Surprising fame: Renaissance gender ideologies and women's lyric," in Nancy Miller, *The Poetics of Gender* (New York, Columbia University Press, 1986), pp. 74–95; François Rigolot, "Gender vs. sex difference in Louise Labé's grammar of love" and Ann Rosalind Jones, "City women and their audiences: Louise Labé and Veronica Franco" both in Margaret Ferguson et al. (eds.), *Rewriting the Renaissance: The Discourses of Sexual Difference in Early Modern Europe* (Chicago, University of Chicago Press, 1986), pp. 287–98, 299–316; Elissa Weaver, "Spiritual fun: a study of sixteenth-century Tuscan convent theater" and Tilde Sankovitch, "Inventing authority of origin: the difficult enterprise" (on the Mesdames des Roches) both in Mary Beth Rose, *Women in the Middle Ages and the Renaissance: Literary and Historical Perspectives* (Syracuse, N.Y., Syracuse University Press, 1986), pp. 173–206, 227–44; Elissa Weaver, "The convent wall in Tuscan convent drama," E. Ann Matter, "The personal and the paradigm: the book of Maria Domitilla Galluzzi", and Anne Jacobsen Schutte, "Inquisition and female autobiography: the case of Cecilia Ferrazzi" all in Monson, *Crannied Wall*, cited above; Ann Rosalind Jones, *The Currency of Eros: Women's Love Lyric in Europe 1540–1620* (Bloomington, Indiana University Press, 1990); Joan DeJean, *Tender Geographies: Women and the Origin of the Novel in France* (New York, Columbia University Press, 1991); Margaret Rosenthal, *The Honest Courtesan: Veronica Franco, Citizen and Writer in Sixteenth Century Venice* (Chicago, University of Chicago Press, 1992); Sara F. Matthews Grieco, "Georgette de Montenay: a different voice in sixteenth-century emblematics," *Renaissance Quarterly* 47 (1994), 793–871; several of the essays in Maria Ornella Marotti, *Italian Women Writers from the Renaissance to the Present* (University Park, Pennsylvania State University Press, 1996); Anne R. Larsen, "Paradox and the praise of women: from Ortensio Lando and Charles Estienne to Marie de Romieu," *Sixteenth Century Journal* 28 (1997), 759–74.

The works of German and Dutch women authors have received many fewer analyses in English or translations. See: Barbara Becker-Cantarino, "'Outsiders': women in German literary culture of absolutism," *Jahrbuch für Internationale Germanistik* 16/2 (1982), 147–57; Jeannine Blackwell and Susanne Zantop, *Bitter Healing: German Women Writers 1700–1840* (Lincoln, University of Nebraska Press, 1990); Ute Brandes, "Baroque women writers and the public sphere," *Women in German Yearbook* 7 (Lincoln, University of Nebraska Press, 1991); Katherine R. Goodman and Edith Waldstein (eds.), *In the Shadow of Olympus: German Women Writers Around 1800* (Albany, State University of New York Press, 1992); Anna Cardus, "Consolation arguments and maternal grief in seventeenth-century verse: the example of Margarethe Susanna von Kuntsch, *German Life and Letters* 47 (1994), 135–151; Lynne Tatlock and Christine

Bohnert (eds.), *The Graph of Sex and the German Text: Gendered Culture in Early Modern Germany 1500–1700*, Chloe: Beihefte zum Daphnis, 19 (Amsterdam, Rodolpi, 1994); Hermina Joldersma, "Anna Bijns" in K. P. Aercke (ed.), *Women Writing in Dutch* (New York, Garland, 1994), pp. 93–146; Florence Koorn, "A life of pain and struggle: the autobiography of Elizabeth Strouven (1600–1661)," in Magdalene Heuser (ed.), *Autobiographien von Frauen: Beiträge zu ihrer Geschichte* (Tübingen, Max Miemeyer, 1996), pp. 13–24; Merry Wiesner-Hanks, "*Kinder, Kirche, Landeskinder:* women defend their publishing in early modern Germany," in Robin B. Barnes, Robert A. Kolb, and Paula L. Presley (eds.), *Books Have Their Own Destiny* (Kirksville, MO., Sixteenth Century Journal Publishers, 1998), pp. 143–52; Susanne T. Kord, *Little Detours: Letters and Plays by Louise Gottsched (1713–1762)* (Columbia, S.C., Camden House, 2000).

Studies of Spanish women writers in English include: Paul Julian Smith, *The Body Hispanic: Gender and Sexuality in Spanish and Spanish American Literature* (Oxford, Clarendon Press, 1989); Lou Charnon-Deutsch, "The sexual economy in the narrative of María de Zayas," *Letras feminas* 17 (1991), 15–28; Lou Charnon-Deutsch (ed.), *Studies on Hispanic Women Writers in Honor of Georgina Sabat Rivers* (Madrid, Castalia, 1992); Ursula K. Heise, "Transvestism and the stage controversy in Spain and England, 1580–1680," *Theatre Journal* (1992), 357–74; Amy R. Williamsen and Judith A. Whitenack (eds.), *María de Zayas: The Dynamics of Discourse* (Teaneck, N.J., Fairleigh Dickenson University Press, 1995); Valerie Hegstrom and Amy Williamsen, *Engendering the Early Modern Stage: Women Playwrights in the Spanish Empire* (New Orleans, University Press of the South, 1999): Margaret R. Greer, *María de Zayas Tells Baroque Tales of Love and the Cruelty of Men* (University Park, Pennslyvania State University Press, 2000). Translations include: María de Zayas y Sotomayor, *The Enchantments of Love: Amorous and Exemplary Novels,* trans. H. Patsy Boyer (Berkeley, University of California Press, 1990); Amy Kaminsky (ed.), *Water Lilies/Flores del agua: An Anthology of Spanish Women Writers from the Fifteenth through the Nineteenth Century* (Minneapolis, University of Minnesota Press, 1996); Sor Juana Inés de la Cruz, *The Answer/La respuesta, Including a Selection of Poems,* ed. Amanda Powell and Electa Arenal (New York, Feminist Press, 1994) and *Poems, Protest, and a Dream,* trans. Margaret Sayers Peden (London, Penguin, 1997).

Women's autobiographies and letters have received special attention. For the former, see Mary G. Mason, "The other voice: autobiographies of women writers," in James Olney (ed.), *Autobiographies: Essays Theoretical and Critical* (Princeton, Princeton University Press, 1980), pp. 207–35; Estelle C. Jelinek (ed.), *Women's Autobiography: Essays in Criticism* (Bloomington, Indiana University Press, 1980); Estelle C. Jelinek (ed.), *The Tradition of Women's Autobiography from Antiquity to the Present* (Boston, Twayne, 1986); Elsbeth Graham, et al. (eds.), *Her Own Life: Autobiographical Writings by Seventeenth-century Englishwomen* (London, Routledge, 1989). The letters of two of the most important early modern letter writers have been translated and reprinted: Madame de Sévigné, *Selected Letters,* trans. Leonard Tancock (London, Penguin, 1982); Elisabeth Charlotte Duchesse d'Orléans, *A Woman's Life in the Court of the Sun King: Letters of Liselotte von der Pfalz, 1652–1722,* trans. Elborg Forster (Baltimore, The Johns Hopkins University Press, 1984). Women's writing of history has been discussed in: Natalie Zemon Davis, "Gender and genre: women as historical writers, 1400–1820," in Patricia Labalme (ed.), *Beyond Their Sex: Learned Women of the European Past* (New York, New York University Press, 1980), pp. 153–82 and "History's Two Bodies," *American Historical Review* 93 (1988), 1–30; Gianna Pomata, "History, particular and universal: on reading some recent women's history textbooks," *Feminist Studies* 19 (1993): 7–50; Charlotte Woodford, "Women as historians: the case of early modern German convents," *German Life and Letters* 52 (1999), 271–80.

Women's role in print culture and the book trade have been discussed in Elizabeth Goldsmith and Dena Goodman (eds.), *Going Public: Women and Publishing in Early Modern France* (Ithaca, Cornell University Press, 1995); Paula McDowell, *The Women of Grub Street: Press, Politics, and Gender in the London Literary Marketplace 1678–1730* (Oxford, Clarendon Press, 1998); Axel Erdmann, *My Gracious Silence: Women in the Mirror of Sixteenth-Century Printing in Western Europe* (Luzerne, Gilhofer and Ranschberg, 1998).

Women's activities as natural philosophers and the effects of the Scientific Revolution on women and ideas about women have been the subject of several major studies. Carolyn Merchant, *The Death of Nature: Women, Ecology and the Scientific Revolution* (New York, Harper & Row, 1980), which examines many facets of the change from an organic to a mechanistic view of the world, is extremely thought-provoking, controversial, and essential reading in the field. Londa Schiebinger, *The Mind Has No Sex? Women in the Origins of Modern Science* (Cambridge, Harvard University Press, 1989), looks at changes in the organization and definition of "science" which worked to exclude women. Patricia Phillips, *The Scientific Lady: A Social History of Women's Scientific Interests, 1520–1918* (London, Weidenfeld and Nicolson, 1990) takes a more biographical approach, as does the more general survey, Margaret Alic, *Hypatia's Heritage: A History of Women in Science from Antiquity through the Nineteenth Century* (Boston, Beacon, 1986). Lynette Hunter and Sarah Hutton (eds.), *Women, Medicine and Science 1500–1700: Mothers and Sisters of the Royal Society* (London, Sutton, 1998) looks at the writings and activities of women practicing medicine and science, and Laurinda Dixon, *Perilous Chastity: Women and Illness in Pre-Enlightenment Art and Medicine* (Ithaca, Cornell University Press, 1995) at images of women in medical works. The works of women philosophers have been reprinted in Margaret Atherton (ed.), *Women Philosophers of the Early Modern Period* (Indianapolis, Hackett, 1994). Biographies of women philosophers may be found in Mary Ellen Waithe (ed.), *A History of Women Philosophers, vol. III* (Dordrecht, Kluwer Academic Publishers, 1991) and analyses of their works in Linda McAllister (ed.), *Hypatia's Daughters* (Bloomington, Indiana University Press, 1995). More specialized studies include: Sarah Hutton, "Damaris Cudworth, Lady Masham: between Platonism and Enlightenment," *The British Journal for the History of Philosophy* 1 (1993), 29–54; Lisa T. Sarasohn, "A science turned upside down: feminism and the natural philosophy of Margaret Cavendish," *Huntington Library Quarterly* 47 (1994), 299–307; Eileen O'Neill, "Disappearing ink: early modern women philosophers and their fate in history," in Janet A. Kourany (ed.), *Philosophy in a Feminist Voice* (Princeton, Princeton University Press, 1998); Anna Battigelli, *Margaret Cavendish and the Exile of the Mind*

(Lexington, University Press of Kentucky, 1998); Andrea Nye, *The Princess and the Philosopher* (on Princess Elizabeth of Bohemia) (London, Rowman and Littlefield, 1999); Susan Bordo (ed.), *Feminist Interpretations of René Descartes* (University Park, Pennsylvania State University Press, 1999). Several of the essays in *Hypatia* 4 (Spring 1989), special issue on the history of women, focus on early modern women. An excellent bibliography on Margaret Cavendish can be found at: jan.ucc.nau.edu/~jbf/CavBiblio.html.

Part III

Spirit

Lord of my soul, you did not hate women when You walked in the world; rather you favored them always with much pity and found in them as much love and more faith than in men. Is it not enough, Lord, that the world has intimidated us. . . so that we may not do anything worthwhile for You in public?

St. Teresa of Avila, *The Way of Perfection*, (1560s) quoted and translated in Alison Weber, *Teresa of Avila and the Rhetoric of Femininity* (Princeton, Princeton University Press, 1990), p. 41.

Since it were very pernicious that the opinions of men, although good and holy, should be put in the place of the commandment of God, I desire that this matter [the decision by the Protestant consistory of her town, a disciplinary body made up of clergy, to excommunicate her and her entire household because she wore her hair in curls] may be cleared up for the well-being and the concord of the churches.

Charlotte Arbaleste, 1584, quoted and translated in James Anderson, *Ladies of the Reformation: In Germany, France, and Spain* (London, Blackie and Sons, 1857), p. 466.

The second quotation above comes from a speech by Charlotte Arbaleste, a French noblewoman and Calvinist Protestant, to the consistory of her town. Matters such as the style of one's hair, Arbaleste continued, were no grounds for the exclusion of someone from church ceremonies and services, and she as a noblewoman was certainly not going to obey the middle-class pastors on an issue that had nothing to do with her or anyone else's salvation.

This conflict and Arbaleste's comments about it highlight many of the issues involving women's religious life in the early modern period. First, though we may view the arrangement of women's hair as trivial, it had tremendous social and symbolic importance. Immediately upon marriage, women covered their hair, for long flowing hair was the mark of someone who was sexually available, either as a virgin or prostitute. Both the New Testament and early Christian writers such as Tertullian had ordered women to cover their heads, not simply as a gesture of respect but also specifically to lessen their sexual attractiveness. Thus the pastors claimed biblical authority for their position, and at the heart of the issue was the control of female sexuality and the maintenance of a moral order in which women were subservient. These factors will emerge in nearly all the religious conflicts involving women in the early modern period, even when the participants did not articulate them.

Second, the key question for women was often the conflict between the authorities Arbaleste mentions: the opinions of men and the commandment of God. Women had to choose between what male political and religious authorities, and sometimes even their fathers and husbands, told them to do, and what they perceived as God's plan for their lives. Third, Arbaleste and the pastors disagreed about the boundaries between public and private; early modern women frequently argued that their religious actions were private matters and that only God could be the true judge. Finally, Arbaleste's confidence in challenging the pastors, and the source of some of her irritation, came from her status as a noblewoman; the women whose religious choices had the most impact in early modern Europe were usually noblewomen or rulers, whose actions affected their subjects as well as themselves and their families. For women of all classes, however, religion provided the most powerful justification for independent action.

It may seem somewhat odd to think of Christianity, Judaism, or Islam as religions that empowered women, for all contain strong streaks of misogyny and were in the early modern period totally controlled by male hierarchies with the highest (or all) levels of the clergy reserved for men. In all three, God is thought of as male, the account of creation appears to ascribe or ordain a secondary status for women, and women are instructed to be obedient and subservient; all three religious traditions were used by men as buttresses for male authority in all realms of life, not simply religion. Nevertheless, it was the language of religious texts, and the examples of pious women who preceded them, which were used most often by women to subvert or directly oppose male directives. Religion was even used as the reason why women should study secular philosophy; Mary Astell, the English feminist and scholar writing in the first part of the eighteenth century, justified her call for women to learn Cartesian philosophy in part by stressing that this could help a woman not only to love God "with all her Heart and Strength" but also to "love Him with all her Mind and Soul."[1]

---

[1] Mary Astell, *The Christian Religion, As Profess'd by a Daughter of the Church of England* (1705) quoted in Hilda Smith, *Reason's Disciples: Seventeenth-century English Feminists* (Urbana, University of Illinois Press, 1982), p. 119.

In exploring early modern women's religious ideas and actions, it will be useful to follow the standard religious chronology and divisions of the period, as these determined the types of ideology and institutions within or against which women could operate. For Christianity, we will start with a look at the late medieval Catholic and Orthodox churches, then at the Protestant and Catholic Reformations in western Europe, developments in Orthodoxy, and the broadening of religious options in the seventeenth and early eighteenth centuries with such movements as quietism, pietism, and the radical sects which were part of the English Civil War. This will be followed by a much briefer discussion of women in early modern Judaism and Islam, whose fate in Europe was shaped to a great degree by the Christian authorities under whose control they largely lived.

The role of women in late medieval Christianity

We have already examined in some detail the ideas about women held by medieval theologians and clerics, but before we can assess the changes for women brought about by the Protestant and Catholic Reformations, and the role of women in both of these movements, we must have some idea of their role in the late medieval church. Here we must distinguish, as would any of their contemporaries, between nuns and other women who had taken religious vows, the majority of lay women who were married or lived with other family members, and women whose status was somewhere in between, who attempted to live a communal life of religious devotion without formal vows or rules.

The most powerful and in many ways independent women in the late medieval church were the abbesses of certain convents, who controlled large amounts of property and often had jurisdiction over many subjects. This was particularly true in Germany, where abbesses of free imperial convents had no secular overlord except the Emperor, but was also true elsewhere in Europe where certain convents were aligned with powerful noble families. Though every convent had to have a priest available to say mass and hear confessions because the Catholic church ruled these were functions that no woman could perform, all of the other administrative duties and much of the spiritual counseling of novices and residents were carried out by women. Since their foundings in the early and high Middle Ages, many convents had been open only to members of the nobility and were thus socially exclusive; lower-class women might be associated with a convent as lay sisters to do the harder physical labor or routine maintenance, but they could not become professed nuns.

The high point of many convents in terms of intellectual accomplishments and political power was the tenth and eleventh centuries, when Hroswitha of Gandersheim wrote the first original dramas since the end of the Roman Empire for the nuns in her convent, and abbesses corresponded and visited with prominent political leaders. Beginning in the late eleventh century, a reform movement usually termed the "Gregorian reform" after one of its most vocal proponents, Pope Gregory VII (pontificate 1073–1085) attempted to cut the conncetions between the church and secular leaders, and also to restrict all links between male clergy and women. Decrees were passed ordering clerical celibacy and declaring priestly marriages that did exist invalid. Reform-minded officials began a campaign against clerical families, driving women and children from their homes. Though there were protests against this change in policy, they were not effective, and clerical celibacy became the policy of the western church from that point on. Priests were ordered to live separately from their female relatives, and convents that had both male and female residents (these were termed "double monasteries," with the men and women in separate sections) were dissolved. Women religious were to be cut off from the world, a practice known as enclosure, which became official policy in the papal decree *Periculoso* promulgated in 1298 by Pope Boniface VIII, though it was never successfully enforced until centuries later. These moves reduced the abbesses' power and visibility in the surrounding community, and at the same time, universities, which were closed to women, replaced monasteries as the main intellectual centers of Europe. In their writings and in their spiritual life, nuns in the late Middle Ages turned to mysticism and personal devotions, rather than giving political advice or writing plays for public performance.

By the fifteenth century, it appeared to some church officials and the more rigorous nuns as if many convents had forgotten their spiritual focus. In many ways this is not surprising, as some convent residents were not there willingly, but had been placed in a convent by their parents because the cost of a dowry for marriage was too high; the entrance fees demanded by convents were generally lower than the dowry that a husband of one's own social class would expect. Such nuns often continued to live as they would outside the convent – they wore secular clothing and jewelry, entertained visitors, ate fancy food, retained servants, and frequently left the convent to visit family or friends. In many areas of Europe, leaders of the orders with which convents were affiliated or reform-minded abbesses attempted to halt such behavior and enforce strict rules of conduct and higher standards of spirituality. These fifteenth-century reforms had both positive and negative results for the nuns. On the negative side, they often put the convent more closely under the control of a local male bishop, taking away some of the abbess's independent power, and decreased the contact that the women had with the outside world, which also decreased their opportunities to get donations. On the positive side, they often built up a strong sense of group cohesion among the nuns and gave them a greater sense of the spiritual worth of their lives, particularly if an abbess herself had led the reform; this would lead, as we will see, to these reformed convents being the most vigorous opponents of the Protestant Reformation in the areas in which it was introduced.

In areas of Europe where Orthodox Christianity was dominant, such as eastern Europe and Russia, women's convents were rarely enclosed and the women did not live communally, but retained their own incomes, clothing, and food. Many of these convents were wealthy centers of pilgrimage, holding huge estates, and had close ties with noble and royal families. A larger share of the nuns in Orthodox convents were widows than was true in western Europe, for widows often entered convents for social and economic security, deeding their goods or property to the convent rather than fighting legal battles for it with other heirs. The abbesses of major convents, who were elected by the nuns, were often very powerful, entertaining secular and ecclesiastical officials and handling relations with the tsar. Unlike western convents, the women in Orthodox convents were not expected to have a strong religious vocation, but simply lead respectable lives; as the accounts of Russian saints' lives demonstrate, the ideal holy woman in Russia was not a nun, as she was in the West, but a devout mother who lived quietly at home and did her miracles and good deeds in private. Orthodoxy was not affected by the Protestant or Catholic Reformations, so that women's convents in eastern Europe continued to operate into the eighteenth century just as they had in the Middle Ages.

In addition to living in convents, a number of women in the late Middle Ages lived in less structured religious communities. Because a dowry was required for either marriage or entrance into a convent, many poor women remained unmarried all their lives, and some chose to live communally in informal religious groups, supporting themselves by weaving, sewing, or caring for the sick. These women were often called Beguines, and were initially ignored by the church, but in the fourteenth century were increasingly regarded as suspect because they were not under male supervision nor did they take formal vows. They were also regarded as cheap competition in the labor market by the craft guilds which were establishing themselves in many cities, and so attempts were made to forbid women to live together unless they were cloistered in a convent. These attempts were sporadically successful, particularly in areas where Beguines were also charged with heresy, but groups of unmarried women and widows continued to live together in many cities because there was simply no other way they could survive. In the Netherlands in the fifteenth century a religious reform movement known as the Devotio Moderna led to the establishment of yet another alternative for unmarried women and widows, the Sisters of the Common Life. Like the Beguines, the Sisters took no vows and supported themselves by copying manuscripts, teaching children, and weaving; the movement was wildly popular, for one house is recorded as having 600 residents, each with her own loom. In fifteenth-century Italy, what were termed open monasteries for women could be found in every town, in which widows, unmarried women, and sometimes even former prostitutes and concubines chose to live a life of religious purpose but without formal vows.

Not all women who felt the call to lead a religious life in the late Middle Ages chose to do so in a community. Anchoresses, who were especially common in England, had themselves walled up in small cells attached to churches or cathedrals, where they could pray and meditate without outside distractions; their contact with the world was often limited to those who brought them food, though some, such as Julian of Norwich, were also sought out for their spritual advice. Some women who felt a special religious calling remained with their families, devoting themselves to helping others, to fighting heresy, or to prayer, and perhaps attaching themselves to the Dominicans or Franciscans as lay followers called tertiaries. In the early Middle Ages women who were regarded as particularly holy were almost all virgins, but by the late Middle Ages there were even a number of saints who were wives and mothers. Some of these women convinced their husbands to live chastely within marriage, a few left their husbands, and others continued to have sexual relations and bear children. Given official church attitudes about the greater worth of virginity, motherhood often troubled women who felt they had a special religious calling, but they took heart in the example of Mary, the mother of Christ. Margery Kempe, a fifteenth-century English mystic who had fourteen children, despaired about being pregnant again, but was relieved by a vision of Christ saying to her, "Forasmuch as thou art a maiden in thy soul, I shall take thee by the one hand, and my Mother by the other hand, and so shalt thou dance in Heaven with other maidens and virgins."[2]

Mary and other female saints also served as inspirations for the vast majority of women in late medieval Christianity who were not nuns,

---

[2] *The Book of Margery Kempe,* ed. William Butler-Bowdon (New York, Devin-Adair, 1944), p. 42.

Beguines, or mystics, but daughters, wives, and mothers living in families. Though all priests and the entire church hierarchy outside of the
convents were male, stories about holy women who had been martyrs or
shown special qualities of piety and devotion circulated orally, as part of
manuscript and later printed collections of saints' lives, or were depicted
in stained-glass windows, church statuary, and paintings. Mary was a
particularly popular subject, being shown so often that many people felt
she was one member of the Trinity. Because of her singular status as both
virgin and mother, Mary was a problematic model for normal women,
who could never hope to achieve what she had. In fact, the cult of the
Virgin was often strongest among celibate male misogynists such as
Bernhard of Clairvaux who used her example to castigate all other
women. According to tradition, however, Mary's mother Anne, a non-
biblical figure whose life was first discussed in written documents in the
second century, had had a perfectly normal pregnancy, and she became
one of the patron saints of childbirth. The saints served medieval
Christians in the same way that minor gods and goddesses had served
Greeks and Romans – as patrons of certain activities and individuals to
turn to with supplications. Female saints were often regarded, not surprisingly, as having special powers over family and household matters, in
the same way that goddesses had.

Veneration of Anne grew throughout the Middle Ages, when her life
story was embellished with legends about her own mother Emerentia,
her three marriages, and her children other than Mary. Stories of her life,
frequently reprinted in the fifteenth and sixteenth centuries in vernacular languages as small pamphlets, were popular with the urban middle
classes as they portrayed family life in a positive way. Though we have no
way of knowing exactly who purchased or read such stories, they were
often illustrated with a female trinity – Mary, Anne, and Emerentia – and
provided examples of normal human women, even older ones, acting in
divinely approved ways.

Late medieval Christianity offered believers a number of opportunities
to improve their likelihood of going to Heaven or ask God to solve their
problems here on earth. Women and men went on pilgrimages, bought
and viewed relics, paid for memorial masses or special prayers, lit candles,
founded lay confraternities dedicated to certain saints or devotional practices such as the rosary, and carried out a variety of other acts for religious reasons. Their lives were punctuated by ceremonies with religious
meaning – baptisms, weddings, funerals – and the entire calendar was
structured according to the Church year, with feasts and fasts celebrated
with family and community ceremonies. Married and single women
formed all-female parish guilds that raised funds, decorated the church,

organized activities, and worshipped together. Even daily acts such as baking bread were given religious significance when women made the sign of the cross before kneading their dough. Scholars are only beginning to ask in what ways women's understanding of Christianity differed from men's and whether there were certain religious activities and ideas that were particularly attractive to women. Sources that discuss popular devotion are often difficult to find because the very frequency and normality of private or family religious activities meant contemporaries rarely commented on them; women's religious actions received even less notice unless they were perceived as threatening.

Careful sifting of visual and written sources does allow us to make a few general statements about how lay women's religious life differed from men's. Other than a few noblewomen or queens who governed territories, no lay woman had any say in the financial or political affairs of the institutional church, though by 1500 city councils and other lay male officials played a large role in running the church in many parts of Europe. Men also oversaw municipal or church agencies for poor relief, whereas women tended to carry out less formal acts of charity, giving food to beggars or taking care of poorer women during illness or childbirth. Because all church services were in Latin, the vast majority of people could not comprehend the words, but simply watched and listened to the music or chanting. Woodcuts and engravings of late medieval services show women more often than men carrying out an alternative religious action, such as saying a rosary or reading in a prayer book, while the priest is conducting the service. It is difficult to know, however, if the artist was representing reality or implicitly criticizing women for not paying attention. Both women and men honored female saints, though, judging by later Protestant criticism, women were more adamant in their loyalty to them, especially during childbirth; praying to Christ, a celibate male, during a difficult birth was simply not as satisying as praying to Anne or another female saint who had been a mother.

The Protestant Reformation

The Protestant Reformation was sparked by one of the many ways the late medieval church offered believers to affect their own salvation – giving money in return for indulgences, which substituted for earthly penance or shortened one's time in Purgatory. Martin Luther, Ulrich Zwingli, John Calvin, and most of the other prominent Protestant leaders, though they disagreed on a great many things, all thought that the Catholic Church placed too great an emphasis on good works; for them,

12 Lucas Cranach d. A., *Women Assaulting Clergy*, after 1537. This is a detail from a larger drawing in which women attack members of the clergy with agricultural implements; here they are beating a bishop and a cardinal with a flail. This probably does not show an actual event, but women are reported to have participated in Protestant riots and actions against clergy in many parts of Europe.

an individual's access to salvation was determined by God alone, and not by any human actions. The God of the Protestant reformers was a transcendent one, not influenced by pilgrimages or surrounded by a group of semi-divine saints who could serve as intermediaries. In their opinion, the clergy were no better than anyone else – the standard phrase expressing this is "the priesthood of all believers" – and the Bible and all church services should be in the vernacular so that all Christians could have access to them.

Like Christianity itself, the Protestant Reformation both expanded and diminished women's opportunities. The period in which women were the most active was the decade or so immediately following an area's decision to break with the Catholic Church or while this decision was being made. In Germany and many other parts of Europe, that decision was made by a political leader – a prince, duke, king, or city council – who then had to create an alternative religious structure. During this period, many groups and individuals tried to shape the new religious institutions. Sometimes this popular pressure took the form of religious riots, in which women and men destroyed paintings, statues, stained-glass windows or other objects that symbolized the old religion, or protected such objects from destruction at the hands of government officials; in 1536 at Exeter in England, for example, a group of women armed with shovels and pikes attacked workers who had been hired by the government to dismantle a monastery. Sometimes this popular pressure took the form of writing when women and men who did not have formal theological training took the notion of the "priesthood of all believers" literally and preached or published polemical religious literature explaining their own ideas.

Women's preaching or publishing religious material stood in direct opposition to the words ascribed to St. Paul (1 Timothy 2: 11–15) which ordered women not to teach or preach, so that all women who published felt it necessary to justify their actions. The boldest, such as Argula von Grumbach, a German noblewoman who published eight works in 1523 and 1524, including a defense of a teacher accused of Lutheran leanings, commented that the situation was so serious that Paul's words should simply be disregarded: "I am not unfamiliar with Paul's words that women should be silent in church but when I see that no man will or can speak, I am driven by the word of God when he said, He who confesses me on earth, him will I confess and he who denies me, him will I deny."[3] Ursula Weyda, a middle-class German woman who attacked the abbot

[3] Ludwig Rabus, *Historien der heyligen Außerwolten Gottes Zeugen, Bekennern und Martyrern* (n.p., 1557), fol. 41. My translation.

of Pegau in a 1524 pamphlet, agreed: "If all women were forbidden to speak, how could daughters prophesy as Joel predicted? Although St. Paul forbade women to preach in churches and instructed them to obey their husbands, what if the churches were full of liars?"[4] Marie Dentière, a former abbess who left her convent to help the cause of the Reformation in Geneva, published a letter to Queen Margaret of Navarre in 1539 defending some of the reformers exiled from that city, in which she gives ringing support to this view:

> I ask, didn't Jesus die just as much for the poor illiterates and the idiots as for the shaven, tonsured, and mighty lords? Did he only say, "Go, preach my Gospel to the wise lords and grand doctors?" Did he not say, "To all?" Do we have two Gospels, one for men and the other for women?. . . For we ought not, any more than men, hide and bury within the earth that which God has. . . revealed to us women?[5]

Katherine Zell, the wife of one of Strasbourg's reformers and a tireless worker for the Reformation, supported Dentière in this, asking that her writings be judged, "not according to the standards of a woman, but according to the standards of one whom God has filled with the Holy Spirit."[6]

Zell's wish was never granted, and women's writings were always judged first on the basis of gender. Argula von Grumbach's husband was ordered to force her to stop writing, and Marie Dentière's pamphlets were confiscated by the very religious authorities she was defending. Once Protestant churches were institutionalized, polemical writings by women (and untrained men) largely stopped. Women continued to write hymns and devotional literature, but these were often published posthumously or were designed for private use.

Women's actions as well as their writings in the first years of the Reformation upset political and religious authorities. Many cities prohibited women from even getting together to discuss religious matters, and in 1543 an Act of Parliament in England banned all women except those of the gentry and nobility from reading the Bible; upper-class women were also prohibited from reading the Bible aloud to others. Class as well as gender hierarchies were to be maintained at all costs,

---

[4] Translated and quoted in Paul A. Russell, *Lay Theology in the Reformation: Popular Pamphleteers in Southwest Germany 1521–1525* (Cambridge, Cambridge University Press, 1986), p. 203.

[5] Translated and quoted in Thomas Head, "Marie Dentière: a propagandist for the reform," in Katharina M. Wilson (ed.), *Women Writers of the Renaissance and Reformation* (Athens, University of Georgia Press, 1987), p. 260.

[6] Quoted in Robert Stupperich, "Die Frau in der Publizistik der Reformation," *Archiv für Kulturgeschichte* 37 (1927), 226. My translation.

though from women's diaries we have learned that this restriction was rarely obeyed.

The ability of a woman to act out her religious convictions was largely dependent on class in reality as well as theory. Though none of the reformers differentiated between noblewomen and commoners in their public advice or writings, in private they recognized that noblewomen had a great deal of power and made special attempts to win them over. Luther corresponded regularly with a number of prominent noble-women, and Calvin was even more assiduous at trying to win noble-women to his cause. Their efforts met with results, for in a number of cases, female rulers converted their territories to Protestantism or influenced their male relatives to do so. In Germany, Elisabeth of Brunswick-Calenburg brought in Protestant preachers and established a new church structure; in France, Marguérite of Navarre and her daughter Jeanne d'Albert supported Calvinism through patronage and political influence; in Norway, Lady Inger of Austraat, a powerful and wealthy noblewoman, led the opposition to the Norwegian archbishop who remained loyal to Catholicism. The most dramatic example of the degree to which a woman's personal religious convictions could influence events occurred in England, of course, when Mary Tudor attempted to wrench the country back to Catholicism and Elizabeth created a moderately Protestant Church. In all of these cases political and dynastic concerns mixed with religious convictions, in the same way they did for male rulers and nobles.

Once the Reformation was established, most women expressed their religious convictions in a domestic, rather than public setting. They prayed and recited the catechism with children and servants, attended sermons, read the Bible or other devotional literature if they were literate, served meals that no longer followed Catholic fast prescriptions, and provided religious instruction for their children. Women's domestic religion often took them beyond the household, however, for they gave charitable donations to the needy and often assisted in caring for the ill and indigent. As it had been before the Reformation, most women's charity was on a case-by-case basis, but there are also examples from Protestant areas of women who established and supported almshouses, schools, orphanages, funds for poor widows, and dowry funds for poor girls. In a few places, such as Amsterdam, women who assisted widows and other poor women were given the title of female deacon *(deaconessen)*, but they did not participate in church governing bodies as male deacons did. The secularization of public welfare that accompanied the Reformation did give some women the opportunity to create permanent institutions to deal with social problems; evidence from wills indicates that women were, perhaps not surprisingly, more likely than men to make bequests which specifically benefitted other women.

Such domestic and charitable activities were widely praised by Protestant reformers as long as husband and wife agreed in their religious opinions. If there was disagreement, however, continental Protestants generally urged the wife to obey her husband rather than what she perceived as God's will. She could pray for his conversion, but was not to leave him or actively oppose his wishes; in Calvin's words, a woman "should not desert the partner who is hostile."[7] English Puritans were less restrictive, urging their female followers to act as "domestic missionaries" and attempt to convert their children, servants, and husbands. During the first decades after the Reformation, marriages between spouses of different faiths were much more common than they would be later in the century when the lines of religious confession hardened. Such mixed marriages occasioned less comment than one would assume given the violence of religious disagreements in general, because for the nobility and gentry, dynastic concerns continued to override those of religion, and even among middle-class urban dwellers, neither spouse appeared to feel the need necessarily to convert the other. By the seventeenth century official opinion had changed, with authorities in many areas prohibiting their citizens from marrying those of different denominations, or at least prohibiting female citizens from doing so, though sometimes they made distinctions on the basis of gender. In 1697, for example, the Irish Parliament revived decrees that had first been issued as part of the Statutes of Kilkenney in 1366 – designed at that point to keep the Gaelic and Norman populations of Ireland apart – and ordered that any Protestant heiress who married a Catholic would lose her property to her Protestant next of kin. Her marriage would be considered treasonous if her husband had not signed the Oath of Succession in support of the English rulers of Ireland.

The women whose domestic religious activities were most closely scrutinized in the first generation of the Protestant Reformation were the wives of the reformers. During the first few years of the Reformation, they were still likened to priests' concubines in the public mind and had to create a respectable role for themselves, a task made even more difficult by the fact that many were former nuns themselves. They did this largely – and quite successfully, within a generation or so – by being models of wifely obedience and Christian charity, living demonstrations

---

[7] Translated and quoted in John H. Bratt, "The role and status of women in the writings of John Calvin," in Peter de Klerk (ed.), *Renaissance, Reformation, Resurgence* (Grand Rapids, Calvin Theologial Seminary, 1976), p. 9.

of their husbands' convictions whose households were the type of orderly "little commonwealths" that their husbands were urging on their congregations in sermons. Whereas priests' concubines had generally been from a lower social class, by the second generation Protestant pastors had little difficulty finding wives from among the same social class as themselves, a trend that further aided the acceptance of clerical marriage. Maintaining an orderly household was just as important for Protestant pastors as teaching and preaching correct doctrine, with visitation teams and other officials investigating charges of sexual improprieties or moral laxness just as thoroughly as charges of incorrect doctrine. The women whose status was most tenuous were the wives of English bishops. Not only were many forced into exile or, worse yet, repudiated by their husbands during Mary's reign, but their marriages were not formally approved by Elizabeth, so that their children could always be declared bastards. Bishops were expected to live like wealthy noblemen and were accorded high rank at all ceremonial occasions, but their wives had no rank whatever. Long after continental pastors' wives had succeeded in making theirs a respectable position, bishops' wives in England still had not achieved even legal recognition despite all of their efforts at maintaining pious households.

No matter how much it was extolled in Protestant sermons and domestic conduct books, the vocation of mother and wife was not enough for some women, whose religious convictions led them to leave their husbands and continue to express their religious convictions publicly, even at the cost of their lives. One of the most famous of these was Anne Askew, an English woman who was tortured and then executed for her religious beliefs in 1546. Like Argula von Grumbach and Marie Dentière, she defended her actions, using the Bible against her inquisitors effectively throughout her trial; her standard response to their questioning was one that affirmed the right of every Christian to read and interpret the Bible on her own: "I beleue as the scripture doth teche me."[8] Askew was one of the few women martyrs to come from a gentry or middle-class background. Of the people martyred during the reign of Mary, one-fifth were women, and most of these were quite poor; wealthy people who opposed Mary fled to the Continent.

Most of the women executed for religious reasons in early modern Europe were Anabaptists, religious radicals who were hated and hunted by Catholics and Protestants alike. Most Anabaptist groups were very

---

[8] Quoted in Diane Willen, "Women and religion in early modern England," in Sherrin Marshall (ed.), *Women in Reformation and Counter-Reformation Europe: Public and Private Worlds* (Bloomington, Indiana University Press, 1989), p. 144.

small, and they had widely divergent ideas, so it is difficult to make generalizations that apply to all. Some groups emphasized divine revelation and spiritual experiences, and took the visions of women prophets very seriously. Others allowed believers to leave their unbelieving spouses, but women who did so were expected to remarry quickly and thus come under control of a male believer. In 1534, Anabaptists took over the northern German town of Münster, and attempted to create their vision of a perfect community. Part of this vision was polygamy and enforced marriage for all women, for the male Anabaptist leaders took literally the statement in the Book of Revelations that the Last Judgment would come once 144,000 "saints" (true believers) were in the world. These most radical of Anabaptists looked to the Old Testament, rather than the Gospels, for their models of gender relations.

The interrogations of Anabaptists are one of the few sources we have for the religious ideas of people who were illiterate; from these records, we learn that many women could argue complicated theological concepts and had memorized large parts of the Bible by heart. As Claesken Gaeledochter, who was drowned at Leeuwarden in 1559, put it, "Although I am a simple person before men, I am not unwise in the knowledge of the Lord."[9] Anabaptist women actively chose the path of martyrdom, often against the pressure of family members, and the records of their trials, which often appeared in print shortly after their executions, reveal a strong sense of determination. Their actions were praised after their deaths in special hymns which were later sung by fellow believers, full of the details about their martyrdoms and testimonies to women who were "in their faith strong, as men might be."[10] Though their strength of purpose may now appear heroic, in other ways the interrogations of Anabaptists parallel later witchcraft interrogations. In both cases, young women were stripped naked before they were tortured, and were asked not only to confess their beliefs, but also to name accomplices; the beliefs they were accused of were viewed as so pernicious that normal rules of legal procedure did not apply; most of those accused were poor women.

So far we have been examining new roles for women brought about by the Protestant Reformation: religious polemicist, pastor's wife, domestic missionary, philanthropist, martyr (which we may not view as positive,

[9] T. J. van Braght, *The Bloody Theatre or Martyrs Mirror*, ed. Edward Bean Underhill (London, Hanserd Knollys Society, 1850), vol. II, p. 33.

[10] "Six women of Antwerp" (written about six Anabaptist women executed in Antwerp in 1559), translated and quoted in Hermoine Joldersma and Louis Grijp (eds. and trans.) *"Elisabeth's Manly Courage": Testimonials and Songs by and about Martyred Anabaptist Women* (Milwaukee, Marquette University Press, 2001).

but which was viewed as such by most of the women who were). Protestant teachings also rejected many of the activities that had given women's lives religious meaning, however. Religious processions which had included both men and women, such as that of Corpus Christi, were prohibited, and sumptuary laws restricted the celebrations of baptism, weddings, and funerals, all ceremonies in which women had played a major role. Lay female confraternities, which had provided emotional and economic assistance for their members and charity for the needy, were also forbidden, and no all-female groups replaced them. The new charitable funds founded by women for women often had men as their overseers, and in any case did not bring together women of different classes as co-members the way confraternities did, but made sharp distinctions between the bestower and recipient of charity. The reformers attempted to do away with the veneration of Mary and the saints, though women continued to pray to Mary and Sts. Anne and Margaret, the patron saints of childbirth, for centuries. The Protestant martyrs replaced the saints to some degree as models worthy of emulation, but they were not to be prayed to and did not give their names to any days of the year, which stripped the calendar of celebrations honoring women.

The Protestant rejection of celibacy had the greatest impact on female religious, both cloistered nuns and women who lived in less formal religious communities. One of the first moves of an area rejecting Catholicism was to close the monasteries and convents, either confiscating the buildings and land immediately or forbidding new novices and allowing the current residents to live out their lives on a portion of the convent's old income. In England and Ireland, where all monasteries and convents were taken over by the Crown, most nuns got very small pensions and were expected to return to their families, though not all did. Many Irish and English nuns fled to religious communities on the Continent, or continued to fulfill their religious vows in hiding while they waited for the chance to emigrate. In many cities of the Dutch Republic, the convents were closed, their assets liquidated, and the women given their dowries and a pension. Though some returned to their families, others continued to live together in small, informal domestic groups. Because Catholic ceremonies and organizations were banned, it is difficult to find information about the religious life of these women, termed *kloppen* or *geestelijke maagden* (holy maidens). From land ownership records and family genealogies we do know that groups of them lived together or near one another long after areas became officially Protestant; one recent study estimates that *kloppen* made up about 2 percent of the Catholic population of the Dutch Republic in the seventeenth century. Many were members of wealthy and prominent upper-class families who had only slowly accepted the Reformation, so were supported by their families in their decisions to remain unmarried and devote themselves to religious activities. *Kloppen* could also be found in the Catholic Spanish Netherlands, where their status as an intermediate group between nuns and lay women made Catholic authorities increasingly uneasy.

Even when prominent families did become Protestant, they sometimes continued to support convents because of long-standing traditions. The convent at Vadstena in Sweden, for example, had long housed female members of the Swedish royal family, and when Swedish rulers became Protestant in the 1520s they thought it inappropriate simply to close it down. Instead they attempted to convince the nuns to accept Protestantism willingly, but the nuns resisted, stuffing wool and wax in their ears when they were forced to attend Lutheran services. The convent survived until the 1590s, when royal patience gave out; the nuns were then forcibly evicted and the convent's treasures and library confiscated.

This link between convents and prominent families was most pronounced in the Holy Roman Empire, where many convents had been established by regional ruling houses or by the wives and daughters of emperors. Many of them had been reformed in the fifteenth century, and long traditions of power, independence, and prestige combined with a reinvigorated spiritual life to make reformed convents the most vocal and resolute opponents of the Protestant Reformation. This was recognized by their contemporaries, as, for example, a papal nuncio who reported that "the four women's convents [in Magdeburg] have remained truer to their beliefs and vows than the men's monasteries, who have almost all fallen away."[11] The nuns' determination had social and political as well as religious roots, however, for they recognized that as women they could have no office in any Protestant Church; the role of a pastor's wife was an unthinkable decrease in status for a woman of noble standing.

In some territories of central Germany, the nuns' firmness combined with other religious and political factors to allow many convents to survive for centuries as Catholic establishments within Protestant territories. In the bishoprics of Magdeburg and Halberstadt, which became Protestant, half of the female convents survived, but only one-fifth of the monasteries. Some of this was certainly due to the women's zeal noted

---

[11] Quoted in Franz Schrader, *Ringen, Untergang und Überleben der katholischen Klöster in den Hochstiften Magdeburg und Halberstadt von der Reformation bis zum Westphalischen Frieden*, Katholisches Leben und Kirchenreform im Zeitalter der Glaubensspaltung, 37 (Münster, Aschendorff, 1977), p. 74. My translation.

by papal nuncio, but also to the fact that religious and political authorities did not regard the women's institutions as as great a threat as the men's. The marriage market for upper-class women also played a role. The cost of dowries was rising in early modern Germany, and even wealthy families could often not afford to marry off all their daughters to appropriate partners. As six noblemen who wrote to one of the Dukes of Brunswick when he was contemplating closing the convents in his territory put it, "What would happen to our sisters' and relatives' honor and our reputation if they are forced to marry renegade monks, cobblers, and tailors?"[12] And these were Lutheran nobles!

Some convents also survived as religious institutions by accepting Lutheran theology except for its rejection of the monastic life. Anna von Stolberg, for example, was the abbess of the free imperial abbey of Quedlinburg, and so governed a sizable territory including nine churches and two male monasteries. When she became Protestant in the 1540s she made all priests swear to Luther's Augsburg Confession and turned her Franciscan monastery into an elementary school for both boys and girls, an interesting gender reversal of the usual pattern of male authorities transforming female convents into schools or using convent property to fund (male, of course) scholars at universities. She continued to receive both imperial and papal privileges, for Catholic authorities were unwilling to cut off support from what was, at any rate, still a *convent*. She was also not uniformly criticized by Lutheran leaders, however, who emphasized that she was, at any rate, *Lutheran*. Quedlinburg was not the only abbey in this situation. At least fourteen Lutheran convents in the relatively small territory of Brunswick/Lüneburg survived into the nineteenth century, most of which are still religious establishments for unmarried women today.

It is very difficult to determine how many convents throughout the Empire were able to survive as either Catholic or Protestant institutions, because their existence was in some ways an embarrassment to secular and religious authorities attempting to enforce a policy of religious uniformity. Many of the urban convents in south Germany, such as those in Strasbourg and Nuremberg, fought disbanding as long as they could, despite being forced to listen to daily sermons, being denied confessors and Catholic ceremonies, and even having residents forcibly dragged out by their families. (The few male monasteries that actually opposed the Reformation were simply ordered shut and their residents banished from

---

[12] Quoted in Johann Karl Seidemann, *Dr. Jacob Schenk, der vermeintlicher Antinomer, Freibergs Reformator* (Leipzig, C. Hinrichs'sche, 1875), Appendix 7, p. 193. My translation.

the territory, an action that could not be used against convents as their reisdents were usually the daughters of local families and would have nowhere outside the territory to go.) Finally urban authorities often gave up their direct attacks, and simply forbade the taking in of new novices so that the convents slowly died out. A few also followed the central German pattern of becoming Protestant; one convent in Ulm, for example, survived as a Protestant institution until the nineteenth century.

The distinction between Protestant and Catholic that is so important in understanding the religious and intellectual history of sixteenth-century Europe may have ultimately been less important to the women who lived in convents or other communal groups than the distinction between their pattern of life and that of the majority of lay women. Evidence from convents in Brunswick and Augsburg indicates that Protestant and Catholic women lived together quite peacefully for decades, protected by the walls of their convent from the religious conflicts surrounding them. Women in the Netherlands and England, denied the possibility of continuing in their convents, continued to live together, letting their formal religious affiliation remain a matter of speculation, both for contemporaries and for historians. The Protestant championing of marriage and family life, which some nuns accepted with great enthusiasm as a message of liberation from the convent, was viewed by others as a negation of the value of the life they had been living; they thus did all in their power to continue in their chosen path.

The Catholic Reformation

The response of the Catholic Church to the Protestant Reformation is often described as two interrelated movements. One, a Counter-Reformation which attempted to win territory and people back to loyalty to Rome and prevent further spread of Protestant ideas, and the other a reform of abuses and problems within the Catholic Church which had been recognized as problems by many long before the Protestant Reformation. Thus the Catholic Reformation was both a continuation of medieval reform movements and a new crusade. Women were actively involved in both movements, but their actions were generally judged more acceptable when they were part of a reform drive; even more than the medieval crusades, the fight against Protestants was to be a masculine affair.

The masculine nature of the Counter-Reformation was intimately related to one of the key aspects of church reform – an enforcement of cloistering for women. Reforms of the church beginning with the Gregorian in the eleventh century had all emphasized the importance of the control of female sexuality and the inappropriateness of women religious being in contact with lay society; claustration was a key part of the restrictions on Beguines in the fourteenth century and of the fifteenth-century reform of the convents. The problem became even more acute after the Protestant Reformation, for numerous women in Europe felt God had called them to oppose Protestants directly through missionary work, or to carry out the type of active service to the world in schools and hospitals that the Franciscans, Dominicans, and the new orders like the Jesuits were making increasingly popular with men. For example, Angela Merici founded the Company of St. Ursula in Brescia, Italy. The Company was a group of lay single women and widows dedicated to serving the poor, the ill, orphans, and war victims, earning their own living through teaching or weaving. Merici received papal approval in 1535, for the pope saw this as a counterpart to the large number of men's lay confraternities and societies that were springing up in Italy as part of the movement to reform the church.

Similar groups of lay women dedicated to charitable service began to spring up in other cities of Italy, Spain, and France, and in 1541, Isabel Roser decided to go one step further and ask for papal approval for an order of religious women with a similar mission. Roser had been an associate of Ignatius Loyola, the founder of the Jesuits, in Barcelona. She saw her group as a female order of Jesuits which, like the Jesuits, would not be cut off from the world but would devote itself to education, care of the sick, and assistance to the poor, and in so doing win converts back to Catholicism. This was going too far, however. Loyola was horrifed at the thought of religious women in constant contact with lay people and Pope Paul III refused to grant his approval. Despite this, her group continued to grow in Rome and in the Netherlands, where they spread Loyola's teaching through the use of the Jesuit catechism.

The Council of Trent, the church council that met between 1545 and 1563 to define what Catholic positions would be on matters of doctrine and discipline, reaffirmed the necessity of cloister for all women religious and called for an end to open monasteries and other uncloistered communities. Enforcement of this decree came slowly, however, for several reasons. First, women's communities themselves fought it or ignored it. Followers of Isabel Roser, for example, were still active into the seventeenth century, for in 1630 Pope Urban VIII published a bull to suppress them, and reported that they were building convents and choosing abbesses and rectors. The residents of some of Roser's communities and other convents that fought strict claustration were often from wealthy urban families who could pressure church officials. Second, church officials themselves recognized the value of the services performed by such communities, particularly in the area of girls' education and care of the sick. Well after Trent, Charles Borromeo, a reforming archbishop in Milan, invited in members of the Company of St. Ursula, and transformed the group from one of lay women into one of religious who lived communally, though they still were not cloistered. From Milan, the Ursulines spread throughout the rest of Italy and into France, and began to focus completely on the education of girls. They became so popular that noble families began to send their daughters to Ursuline houses for an education, and girls from wealthy families became Ursulines themselves.

The very success of the Ursulines led to the enforcement of claustration, however, as well as other Tridentine decrees regulating women religious. Wealthy families were uncomfortable with the fact that because Ursulines did not take solemn vows, their daughters who had joined communities could theoretically leave at any time and make a claim on family inheritance. (Solemn vows bound one permanently to a religious establishment, and made an individual legally dead in the secular world.) Gradually the Ursuline houses in France and Italy were ordered to accept claustration, take solemn vows, and put themselves under the authority of their local bishop, thus preventing any movement or cooperation between houses. They were still allowed to teach girls, but now only within the confines of a convent. Some houses fought this as long as they could, though others accepted claustration willingly, having fully internalized Church teachings that the life of a cloistered nun was the most worthy in the eyes of God.

Extraordinary circumstances occasionally led church leadership to relax its restrictions, but only to a point. The situation of English Catholics under Protestant rulers was viewed as a special case, and a few women gained approval to go on their own as missionaries there. One of these was Luisa de Carvajal y Mendoza, a Spanish noblewoman who opposed her family's wishes and neither married nor entered a convent. She was quite effective at converting non-Catholics and bolstering the faith of her co-religionists, and later commented that being a woman helped her, as the English never suspected a woman could be a missionary. Paul V, pope from 1605 to 1621, was relatively open to female initiatives and in 1616 granted Mary Ward, who had run a school for English Catholic girls in exile in the Spanish Netherlands, provisional approval for her Institute of the Blessed Virgin Mary. She wanted women in her Institute to return to England as missionaries, for "it seems that the female sex also in its own measure, should and can. . . undertake something more than ordinary in this great common spiritual undertaking."[13] She openly modeled the Institute on the Jesuits and began to minister to the poor and sick in London, visiting Catholic prisoners and teaching in private homes.

The reports of Ward's successes proved too much for church leadership, and she was ordered to stop all missionary work, for "it was never heard in the Church that women should discharge the Apostolic Office."[14] Undaunted, Ward shifted her emphasis, and the Institute began to open houses in many cities throughout Europe in which women who took no formal vows operated free schools for both boys and girls, teaching them reading, writing, and a trade. The Institute needed constant donations, for which Ward and her associates traveled extensively and corresponded with secular and church authorities. Ward recognized that this public solicitation of funds was necessary in order for her schools to flourish, and so asked that the Institute never be under the control of a bishop, but report directly to the pope. She also realized that this sort of public role for women was something new in Catholicism, in her words, "a course never thought of before," but she stressed that there "is no such difference between men and women that women may not do great things as we have seen by the example of many saints."[15] Her popularity and independence proved too much for the Church hierarachy, however, and the year after the Bull was published against Roser Ward's schools and most of her houses were ordered closed, and Ward herself imprisoned by the Inquisition in Munich. "Jesuitesses," as Ward's Institute was termed by her enemies, were not to be tolerated, and similar other uncloistered communities of women, such as the Visitation, started to serve the poor by Jeanne de Chantal, a French lay woman, and Francis de Sales, a priest, were ordered to accept claustration or be closed.

Thus the only active apostolate left open to religious women was the instruction of girls, and that only within the convent. No nuns were sent to the foreign missions for any public duties, though once colonies were established in the New World and Asia cloistered convents quickly followed. The exclusion of women from what were judged the most exciting and important parts of the Catholic Reformation – countering Protestants and winning new converts – is reflected in the relative lack of women from the sixteenth century who were made saints. Luisa de

---

[13] Quoted in Elizabeth Rapley, *The Dévotes: Women and Church in Seventeenth-Century France* (Montreal and Kingston, McGill-Queen's University Press, 1990), p. 29.
[14] Ibid., p. 31.
[15] Quoted in Marie B. Rowlands, "Recusant women 1560–1640," in Mary Prior (ed.), *Women in English Society, 1500–1800* (London and New York, Methuen, 1985), p. 173.

Carvajal was raised to the status of Venerable, the first rung on the ladder to sanctity, but only 18.1 percent of those who reached the top of the ladder from the sixteenth century were women, whereas 27.7 percent of those from the fifteenth century had been female. Most of the women who did achieve sainthood followed a very different path, one of mysticism or reforming existing orders, a path in some ways set by the most famous religious woman of the sixteenth century, Teresa of Avila.

Teresa was a Carmelite nun who took her vows at twenty, and then spent the next twenty-five years in relative obscurity in her convent at Avila. During this time of external inaction, she went through great spiritual turmoil, similar to that experienced by Loyola and Luther, but came to feel the presence of God not through founding a new denomination or new order, but by mystical union with the divine. She went through extremes of exaltation and melancholy, suffering physical effects such as illness, trances, and paralysis. Her mystical path was not one of extreme mortification of the flesh, but of prayer, purification of the spirit, and assistance to the women of her convent. At other times or places she might have spent her life unnoticed, but this was Spain during the sixteenth century, when the Spanish crown was using its own Inquisition to stamp out any sign of humanist, Lutheran, or other deviant ideas. Other nuns and lay women who felt a sense of religious vocation *(beatas)* had been accused of heresy and questioned, so Teresa's confessors ordered her not only to describe her mystical experiences in writing, but to reflect on them and try to explain why she thought these were happening to her. Though Teresa complained about having to do this, she also clearly developed a sense of passion about her writing, for she edited and refined her work, transforming it into a full spiritual autobiography. Like many of the authors discussed in the last chapter, she manipulated stereotypes of femininity, conceding women's weakness, powerlessness, and inferiority so often that it appears ironic, and using informal language both to appeal to a wider audience and deflect charges that she was teaching theology.

Like Angela Merici and Mary Ward, Teresa also yearned for some kind of active ministry, and explicitly chafed at the restrictions on her because of her sex, as the quotation at the beginning of this chapter makes clear. In part she solved this by interpreting her prayers and those of other nuns as public actions: "we shall be fighting for Him [God] even though we are very cloistered."[16] When she was fifty-two, she also began to

---

[16] *The Way of Perfection,* translated and quoted in Jodi Bilinkoff, *The Avila of St. Teresa: Religious Reform in a Sixteenth-Century City* (Ithaca, Cornell University Press, 1989), p. 136.

reform her Carmelite order, attempting to return it to its original standards of spirituality and poverty. To do this she traveled all around
Spain, founding new convents, writing meditations, instructions for
monastic administrators, and hundreds of letters, provoking the wrath or
annoyance of some church authorities; a papal nuncio called her a "rest-
less gadabout, a disobedient and obstinate woman, who invented wicked
doctrines and called them devotion. . . and taught others against the
commands of St. Paul, who had forbidden women to teach."[17]

Teresa's success in reforming the Carmelites won her more supporters than critics within the church, however, for, unlike Angela Merici
and Mary Ward, she did not advocate institutionalized roles for women
outside of the convent. Her frustration at men's alterations of Christ's
view of women did not lead her to break with the male Church hierarchy, and the words quoted at the beginnning of this chapter which
expressed that frustration were expunged from her works by church cen-
sors. The version of Teresa that was presented for her canonization proceedings, held very shortly after her death, was one that fit her into the
acceptable model of woman mystic and reformer, assuming a public role
only when ordered to do so by her confessor or superior; only recently
have we begun to understand that Teresa thought of herself as a
Counter-Reformation fighter, viewing the new religious houses she
established as answers to the Protestant takeover of Catholic churches
elsewhere in Europe.

It is easy to view Teresa as a complete anomaly, but in many ways she
fits into a pattern of women's religious experience that was quite common in Spain, the Spanish colonies, and Italy. Other nuns also composed spiritual autobiographies and shared them with others, and they,
as well as lay holy women *(beatas)*, acted as reformers and social critics, combining mysticism and activism. Their visions and ecstatic
trances sometimes led to their being investigated by the Inquisition,
which was also concerned about their modesty and chastity. Diego
Pérez de Valdivia, a professor at the University of Barcelona, complained that some beatas had "much freedom and little modesty" and
were easily tempted by "the devil, the world, and their own flesh."[18]
Women who were religiously scrupulous, whether nuns or lay women,
confessed often and developed intense emotional relationships with

---

[17] Translated and quoted in Alison Weber, *Teresa of Avila and the Rhetoric of Femininity*
(Princeton, Princeton University Press, 1990), pp. 3–4.
[18] Diego Pérez de Valdivia, *Aviso de gente recogida* (1585), translated and quoted in Stephen
Haliczer, *Sexuality in the Confessional: A Sacrament Profaned* (New York, Oxford
University Press, 1996), p. 111.

their confessor. By the seventeenth century, church authorities recognized that this emotional intimacy might lead to physical intimacy, especially as confession was to entail a detailed examination of one's conscience and a minute accounting of sins, including sexual sins. Thus they paid close attention to the relationship between women and their confessors, and sometimes excluded nuns and women under forty from a priest's first license to hear confessions. These relationships led sometimes to charges of rape, seduction, or solicitation on the part of the priest or to charges of fraud and falsifying miracles on the part of the women. Despite examples of such "false saints," however, many women retained their reputations as, in the words of the time, "living saints." They resolved local conflicts and were sought for advice on personal, political, and religious matters, gaining power over political leaders, who in turn used the approval of such women as an endorsement of their policies and an enhancement of their prestige.

The respect accorded to Teresa and other "holy women" did not lead to any lessening of the call for the cloistering of religious women, however. Their separation from the world lessened the ability of women's communities to solicit funds, and the post-Tridentine emphasis on the sacraments meant that most benefactors preferred to give donations to a male house whose residents could say Mass. Thus many female houses grew increasingly impoverished, or more interested in the size of the dowry of a prospective entrant than the depth of her religious vocation. By the seventeenth century, convents in many parts of Europe were both shrinking and becoming increasingly aristocratic; in Venice, for example, nearly 60 percent of all women of the upper class joined convents. The long-range effects of claustration were not an increase but a decrease in spiritual vigor.

The effects of the Catholic Reformation on religious women were thus to a great degree restrictive. What about lay women in Catholic Europe? Here the balance sheet is more mixed, in large part because of the ambivalent attitude of church leadership about marriage. Catholic authors did begin to publish manuals for husbands and wives to counteract those written by Protestants, and emphasized their continued view of the sacramental nature of marriage. On the other hand, virginity continued to be valued over marriage, and spouses who took mutual vows of chastity within a marriage or left marriage to enter cloisters were praised. Catholic authors criticized the veneration of Anne, seeing the intercession of an older woman as no longer an appropriate avenue to God; the depiction of an all-female trinity disappeared from religious pamphlets, replaced by illustrations of Mary with both of her parents. Mary herself was also portrayed differently. Up to the early sixteenth century she was generally shown as an adult woman, capably caring for the infant Jesus while an older Joseph hovered in the background or was not shown at all. By the late sixteenth she was depicted as an adolescent girl, clearly under the protection of a strong and vigorous Joseph, who was now a much more dominant figure. Joseph replaced Anne as the fully human individual most often held up for emulation, and his cult grew in popularity with the spread of the Catholic Reformation.

In Italian cities, Catholic reformers began to open institutional asylums for repentent prostitutes *(convertite),* and also asylums for women who were felt to be at risk of turning to prostitution or losing their honor, such as orphans, poor unmarried women and widows, or those whose marriages had failed, called *malmaritate.* As we saw in Chapter 2, women in these institutions were taught basic skills with which to support themselves, usually weaving, and given large doses of religious and moral instruction. The drive to cloister all women's communities affected them as well, though some were able to remain uncloistered, with the residents even allowed to keep any wages earned, because it was seen as so important to prevent the women from landing back on the streets. In Catholic theory marriage was indissoluble, but in practice the Malmaritate houses offered women who had been abandoned or victimized by their husbands a respectable place to live, an alternative that was unavailable in Protestant areas.

No Catholic author went so far as to recommend that Catholic wives leave Protestant husbands, but in practice Catholic authorities put fewer blocks in the path of a woman who did. Protestant city councils in Germany were suspicious of any woman who asked to be admitted to citizenship independently and questioned her intently about her marital status. Catholic cities such as Munich were more concerned about whether the woman who wanted to immigrate had always been a good Catholic than whether or not she was married, particularly if she wanted to enter a convent. Catholic writers were also more open in their support of women working to convert their Protestant or indifferent husbands than were continental Protestant writers, or even of daughters converting or inspiring their parents. "Young girls will reform their families, their families will reform their provinces, their provinces will reform the world."[19] It was during this period that the confessional box was used more widely, for the Counter-Reformation church saw private confession as a way to combat heresy. Catholic women married to Protestant men could find in the priest hearing their confession a man who could

[19] Quoted in Rapley, *Dèvotes,* p. 157.

give them a source of authority to overrule or disobey their husbands. The husbands recognized this, for court records in Venice indicate that men charged with heresy often beat their Catholic wives after they came home from confession.

England and Ireland provided the most dramatic example of the importance of Catholic women's domestic religious activities. In 1559 Queen Elizabeth ordered that everyone attend services in the Anglican church or be penalized with fines or imprisonment. Many English and Irish Catholics outwardly conformed, but others did not, becoming what were termed recusants. Among these were a large percentage of women, who posed a special problem for royal officials. A single woman or widow found guilty of recusancy could be fined, but a married women, according to common law, controlled no property, and imprisoning her would disrupt her family life and harm her husband, who might not even share her religious convictions. The crown tried a variety of tactics to solve the problem, but only the most adamant Protestant men were willing to back measures that would allow a wife to be legally responsible as an individual for her religious choices and put her husband's property at risk. Catholic husbands often outwardly conformed and attended services, leaving their wives to arrange for private masses held in the home, or even to shelter illegal Catholic missionaries. A few women, such as Margaret Clitherow and Anne Line, were executed for their Catholic faith, but most recusant women were able to avoid strict punishment. Because of this, while continental Catholicism was becoming increasingly parish-oriented after the Council of Trent, Catholicism in England and Ireland grew increasingly domestic. As stories were collected about the persecution of Catholics, a new type of Catholic heroine emerged – capable, benevolent, intelligent, and in many ways crafty in her dealings with authorities; an idealization, but one modeled on real recusant women, for judges and the Privy Council frequently complained about the influence such women had on their husbands, children, and servants.

Beginning in the seventeenth century, lay women in some parts of Europe were slowly able to create what had been so forcibly forbidden to religious women – a community of women with an active mission out in the world. The *kloppen* of the Spanish Netherlands did this on a small scale, and the Daughters of Charity, begun by Vincent de Paul and Mademoiselle de Gras, spread this model more broadly; though both founders privately thought of the group as a religious community, they realized that outwardly maintaining secular status was the only thing that would allow them to serve the poor and ill. The Daughters took no public vows and did not wear religious habits, and constantly stressed that they would work only where invited by a bishop or priest. This sub-version of the rules was successful, for the Daughters of Charity received papal approval and served as the model for other women's communities that emphasized educating the poor or girls; by 1700 numerous teaching and charitable "congregations" were found throughout Catholic Europe. They explicitly used the Virgin Mary as their model, stressing that she, too, had served as a missionary when she had visited her cousin Elizabeth during Elizabeth's pregnancy with John the Baptist, revealing to Elizabeth that they would both give birth to extraordinary sons.

The Daughters of Charity and other congregations were often backed by larger women's religious confraternities, in which elite women supported a congregation financially or engaged in charitable works themselves. Such confraternities were patterned after the much more common men's confraternities, which had been founded by Jesuits as a key part of both combating Protestantism and deepening Catholic spiritual life. Their popularity among Catholic women showed that women continued to have a desire for religious life and activities not connected with the household, just as they had had in pre-Reformation Christianity. Congregations and confraternities provided women with companionship, devotional practices, and an outlet for their energies beyond the household, and may partly be responsible for women's greater loyalty to the church with the growing secularism of the eighteenth century. The choice that the Council of Trent had attempted to impose on women, *maritus aut murus* (a husband or a cloister), was simply not acceptable to many women, and had by the seventeenth century been transformed by them into a range of religious options.

The seventeenth and early eighteenth centuries

Orthodox Christianity in eastern Europe did not experience a permanent division in the sixteenth century as did western Christianity, although during the seventeenth century, a number of reformers emerged in the Russian Orthodox Church. Like both Protestants and Catholics who were their inspiration, they wanted to strengthen the role of the clergy in parish life and rid popular piety of its – to their eyes – non-Christian elements and immoral excesses. Church ceremonies became an increasingly important part of weddings, and confession and penance were required. The consent of the spouses and their parents were required for a valid marriage, and divorce was allowed, for incompatability, drunkenness, and violence as well as adultery, though it was frowned on, as was remarriage. Modest reforms in church liturgy, prayers, and rituals advocated by some Orthodox leaders – which would make them more like those of western Christianity – were violently opposed by those who wanted to stay with traditional practices, termed Old Believers. Old Believers were convinced that the reforms were the work of the Antichrist and that the Apocalypse was at hand. Consequently they saw little purpose in marriage and procreation, although they moderated this position when it became apparent that the end of the world was more distant than they had originally calculated. Because they cast the tsar and the government as the "spirit of the Antichrist" and rejected their authority, they were subjected to persecution, often severe. Some Old Believers chose the route of martyrdom, usually by self-immolation; others fled to the fringes of the enormous Russian Empire or even abroad; still others found ways of accommodation, politically and ideologically, with the Russian state.

The modest adoption of western practices which so horrified Old Believers paled in comparison with those demanded in the late seventeenth century by tsar Peter I (ruled 1682–1725), who became known as Peter the Great. Peter was intent on modernizing and westernizing Russia, in order to make it a larger and more powerful state. To this end he engaged in nearly constant warfare, and so favored anything that would increase the Russian population. Peter was convinced that unhappy marriages produced fewer children, so in 1722 he added his voice to that of the Orthodox Church forbidding forced marriages at all social levels. Landlords were not to force their serfs to marry against their wishes – a common practice despite church opposition – and elite women were to appear in public and have a voice in the choice of their spouse. The state established foundling homes, and encouraged desperate mothers to bring their newborns there, instead of abandoning their babies or practicing infanticide, which was criminalized. Peter regarded marriages between social equals as preferable, and so required spouses to be of the same social class. Religious differences, on the other hand, were not an issue; over the objections of the church, he allowed marriages between spouses of different Christian denominations, demanding only that the children be baptized into the Orthodox faith. Because Peter saw no purpose in wasting human resources on monastic life, he forbade physically capable men and women of childbearing years from taking vows.

Although the church and state of Peter's era issued many new regulations, it proved much more difficult to alter ingrained attitudes and behavior. Nobles successfully lobbied Peter's successors to undo some of his laws concerning parental consent to marriage and effectively prevented their serfs from marrying. Rules concerning entrance into monasteries were relaxed, and displaced middle-aged women in particular sought this alternative. Orthodox convents continued to house a wide range of women, as they had in the Middle Ages, and their abbesses were powerful individuals. The spiritual life in these convents is only beginning to be studied, and we will no doubt learn more in the future about their residents' religious aims and ideas.

In contrast to eastern Europe, we know a great deal about women's religious ideas in western Europe during the seventeenth and eighteenth centuries. Some analysts see this period as one in which western European religion was feminized, in the same way that American religious life was feminized in the nineteenth century. Large numbers of people thought the established churches, both Protestant and Catholic, had lost their spiritual vigor, and turned to groups that emphasized personal conversion, direct communication with God, and moral regeneration. Some of these groups survived only briefly, others became involved in social and political changes, such as the Quakers and other radical sects active during the English Civil War, others ultimately shaped the institutionalized churches, such as the Quietists and Jansenists, and others became institutionalized themselves, such as the pietists. Many of these groups were inspired by or even founded by women, and had a disproportionate number of women among their followers. This female influence was recognized by contemporaries and seen as a reason for criticism. Among the "errors, heresies, blasphemies and pernicious practices of the sectaries," described by Thomas Edwards in *Gangraena* (London, 1646) was the fact that they allowed women to preach. Johann Feustking, a German theologian, turned his attention entirely to women in *Gynaeceum Haeretico Fanaticum* (Frankfurt and Leipzig, 1704), spending 700 pages describing, as his full title reads, the "false prophetesses, quacks, fanatics and other sectarian and frenzied female persons through whom God's church is disturbed."

The uncertainty and turmoil surrounding the English Civil War provided the most dramatic field for women's leadership and action, and the hiatus in censorship during the war allowed many religious works by women to be published. As a result, there has been more research on women's religious experiences during this brief period than on any comparable period elsewhere.

Though most Puritan writers and preachers did not break with Anglicans or continental Protestants on the need for wifely obedience or women's secondary status, certain aspects of Puritan theology and practice prepared women for a more active role. All believers, male and female, were to engage in spiritual introspection, and in particular to focus on their experience of conversion. This experience was an indication that one was among the elect, and in more established Puritan communities such as those of New England became a requirement for membership in a congregation. A particularly dramatic conversion could give one a certain amount of power, especially if it resulted in the healing of an illness or a continuing experience of divine revelation. Women's conversion narratives are often very personal and physical, such as that of Sarah Wight published as *The Exceeding Riches of Grace Advanced* (London, 1647): "Now I have my desire; I desired nothing but a crucified Christ and I have him; a crucified Christ, a naked Christ; I have him and nothing else. . . *I am so full of the Creator, that I now can take in none of the Creature. I am filled with heavenly Manna.*"[20] Though Wight appears in some ways as passive, she is discussing her own spiritual development publicly in a way that was new for Protestant women; nuns were the only other women whose spiritual growth and trials had been viewed as at all important, and not even St. Teresa's autobiography made it into print during her lifetime.

Puritans shared something else with St. Teresa, the conviction that prayer was an active force that could influence state affairs. Puritan women (and men) privately and publicly prayed for certain political changes, and were firmly convinced that prayer aided one's family, community, and political allies. For Puritans, who had rejected the efficacy of exorcism, group prayer was the most powerful weapon in cases of possession, and many tracts report on the efficacy of such prayers against that worst of enemies, Satan.

Women's prayers and conversion narratives often grew into more extended prophecies in seventeenth-century England, some of which were described by others (often hostile to the woman or the message) and some of which were published by the women themselves. Many of these were very general warnings to repent, though some were quite specific; Elizabeth Poole, for example, came to a meeting of the leaders of the Parliamentary Army in 1648 with a message from God not to execute the king, and after the execution published a tract foretelling God's judgment on the Army for that action. Some female prophets acted completely independently and made a career of prophecy; Lady Eleanor Douglas published thirty-seven pamphlets during her life, despite frequent imprisonments for sedition. Others belonged to the radical groups such as the Levellers or Fifth Monarchists which were more open to divine revelation in the mouths of untrained persons than more moderate Puritans.

Female prophets were occasionally criticized for speaking out publicly on political and religious matters, but they had Old Testament and clas-

---

[20] Quoted in Barbara Ritter Dailey, "The visitation of Sarah Wight: holy carnival and the revolution of the saints in civil war London," *Church History* 55 (1986), 447.

sical precedents for what they were doing, and were usually viewed in the way they viewed themselves – as mouthpieces of God, as, in the words of some, "impregnated with the Holy Spirit." Women who went beyond prophecy to actual preaching also emphasized the strength of their calling, but this was not enough in the eyes of most observers to justify such a clear break with the deutero-Pauline injunction forbidding women to teach. It is difficult to know how common female preaching actually was during the Civil War decades, for most reports of it come from extremely hostile observers such as Thomas Edwards who were in turn criticized for making up some of their accounts. Women tended to preach spontaneously at informal or clandestine meetings, and their listeners never thought to record the content of their sermons, so it is unclear how much sustained influence they exerted.

Women clearly did have an impact on the spread of more radical religious ideas through two other activities, organizing what were known as "gathered" churches in their own homes and publishing pamphlets. Puritan women had often organized prayer meetings and conventicles in their houses during the early part of the seventeenth century, and after the Restoration (which restored the Anglican Church as the official religion of England when it restored the monarchy) continued to open their homes to Baptists, Presbyterians, Quakers, and other groups. Post-Restoration commentators belittled such groups by pointing out the large number of women they attracted, though again we have few objective records with which to judge the actual gender balance. Political and religious pamphlets authored by women appeared most frequently during the two decades (1641–1660) when censorship was not rigorously enforced, as part of a more general explosion of pamphlet literature by a wide range of authors. Though most female authors deprecate their own abilities and describe themselves as "instruments of God's power," they clearly intended their works to be read by men and felt no limits as to subject matter, delving into complex theological and doctrinal matters and directly challenging the actions of the King or Parliament.

A sense of urgency pervades most women's pamphlets, an urgency that occasionally led women to more overtly political actions. Several times during the Civil War decades, women petitioned Parliament directly; in 1649 hundreds of women petitioned for the release of the Leveller leader John Lilburne, and 7,000 Quaker women signed a petition to Parliament in 1659 for the abolition of tithes, a type of religious tax. The language of the Leveller women clearly indicates that they felt a right to operate as political actors: "We cannot but wonder and grieve that we should appear so despicable in your eyes as to be thought unworthy to Petition or represent our Grievances to this Honourable House.

Have we not an equal interest with the men of the Nation, in those liberties and securities contained in the Petition of Right, and other good Laws of the Land?"[21] As we will discuss more fully in Chapter 8, a statement such as this claiming political rights for women who were not rulers was extremely rare in early modern Europe.

Such actions came to an abrupt end with the Restoration, and most of the radical groups in which women had participated died out. The most important exception to this were the Quakers, who had been the most supportive of women's independent religious actions throughout the decades of the Civil War. John Fox, the founder of the Quakers, did not advocate women's social or political equality, but did support women's preaching and separate women's meetings charged with caring for the poor, ill, prisoners, and children. Quakers taught that the spirit of God did not differentiate between men and women, and advocated qualities for all believers similar to those which most Protestants stressed for women: humility, self-denial, piety, devotion, modesty. These were not to make one weak in the face of persecution, however, and Quakers were the most viciously persecuted of all the radical groups, perhaps because they were the most adamant in proclaiming their beliefs. Quaker women preached throughout England and the English colonies in the New World, and were active as missionaries also in Ireland and continental Europe well into the eighteenth century. They were whipped and imprisoned for preaching, refusing to pay tithes or take oaths, or holding meetings in their houses; no special treatment was accorded women for age, illness, pregnancy, or the presence of young children. Quaker women also published a large number of pamphlets, most of them apocalyptic prophecies or "encouragements" for co-believers, and wrote spiritual autobiographies, which are one of the few sources we have from the seventeenth century written by middle- or lower-class women. Margaret Fell Fox, who eventually married John Fox after years of organizing, preaching, visiting prisoners, and being imprisoned herself for her Quaker beliefs, published *Women's Speaking Justified* in 1669, which argued that Paul's prohibition of women's preaching had only been meant for the "busie-bodies and tatlers" of Corinth, and provided a host of Biblical examples of women who publicly taught others. Fell did not argue for women's equality in secular matters, but for Quakers spiritual matters were more important anyway. The women's meetings she organized gave many women the opportunity to speak in public and to engage in philanthropic activities for persons outside of their own fami-

---

[21] Quoted in Smith, *Reason's Disciples*, p. 55.

lies. Though Quakers as a group became increasingly apolitical in the eighteenth century, social action by Quaker women continued; many of the leaders of the abolitionist and women's rights movements in nineteenth-century America were women who had been brought up as Quakers.

Though many areas of Europe experienced social and political revolts in the seventeenth century (leading some historians to suggest that this was a time of "general crisis"), female religious writers and thinkers on the Continent were generally not involved in them in the way Leveller and Quaker women in England were. Most continental women religious thinkers were mystics and ecstatics, who might have visions of political events, but did not work to bring these about. They tended to emphasize the inner life of the spirit and downplay the importance of the Bible, an ordained clergy, outward ceremonies or sacraments, higher education, and sometimes reason. Jane Lead, for example, wrote that true religious knowledge came only through turning inward and finding one's own inner light; she urged her followers to seek the "virgin wisdom of God" and not go "whoring after Lord Reason." Antoinette Bourignon believed spiritual rebirth more important than baptism so that Jews and Muslims might also be blessed and resurrected; she refused to be associated with any group, saying that the divisions within Christianity were signs of the coming end of the world. Madame Guyon carried this emphasis on interiority further, teaching that one should try to lose one's individual soul in God, reaching inner peace through pure disinterested love of God, an idea generally termed quietism.

Many of these female religious thinkers drew large numbers of followers. Jane Lead organized a circle of like-minded people called the Philadelphian Society; like the Quakers, whose official name is the Society of Friends, she did not want to describe her associates as a "church." Madame Guyon's quietism attracted women and men, including high church officials such as Archbishop Fenelon, who wrote that he had learned more from her than any theologian. Some of the works of female religious writers went through numerous editions and translations, so they were apparently widely read.

Most church and state officials reacted with horror to such women, however, both for their independence in expressing their ideas and for the content of what they were saying or writing. Madam Guyon was imprisoned several times on the orders of Bishop Bossuet, the most powerful conservative French cleric, who was particularly incensed that her quietism, detachment, and lack of concern for external religious structures took her in spiritual terms out of his power; if such ideas spread further, wrote Bossuet, they would lead to an intolerable lack of respect for authority. Many women and the groups they were associated with were driven from place to place seeking more tolerant political authorities. Antoinette Bourignon was forced from France to Flanders to Germany and finally to the Netherlands, which provided a refuge for Philadelphians and Quakers as well. The Netherlands was the most tolerant part of Europe so that it was also the most common place of publication for the works of these women and those of other radical religious thinkers.

Not all continental female religious thinkers were mystics, however. Anna Hoyer was similar to Jane Lead and Madame Guyon in coming to her religious insights after being widowed with children to care for, and in suffering persecution for them, but she confronted the established state church leaders much more directly. She published sharp religious-political satire, blaming the Thirty Years' War on the "devil pastors," and attacking the Lutheran clergy for laxness, pride, greed, and trust in wordly learning. She often used literary forms normally supportive of traditional piety, such as the conversation between parent and child, but turned them into bitter polemical pieces. In her *Spiritual Conversation Between a Mother and Child About True Christianity* the mother first asks "'What did you learn about salvation and the Bible in church today?' 'Nothing.' 'About the prophets and Revelation?' 'Nothing.'" The mother then launches into a harsh critique of the clergy's monopoly of religious discourse despite their lack of spiritual understanding:

> No one is allowed to contradict him
> Even if he says that crooked is straight
> And black is white. He must be right.[22]

In her other writings as well, Hoyer recommends that women act independently to make sure their children and others gain true religious knowledge, and not put too much trust in male institutions or authorities. She followed her own recommendation, gathering a group of like-minded associates as well as publishing, for which she was forced out of her native Schleswig-Holstein and eventually found refuge in Sweden.

Though many groups that welcomed female religious thinkers were quite small and dismissed by their contemporaries (and some modern historians) as "enthusiastic" or "fringe," women were also instrumental in several broader movements, though their contributions were often minimized by later historians of these movements. Jansenism, a movement primarily within the French Catholic church which empha-

---

[22] Gottfried Arnold, *Unpartheiische Kirchen und Ketzerhistorie. . .* (Frankfurt, Fritschens sel. Erben, 1729), p. 106. My translation.

sized personal holiness and spiritual renewal, attracted many women, and the convent of Port Royal in Paris became the movement's spiritual center. Nuns from Port Royal became renowned for their piety, and their help was sought all over France for the reform of convent discipline. Jansenism was not simply a movement for clergy, however, but also for lay people, for it advocated lay reading of and meditation on Scripture, lay participation in church services, and scrupulous attention to morality; Jansenists also discouraged frequent communion for the faithful. This last idea and disagreements about predestination led it into conflict with the Jesuits, and the movement was condemned in the papal bull *Unigenitus* (1713). Most Jansenist priests fled France, leaving Jansenist nuns to officiate at their own services and sometimes to suffer papal interdict for refusing to accept the bull; the nuns at Port Royal were expelled. Jansenist laity continued to hold underground prayer meetings, and there is some evidence that women read and commented on Scripture at these meetings; women were also imprisoned for distributing prohibited Jansenist literature. Despite its official prohibition, Jansenism continued to shape the religious life of many women in France, encouraging them not only to become literate but to become frequent readers, to develop their children's spiritual lives through family devotions, and to accept Catholic doctrine not simply as a matter of emotional commitment and habit, but also of intellectual conviction.

In Germany, the movement termed pietism was in some ways similar to Jansenism in that both emphasized morality, Bible study, and personal spiritual regeneration. The history of pietism is often written as the history of its best-known leaders, Philipp Spener and August Francke, but in many ways it was a grass-roots movement of lay people who met in prayer circles and conventicles, among which were many women. Eleanore Petersen organized several pietist circles and wrote a huge number of tracts, including a commentary on the Book of Revelations. Erdmuthe von Zinzendorf was largely responsible for the financial security and day-to-day operations of her husband's colony of Moravian Brethren at Herrnhut in Germany. Count von Zinzendorf had orginally wanted the Herrnhutters to be simply a group within the Lutheran Church which encouraged deeper religious sensibilities, but they became instead a separate body, and Zinzendorf was banished from Germany for more than ten years and traveled to America and England to set up Moravian congregations. During this time Erdmuthe handled missionary work in Denmark and Livonia, established orphanages and ran the home colony; her dowry and family money provided most of the support for all Herrnhutter activities.

Some of Count von Zinzendorf's writings, like those of other pietist and mystic men, may be seen as more positive toward women than those of more traditional Protestant or Catholic writers. Zinzendorf thought, for example, that Adam was androgynous before the fall and that men had to recover the feminine part of their soul in order to be saved. For many pietists, Christ was also androgynous; male, yes, but a virgin, so that he was not fully a man. The pietist emphasis on devotion rather than doctrine also led some writers (including Eleanore Petersen as well as male writers) to view women as the clearest embodiment of proper piety. This championing of female or androgynous qualities in theory did not lead to permanent female church leadership in practice, however. Once pietist groups were established, women were informally or formally excluded from leadership roles; in 1764 a Herrnhutter synod explicitly forbade women from all governing offices except the most minor, noting that this would help them control their "desire for power." *(Herrnsucht)* Zinzendorf himself criticized Erdmuthe for her independence, which he called pride; his second wife was a much younger woman who had long been his traveling companion. Gottfried Arnold, a pietist himself and one of the few eighteenth-century historians sympathetic to individuals outside of the state churches, wrote that women had to be particularly careful if they were religious individualists; Satan could easily lead them from religious freedom to sexual license. Pietist historians who did include women such as Eleanore Peterson and Erdmuthe von Zinzendorf in their histories were careful to describe them as "help-mates." Thus two centuries after the Protestant Reformation, and even among those who had greatly benefited from women's independent actions, control of female sexuality and maintenance of female sub-servience were still as important as they had been for Charlotte Arbaleste's consistory.

Jewish and Muslim women's religious life

Judaism in the early modern period did not go through the same type of schism that western Christianity did, but did suffer from increasing repression, restriction, and in some cases outright prohibition; Jews thus gathered in cities that were less hostile, such as those of Italy and the Low Countries. In 1492, Ferdinand and Isabella of Spain ordered all Jews to leave Spain or convert, and during the next several centuries those who converted and their descendants (termed "New Christians") were frequently targets of the Inquisition. Women as well as men were questioned, tortured, physically punished, and in some cases executed, leading Jews in other parts of Europe to make special efforts to help women of Jewish ancestry leave Spain and Portugal. Portuguese Jews in Amsterdam, for example, set up a special dowry fund in 1615 for poor women and girls from the Iberian peninsula who were willing to migrate to Amsterdam, readopt Judaism and marry Jewish men, though women often had to wait ten years before enough money became available for them. Gracia Nasi (1510–1569), who after fleeing Portugal ran her family business from Antwerp, Venice, Ferrara, and Constantinople, helped establish an "underground railway" to get Jews out of Portugal and Spain, and organized a boycott against Ancona when that city began to persecute Jews. She supported rabbis and scholars and encouraged book publications; a number of Jewish scholarly works from the sixteenth century were dedicated to her.

Women were often particularly suspect in the eyes of Spanish authorities because they were responsible for religious rituals that took place in the home or that involved their own bodies, both more difficult to control than the public rituals which were the province of men. This was true not only in Spain, but in all of Europe and in the Spanish New World. Like Christian women, Jewish women were excluded from public religious life; they rarely learned Hebrew, did not receive training in Jewish law *(halakhah)* or religious literature (the Torah and Talmud), and were excluded from rabbinical courts. They did have three very specific religious duties, however: separating a portion of dough each time they baked and burning it in the oven in memory of priestly tithes; lighting the Sabbath candles; avoiding sexual relations with their spouses during menstruation and for seven days afterward.

This last duty, termed *niddah*, fostered a very elaborate group of menstrual laws and practices. The woman herself was responsible to know when she was menstruating, count seven "clean" days after the last issue of blood, and if possible, take a ritual bath *(mikvah)* before beginning sexual relations again. *Niddah* stemmed from ideas of ritual impurity which had originally required a menstruating woman to avoid many other types of contacts along with sexual, but by the medieval and early modern periods only sexual relations and a few other contacts between husband and wife were forbidden. Popular beliefs had also developed which interpreted *niddah* more positively; proper observance was thought to foster conception, easy childbirth, and male children. The first of these actually has biological basis, for most women ovulate roughly fourteen days after the beginning of their menstrual period, the day *niddah* allowed sexual relations again.

Women were not required to take part in public formal prayers and were in some cases excluded from them, but they did develop special voluntary prayers for events that had special meaning for them. These prayers, termed *thkines*, began to be published in the seventeenth century, and we can gain an insight into Jewish women's spiritual lives from them. They were written in Yiddish by a variety of authors, some of whom were probably female and who vary in their level of knowledge of Jewish tradition. They often concern biological and cultural events particularly important for women, such as menstruation, pregnancy, childbirth, baking bread, or visiting cemeteries. Though they were meant to be said in private, they exhibit a sense of community with generations of Jewish women who had done the same thing, and often transform folk rituals not mentioned in Jewish law, such as making candles for Yom Kippur, into true religious duties. This dignified women's folk rituals, and enabled women to compare themselves to priests in their carrying out of religious duties. Unlike much of the religious literature by Christian women during the seventeenth century, the *thkines* were not mystical, for women were excluded from most Jewish mysticism just as they were from official Hebrew prayer services. Jewish mysticism in the early modern period centered on the kabbalah, a group of writings from various ancient authors in which women were generally associated with the demonic; women occasionally took part in mass outbursts of mystical enthusiasm, such as that sparked by the pseudo-Messiah Sabbatai Zevi in the seventeenth century, but were not leaders or even regular participants in the secret meetings (conventicles) held by kabbalists.

Occasionally individual Jewish women did step beyond their domestic religious roles. A few women learned Hebrew, generally from their fathers or brothers, and recited group prayers along with men. Sarra Copia Sullam (1592–1641), who had established a literary salon in Venice, published a pamphlet defending herself against charges that she did not believe in the immortality of the soul, an essential part of both Jewish and Christian teachings. She was accused of plagiarism, for her work was considered too learned to be that of a woman, although several years later some of her literary admirers also wrote in her defense. Women sometimes served as ritual slaughterers, which required a high level of training, though usually they were granted permission only in unusual circumstances such as periods of persecution or disruption when their families might otherwise go hungry. Though Jewish women in Italy were normally confined to a balcony during services, they could and did enter the main floor if they had a specific grievance against one of the male members of the congregation. Women used this opportunity to charge men with abandonment, physical abuse, broken engagements, or the refusal to acknowledge children born out of wedlock, a practice that custom allowed as a sort of appeals court of last resort. Men could also use the service to air their grievances, however, particularly in cases where their wives refused to have intercourse with them.

Public religious activities by Jewish women are even rarer than those of Christian women, however, and, because men were charged with overseeing the early religious training of their sons within the household, domestic religious activities were also not solely women's sphere. As in Christianity, women were responsible for the ultimate destination of their souls; some medieval and early modern popular spiritual works even describe a separate Paradise for women, where they will have the opportunity for prayer, study, and contemplation and not be burdened by domestic responsibilities. No suggestions were made for the establishment of such a place on earth, however, giving such ideas as little practical impact as the concept of spiritual equality had for most Christian women.

Jews lived in many parts of Europe during the early modern period, but Muslims lived primarily in the Iberian peninsula and southeastern Europe, where the Ottoman Turks were expanding their territory. At roughly the same time that they ordered Jews to leave or convert, Spanish and Portuguese authorities also outlawed the practice of Islam, and gave the Inquisition jurisdiction over those suspected of Muslim practices as well as Jewish. Muslims – termed "Moriscos" – made up a large share of the population in many parts of Spain, however, and many lived in rural areas, so that it was difficult for the Inquisition actually to exert control, although persecutions and forced conversions increased throughout the early modern period. Many Moriscos in the Kingdoms of Valencia and Granada in southern Spain spoke only Arabic and had practically no contact with Christians, and Muslim clergy, teachers, and legal authorities continued to operate in these areas.

In places where Islam was more heavily persecuted, such as Aragon, women were extremely important in its survival. Like English recusants and Jews, Spanish Muslim women (termed "Moriscas") carried out religious rituals in their homes and taught them to their children. According to the records of the Inquisition, Moriscas observed the Muslim holy month of Ramadan, performed daily prayers, wore Muslim dress while Morisco men adopted Christian-style clothing, hid religious books and amulets written in Arabic in their clothing and furniture, taught Muslim ideas and practices to Christian women who married Muslim men, and organized funerals, weddings, and other ceremonies. Muslim midwives circumcised baby boys, and failed to report births to Christian priests, as they were required to do. Though they generally stayed away from controversy, a few Moriscas publicly argued with their Christian neighbors about points of theology; through this, or other actions, they came to the attention of the Inquisition. Like Muslim men, they were whipped, imprisoned (often in convents), subjected to rituals of public humiliation, and occasionally executed at ceremonies termed *autos de fe*. In Saragossa, the Inquisitors complained that "the Moriscas of this kingdom are worse than the men, many of whom do not dare drink wine or eat bacon [both practices forbidden to Muslims] or do other Christian things from fear of their wives."[23]

The Inquisition paid special attention to marriages between Christians and Moriscos, which were generally allowed, and at times even promoted, as long as the Muslim spouse converted; in 1548, for example, an edict of the Spanish Crown ordered converted Muslims to marry Old Christians. (Old Christians were those whose ancestors were not known to have been Jewish or Muslim.) At the same time, however, laws that favored "purely" Old Christian families (generally termed "purity of the blood" laws) worked against intermarriage, and also led couples in which the husband was of Muslim background to adopt the wife's Christian surname in order to disguise his Muslim ancestry. In the Turkish areas of southeastern Europe, conversion went the opposite direction, with women who had been Orthodox converting to Islam in order to marry Muslim men. In a few cases Orthodox women who were already married divorced their husbands and married Muslim men, though to do this they had to swear in a Muslim court that they had converted of their own volition and that their husbands had refused conversion. Little is known about the religious practices of either Orthodox or Muslim women in these areas as the Turkish authorities were largely tolerant in matters of religion, and there were thus no investigations comparable to those of the Inquisition.

In Christianity, Judaism, and Islam, the early modern period was a time when the domestic nature of women's acceptable religious activities was reinforced. The proper sphere for the expression of women's religious ideas was a household, whether the secular household of a Jewish, Orthodox, Catholic, Protestant, or Muslim marriage, or the spiritual household of an enclosed Catholic convent. Times of emergency and instability, such as the expulsion of the Jews and Muslims from Spain, the first years of the Protestant Reformation, or the English Civil War, offered women opportunities to play a public religious role, but these were clearly regarded as extraordinary by male religious thinkers and by many of the women who wrote or spoke publicly during these times.

---

[23] Translated and quoted in William Monter, *Frontiers of Heresy: The Spanish Inquisition from the Basque Lands to Sicily* (Cambridge, Cambridge University Press, 1990), p. 227.

Women who were too assertive in expressing themselves during more stable times, or who were too individualistic in their ideas, risked being termed insane (as were Lady Eleanor Douglas and Antoinette Bourignon) or being imprisoned by religious or secular courts (as were Mary Ward and Madame Guyon). Both of these judgments were also leveled against women who were charged with witchcraft, that is, with inverting and destroying, rather than simply improperly reinforcing, religious tradition in Europe. Though many general histories of religious developments in early modern Europe oddly make no mention of witchcraft, our discussion of women's spirit would be highly skewed if we avoided this, and so we will turn to witchcraft as the final chapter in our analysis of women's lives.

Bibliography

Wide-ranging collections of articles provide a good place to begin if you wish an overview of women's role in religion. Some of the best include: Rosemary Radford Ruether, *Religion and Sexism: Images of Woman in the Jewish and Christian Traditions* (New York, Simon and Schuster, 1974); Rosemary Radford Ruether and Eleanore McLaughlin (eds.), *Women of Spirit: Female Leadership in the Jewish and Christian Traditions* (New York, Simon and Schuster, 1979); Richard L. Greaves (ed.), *Triumph Over Silence: Women in Protestant History* (Westport, Conn., Greenwood, 1985); Lynda L. Coon, et al. (eds.), *That Gentle Strength: Historical Perspectives on Women in Christianity* (Charlottesville: University of Virginia Press, 1990); W. J. Shields and Diana Wood (eds.), *Women in the Church*, Studies in Church History, vol. 27 (Oxford, Basil Blackwell, 1990); Judith Baskin (ed.), *Jewish Women in Historical Perspective* (Detroit, Wayne State University Press, 1991); Kari Elizabeth Borreson and Kari Vogt (eds.), *Women's Studies of the Christian and Islamic Traditions: Ancient, Medieval, and Renaissance Foremothers* (Dordrecht, Kluwer, 1993); Daniel Bornstein and Roberto Rusconi (eds.), *Women and Religion in Medieval and Renaissance Italy* (Chicago, University of Chicago Press, 1996). A recent collection focusing only on the Reformation period, with articles about women in many countries, is Sherrin Marshall (ed.), *Women in Reformation and Counter-Reformation Europe: Public and Private Worlds* (Bloomington, Indiana University Press, 1989).

Bibliographies provide another place to look for further information, and include F. Ellen Weaver, "Women and religion in early modern France: a bibliographic essay on the state of the question," *Catholic Historical Review* 67 (1981), 50–59; Merry E. Wiesner, *Women in the Sixteenth Century: A Bibliography*, Sixteenth Century Bibliography, 23 (St. Louis, Center for Reformation Research, 1983); Kathryn Norberg, "The Counter-Reformation and women, religious and lay," in John O'Malley, S.J. (ed.), *Catholicism in Early Modern History: A Guide to Research* (St. Louis, Center for Reformation Research, 1988), pp. 133–46; Merry E. Wiesner, "Studies of women, the family and gender," in William S. Maltby (ed.), *Reformation Europe: A Guide to Research II* (St. Louis, Center for Reformation Research, 1992), pp. 159–87; the *Journal of Feminist*

Studies in Religion, which began publication in 1984, always contains the most current research.

Women in medieval Christianity have been the focus of a number of fascinating studies. Among the most important are: Caroline Bynum, *Jesus as Mother: Studies in the Spirituality of the High Middle Ages* (Berkeley, University of California Press, 1982) and *Holy Feast and Holy Fast: The Religious Significance of Food for Medieval Women* (Berkeley, University of California Press, 1987); Barbara Newman, *From Virile Woman to WomanChrist* (Philadelphia, University of Pennsylvania Press, 1995); Shannon McSheffrey, *Gender and Heresy: Women and Men in Lollard Communities, 1420–1530* (Philadelphia, University of Pennsylvania Press, 1995); Jane Schulenberg, *Forgetful of their Sex: Female Sanctity and Society, ca. 500–1100* (Chicago, University of Chicago Press, 1998). Useful collections of articles include Derek Baker (ed.), *Medieval Women* (Oxford, Basil Blackwell, 1978) and Julius Kirshner and Suzanne Wemple (eds.), *Women of the Medieval World: Essays in Honor of John H. Mundy* (New York and London, Basil Blackwell, 1985). Elizabeth Makowski, *Canon Law and Cloistered Women: Periculoso and Its Commentators 1298–1545* (Washington, D.C., The Catholic University of America Press, 1997) explores ideas about the cloistering of women. Penelope D. Johnson, *Equal in Monastic Profession: Religious Women in Medieval France* (Chicago, University of Chicago Press, 1991), Roberta Gilchrist, *Gender and Material Culture: The Archaeology of Religious Women* (London, Routledge, 1994), Patricia Ranft, *Women and the Religious Life in Premodern Europe* (New York, St. Martin's, 1996), Marilyn Oliva, *The Convent and Community in Late Medieval England: Female Monasteries in the Diocese of Norwich, 1350–1540* (Rochester, N.Y., Boydell & Brewer, 1997) and Bruce Venarde, *Women's Monasticism and Medieval Society: Nunneries in France and England, 890–1215* (Ithaca, Cornell University Press, 1997) explore the actual situation for monastic women, and Katherine L. French, "Maidens' lights and wives' stores: women's parish guilds in late medieval England," *Sixteenth Century Journal* 29 (1998), 399–426 looks at the activities of lay women. Because so many of the records by or about medieval women concern their religious life, most of the suggestions of general works on medieval women mentioned in the bibliography that follows Chapter 1 can also give you information about religion.

Recent scholarship on women and the Reformation began with Roland H. Bainton's three volumes, *Women of the Reformation* (Minneapolis, Augsburg Publishing House, 1971, 1973, 1977), which are completely biographical, but include information on many little-known women. More analytical early studies that still provide important theoretical frameworks include three articles in a special issue of *Archive for Reformation History* 63 (1972): Miriam U. Chrisman, "Women of the Reformation in Strasbourg 1490–1530," Charmarie Jenkins-Blaisdell, "Renée de France between reform and counter-reform," and Nancy Roelker, "The role of noblewomen in the French Reformation"; Nancy Roelker, "The appeal of Calvinism to French noblewomen in the sixteenth century," *Journal of Interdisciplinary History* 2 (1972), 391–418; Natalie Zemon Davis, "City women and religious change," in her *Society and Culture in Early Modern France* (Stanford, Stanford University Press, 1975), pp. 65–96; Patrick Collinson, "The role of women in the English Reformation illustrated by the life and friendships of Anne Locke," in G. J. Cuming (ed.), *Studies in Church History,* vol. 2 (London, Thomas Nelson, 1975), pp. 258–72; Sherrin Marshall (Wyntges), "Women in the Reformation Era," in Renate Bridenthal and Claudia Koonz (eds.), *Becoming Visible: Women in European History*, 1st ed. (Boston, Houghton-Mifflin, 1977), pp. 165–91.

The bibliography that follows Chapter 1 gives many suggestions as to readings on the reformers' ideas about women. In addition to these, Margaret Miles, *Carnal Knowing: Female Nakedness and Religious Meaning in the Christian West* (Boston, Beacon Press, 1989), discusses ideas about the female body and sexuality. John H. Bratt, "The role and status of women in the writings of John Calvin," and Charmarie Jenkins Blaisdell, "Response to Bratt," both in Peter de Klerk (ed.), *Renaissance, Reformation, Resurgence* (Grand Rapids, Calvin Theologial Seminary, 1976) is a good example of disputes that have arisen over how the reformers' ideas are to be interpeted. The ways in which reformers' relationships with women shaped their theology have been discussed in Charmarie Blaisdell, "Calvin's letters to women: the courting of ladies in high places," *Sixteenth Century Journal* 13 (1982), 67–84 and A. Daniel Frankforter, "Elizabeth Bowes and John Knox: a woman and Reformation theology," *Church History* 56 (1987), 333–47. Two good studies of one aspect of popular religious ideas are Ton Brandenburg, "St. Anne and her family: the veneration of St. Anne in connection with concepts of marriage and the family in the early modern period," in Lène Dresen-Coenders (ed.), *Saints and She-Devils: Images of Women in Fifteenth and Sixteenth Centuries* (London, Rubicon, 1987), pp. 101–27 and Kathleen Ashley and Pamela Schiengorn (eds.), *Interpreting Cultural Symbols: St. Anne in Late Medieval Society* (Athens, University of Georgia Press, 1990). Lyndal Roper's "'The common man,' 'the common good,' 'common women': reflections on gender and meaning in the Reformation German commune," *Social History* 12 (1987), 1–21 is the best example of an analysis of the interplay between Reformation ideas and notions of gender.

The actual effects of the Reformation on women's religious and family life have been examined in a number of studies, including several books: Retha Warnicke, *Women of the English Renaissance and Reformation* (Westport, Conne., Greenwood Press, 1983); Lyndal Roper, *The Holy Household: Women and Morals in Reformation Augsburg* (Oxford, Clarendon Press, 1989) and *Oedipus and the Devil: Witchcraft, Sexuality, and Religion in Early Modern Europe* (London, Routledge, 1994); Patricia Crawford, *Women and Religion in England, 1500–1750* (London, Routledge, 1993). Important articles include: Susan C. Karant-Nunn, "Continuity and change: some effects of the Reformation on the women of Zwickau," *Sixteenth Century Journal* 13 (1982), 17–42, "The transmission of Luther's teachings on women and matrimony: the case of Zwickau," *Archive for Reformation History* 77 (1986), 31–46, "The Reformation of women," in Renate Bridenthal, Susan Mosher Stuard, and Merry E. Wiesner, *Becoming Visible: Women in European History*, 3rd ed. (Boston, Houghton-Mifflin, 1998), pp. 175–202; Grethe Jacobsen, "Women, marriage and magisterial Reformation: the case of Malmø, Denmark," in Kyle C. Sessions and Phillip N. Bebb (eds.), *Pietas et Societas: New Trends in Reformation Social History* (Kirksville, Mo., Sixteenth Century Journal Press, 1985), pp. 57–78; Merry E. Wiesner, "Ideology meets the Empire: reformed convents and the Reformation," in Susan Karant-Nunn and Andrew Fix (eds.), *Germania Illustrata: Essays Presented to Gerald Strauss*

(Kirksville, Mo., Sixteenth Century Essays and Studies, 1991), pp. 181–96; Jill Bepler, "Women in German funeral sermons: models of virtue or slice of life?" *German Life and Letters* 44 (1991), 392–403; Jeffrey R. Watt, "Women and the consistory in Calvin's Geneva," *Sixteenth Century Journal* 24 (1993), 429–39; D. Jonathan Grieser, "A tale of two convents: nuns and Anabaptists in Münster, 1533–1535," *Sixteenth Century Journal* 26 (1995), 31–48.

The role of women in the radical Reformation is becoming a focus of much research. Joyce Irwin (ed.), *Womanhood in Radical Protestantism* (New York, E. Mellen, 1979) provides extensive examples of (male) Anabaptist ideas. For analyses, see: Marion Kobelt-Groch, "Why did Petronella leave her husband? Reflections on marital avoidance among the Halberstadt Anabaptists," *Mennonite Quarterly Review* 62 (1988), 26–41; Wes Harrison, "The role of women in Anabaptist thought and practice: the Hutterite experience of the sixteenth and seventeenth centuries," *Sixteenth Century Journal* 23 (1992), 49–70; C. Arnold Snyder and Linda A. Heubert Hecht (eds.), *Profiles of Anabaptist Women: Sixteenth-Century Reforming Pioneers* (Waterloo, Ontario, Wilfried Laurier University Press, 1996); Craig D. Atwood, "Sleeping in the arms of Christ: sanctifying sexuality in the eighteenth-century Moravian church," *Journal of the History of Sexuality* 8 (1997), 25–47.

Studies that focus on the impact of the Reformation on marriage and the family include: Miriam Chrisman, "Family and religion in two noble families: French Catholic and English Puritan," *Journal of Family History* 8 (1983), 190–213; Thomas Max Safley, "Protestantism, divorce, and the breaking of the modern family," in Sessions and Bebb, *Pietas et Societas*, pp. 35–56 and *Let No Man Put Asunder: The Control of Marriage in the German Southwest* (Kirksville, Mo., Sixteenth Century Publishers, 1984); Martin Ingram, *Church Courts, Sex and Marriage in England 1570–1640* (Cambridge, Cambridge University Press, 1987); James R. Farr, "The pure and disciplined body: hierarchy, morality, and symbolism in France during the Catholic Reformation," *Journal of Interdisciplinary History* 21 (1991), 391–414 and *Authority and Sexuality in Early Modern Burgundy* (New York, Oxford University Press, 1995); Jeffrey R. Watt, *The Making of Modern Marriage: Matrimonial Control and the Rise of Sentiment in Neuchâtel, 1550–1800* (Ithaca, Cornell University Press, 1992); Eric Josef Carlson, *Marriage and the English Reformation* (Oxford, Basil Blackwell, 1994); Joel F. Harrington, *Reordering Marriage and Society in Reformation Germany* (Cambridge, Cambridge University Press, 1995); Robert Kingdon, *Adultery and Divorce in Calvin's Geneva* (Cambridge, Mass., Harvard University Press, 1995); Richard Adair, *Courtship, Illegitimacy and Marriage in Early Modern England* (Manchester, Manchester University Press, 1996); Michael F. Graham, *The Uses of Reform: "Godly Discipline" and Popular Behavior in Scotland and Beyond 1560–1610* (Leiden, Brill, 1996); Helen Parish, *Clerical Marriage and the English Reformation: Precedent, Policy and Practice* (London, Ashgate, 2000); Merry E. Wiesner-Hanks, *Christianity and the Regulation of Sexuality in the Early Modern World: Regulating Desire, Reforming Practice* (London, Routledge, 2000).

Changes in engagement and wedding ceremonies have been explored most fully in: Susan C. Karant-Nunn, *The Reformation of Ritual: An Interpretation of Early Modern Germany* (London, Routledge, 1997) and David Cressy, *Birth, Marriage and Death: Ritual, Religion, and the Life-Cycle in Tudor and Stuart*

England (Oxford, Oxford University Press, 1997); see also Lyndal Roper, "Going to church and street: weddings in Reformation Augsburg," *Past and Present* 106 (1985), 62–101.

Women's own religious ideas and actions in religious matters have been discussed in Sherrin Marshall, "Women and religious choices in the sixteenth-century Netherlands," *Archive for Reformation History* 75 (1984), 276–89; Florence Koorn, "Women without vows: the case of the Beguines and Sisters of the Common Life in the northern Netherlands," in E. Schulte van Kessel (ed.), *Women and Men in Spiritual Culture XIV–XVII Centuries: A Meeting of South and North* (The Hague, Staatsuitgeverij, 1986), 135–47; K. E. Christopherson, "Lady Inger and her family: Norway's exemplar of mixed motives in the Reformation," *Church History* 55 (1986), 21–38; Merry E. Wiesner, "Women's response to the Reformation," in R. Po-Chia Hsia, *The German People and the Reformation* (Ithaca, Cornell University Press, 1988), pp. 148–72; Retha Warnicke, "Lady Mildmay's journal: a study in autobiography and meditation in Reformation England," *Sixteenth Century Journal* 22 (1989), 55–68; Elsie Anne McKee, *Reforming Popular Piety in 16th Century Strasbourg: Katherine Schütz Zell and Her Hymnbook,* Studies in Reformed Theology and History, Princeton Theological Seminary 2/4 (Fall 1994), and "Katherina Schütz Zell: Protestant Reformer," in Timothy J. Wengert and Charles W. Brockwell (eds.), *Telling the Churches' Story: Ecumenical Perspectives on Writing Christian History* (Grand Rapids: Eerdmans, 1995), pp. 73–90; Merry E. Wiesner, "Katherine Zell's 'Answer to Ludwig Rabus' as autobiography and theology," *Colloquia Germanica* 28 (1995), 245–54; Paula S. Datsko Barker, "Charitas Pirckheimer: a female humanist confronts the Reformation," *Sixteenth Century Journal* 26 (1995), 259–72; Peter Matheson, "Breaking the silence: women, censorship and the Reformation," *Sixteenth Century Journal* 27 (1996), 97–109 and "A Reformation for women? Sin, grace, and gender in Argula von Grumbach," *Scottish Journal of Theology* 49 (1996), 1–17. Studies of the special opportunities offered to women through martyrdom include Carole Levin, "Women in the *Book of Martyrs* as models of behavior in Tudor England," *International Journal of Women's Studies* 4 (1981), 196–207; John Klassen, "Women and the family among Dutch Anabaptist martyrs," *Mennonite Quarterly Review* 60 (1986), 548–71; Ellen Macek, "The emergence of a feminine spirituality in the *Book of Martyrs,*" *Sixteenth Century Journal* 19 (1988), 63–80; Jenifer Umble, "Women and choice: an examination of the *Martyr's Mirror,*" *Mennonite Quarterly Review* 64 (1990), 135–45.

There are several book-length studies in English on women and the Catholic Reformation, including: Elizabeth Rapley, *The Dévotes: Women and Church in Seventeenth-Century France* (Montreal and Kingston, McGill-Queen's University Press, 1990); Craig Harline, *The Burdens of Sister Margaret: Private Lives in a Seventeenth-century Convent* (New York, Doubleday, 1994); Ronald E. Surtz, *Writing Women in Late Medieval and Early Modern Spain: The Mothers of Saint Teresa of Avila* (Philadelphia, University of Pennsylvania Press, 1995); Sherry M. Velasco, *Demons, Nausea and Resistance in the Autobiography of Isabel de Jesús 1611–1682* (Albuquerque, University of New Mexico Press, 1996); Jeanne Cover, IBVM, *Love, The Driving Force: Mary Ward's Spirituality: Its Significance for Moral Theology* (Milwaukee, Marquette University Press, 1997). There are also a number of good articles, including several in Marshall, *Women in Reformation,* cited above, and in Mary G. Giles, *Women in the Inquisition: Spain and the New World* (Baltimore, The Johns Hopkins University Press, 1998). In addition, see Ruth Liebowitz, "Virgins in the service of Christ: the dispute over an active apostolate for women during the Counter-Reformation," in Ruether and McLaughlin, *Women of Spirit,* cited above, pp. 132–52; John Martin, "Out of the shadow: heretical and Catholic women in Renaissance Venice," *Journal of Family History* 10 (1985), 21–33; Marie B. Rowlands, "Recusant women 1560–1640," in Mary Prior (ed.), *Women in English Society 1500–1800* (London, Methuen, 1985), pp. 149–80; E. William Monter, "Women and the Italian Inquisition," in Mary Beth Rose (ed.), *Women in the Middle Ages and the Renaissance* (Syracuse, Syracuse University Press, 1985), pp. 73–87; Phil Kilroy, "Women and the Reformation in seventeenth-century Ireland," in Margaret MacCurtain and Mary O'Dowd, *Women in Early Modern Ireland* (Edinburgh, Edinburgh University Press, 1991); Mary Elizabeth Perry, "Magdalens and Jezebels in Counter-Reformation Spain," in Anne J. Cruz and Mary Elizabeth Perry (eds.), *Culture and Control in Counter-Reformation Spain* (Minneapolis, University of Minnesota Press, 1992); Monica Chojnacka, "Women, charity and community in early modern Venice: the Casa dell Zitelle," *Renaissance Quarterly* 51 (1998), 68–89; Jodi Bilinkoff, "Elite widows and religious expression in early modern Spain: the view from Avila," in Sandra Cavallo and Lyndan Warner (eds.), *Widowhood in Medieval and Early Modern Europe* (London, Longman, 1999); Caroline Bowden, "The abbess and Mrs. Brown: Lady Mary Knatchbull and royalist politics in Flanders in the late 1650s," *Recusant History* 24 (1999); Claire Walker, "Combining Mary and Martha: gender and work in seventeenth-century English cloisters," *Sixteenth Century Journal* 30 (1999), 397–417; Ulrike Strasser, "Bones of contention: cloistered nuns, decorated relics, and the contest over women's place in the public sphere of counter-reformation Munich," *Archive for Reformation History* 90 (1999), 255–88.

The relationship between family politics and women's entry into convents has been explored in: Elizabeth Rapley, "Women and the religious vocation in seventeenth-century France," *French Historical Studies* 18 (1994), 613–31; P. Renée Baernstein, "In widow's habit: women between convent and family in sixteenth-century Milan," *Sixteenth Century Journal* 25 (1994), 787–807; Barbara Diefendorf, "Give us back our children: patriarchal authority and parental consent to religious vocation in early Counter-Reformation France," *Journal of Modern History* 68 (1996), 265–307; Joanne Baker, "Female monasticism and family strategy: the Guises and Saint Pierre de Reims," *Sixteenth Century Journal* 28 (1997), 1091–1108; Thomas Worcester, "'Neither married nor cloistered': blessed Isabelle in Catholic Reformation France," *Sixteenth Century Journal* 30 (1999), 457–76; Jutta Gisela Sperling, *Convents and the Body Politic in Renaissance Venice* (Chicago, University of Chicago Press, 2000). The ways in which nuns expressed their religious ideas through artistic patronage have been explored in: Craig Monson (ed..), *The Crannied Wall: Women, Religion and the Arts in Early Modern Europe* (Ann Arbor, University of Michigan Press, 1992); E. Ann Matter and John Coakley (eds.), *Creative Women in Medieval and Early Modern Italy* (Philadelphia, University of Pennsylvania Press, 1994); Jeryldene M. Wood, *Women, Art, and Spirituality: The Poor Clares of Early Modern Italy* (Cambridge,

Cambridge University Press, 1996). Rudolph M. Bell and Donald Weinstein, *Saints and Society: The Two Worlds of Western Christendom, 1000–1700* (Chicago, University of Chicago, 1982) discusses the differing opportunities for male and female sanctity. Ruth El Saffar, *Rapture Encaged: The Suppression of the Feminine in Western Culture* (London, Routledge, 1994) explores the darker side of monastic life, while JoAnn Kay McNamara, *Sisters in Arms: Catholic Nuns Through Two Millennia* (Cambridge, Harvard University Press, 1996) stresses women's agency in monasticism and includes several chapters on the early modern period.

There are several recent excellent studies of various aspects of the life of St. Teresa, including: Jodi Bilinkoff, *The Avila of St. Theresa* (Ithaca, Cornell University Press, 1989); Alison Weber, *Teresa of Avila and the Rhetoric of Femininity* (Princeton, Princeton University Press, 1990); Janice Mary Luti, *Teresa of Avila's Way* (Collegeville, Minn., Liturgical Press, 1991); Carole Slade, *Saint Teresa of Avila: Author of a Heroic Life* (Berkeley, University of California Press, 1995); Gillian T. W. Ahlgren, *Teresa of Avila and the Politics of Sanctity* (Ithaca, Cornell University Press, 1996). John Sullivan, OCD (ed.), *Carmelite Studies: Centenary of St. Teresa,* Carmelite Studies, 3 (Washington, Institute of Carmelite Studies, 1984) contains a number of useful articles.

Recent studies of *beatas* and "living saints" in southern Europe include: Richard Kagan, *Lucrecia's Dreams: Politics and Prophecy in Sixteenth Century Spain* (Berkeley, University of California Press, 1990); Jodi Bilinkoff, "A Spanish prophetess and her patrons: the case of María de Santo Domingo," *Sixteenth Century Journal* 23 (1992), 21–34; Fulvio Tomizza, *Heavenly Supper: The Story of Maria Janis,* trans. Anne Jacobsen Schutte (Chicago, University of Chicago Press, 1993); Luisa Ciammitti, "One saint less: the story of Angela Mellini, a Bolognese seamstress (1667–17[?])," in Edward Muir and Guido Ruggiero (eds.), *Sex and Gender in Historical Perspective; Selections from Quaderni Storici* (Baltimore, The Johns Hopkins University Press, 1990), 141–76; Gabriella Zarri, "Living saints: a typology of female sanctity in the early sixteenth century," in Bornstein and Rusconi, *Women and Religion in Medieval and Renaissance Italy,* pp. 219–303. Studies of the relationships between female penitents and their confessors include: Rudolph M. Bell, "Telling her sins: male confessors and female penitents in Catholic Reformation Italy," in Coon, *Gentle Strength,* 118–33; Jodi Bilinkoff, "Confessors, penitents, and the construction of identities in early modern Avila," in Barbara B. Diefendorf and Carla Hesse, *Culture and Identity in Early Modern Europe (1500–1800): Essays in Honor of Natalie Zemon Davis* (Ann Arbor, University of Michigan Press, 1993); Patricia Ranft, "A key to Counter-Reformation women's activism: the confessor-spiritual director," *Journal of Feminist Studies in Religion* 10 (1994), 7–26; Stephen Haliczer, *Sexuality in the Confessional: A Sacrament Profaned* (New York, Oxford University Press, 1996).

Women's religious writings from the Reformation period are beginning to see translations and reprints. Electa Arenal and Stacey Schlau, *Untold Sisters: Hispanic Nuns in their Own Works* (Albuquerque, University of New Mexico Press, 1989) provides long selections in both Spanish and English from the works of many Spanish and New World nuns, as well as interpretations of their writings. Elsie Anne McKee, *Katharina Schütz Zell* (Leiden, Brill, 1999) includes one volume of biography and interpretation (Vol. 1: The Life and Thought of a

Sixteenth-Century Reformer) and one of edited texts (Vol. 2: The Writings: A Critical Edition). Peter Matheson has edited and translated, *Argula von Grumbach: A Woman's Voice in the Reformation* (Edinburgh, T. & T. Clark, 1995), and Dayle Seidenspinner-Núñez, *The Writings of Teresa de Cartagena* (Rochester, Boydell & Brewer, 1998). Two new series include translations of women's religious writings. The Other Voice in Early Modern Europe, edited by Albert Rabil and Margaret King, and published by the University of Chicago Press, has issued or will soon issue: Cecelia Ferrazzi, *Autobiography of an Aspiring Saint*, ed. and trans. Anne Jacobson Schutte (1996); Antonia Pulci, *Florentine Drama for Convent and Festival*, ed. and trans. James Wyatt Cook and Barbara Collier Cook (1996); Bartolomea Riccoboni, *Spiritual Letters*, ed. and trans. Daniel Bornstein (2000); Lucrezia Tornabuoni, *Sacre Rappresentazioni*, ed. and trans. Jane Tylus (2001). Reformation Texts with Translation (1350–1600) Women of the Reformation Series, edited by Kenneth Hagen and Merry Wiesner-Hanks and published by Marquette University Press, has issued or will soon issue: Merry Wiesner-Hanks and Joan Skocir (ed. and trans.), *Convents Confront the Reformation: Catholic and Protestant Nuns in Germany* (1996); Elizabeth Rhodes (ed. and trans.), *"This Tight Embrace": Luise de Carvajal y Mendoza* (2000), Hermoine Joldersma and Louis Grijp (eds. and trans.), *"Elisabeth's Manly Courage": Testimonials and Songs by and about Martyred Anabaptist Women* (2001).

Among all topics from the seventeenth and early eighteenth centuries, women's role in radical sects in England has received the most attention. This began with Ethyn Morgan Williams, "Women preachers in the Civil War," *Journal of Modern History* 1 (1929), 561–69 and Keith Thomas, "Women and the Civil War sects," *Past and Present* 13 (1958), 42–62 and has continued with Dorothy Ludlow, "Shaking patriarchy's foundations: sectarian women in England, 1641–1700," in Greaves, *Triumph Over Silence*, cited above, pp. 93–123; Barbara Ritter Dailey, "The visitation of Sarah Wight: holy carnival and the revolution of the saints in civil war London," *Church History* 55 (1986), 438–55; Margaret George, *Women in the First Capitalist Society: Experiences in Seventeenth-Century England* (Urbana, University of Illinois Press, 1988); Phyllis Mack, *Visionary Women: Ecstatic Prophecy in Seventeenth-Century England* (Berkeley, University of California Press, 1992); Diane Watt, *Sectaries of God: Women Prophets in Late Medieval and Early Modern England* (Rochester, N.Y., Boydell & Brewer, 1997). Quaker women have been especially well studied, and their writings reprinted and analyzed. See: Emily Manners, *Elizabeth Hooton: First Quaker Woman Preacher (1600–1672)* (London, Headley Bros., 1914); Catherine La Courreye Blecki, "Alice Hayes and Mary Penington: personal identity within the tradition of Quaker spiritual autobiography," *Quaker History* 65 (1976), 19–31; Phyllis Mack, "Feminine behavior and radical action: Franciscans, Quakers, and the followers of Gandhi," *Signs* 11 (1986), 457–77 and "Teaching about gender and spirituality in early English Quakerism," *Women's Studies* 19 (1991), 223–38; Bonnelyn Young Kunze, *Margaret Fell and the Rise of Quakerism* (Stanford, Stanford University Press, 1994); Catherine M. Wilcox, *Theology and Women's Ministry in Seventeenth-Century English Quakerism: Handmaids of the Lord* (London, E. Mellen, 1995). For the religious writings of Englishwomen who were not Quakers, see: Vera Camden (ed.), *The Narratives of the Persecutions of Agnes Beaumont* (East Lansing, Mich., Colleagues Press,

1991); Esther S. Cope, *Handmaid of the Holy Spirit: Dame Eleanor Davies, Never So Mad a Ladie* (Ann Arbor, University of Michigan Press, 1993); Effie Botonaki, "Seventeenth-century Englishwomen's spiritual diaries: self-examination, covenanting, and account keeping," *Sixteenth Century Journal* 30 (1999), 3–22.

Continental developments have been studied in George Balsama, "Madame Guyon, heterodox," *Church History* 42 (1973): 350–65; B. Robert Kreiser, "Religious enthusiam in early 18th-century Paris: The convulsionaries of Saint-Médard," *Catholic Historical Review* 61 (1975), 353–85; Marie-Florine Bruneau, "The writing of history as fiction and ideology: the case of Madame Guyon," *Feminist Issues* 5 (1985), 27–38; Elissa Weaver, "Erudition, spirituality, and women: the Jansenist contribution," in Marshall, *Women in Reformation,* cited above, pp. 189–206; Kathleen Foley-Beining, *The Body and Eucharistic Devotion in Catharina Regina von Greiffenberg's "Meditations"* (Columbia, S.C., Camden House, 1997). Studies of Anna Hoyer or German pietist women are all to date in German.

There are beginning to be a few studies in English of women in eastern European religious life. See: Marie A. Thomas, "Managerial roles in the Suzdal'skii Pokrovski convent during the seventeenth century," *Russian History* 7 (1980), 92–112 and "Muscovite convents in the seventeenth century," *Russian History* 10 (1983), 230–42; Georg Michels, "Muscovite elite women and Old Belief," *Harvard Ukrainian Studies* 19 (1995), 428–50.

Along with the collection edited by Baskin, there are several other good articles on the experiences of early modern Jewish women, especially Chava Weissler, "The traditional piety of Ashkenazic women," in Arthur Greene (ed.), *Jewish Spirituality II* (New York, Crossroad, 1987), pp. 245–75 and "'For women and for men who are like women': the construction of gender in Yiddish devotional literature," *Journal of Feminist Studies in Religion* 5 (1989), 7–25; Howard Adelman, "Rabbis and reality: public activities of Jewish women in Italy during the Renaissance and Catholic Restoration," *Jewish History* 5 (1992); Deborah Hertz, "Women at the edge of Judaism: female converts in Germany, 1600–1750," in Menachem Mor (ed.), *Jewish Assimilation, Acculturation and Accommodation: Past Traditions, Current Issues and Future Prospects* (Lanham, Md., University Press of America, 1992), pp. 87–109. Gracia Nasi has received full biographical treatment in Cecil Roth, *The House of Nasi: Dona Gracia* (Philadelphia, Jewish Publication Society of America, 1948).

Muslim women in Europe are just beginning to receive the attention of scholars. See: Mary Elizabeth Perry, "Behind the veil: moriscas and the politics of resistance and survival," in Magdalena S. Sánchez and Alain Saint-Saëns (eds.), *Spanish Women in the Golden Age: Images and Realities* (Westport, Conn., Greenwood Press, 1996); several of the essays in Gavin R. G. Hambly (ed.), *Women in the Medieval Islamic World: Power, Patronage, and Piety* (New York, St. Martin's, 1998). For the Ottomans, see: Leslie Peirce, *The Imperial Harem: Women and Sovereignty in the Ottoman Empire* (New York, Oxford University Press, 1993); Judith Tucker, *In the House of the Law: Gender and Islamic Law in Ottoman Syria and Palestine* (Berkeley, University of California Press, 1998). For studies of Muslim women more generally, see: Nikki R. Keddie and Beth Baron (eds.), *Women in Middle Eastern History: Shifting Boundaries in Sex and Gender* (New Haven: Yale University Press, 1991); Judith Tucker, *Gender and Islamic History* (Washington D.C., American Historical Association, 1995); Amire El Azhary Sonbol (ed.), *Women, the Family and Divorce Laws in Islamic History* (Syracuse, Syracuse University Press, 1996).

7 Witchcraft

As for the first question, why a greater number of witches is found in the fragile feminine sex than among men. . . the first reason is, that they are more credulous, and since the chief aim of the devil is to corrupt faith, therefore he rather attacks them. . . the second reason is, that women are naturally more impressionable, and. . . the third reason is that they have slippery tongues, and are unable to conceal from their fellow-women those things which by evil arts they know. . . But the natural reason is that she is more carnal than a man, as is clear from her many carnal abominations. And it should be noted that there was a defect in the formation of the first woman, since she was formed from a bent rib, that is, a rib of the breast, which is bent as it were in a contrary direction to a man. And since through this defect she is an imperfect animal, she always deceives. . . And this is indicated by the etymology of the word; for *Femina* comes from *Fe* and *Minus,* since she is ever weaker to hold and preserve the faith. . . To conclude. All witchcraft comes from carnal lust, which is in women insatiable.

> *Malleus Maleficarum* (1486) translated and quoted in Alan C. Kors and Edward Peters (eds.), *Witchcraft in Europe 1100–1700: A Documentary History* (Philadelphia, University of Pennsylvania Press, 1972), pp. 114–127.

It is commonly the nature of women to be timid and to be afraid of everything. That is why they busy themselves so much about witchcraft and superstititions and run hither and thither, uttering a magic formula here and a magic formula there.

> Sermon by Martin Luther on I Peter, translated and quoted in Sigrid Brauner, "Martin Luther on witchcraft: a true reformer?" in Jean R. Brink, et al. (eds.), *The Politics of Gender in Early Modern Europe,* Sixteenth Century Essays and Studies, 12 (Kirksville, Mo., Sixteenth Century Journal Publishers, 1989), p. 34.

And then the Devil said, "Thee art a poor overworked body. Will thee be my servant and I will give thee abundance and thee shall never want."

> Confession of Bessie Wilson, quoted in Christina Larner, *Enemies of God: The Witch Hunt in Scotland* (Baltimore, The Johns Hopkins University Press, 1981), p. 95.

These three statements, the first by two Dominican monks in the most influential witch-hunters' manual of the early modern period, the second by Martin Luther in a sermon on Christian marriage, and the third by a Scottish woman during her interrogation for witchcraft, represent widely varying assessments of the reasons why women were so much more likely to be accused and found guilty of witchcraft during the early modern period. Though they disagree, the three things they point to – sex, fear, and poverty – can in many ways be seen as the three most important reasons why between 75 and 85 percent of those questioned, tried, and executed for witchcraft after 1500 were women.

Anthropologists and historians have demonstrated that nearly all premodern societies believe in witchcraft and make some attempts to control witches. It was only in early modern central and northern Europe and the English colony in Massachusetts, however, that these beliefs led to wide-scale hunts and mass executions. Because so many records have been lost or destroyed, it is difficult to make an estimate for all of Europe, but most scholars agree that during the sixteenth and seventeenth centuries somewhere between 100,000 and 200,000 people were officially tried and between 50,000 and 100,000 executed. Given the much smaller size of the European population in comparison with today, these are enormous numbers.

Explanations for the witch hunts

This dramatic upsurge in witch trials, often labeled the "Great Witch Hunt" or the "Witch Craze," has been the subject of a huge number of studies during the last thirty years, and a variety of explanations have been suggested. Some scholars have chosen to emphasize intellectual factors: During the late Middle Ages, Christian philosophers and theologians developed a new idea about the most important characteristics of a witch. Until that period in Europe, as in most cultures throughout the world, a witch was a person who used magical forces to do evil deeds (*maleficia*). One was a witch, therefore, because of what one *did*, causing injuries or harm to animals and people. This notion of witchcraft continued in Europe, but to it was added a demonological component. Educated Christian thinkers in some parts of Europe began to view the essence of witchcraft as making a pact with the devil, a pact that required the witch to do the devil's bidding. Witches were no longer simply people who used magical power to get what they wanted, but people used by the devil to do what *he* wanted. (The devil is always described and portrayed visually as male.) Witchcraft was thus not a question of what one *did*, but of what one *was*, and proving that a witch had committed maleficia was no longer necessary for conviction. Gradually this demonological or Satanic idea of witchcraft was fleshed out, and witches were thought to engage in wild sexual orgies with the devil, fly though the night to meetings called sabbats which parodied the Mass, and steal communion wafers and unbaptized babies to use in their rituals. Some demonological theorists also claimed that witches were organized in an international conspiracy to overthrow Christianity, with a hierarchy modeled on the hierarchy of angels and archangels constructed by Christian philosophers to give order to God's assistants. Witchcraft was thus spiritualized, and witches became the ultimate heretics, enemies of God.

This demonology was created by Catholic thinkers during the fifteenth century, and is brought together in the *Malleus Maleficarum (The Hammer of [Female] Witches)*, quoted above, written by two German Dominican inquisitors, Heinrich Krämer and Jacob Sprenger, and published in 1486. This book was not simply a description of witchcraft, however, but a guide for witch-hunters, advising them how to recognize and question witches. It was especially popular in central Europe, and the questions that it taught judges and lawyers to ask of witches were asked over a large area; the fact that they often elicited the same or similar answers fueled the idea that witchcraft was an international conspiracy. Though witch trials died down somewhat during the first decades after the Protestant Reformation when Protestants and Catholics were busy fighting each other, they picked up again more strongly than ever about 1560. Protestants rejected many Catholic teachings, but not demonology, and the *Malleus* was just as popular in Protestant areas as Catholic. Protestants may have felt even more at the mercy of witches than Catholics, for they rejected rituals such as exorcism which Catholics believed could counter the power of a witch. The Reformations may have contributed to the spread of demonological ideas among wider groups of the population, for both Catholics and Protestants increased their religious instruction of lay people during the sixteenth century. As part of their program of deepening popular religious understanding and piety, both Protestants and Catholics attempted to suppress what the elites viewed as superstition, folk belief, and more open expressions of sexuality; some historians, most notably Robert Muchembled, view the campaign against witches as part of a larger struggle by elite groups to suppress popular culture, to force rural residents to acculturate themselves to middle-class urban values. The fact that women were the preservers and transmitters of popular culture, teaching their children magical sayings and rhymes along with more identifiably Christian ones, made them particularly suspect.

The Reformation also plays a role in political explanations of the upsurge in witch trials. Christina Larner has effectively argued that with the Reformation, Christianity became a political ideology, and rulers felt compelled to prove their piety and the depth of their religious commitment to their subjects and other rulers. They could do this by fighting religious wars or by cracking down on heretics and witches within their own borders. Because many of the people actually accused or tried were old, poor women, political authorities felt compelled to stress the idea of an international conspiracy of witches so as not to look foolish and to justify the time, money, and energy spent on hunting witches. Witchcraft was used as a symbol of total evil, total hostility to the community, the state, the church, and God. Only when authorities came to be more concerned with purely secular aims such as nationalism, the defense of property, or the creation of empires did trials for witchcraft cease.

Legal changes were also instrumental in causing, or at least allowing for, massive witch trials. One of these was a change from an accusatorial legal procedure to an inquisitorial procedure. In the former, a suspect knew her accusers and the charges they had brought, and an accuser could in turn be liable for trial if the charges were not proven; in the latter, legal authorities themselves brought the case. This change made people much more willing to accuse others, for they never had to take personal responsibility for the accusation or face the accused's relatives. Inquisitorial procedure involved intense questioning of the suspect, often with torture, and the areas in Europe that did not make this change saw very few trials and almost no mass panics. Inquisitorial procedure came into Europe as part of the adoption of Roman law, which also (at least in theory) required the confession of a suspect before she or he could be executed. This had been designed as a way to keep innocent people from death, but in practice in some parts of Europe led to the adoption of ever more gruesome means of inquisitorial torture; torture was also used to get the names of additional suspects, as most lawyers trained in Roman law firmly believed that no witch could act alone.

The use of inquisitorial procedure did not always lead to witch-hunts, however. The most famous Inquisitions in early modern Europe, those in Spain, Portugal, and Italy, were in fact very lenient in their treatment of those accused of witchcraft: the Inquisition in Spain executed only a handful of witches, the Portuguese Inquisition only one, and the Roman Inquisition none, though in each of these areas there were hundreds of cases. Inquisitors firmly believed in the power of the devil and were no less misogynist than other judges, but they doubted very much whether the people accused of doing maleficia had actually made a pact with the devil that gave them special powers. They viewed them not as diabolical devil-worshippers, but as superstitious and ignorant peasants who should be educated rather than executed. Their main crime was not heresy, but rather undermining the church's monopoly on supernatural remedies by claiming they had special powers. Thus Inquisitors set witchcraft within the context of false magical and spiritual claims, rather than within the context of heresy and apostasy, and sent the accused home with a warning and a penance. This view was not shared by Catholic authorities in central and northern Europe, however. The most eminent demonologists of the late sixteenth century were Catholic, including the French jurist Jean Bodin and the Flemish Jesuit Martin Del Rio, and certain parts of Catholic Europe, such as the Duchy of Lorraine in eastern France along with the Rhineland and territories ruled by prince-bishops in Germany, saw mass panics and the execution of hundreds or thousands of people. In these areas, as well as in the Protestant areas that saw mass trials, secular or bishop's courts using inquisitorial procedure proved much deadlier than the Inquisition itself.

Many historians see social and economic changes as also instrumental in the rise of witch trials. Europe entered a period of dramatic inflation during the sixteenth century and continued to be subject to periodic famines resulting from bad harvests; increases in witch accusations generally took place during periods of dearth or destruction caused by religious wars. This was also a time when people were moving around more than they had in the previous centuries, when war, the commercialization of agriculture, enclosure, and the lure of new jobs in the cities meant that villages were being uprooted and the number of vagrants and transients increased. These changes led to a sense of unsettledness and uncertainty in values, with people unwilling or unable to assist their neighbors, yet still feeling they should. The initial accusation in many witch trials often came from people who had refused to help a fellow villager, and then blamed later misfortune on her anger or revenge; Keith Thomas has suggested that in such a scenario, witchcraft accusations were used as a way of assuaging guilt over uncharitable conduct. This explanation can help us understand the first accusation in a trial, but not the mass trials that might involve scores or hundreds of people.

Demographic changes may have also played a part. During the sixteenth century, the age at first marriage appears to have risen, and the number of people who never married at all increased. The reasons for these changes are not entirely clear, but this meant that there was a larger number of women unattached to a man, and therefore more suspect in the eyes of their neighbors. Female life expectancy may also have risen during the sixteenth century, either in absolute terms or at least in comparison with male life expectancy during this period when many men lost their lives in religious wars.

Misogyny clearly played a role in shaping the witch-hunts, and some analysts view hatred or suspicion of women as the main driving force. Mary Daly, for example, views the witch-hunts as an attempt by male authorities to suppress independent women, especially those who had spiritual knowledge or were midwives, herbalists, or healers. Marianne Hester has suggested that the issue of male control of medicine may be too narrow, and argues that the emphasis should be placed on male sexual violence and the maintenance of male power through the eroticization of male-female relations. Other historians acknowledge the role of misogyny, but note that negative ideas about women were just as prevalent in areas that saw few trials, such as southern Europe, as in areas that saw many. They stress that local factors played a far greater role in shaping the level of persecution and the gender balance among the accused. These local factors could include gender relations, however, as Carol Karlsen notes in her study of the New England witchcraft persecutions; she finds that many of the women accused of witchcraft were widows or unmarried women who were a potential challenge to male economic control as they had inherited property or might do so, and that older women received harsher sentences than younger.

Medical issues have also been part of another area of investigation related to the witch craze. Witches were often accused of mixing magic potions and creams, leading some scholars to explore the role that hallucinogenic drugs such as ergot and belladonna may have played, particularly in inducing feelings of flying. Such hallucinogens could have been taken inadvertently by eating bread or porridge made from spoiled grain. A problem with this is that witches were rarely accused of eating their concoctions or rubbing them on their bodies, but of spreading them on brooms or pitchforks, which they then rode to a sabbat. If delusions of flying came from eating spoiled grain, why was not the whole population of an area equally affected?

No one factor alone can explain the witch-hunts, but taken together, intellectual, religious, political, legal, social, and economic factors all created a framework that proved deadly to thousands of European women. In the rest of this chapter, I would like to consider why the vast majority of European witches were women; to do this we must first examine how the stereotype of witch-as-woman developed, and then explore actual witch trials to develop a more refined view as to what types of women were actually accused and convicted.

The stereotype

The idea that women were more likely to engage in witchcraft had a number of roots in European culture. Women were widely recognized as having less physical, economic, or political power than men, so that they were more likely to need magical assistance to gain what they wanted. Whereas a man could fight or take someone to court, a woman could only scold, curse, or cast spells. Thus in popular notions of witchcraft, women's physical and legal weakness was a contributing factor, with unmarried women and widows recognized as even more vulnerable because they did not have a husband to protect them. Because women often married at a younger age than men and female life expectancy may have been increasing, women frequently spent periods of their life as widows. If they remarried, it was often to a widower with children, so that they became stepmothers; resentments about preferential treatment were very common in families with step-siblings, and the evil stepmother became a stock figure in folk tales. If a woman's second husband died, she might have to spend her last years in the house of a stepson or step-daughter who resented her demands but was bound by a legal contract to provide for her; old age became a standard feature of the popular stereotype of the witch.

Women also had close connections with many areas of life in which magic or malevolence might seem the only explanation for events – they watched over animals that could die mysteriously, prepared food that could become spoiled unexplainably, nursed the ill of all ages who could die without warning, and cared for children who were even more subject to disease and death than adults in this era of poor hygiene and unknown and uncontrollable childhood diseases. Some women consciously cultivated popular notions of their connection with the supernatural, performing rituals of love magic with herbs, wax figures, or written names designed to win a lover or hold a spouse. Though learned notions of witchcraft as demonology made some inroads into popular culture, the person most often initially accused of witchcraft in any village was an older woman who had a reputation as a healer, a scold, or a worker of both good and bad magic.

We might assume that women would do everything they could to avoid such a reputation, but in actuality the stereotype could protect a woman for many years. Neighbors would be less likely to refuse assistance, and the wood, grain, or milk which she needed to survive would be given to her or paid as fees for her magical services such as finding lost objects, attracting desirable suitors, or harming enemies. This can help explain the number of women who appear to have confessed to

13 Hans Baldung Grien, *The Witches,* 1510. In this woodcut, Grien depicts many elements of both the popular and learned stereotype of the witch: animal familiars, night-flying, the concoction of poisonous brews, and the link with female sexuality.

being witches without the application or even threat of torture; after decades of providing magical services, they were as convinced as their neighbors of their own powers. Though we regard witchcraft as something that has no objective reality, early modern women and men were often absolutely convinced they had suffered or caused grievous harm through witchcraft.

This popular stereotype of the witch existed long before the upsurge in witch trials, and would continue in Europe centuries after the last witch was officially executed; in some more isolated parts of Europe people still mix magical love potions and accuse their neighbors of casting the evil eye. The early modern large-scale witch-hunts resulted much more from learned and official ideas of witchcraft than popular ones, and in the learned mind, witches were even more likely to be women than they were in popular culture.

The quotations from the *Malleus* and Luther which opened this chapter demonstrate that the connections between women and witchcraft for Europe's intellectual elite came from the two main bases of their intellectual tradition, Aristotle and Christianity. As we have seen in Chapter 1, Aristotle regarded women as defective males, as more passive and weaker not just physically but also morally and intellectually, making them more likely to give in to the devil's offers. Aristotle's biological ideas provided added grounds for the connections. He viewed the woman's role in reproduction as totally passive, with male semen providing all the active force needed for conception. Late medieval and Renaissance authors used this and women's capacity for multiple orgasm as an explanation for what they regarded as female sexual voraciousness; in the words of the *Malleus*, "Proverbs XXX says there are three things which are never satisfied, but yea, there is a fourth thing which says not, It is enough; that is the mouth of the womb. Wherefore for the sake of fulfilling their lusts they [women] consort even with devils."[1] Male authors also worried about the effects of too much sexual intercourse on their own sex, for brain tissue, bone marrow, and semen were widely regarded as the same thing. Sexual intercourse was thought to draw brain tissue down the spine and out the penis, making all intercourse a threat to a man's reason and health. This worried even such leading intellectuals as Leonardo da Vinci and Francis Bacon, and men were advised to limit their sexual relations if they wished to live a long life. Intercourse with female demons *(succubi)* was especially threaten-

---

[1] Translated and quoted in Alan C. Kors and Edward Peters (eds.), *Witchcraft in Europe 1100–1700: A Documentary History* (Philadelphia, University of Pennsylvania Press, 1972), p. 127.

ing, for such creatures attempted to draw out as much semen as possible, thus drastically debilitating any man. (Because the devil and his demons were regarded as impotent, learned demonologists had to figure out where they got semen to impregnate witches; the theory developed that because demons could change shape they would appear as a woman *(succubus)* in order to draw semen out of a human man, then change into a male demon *(incubus)* for intercourse with female witches. Because the semen had spent time in a devil's body, it produced demonic children.)

This anatomically based suspicion of sexuality was enhanced by the writings of Christian authors such as Jerome, Augustine, and Tertullian which expressed not simply suspicion, but hostility and loathing. Because women were the source of their sexual temptations, their hostility to sexuality was often expressed as a more general hatred of women. Christian misogyny continued throughout the Middle Ages when the western church attempted to enforce celibacy for all clerics, and, as we saw in Chapter 1, though Protestants rejected celibacy and championed marriage, they were at best ambivalent about sexual pleasure and affirmed that procreation was the one justification for intercourse. Female sexual drive was viewed as increasing throughout a woman's life, making, in learned eyes, the post-menopausal woman most vulnerable to the blandishments of a demonic suitor. If this older woman was widowed or single, she of course had no legitimate sexual outlets, and even if she was married, sex with her husband was officially frowned upon because it could not result in children.

This obsession with the sexual connection between witches and the devil is something quite new in late medieval ideas of witchcraft. Many commentators have pointed out that the *Malleus* is much more misogynist than earlier works on demonology, and a recently discovered letter written by Heinrich Krämer, one of its authors, to the pope, suggests that Krämer may have had an unusually gender-specific view of Satanic witches. In this letter he talks about the unsatisfactory measures taken against heretics in his day, which he defines as male conciliarists (theologians who advocated that the highest authority in the church should be a council rather than the pope) and "certain other heretics, especially some women who abjure their Catholic faith in front of male demons *(incubi)*."[2] No mention is made at all of *maleficia*, indicating that in Krämer's mind the essence of witchcraft was an abjuration of faith by women, and an abjuration directly connected to sex with demons, for

---

[2] Quoted in Jürgen Petersohn, "Konziliaristen und Hexen. Ein unbekannter Brief des Inquisitors Heinrich Institorius an Papst Sixtus IV. aus dem Jahre 1484," *Deutsches Archiv für Erforschung des Mittelalters* 44 (1988), 120–60. My translation.

the word *incubi* always has a sexual connotation. Female heresy is thus demonic and sexual, whereas male heresy, that of the conciliarists, is intellectual and theological, with no connection either to the devil or the body. Krämer was not the only one to see sexual relations with the devil as limited to women, however, for in Scotland no man was ever accused of such actions, though men were tried and executed for witchcraft; perhaps the judges could simply not bring themselves to imagine members of their own sex doing such things. In France, on the contrary, demonologists thought witches of both sexes engaged in sexual intercourse with the devil, and were much less concerned than the authors of the *Malleus* about why witches were women.

In demonological theory, sex with the devil was not satisfying, for his penis was cold and hard, and so witches also had sex with other demons, their animal familiars, and with each other. These orgiastic sexual relations left their mark on a witch's body, which was either an extra nipple for the animal familiar to suckle or a place that did not feel pain. During the course of questioning, judges and inquisitors in some parts of Europe sought the exact details of a witch's demonic sexual contacts. Suspects were generally stripped and shaved in a search for this "witch's mark"; if no wart or mole could be found that could be viewed as such a mark, she might be "pricked" with a needle in an attempt to discover a spot that was insensitive to pain, also regarded as a sign from the devil. These investigations were generally carried out by a group of male officials – judges, notaries who recorded the witch's answers, the executioner who did the actual pricking or other types of torture – with the witch at least partially naked, so that it is difficult not to view them as at least partly motivated by sexual sadism. This concentration on sexuality in central Europe may have partly resulted from the fact that so many interrogations there were based on the questions posed in the *Malleus,* and partly also because the middle- and upper-class authorities doing the questioning were suspicious of lower-class sexual mores in general.

Sexual relations with the devil rarely (and in some parts of Europe, especially Scandinavia, never) formed part of popular ideas about witchcraft, and other aspects of the learned stereotype of the witch also never became part of the popular stereotype. The *Malleus* is convinced that witchcraft is particularly rampant among midwives, "who surpass all others in wickedness. . . No one does more harm to the Catholic Faith than midwives."[3] This is not reflected in popular denunciations for witchcraft, and considering that most midwives were part of the population group from which the majority of witches were drawn – older

---

[3] Translated and quoted in Kors and Peters, *Witchcraft in Europe*, pp. 114, 129.

women – their numbers are probably not overrepresented among the accused. As we noted in our discussion of midwifery in Chapter 2, female midwives remained the primary birth assistants throughout the early modern period, even in the areas of Europe such as the Holy Roman Empire where witch persecutions were most widespread.

Though at the popular level people continued to be primarily concerned with the *effects* of a witch's powers while at the learned level they were concerned with the *origins* of these, the learned stereotype gradually began to infiltrate popular understanding of what it meant to be a witch. Illustrated pamphlets and broadsides portrayed witches riding on pitchforks to sabbats where they engaged in anti-Christian acts such as spitting on the communion host and sexual relations with demons. Though witch trials were secret, executions were not; they were public spectacles witnessed by huge crowds, with the list of charges read out for all to hear. By the late sixteenth century, popular denunciations for witchcraft in many parts of Europe involved at least some parts of the demonic conception of witchcraft. This spread of diabolism led inevitably to a greater feminization of witchcraft, for witches were now the dependent agents of a male devil rather than independently directing demons themselves, and it fit general notions of proper gender roles to envision women in this dependent position; even witches could not break fully with masculine norms. In areas of Europe in which the demonic concept of witchcraft never took hold, such as Finland, Iceland, Estonia, and Russia, witchcraft did not become female-identified and there were no large-scale hunts. In Finland and Estonia about half of those prosecuted for witchcraft cases were male, and in Iceland and Muscovite Russia, the vast majority of those prosecuted were men charged with sorcery or using their skills as healers to harm people or animals instead.

In the same way that they have analyzed factors contributing to the upsurge in witch trials in general, modern scholars have searched for underlying intellectual concepts which would have supported the link between women and witchcraft. One of these was the dichotomy between order and disorder, one of the primary polarities of both Greek and Christian thought. In both the classical and Christian traditions, women were thought to be more disorderly, and witches both disorderly and actively bent on destroying order. Witches disturbed the natural order of the four elements and the four humors in the body by causing storms and sickness. They disrupted patriarchal order by making men impotent through spells or tying knots in a thread, and subjecting their minds to their passions in a double emasculation. The disorder they caused was linked to the first episode of disorder in the Judeo-Christian tradition, the rebellion and fall of Satan. Related to this order versus disorder dichotomy were those of culture versus nature, reason versus emotion, mind versus body, all dichotomies in which men were linked to the first term and women to the second. In every case, witches were women who let these qualities – links with nature, their emotions, and their bodily drives – come to dominate them completely, but no woman was free from them. Thus all women, even the most outwardly pious, were, in the minds of demonologists, potential witches.

Witchcraft also represented an inversion of the normal order, with witches often portrayed riding backwards on animals or their pitchforks to sabbats where they did everything with their left hand, ate nauseating food, and desecrated rather than honored Christian symbols; witches also often passed on their powers from mother to daughter, an inversion of the way property normally passed from father to son. The witch was also the inversion of a "good woman," and set a negative standard for women; she was argumentative, willful, independent, aggressive, and sexual, rather than chaste, pious, silent, obedient, and married. As the indictment of Margaret Lister in Scotland in 1662 put it, she was "a witch, a charmer, and a libber."[4] The last term carried the same connotation and negative assessment of "liberated woman" that it does today. The witch did not fulfill her expected social role as a wife; the sixteenth-century scientist and physician Theophrastus Paracelsus describes witches as "turning away from men, fleeing men, hiding, wanting to be alone, not attracting men, not looking men in the eye, lying alone, refusing men."[5] The witch was an inversion of the good mother as well as the good woman. She might in actuality be a stepmother, or simply charged with actions that destroyed, rather than sustained, infants and children, such as drying up a woman's milk or menstrual flow, or poisoning children with food. Lyndal Roper and Deborah Willis have recently pointed out that issues of maternity and images of bad mothers emerge more often in witch trials than do those of male/female sexuality.

Positive and negative standards for female behavior in early modern Europe were of course set by men, but women internalized these cultural values as well, which helps explain why women also joined, and sometimes led, the attacks on witches. Women gained economic and

---

[4] Quoted in Christina Larner, *Witchcraft and Religion: The Politics of Popular Belief* (London, Basil Blackwell, 1984), p. 85.

[5] *De sagis,* translated and quoted in Gerhild Scholz Williams, "On finding words: witchcraft and the discourses of dissidence and discovery," in Lynne Tatlock and Christiane Bohnert (eds.), *The Graph of Sex and the German Text: Gendered Culture in Early Modern Germany 1500–1700,* Chloe: Beihefte zum Daphnis, 19 (Amsterdam, Rodolpi, 1994), p. 55.

social security by conforming to the standard of the good wife and mother, and by confronting women who deviated from it. Witch-hunting was thus not simply women-hunting, but the tracking down of a certain type of woman. Because this type of woman often used words as a weapon, witchcraft has also been analyzed in the context of language, speech, and meaning, for in witchcraft words have the power of waging war. The language of the witch-hunts provided a vocabulary for educated Europeans to describe the natives of the New World; in 1585, for example, the French explorer Jéan Lery described religious rituals of Brazilian women in words he had taken from a contemporary French demonological guide. Like women in Europe, the women of the New World were regarded as especially likely to give in to demonic suggestion; linking their practices with those of European women charged with witchcraft also made European witches appear even more exotic and dangerous, representatives of a truly worldwide conspiracy.

The actualities of persecutions for witchcraft

How well did the people who were actually accused, charged, and executed for witchcraft fit the popular and learned stereotypes of the witch? This question can only be answered by intensive local studies of actual witchcraft trials, which have resulted in a recognition of regional and chronological differences, as well as differences between types of witch-hunts.

To take the last distinction first. Historians now distinguish between two types of hunts, the isolated case or small hunt involving one or only a few suspects and the mass panic. Isolated cases, and in fact most hunts, began with an accusation of *maleficia* in a village or town, and the persons accused most often closely fit the sterotype. They were female, over fifty, often widowed or single, poor, and in some way peculiar – they looked or behaved oddly or were known for cursing or scolding or aberrant sexual behavior. They were often on the margins of village society and dependent on the goodwill of others for their support, suspect because they were not under the direct control of a man. In some parts of Europe and in North America they might also be women suspected of other types of crimes. They might be women who had been troublesome to authorities for different reasons, as, for example, Doritte Nippers, who was convicted and executed for witchcraft in 1571 in Elsinore, in Denmark, despite refusing to confess even when tortured; she was the leader of a group of female traders who refused to stop trading when ordered to by the town council. They might be women who cared for women who had recently given birth and their infants, for though midwives were not more likely to be accused than other women, the older women who hired themselves out temporarily as lying-in maids were.

Local studies have shown that kinship stresses often played a role in these initial accusations, for tensions over property, stepchildren, or the public behavior of a relative or in-law were very common in early modern families. Women were in a more vulnerable position once such strains came out into the open, for marriage had often separated them from their birth families and they were dependent on their husband's family to protect them. Household or neighborhood antagonisms might also lead to an accusation, particularly those between women who knew each other's lives intimately such as servants and mistresses or close neighbors; women number very prominently among accusers and witnesses as well as those accused of witchcraft because the actions witches were initially charged with, such as harming children or curdling milk, were generally part of women's sphere. Witchcraft charges often arose in situations that were largely confined to women – food preparation and preservation, pregnancy and childbirth, the care of young children. As one English witch confessed, "she touch[ed] the said John Patchett's wife in her bed and the child in the grace-wife's [midwife's] arms. And then she sent her said spirits to bewitch them to death, which they did."[6]

Very often the incident that led to the charge was not the first, but for some reason the accuser decided no longer to tolerate the suspect's behavior. Once a first charge was made, the accuser often thought back over the years and augmented the current charge with a list of things the suspect had done in the past. The judges then began to question other neighbors and acquaintances, building up a list of suspicious incidents that might stretch for decades. Historians have pointed out that one of the reasons those accused of witchcraft were often older was that it took years to build up a reputation as a witch. Fear or a desire for the witch's services might lead neighbors to tolerate such actions for a long time, and it is difficult to tell what might finally drive them to make a formal accusation.

At this point, the suspect was brought in for questioning by legal authorities, and here there were great regional differences in the likely outcome. In Spain, Portugal, and much of Italy, all cases of witchcraft were handled by the Spanish, Portuguese, or Roman Inquisitions, which continued to make a distinction between ritual magic and diabolic

---

[6] *The wonderful discoverie of the witchcrafts of Margaret and Philippa Flower,* 1619, printed in Barbara Rosen (ed.), *Witchcraft in England 1558–1618* (Amherst, University of Massachusetts Press, 1991), p. 379.

witchcraft. If there was no evidence the suspect had worshipped the devil or used Christian objects such as crucifixes or communion hosts in her magic, the case was most often simply dismissed. Even if the suspect was found guilty, judges of the Inquisition in many parts of southern Europe preferred punishments of public humiliation such as whipping or standing in the pillory to execution; even these might be foregone or lessened if the woman's husband or relatives pleaded with the judges. In the Friuli, for example, a region in northern Italy, 131 people, 85 percent of them female, were charged with witchcraft between 1596 and 1670, and not a single one put to death; that pattern was not unusual in Italy, for there is no clear evidence the Roman Inquisition ever executed any witches, nor that it allowed secular courts in the areas where it operated to handle witchcraft cases. The numbers from Spain are comparable – more than 4,000 cases of witchcraft from 1550 to 1700, and fewer than a dozen witches executed, most of them in a single trial in Navarre in northern Spain in 1610, when the area came briefly under the influence of the French demonologist Pierre de Lancre.

Why, in comparison with other courts throughout the rest of Europe, was the Inquisition so lenient? We must base our answer on the record of the judges' comments, which may not necessarily represent their true sentiments, but it appears, as noted above, that they simply regarded the women and men charged with witchcraft as pawns of the devil, as misled by the "Father of lies" into thinking they had magical powers. They disagreed with the authors of the *Malleus,* which they never used as a guidebook for questioning as secular and ecclesiastical judges did in central Europe, and agreed with the few northern European commentators who opposed hunting witches, such as Johann Weir and Reginald Scot, that most witches were simply stupid or deluded old women suffering from depression who needed spiritual retraining and (earthly) male guidance. Their testimony was certainly not valid grounds to arrest anyone else, which means there were no mass panics. Inquisitors' attitude toward women was thus more condescending and patronizing than that of northern judges, but the effects of this attitude on women's lives was certainly more positive.

In Europe north of the Alps and Pyrenees the initial accusation might also be dismissed if the judges regarded the evidence as questionable, but here there were wide regional differences, and some parts of Europe have not been investigated fully yet, nor might statistics ever be available. At this point, it appears that more cases were dismissed or led to a punishment less than execution in England and Scandinavia than on the Continent; one set of figures from the Home Assize Circuit court in England shows 513 persons accused of witchcraft between 1559 and

1736, of which 200 were convicted and 109 hanged, with the percentage of convictions and executions declining throughout the period. At the same time, when an English judge asked some of his German counterparts how a person accused of witchcraft could escape conviction, they could not think of a way to answer him. England, the northern Netherlands, and Scandinavia also had fewer trials in total than areas on the Continent with similar populations, and almost no mass panics. Several reasons have been suggested for this: the learned stereotype of witchcraft as a devil-worshipping international conspiracy was never fully accepted by English, Dutch, or Scandinavian judicial authorities, which both led to and resulted from a much more restricted use of torture. (Torture was generally used primarily to find out a witch's accomplices and learn the details of her demonic pact; it was employed most by those convinced of the reality of massive numbers of witches and in turn led to the denunciation of as many other people as the judges thought necessary, for torture was stopped only when the accused supplied what the judges thought was a sufficient number of names.) Witches were also tried by jury in England, which some analysts see as leading to milder sentences, though jury trials did not have this effect in Denmark. Witch-hunts in England were never begun by church or state officials, but only after personal denunciations by neighbors, and rarely grew into mass panics.

Once the initial suspect had been questioned, and particularly if she had been tortured, the people whom she had implicated were brought in for questioning. This might lead to a small hunt, involving from five to ten victims, which was most common in Scotland and parts of Switzerland and Germany. This next round often included the relatives or neighbors of the first suspect, as well as people whose lifestyle made them suspect or who had the reputation of being a witch. Most of those accused in such a hunt also fit the stereotype – female, older, poor; male suspects were generally relatives of the accused women. Many of these small hunts could have grown larger, and it is difficult to say why they did not. Historians speculate that perhaps higher officials were otherwise engaged at that particular point and so did not make available the legal machinery needed for a large hunt, or perhaps the communities themselves realized that a further extension of the circle of suspects might prove to be more dangerous than any possible actions by witches.

Small hunts did grow into large-scale panics in at least one instance in England (in the 1640s, led by the self-proclaimed witch-finder Matthew Hopkins) and in Sweden (beginning in the province of Dalarna during the period 1668–1676), but the part of Europe that saw the most frequent mass hunts was also that which saw the most witch accusations in general – the Holy Roman Empire, Switzerland, and parts of France. There are a number of possible explanations for this: much of this area consisted of very small governmental units, which were jealous of each other and after the Reformation divided by religion. The rulers of these small territories often felt more threatened than did the monarchs of western Europe, and were largely unhindered in their legal or judicial moves by any higher authority. The parts of France that were under tighter control of the French monarchy saw far fewer large witch-hunts than the areas that bordered Switzerland or the Empire. Some of the territories that saw the most devastating hunts were territories within the Empire, such as Würzburg, Bamberg, or Ellwangen, in which a bishop or other church official was the head of both church and state; for them, Christianity was clearly a political ideology and persecuting witches a way to demonstrate their piety and concern for order. They consciously used patriarchy as a model, describing themselves as firm but just fathers, ruling their subjects for their own benefit; a campaign in which most of the accused and convicted were women, and many of them women who did not conform to male standards of female behavior, fit their aims very nicely.

Large-scale panics might begin in a number of ways. Many were the outgrowths of smaller investigations, in which the circle of suspects brought in for questioning simply continued to grow unchecked; in one hunt in Ellwangen, more than 400 people were executed between 1611 and 1618. Some were also the result of legal authorities rounding up a group of suspects together, and then receiving further denunciations. Women continued to be the majority of those accused in such mass panics – in 1585, two villages in Germany were left with one female inhabitant each after such an outburst – but when such large numbers of people began to be accused the stereotype also often broke down. Wives of honorable citizens were taken in, and the number of male suspects increased significantly, though these were still often related to female suspects. Girls and boys as young as seven might be tried, and children used as witnesses though their testimony was not normally accepted in law courts. It was only at this stage that witches were generally accused of causing general problems such as famine or disease; in smaller trials, they were charged only with *maleficia* directed against individuals or small groups. The men accused in mass panics were generally charged with different types of witchcraft than the women – of harming things in the male domain such as horses or crops rather than killing infants or spoiling bread – and only rarely accused of actions such as night-flying or pacts with the devil. In Germany, Sweden, and perhaps elsewhere they were wealthier than accused women, and more likely to be defended successfully by friends and family so that their execution rate was lower.

This breaking down of the stereotype is perhaps the primary reason why any mass panic finally ended; it suddenly or slowly became clear to legal authorities, or to the community itself, that the people being questioned or executed were not what they understood witches to be or that the scope of accusations defied credulity. Some from their community might be in league with Satan, but not this type of person and not as many as this. This realization did not cause them to give up their stereotype, but simply to become skeptical about the course of the hunt in their village or town, and to call for its cessation.

In many ways it was similar skepticism that led to the gradual end of the witch-hunts in Europe. Gradually the same religious and legal authorities who had so vigorously persecuted witches began to doubt whether witches actually existed, or at least whether the people brought before them actually were witches. Their skepticism had its roots in the growth of rationalism among many middle- and upper-class people, which required even religion to follow the dictates of reason, and of pietism among others, which saw witchcraft as a purely theological matter and not something for secular judges. There was also a spreading conviction among people with at least some education that natural explanations should be sought for things that had been attributed to the supernatural. Older women who thought themselves witches were more likely to be regarded as deluded or mentally defective, meriting pity rather then persecution, even by people who still firmly believed in the devil. These intellectual changes resulted in the demand for much clearer evidence and a decreased use of torture, which in turn led to fewer accusations and greater doubts about the reality of witchcraft. Creating a godly society ceased to be the chief aim of governments, and laws were passed that restricted or forbade prosecutions for witchcraft; in some parts of Europe, district and national judges fined local pastors or bailiffs for arresting and torturing women. At the popular level, belief in the power of witches often continued, but this was now sneered at by the elite as superstition, and people ceased to bring formal accusations when they knew they would simply be dismissed. The decline in prosecutions happened earliest in areas that had seen few mass panics and a generally low level of witch trials, and latest in the continental heartland; the last official execution for witchcraft in England was in 1682, but in the Holy Roman Empire not until 1775. This did not mean an end of demands for death to witches, however, for lynchings for witchcraft or sorcery have been recorded in Europe within the last few decades, and as recently as 1998, calls for the pardon of a woman convicted of pretending to be witch made headlines in London.

Though historians have investigated all aspects of the great witch-hunts, few have tackled or even asked what may be the central question for our investigation of the lives of early modern women: What effects might all of this have had on women? As noted above, we must reject one hypothesis that has been made, namely that the witch-hunts were directed primarily at female healers, destroying their opportunities for independent action. Several other hypotheses may be more fruitful. Edward Bever notes that the stereotype of the older woman from the late Middle Ages is one who is bawdy, aggressive, and domineering, while that of the nineteenth century is one who is asexual, passive, and submissive. Because some women accused of witchcraft clearly did act the part and firmly believed in their own powers, he suggests that witch trials may in fact have convinced older women to act less "witch-like." Witch persecutions have also been seen as part of the criminalization of female behavior in early modern Europe, for at the same time that witchcraft accusations increased, accusations of women for other types of crimes also increased, particularly gender-specific ones such as prostitution or infanticide. Christina Larner and Susanna Burghartz both note that along with witch trials, these other sorts of criminal charges were a means of controlling female behavior.

All answers to this central question remain speculative at this point, and may perhaps always be, because the women who could have answered it best, the women accused of witchcraft, had no way of leaving an answer for us. It was one question that religious and legal authorities, either those who persecuted witches or those who stopped the persecutions, never thought of asking.

Bibliography

There is a huge literature on witchcraft, and some studies promote ideas that have since proven to have little basis in fact, such as the idea that witches were members of a pre-Christian cult of worshippers of the goddess Diana, or that witch-hunting was primarily an attempt to wipe out knowledge of birth control. The bibliography that follows includes only the most important basic studies whose conclusions have continued to shape our understanding of the witch-hunts, and works that focus on the issue of the gendered nature of witchcraft. For further suggestions see the bibliographies contained in almost every study and two recent review essays: Garthine Walker, "Witchcraft and history," *Women's History Review* 7/3 (1998), 425–32 and Barbara Becker-Cantarino, "'Feminist consciousness' and 'wicked witches': recent studies on women in early modern Europe," *Signs* 20 (1994), 152–75. For older works, see H. C. Erik Midelfort, "Witchcraft, magic and the occult", in Steven Ozment (ed.), *Reformation Europe: A Guide to Research* (St. Louis, Center for Reformation Reserach, 1982), pp. 183–209. An excellent survey and critique of many schools of witchcraft research is Diane Purkiss, *The Witch in History: Early Modern and Twentieth-Century Representations* (London, Routledge, 1996). Elspeth Whitney, "The witch 'she'/the historian 'he': gender and the historiography of the European witch hunts," *Journal of Women's History* 7 (1995), 77–101 explicitly analyzes the role of gender in witchcraft studies.

Older general studies that continue to be useful include: Julio Caro Baroja, *The World of the Witches* (Chicago, University of Chicago Press, 1964); H. R. Trevor-Roper, *The European Witch Craze of the Sixteenth and Seventeenth Centuries and Other Essays* (Harmondsworth, Penguin, 1969); Alan Macfarlane, *Witchcraft in Tudor and Stuart England* (London, Routledge, 1970); Keith Thomas, *Religion and the Decline of Magic* (New York, Charles Scribners' Sons, 1971); H. C. Erik Midelfort, *Witchhunting in Southwestern Germany 1562–1684: The Social and Intellectual Foundations* (Stanford, Stanford University Press, 1972); Norman Cohn, *Europe's Inner Demons: An Enquiry Inspired by the Great Witch-Hunt* (New York, Basic Books, 1975); E. William Monter, *Witchcraft in France and Switzerland: The Borderlands During the Reformation* (Ithaca, Cornell University Press, 1976). Alan C. Kors and Edward Peters (eds.), *Witchcraft in Europe 1100–1700: A Documentary History* (Philadelphia, University of Pennsylvania Press, 1972) and Barbara Rosen (ed.), *Witchcraft in England 1558–1618* (Amherst, University of Massachusetts Press, 1991) provide source materials.

There are two newer general surveys of the witch-hunts in all of Europe which specifically address the issue of why women were more likely to be accused: Joseph Klaits, *Servants of Satan: The Age of the Witch Hunts* (Bloomington, Indiana University Press, 1985) and Brian P. Levack, *The Witch-Hunt in Early Modern Europe*, 2nd ed. (London, Longman, 1995). Levack has also edited a twelve-volume collection, *Articles on Witchcraft, Magic and Demonology* (New York, Garland, 1992), of which volume 10 looks specifically at women. Another new wide-ranging collection of articles is: Jonathan Barry, Marianne Hester, and Gareth Roberts (eds.), *Witchcraft in Early Modern Europe: Studies in Culture and Belief* (Cambridge, Cambridge University Press, 1996).

Recent work on witchcraft has stressed the fact that patterns of persecution differed widely in different areas of Europe, and many of the best studies are those that focus on a specific city, country, or region. See, for example, Ruth Martin, *Witchcraft and the Inquisition in Venice 1550–1650* (London, Basil Blackwell, 1989); Gustav Henningsen, *The Witch's Advocate: Basque Witchcraft and the Spanish Inquisition* (Reno, University of Nevada Press, 1980); David Gentilcore, *From Bishop to Witch: The System of the Sacred in Early Modern Terra d'Otranto* (Manchester, Manchester University Press, 1992); Christina Larner, *Enemies of God: The Witch Hunt in Scotland* (Baltimore, The Johns Hopkins University Press, 1981); Carlos Nogueria, "Sexuality and desire: the witches of Castille," *Revista Brasileira de Historia* 15 (1987–88), 169–84; Valerie Kivelson, "Through the prism of witchcraft: gender and social change in seventeenth-century Muscovy," in Barbara Evans Clements, et al. (eds.), *Russia's Women: Accommodation, Resistance, Transformation* (Berkeley, University of California

Press, 1991), pp. 74–94 and "Patrolling the boundaries: the uses of witchcraft accusations and household strife in seventeenth-century Muscovy," *Harvard Ukrainian Studies* 19 (1995), 302–23. Sally Scully, "Marriage or a career: witchcraft as an alternative in seventeenth-century Venice," *Journal of Social History* 28 (1995), 857–76; James Sharpe, *Instruments of Darkness: Witchcraft in Early Modern England* (Philadelphia, University of Pennsylvania Press, 1997); Edmund M. Kern, "Quotidian distinctions: women, gender, and witchcraft in Styria, 1550–1750," *Journal of Medieval and Early Modern Studies* (Forthcoming 2000). Bengt Ankarloo and Gustav Henningsen (eds.), *Early Modern European Witchcraft: Centers and Peripheries* (Oxford, Oxford University Press, 1989) presents local studies from throughout Europe, including Scandinavia and Slavic areas.

Single case studies provide fascinating details that general surveys cannot. See, for example, Retha Warnicke, *The Rise and Fall of Anne Boleyn: Family Politics at the Court of Henry VIII* (Cambridge, Cambridge University Press, 1989), which explores the case of one of the most prominent women ever accused of witchcraft. Michael Kunze, *Highroad to the Stake: A Tale of Witchcraft*, trans. Willian E. Yuill (Chicago and London, University of Chicago Press, 1987) provides a gripping narrative of a single case of otherwise obscure people charged with witchcraft in Bavaria; this is a book that is impossible to put down, and, though slightly fictionalized in terms of details, is based on exhaustive archival research. Gilbert Geis and Ivan Bunn, *A Trial of Witches: A Seventeenth-Century Witchcraft Persecution* (London, Routledge, 1997) traces an English case of two women hanged for witchcraft, with in-depth analysis of the court proceedings. Carol Karlsen, *The Devil in the Shape of a Woman* (New York, Norton, 1987) is only one of a score of books that look at the Salem case; it is important to recognize that Salem was the *only* mass trial in North America.

Works that focus specifically on the issue of women and witchcraft have become much more numerous over the last decade than they were earlier. These include several new books, which tend to emphasize misogyny and male control of female sexuality: Marianne Hester, *Lewd Women and Wicked Witches: A Study of the Dynamics of Male Domination* (London, Routledge, 1992); Anne Llewellyn Barstow, *Witchcraze: A New History of the European Witch Hunts* (New York, Pandora, 1994); Sigrid Brauner, *Fearless Wives and Frightened Shrews: The Construction of the Witch in Early Modern Germany* (Amherst, University of Massachusetts Press, 1995). Mary Daly's classic critique of male dominance, *Gyn/Ecology* (London, The Women's Press, 1979), uses the witchcraze as one of its prime examples. Three studies that address the issue of motherhood and witchcraft are Lyndal Roper, "Witchcraft and fantasy in early modern Germany," in her *Oedipus and the Devil: Witchcraft, Religion, and Sexuality in Early Modern Europe* (London, Routledge, 1994), Deborah Willis, *Malevolent Nurture: Witch-Hunting and Maternal Power in Early Modern England* (Ithaca, Cornell University Press, 1995), and Louise Jackson, "Witches, wives, and mothers: witchcraft persecution and women's confessions in seventeenth-century England," *Women's History Review* 4 (1995), 63–83.

Many of the studies that focus on demonology and ideas about witchcraft do not address the issue of gender to a great extent, except to mention general cultural misogyny. Several that do include: Brian Easlea, *Witchhunting, Magic and the New Philosophy: An Introduction to Debates of the Scientific Revolution, 1450–1750* (Sussex, Harvester, 1980); Carolyn Merchant, *The Death of Nature: Women, Ecology and the Scientific Revolution* (New York, Harper & Row, 1980); J. K. Swales and Hugh McLachlan, "Witchcraft and antifeminism," *Scottish Journal of Sociology* 4 (1980), 141–66. The works of Stuart Clark tend to deemphasize the role of misogyny in demonology: "Inversion, misrule and the meaning of witchcraft," *Past and Present* 97 (1980), 98–127, "The 'gendering' of witchcraft in French demonology: misogyny or polarity?" *French History* 5 (1991), 426–37, *Thinking with Demons: The Idea of Witchcraft in Early Modern Europe* (Oxford, Oxford University Press, 1997).

There is a number of recent case studies that directly address the issue of women's role as both accuser and accused: Russell Zguta, "Witchcraft trials in seventeenth-century Russia," *American Historical Review* 82 (1977), 1187–1207; Phyllis Guskin, "The context of witchcraft: the case of Jane Wenham, 1712," *Eighteenth Century Studies* 15 (1981), 48–71; Peter Rushton, "Women, withcraft and slander in early modern England: cases from the church courts of Durham," *Northern History* 18 (1982), 116–32; Susanna Burghartz, "The equation of women and witches: a case study of witchcraft trials in Lucerne and Lausanne in the fifteenth and sixteenth centuries," in Richard Evans (ed.), *The German Underworld: Deviants and Outcasts in German History* (London, Routledge, 1988), pp. 57–74; Richard Horsley, "Who were the witches? The social roles of the accused in European witch trials," *Journal of Interdisciplinary History* 9 (1979), 689–716; Robin Briggs, "Women as victims? Witches, judges and the community," *French History* 5 (1991), 438–50; Clive Holmes, "Women: witnesses and witches," *Past and Present* 140 (1993), 45–78; Marion Gibson, *Reading Witchcraft: Stories of Early English Witches* (London, Routledge, 1999).

Works that consider the issue across a broader geographic area include: Clarke Garrett, "Women and witches: patterns of analysis," *Signs* 3 (1977), 461–70 and comments by Claudia Honegger and Nelly Moia, same issue, pp. 792–804; Alan Anderson and Raymond Gordon, "Witchcraft and the status of women," *British Journal of Sociology* 29 (1978), 171–84 and the response, J. K. Swales and Hugh McLachlan, "Witchcraft and the status of women," *British Journal of Sociology* 30 (1979), 349–58; Ritta Jo Horsley and Richard A. Horsley, "On the trail of the 'witches': wise women, midwives and the European witch hunts", in Mariane Burkhard and Edith Waldstein (eds.), *Women in German Yearbook 3: Feminist Studies and German Culture* (Washington, D.C.: University of America Press, 1987), pp. 1–28; Allison P. Coudert, "The myth of the improved status of Protestant women: the case of the witchcraze", in Jean R. Brink, et al., (eds)., *The Politics of Gender in Early Modern Europe.* Sixteenth Century Essays and Studies, 12 (Kirksville, Mo., Sixteenth Century Journal Publishers, 1989), 61–89. Robin Briggs, *Witches and Neighbours: The Social and Cultural Context of European Witchcraft* (New York: HarperCollins, 1996) provides a thoughtful discussion of the complexities of the link between gender and witchcraft, and also discusses witchcraft within the context of sexual and family relationships.

Thomas Rogers Forbes, *The Midwife and the Witch* (New Haven, Yale University Press, 1966) and Barbara Ehrenreich and Deirdre English, *Witches, Midwives and Nurses: A History of Women Healers* (New York, Feminist Press, 1973) posit a connection between midwifery and witchcraft, while David Harley,

"Historians as demonologists: the myth of the midwife-witch," *Social History of Medicine* 3 (1990), 1–26 is harshly critical of this idea. Leland Estes. "The medical origins of the European witch craze: a hypothesis," *Journal of Social History* 17 (1983), 271–84 looks more broadly at medical issues, and Edward Bever, "Old age and witchcraft in early modern Europe," in Peter Stearns (ed.), *Old Age in Preindustrial Society* (New York, Holmes and Meier, 1982), pp. 150–90 focuses on age.

Studies that put witchcraft into a broader perspective of popular culture also often do not consider the question of gender, but those that do include Robert Muchembled, "The witches of the Cambrésis: the acculturation of the rural world in the sixteenth and seventeenth centuries", in James Obelkevich (ed.), *Religion and the People 800–1700* (Chapel Hill, University of North Carolina Press, 1979), pp. 221–76; Robert Muchembled, *Popular Culture and Elite Culture in France 1450–1750* (Baton Rouge, University of Louisiana Press, 1985); Robin Briggs, *Communities of Belief: Cultural and Social Tensions in Early Modern France* (Oxford, Oxford University Press, 1989). Jeanne Favret-Saada, *Deadly Words: Witchcraft in the Bocage* (Cambridge, Cambridge University Press, 1980), David Sabean, *Power in the Blood: Popular Culture and Village Discourse in Early Modern Germany* (Cambridge, Cambridge University Press, 1984), and Gerhild Scholz Williams, *Defining Dominion: The Discourses of Magic and Witchcraft in Early Modern France and Germany* (Ann Arbor, University of Michigan Press, 1995) explore witchcraft within the context of language and meaning.

Studies that include witchcraft along with other types of crimes investigated by the Inquisition, and that address the issue of women, include E. William Monter, "Women and the Italian Inquisitions", in Mary Beth Rose (ed.), *Women in the Middle Ages and the Renaissance: Literary and Historical Perspectives* (Syracuse, Syracuse University Press, 1986), pp. 73–87; Mary O'Neil, "Magical healing, love magic and the Inquisition in late sixteenth-century Modena," in Stephen Haliczer (ed.), *Inquisition and Society in Early Modern Europe* (London, Croom Helm, 1987), pp. 88–114; several of the essays in Mary Elizabeth Perry and Anne J. Cruz (eds.), *Cultural Encounters: The Impact of the Inquisition in Spain and the New World* (Berkeley, University of California Press, 1991).

8   Gender and power

A woman promoted to sit in the seat of God, that is, to teach, to judge
or to reign above man, is a monster in nature, contumely to God, and
a thing most repugnant to his will and ordinance.

John Knox, *The First Blast of the Trumpet Against the Monstrous Regiment of
Women* (Geneva, 1558), fol. 16r.

If all men are born free, how is it that all women are born slaves?

Mary Astell, *Some Reflections Upon Marriage* (London, 1706), preface.

In the preceding chapters, we have discussed many aspects of women's
lives in the early modern period, but you may have been struck by the
lack of a chapter on women's political role, a topic that would assuredly
be covered in a similar survey of women in the nineteenth or twentieth
centuries. The easiest explanation for this is the one that has traditionally been used to justify ignoring women in discussions of the early modern state or political theory of the period: other than a few rulers and a
few noblewomen and abbesses who chose delegates to representative
institutions, women did not have a formal political role in early modern
society. They did not hold office, sit in representative institutions, serve
as judges, or in any other way participate in formal political institutions,
except for a few odd instances in which they served as sextons or church-
wardens, very minor offices. Their absence from political life was
matched by an absence from most works of political theory. Authors discussing political rights and obligations, whether monarchical or republi-
can, rarely mentioned women at all, setting up the male experience as
universal and subsuming women's rights under those of the male heads
of their household or family. Based on this, political histories of the
period have generally made little mention of women.

This has recently changed somewhat because of two historiographical
trends. One is the broadening of political history to include not only formal politics, but anything in a society having to do with power relationships. Not only are the relationships between king and subject, monarch
and parliament now viewed as political, but also those between master
and servant, landlord and tenant, father and son, husband and wife. The

study of institutions of government is thus just one part of this new political history, which also looks at other ways in which people expressed their opinions and shaped the world around them: voluntary societies, printed materials, clubs and associations, interest groups. This larger political realm has been dubbed the "public sphere" by the social theorist Jürgen Habermas, who sees it as standing somewhat distinct from the formal politics of kings and courts in the early modern period, but eventually forming the basis of the modern public sphere of political participation. Though Habermas paid little attention to women's activities in this new public sphere, more recent historians have pointed out that women were very active in creating it: hosting salons, reading and writing new types of literature, patronizing writers and philosophers. In addition, many of the other aspects of women's lives we have discussed in previous chapters, such as their marriages, sexuality, work opportunities, and religious institutions, are now being examined politically, in both their internal power relationships and their connections with more formal institutions of political power or the public sphere.

Women's informal political power has also begun to receive more attention, in a more sophisticated way than older "power behind the throne" studies of queens and royal mistresses. Political historians make distinctions between power – the ability to shape political events – and authority – power which is formally recognized and legitimated – noting that while women rarely had the latter, they did have the former. Through the arrangement of marriages, they established ties between influential families; through letters or the spreading of rumors, they shaped networks of opinion; through patronage, they helped or hindered men's political careers; through giving advice and founding institutions, they shaped policy; through participation in riots and disturbances, they demonstrated the weakness of male authority structures. As we will see, none of these actions led in the early modern period to a call for formal political rights for women, but they are clearly part of the new wider concept of political history.

The second historiographical trend is the broadening of women's history into the history of gender, which has led to an exploration of the political context within which any society defines what it means to be female or male. As we noted in the introduction, most historians distinguish between sex – physical or biological differences between men and women – and gender – socially constructed differences – though they also recognize that the boundaries between what is understood as "biological" sex and what is "cultural" gender are themselves culturally created and historically changing. Contrasting our own era with the early modern period in Europe provides a good example of such changes, for behaviors that we would define as socially prescribed, such as dominance or dependence, were viewed as "natural" qualities in men and women, inherent in their bodies and beings. (This naturalization of socially determined qualities still goes on, of course, with boys being described as "naturally" better at math, girls as "naturally" better at relating to people, and has even inspired "scientific" investigations of such things as the "math gene.")

Historians, anthropologists, and sociologists have all pointed out that the dichotomy male/female is linked in many societies, at least in theory, to the dichotomy public/private (or domestic) – that is, the male realm is defined as public, and the female realm as private. They see the public realm more broadly than Habermas, defining it as all political, economic, and intellectual institutions that control people's lives, and thus as existing from early in human history. Some theorists, such as Mary O'Brien, argue that men first created a public realm because they felt excluded from the most important human physical process – birth. The public/private split is thus, in her view, based on men's desire to control biological reproduction. Whatever the origins of this broader public realm – and they are difficult to determine because this happened so early in recorded human history – it is clear that the public/private divide has varied in intensity throughout time, and varied somewhat in its association with the gender dichotomy. At certain points, such as in classical Athens and Victorian England, the links between public/private and male/female are very strong, and at other points, such as in early medieval Europe, they are less so. Consideration of these links formed part of the early modern debate about women we discussed in Chapter 1 and the debate about women's education we discussed in Chapter 4. It also formed part of the wider discussions of what we would term gender roles that we will consider in this chapter, as learned and unlearned people debated the boundaries of women's and men's spheres: Did a woman's proper sphere extend beyond the household and family? Did a man's proper sphere require a household and family as its basis? What was the proper power balance between the sexes, and between individual men and women, in private and in public?

We will follow both of these trends in this final chapter, shifting our focus from women to gender in order to explore the ways in which masculinity and femininity were linked with broadly defined political power in the state and household, and then with other hierarchies and relationships that made up what the early modern period termed the "social order," that is, the proper functioning of society. Though other chapters have made comparisons between women's and men's situations, this chapter will do so more extensively, as considerations of power are always relational, that is, they involve power *over* someone or something, along with power *to* carry out a certain action.

Gender and political power

As we saw in Chapter 1, during the fifteenth through the seventeenth centuries male and female writers in many countries of Europe wrote both learned and popular works debating the nature of women. Beginning in the sixteenth century, this debate also became one about female rulers, sparked primarily by dynastic accidents in many countries, which led to women serving as advisers to child kings or ruling in their own right – Isabella in Castile, Mary and Elizabeth Tudor in England, Mary Stuart in Scotland, Catherine de Medici and Anne of Austria in France. The questions vigorously and at times viciously disputed directly concerned what we would term the social construction of gender: could a woman's being born into a royal family and educated to rule allow her to overcome the limitations of her sex? Should it? Or stated another way: which was (or should be) the stronger determinant of character and social role, gender or rank?

The most extreme opponents of female rule were Protestants who went into exile on the Continent during the reign of Mary Tudor. From the safety of Strasbourg and Geneva, Anthony Gilby, Thomas Becon, Christopher Goodman, and John Knox all compared Mary with Jezebel, arguing that female rule was unnatural, unlawful, and contrary to Scripture. Knox titled his treatise *The First Blast of the Trumpet Against the Monstrous Regiment of Women* (1558), directing it against Mary Stuart as well as Mary Tudor. His sentiments can be seen in the quotation that opens this chapter, and the word "monster" was used by the other authors as well to describe female rulers (echoing Aristotle's notion that the female sex in general is monstrous) and asserting that both nature and Scripture placed all women under male authority, "excepting none" (fol. 15r). Thus, for these authors, being female was a condition that could never be overcome, and subjects of female rulers needed no other justification for rebelling than their monarch's sex. This suspicion of female rulers may have been influenced by the recent experiences of the German and Swiss cities in which they were exiled, against which noblewomen such as the Duchesses Bianca Maria Sforza of Milan or Elisabeth of Bavaria-Landshut led military actions, though this line of influence has not been investigated as thoroughly as those linking the Marian exiles' other political ideas with those of their continental hosts.

Gilby, Goodman, and Knox all had the misfortune to publish their works in 1558, the very year that Mary Tudor died and Elizabeth assumed the throne, making their position as both Protestants and opponents of female rule rather tricky. A number of courtiers realized that defenses of female rule would be likely to help them win favor in Elizabeth's eyes, and advanced arguments against viewing a woman's sex as an absolute block to rulership. Thomas Smith in *De Republica Anglorum: The maner of Government or Policie of the Realme of England* (1583) stated bluntly that "an absolute Queene, and absolute Dutches or Countesse" had a clear right to rule, and John Aylmer, in a *Harborowe for Faithfull and Trewe Subjectes* (1559), disputed both the Scriptural and natural law arguments against female rulership. Aylmer argued that Scriptural prohibitions of women teaching or speaking were only relevant for the particular groups to which they were addressed, and that a woman's sex did not automatically exclude her from rule just as a boy king's age or a handicapped king's infirmity did not exclude him. He asserted that even a married queen could rule legitimately, for she could be subject to her husband in her private life, yet monarch to him and all other men in her public – a concept of a split identity that Aylmer and other political theorists described as the ruler's "two bodies" and what we might describe as a distinction between the queenship and the queen. A queen might be thus clearly female in her body and sexuality, but still exhibit the masculine qualities regarded as necessary in a ruler because of traits she had inherited or learned. As Constance Jordan has pointed out, Aylmer and other defenders of female rule were thus clearly separating sex from gender, and even approaching an idea of androgyny as a desirable state for the public persona of female monarchs. It is perhaps not very surprising that they were writing during the rule of Elizabeth, the early modern monarch who most astutely used both feminine and masculine gender stereotypes to her own advantage and expressed the idea of androgyny succinctly: "I know I have the body of a weak and feeble woman, but I have the heart and stomach of a king."[1]

Jean Bodin, the French jurist and political theorist, returned to Scripture and natural law in his opposition to female rule in *The Six Books of the Republic* (1576), but also stressed what would become in the seventeenth century the most frequently cited reason against it: that the state was like a household, and just as in a household the husband/father has authority and power over all others, so in the state a male monarch should always rule. Robert Filmer carried this even further in *Patriarchia,* asserting that rulers derived all legal authority from the

---

[1] Queen Elizabeth I, Tilbury speech, quoted in Frances Teague, "Elizabeth I: Queen of England," in Katharine M. Wilson (ed.), *Women Writers of the Renaissance and Reformation* (Athens, University of Georgia Press, 1987), p. 542.

divinely sanctioned fatherly power of Adam, just as did all fathers. Male monarchs used husbandly and paternal imagery to justify their assertion of power over their subjects, as in James I's statements to parliament: "I am the Husband, and the whole Isle is my lawfull Wife. . . By the law of nature the king becomes a natural father to all his lieges at his coronation. . . A King is trewly *Parens patriae*, the politique father of his people."[2] Criticism of monarchs was also couched in paternal language; pamphlets directed against the crown during the revolt known as the Fronde in seventeenth-century France, for example, justified their opposition by asserting that the king was not properly fulfilling his fatherly duties.

This link between royal and paternal authority could also work in the opposite direction to enhance the power of male heads of household. Just as subjects were deemed to have no or only a very limited right of rebellion against their ruler, so women and children were not to dispute the authority of the husband/father, because both kings and fathers were held to have received their authority from God; the household was not viewed as private, but as the smallest political unit and so part of the public realm. Jean Bodin put it succinctly: "So we will leave moral discourse to the philosophers and theologians, and we will take up what is relative to political life, and speak of the husband's power over the wife, which is the source and origin of every human society."[3]

Many analysts see the Protestant Reformation and, in England, Puritanism as further strengthening this paternal authority by granting male heads of household a much larger religious and supervisory role than they had under Catholicism. The fact that Protestant clergy were themselves generally married heads of household also meant that ideas about clerical authority reinforced notions of paternal and husbandly authority; priests were now husbands, and husbands priests. Most Protestant writers also gave mothers a role in the religious and moral life of the household, but this was always secondary to that of fathers.

The split in Christianity created by the Protestant Reformation heightened male political authority in other ways in both Protestant and Catholic areas. During the sixteenth century, the citizens of many cities and villages increasingly added an oath to uphold the city's religion to the oaths they took to defend it and support it economically.

---

[2] *The Political Works of James I*, ed. Charles Howard McIlwain (New York, Russell and Russell, 1965), pp. 272–307.

[3] Jean Bodin, *Six Books of the Republic*, translated and quoted in Christine Fauré, *Democracy Without Women: Feminism and the Rise of Liberal Individualism in France*, trans. Claudia Gorbman and John Berks (Bloomington, Indiana University Press, 1991), p. 40.

This annual oath-swearing, which had begun when cities were first established in the Middle Ages, probably had never involved female citizens. (There is no explicit discussion of why women, who swore oaths of loyalty on first becoming citizens and were otherwise obligated to perform most of the duties of citizenship, did not participate in the annual oath-swearing, nor are there any records of women who attempted to, as later women such as Susan B. Anthony would attempt to vote.) With the Reformations, however, the annual oath-swearing created an even larger distinction between male and female citizens, and it also created a distinction between male and female *Christians*. (The vast majority of Europe's population was Christian, of course, and there was *never* any discussion of granting citizenship to non-Christians such as Jews or Muslims during this period.) For men, faith was a ritualized civic matter while for women it was not. This led to uncertainty about how to handle the citizenship status of certain women. In Protestant cities, one of the key political effects of the Reformation was the integration of the male clergy into the citizenry, ending the distinction between clerical and lay status. In most cases, these priests also married, but this was not a requirement for obtaining citizenship. For nuns, however, it was. The only way they could become citizens was to marry, which meant, of course, they were no longer nuns. A priest could be both a citizen *and* a priest, but a nun could not be a citizen and a nun. Thus *both* the public political community and the public religious community – which are regarded as the same in sixteenth-century Europe – were for men only, a situation reinforced in the highly gendered language of the Reformers, who extolled "brotherly love" and the religious virtues of the "common man."

The first elections in Europe since the time of the Greeks which involved common "people" rather than knights, nobles, or the residents of religious houses were in villages and towns of south Germany and Switzerland where, as early as the fourteenth century, the men of the parish elected their priest. Thus in church as well as state, democracy marked a division between men and women that had not existed when priests were appointed, for noblewomen as well as noblemen often had the right to appoint priests. (Swiss democracy, so praised in the stories about William Tell, continued that gender division until very recently, for Switzerland was the last country in Europe in which women got the vote – they got the vote only in 1971, after 82 referenda – and they still cannot vote in certain local elections today.) Gender restrictions in electing clergy were eased in a few congregations among the Baptists, Independents, and other radical Protestant groups in seventeenth-century England, where women as well as men raised their hands to approve or disapprove a new pastor. Even in congregations that allowed women to vote, however, positions as pastor or elder were reserved for men.

Protestant women such as Argula von Grumbach or Elinor James occasionally linked authority within the family to authority in the larger community for women as well as men. They argued that because the household was widely regarded as part of the public realm, women already had public duties even if they were not oath-swearing citizens; therefore their speaking out on political or religious matters was simply an extension of their public role as mothers and wives. This line of argument was generally rejected in the early modern period, and when nineteenth-century women's rights advocates again spoke of their duties as wives and mothers, the terms of the debate had shifted. By this time the household was regarded as part of the private sphere rather than the public, and women could not speak of political responsibilities as something they were already doing in the way that Grumbach or James had. Instead they argued that only by gaining political rights would women truly be able to carry out their private familial duties, because the political realm shaped family life so intensely in matters such as temperence, education, and health. These "domestic" or "relational" feminists, as they are termed, thus acknowledged the private nature of the household, though one wonders if in the long run a continued assertion of the public nature of women's domestic responsibilities might have proved a more secure base for the expansion of women's political rights.

Religious divisions were not the only development that enhanced the authority of many men. Rulers intent on increasing and centralizing their own authority supported legal and institutional changes that enhanced the power of men over the women and children in their own families. In France, for example, a series of laws were enacted between 1556 and 1789 which increased both paternal and state control of marriage. Parental consent was required for marriage, and severe penalties, including capital punishment, were prescribed for minors who married against their parents' wishes. (Minors were defined as men under 30 and women under 25.) Marriages without parental consent were defined as *rapt* (abduction), even if they had involved no violence (such cases were termed *rapt de seduction*). Though in actuality they were not executed, young people who defied their parents were sometimes imprisoned by what were termed *lettres de cachet,* documents that families obtained from royal officials authorizing the imprisonment without trial of a family member who was seen as a souce of dishonor. *Lettres de cachet* were also used against young people who refused to go into convents or monasteries when their families wished them to, or against individuals whose behavior was regarded as in some way scandalous, such as wives whose husbands suspected them of adultery or men from prominent families who engaged in homosexual activities; this practice was often abused, and individuals imprisoned for years if their families refused to agree to their release. These laws and practices were proposed and supported by French officials because they increased their personal authority within their own families, and simultaneously increased the authority of the state vis-à-vis the Catholic Church, which had required at least the nominal consent of both parties for a valid marriage. This "family/state compact," as Sarah Hanley terms it, dramatically lessened women's rights to control their own persons and property; these marriage laws would be one of the first things that French women's rights advocates in the nineteenth and twentieth centuries worked to change.

The power of husbands over their wives was rarely disputed in the sixteenth and seventeenth centuries, which was an important reason why women were not included in discussions of political rights; because married women were legally dependent, they could not be politically independent persons, just as servants, apprentices, or tenants could not. Thus even the most eloquent defenders of women, such as Agrippa of Nettesheim, did not suggest practical ways to increase women's political rights and simply avoided the issue of marriage when promoting women's equality or superiority. The strongest supporters of a queen's right to rule, such as Thomas Smith, did not suggest extending political rights to other women: "In which consideration also do we reject women, as those whom nature hath made to keepe home and to nourish their familie and children, and not to medle with matters abroad, nor to beare office in a citie or commonwealth no more than children and infantes."[4]

Husbandly power was not simply a matter of theory. In France, men occasionally used *lettres de cachet* as a means of solving marital disputes, convincing authorities that family honor demanded the imprisonment of their wives, while in Italy and Spain, a "disobedient" wife could be sent to a convent or house of refuge for repentant prostitutes. Courts generally held that a husband had the right to beat his wife in order to correct her behavior as long as this was not extreme, with a common standard being that he did not draw blood, or the diameter of the stick he used did not exceed that of his thumb. (This is the origin of the term "rule of thumb.") A husband accused of abuse in court was generally simply admonished to behave better, and only on a third or fourth court appearance might stricter punishment be set. If the wife had left the

---

[4] Thomas Smith, *De Republica Anglorum* (London, 1583), sig. D2r.

household she was ordered to return, though there are cases in many jurisdictions where this eventually led to a wife's death at the hands of her husband. The reverse situation, in which a wife killed her husband, was much rarer, but the few cases that did exist fascinated people and were often retold many times in illustrated pamphlets and broadsheets with titles such as *Murther, Murther. Or, a Bloody Relation How Anne Hamton. . . by Poyson Murthered Her Deare Husband* (London, 1641). In England, killing a husband was legally defined as "petty treason" and punishable by death at the stake. In the ballad "A Warning for All Desperate Women" (1628), a convicted wife warns others:

> Then hasty hairebraind wives take heed,
> of me a warning take,
> Least like to me in coole of blood,
> you burn't be at the stake.[5]

Accusations of adultery were taken far more seriously than those of domestic violence, because adultery directly challenged the central link between marriage and procreation as well as impugning male honor and husbandly authority. In many ancient and medieval law codes, adultery was defined as sex between a married woman and a man who was not her husband; by the sixteenth century sex between a married man and a woman who was not his wife was also legally defined as adultery. Because adultery by men did not threaten the family and lineage the way that adultery by a married woman did, however, the severity of penalties remained tied to gender. In the 1566 Genevan law, an adulterous married man and his lover were to be punished by twelve days in prison, but an adulterous married woman to be executed; in the 1650 Adultery Act in England, adultery was made a capital offense for a married woman and her partner, but was only punished by three months' imprisonment for a married man. In Geneva, the punishment set for the lover of a married woman explicitly links considerations of gender and class, for he was to be whipped and banished unless he was a servant, in which case he was also to be executed.

Women's dependence on their husbands was used as a reason not to listen to their demands in the few cases where women other than queens actually carried out political actions in early modern Europe. Women's petitions to Parliament during the English Civil War provide the clearest example of this. Several times during the war, large groups of women petitioned Parliament to improve trade and end the debt laws, release

---

[5] Reprinted in Frances E. Dolan, *Dangerous Familiars: Representations of Domestic Crime in England, 1550–1700* (Ithaca, Cornell University Press, 1994), p. 49.

the revolutionary Leveller John Lilburne from prison, or end the application of martial law in times of peace. Though their petitions were occasionally received respectfully, more often they were met with disdain and sarcasm, with Parliament commenting that such matters were beyond female understanding and that the women should go home and ask their husbands; using the standard argument that a husband represented his wife in public matters beyond the household, Parliament commented that women had no right to petition. Later women's petitions noted explicitly that "we are not all wives," and the 1649 petititon against martial law contained the strongest language in the early modern period in favor of women's political rights:

Since we are assured of our Creation in the image of God, and of an interest in Christ, equal unto men, as also of a proportionable share in the Freedoms of this Commonwealth, we cannot help but wonder and grieve that we should appear so despicable in your eyes as to be thought unworthy to petition or represent our grievances to this honorable House. . . Have we not an equal interest with the men of this Nation in those liberties and securities contained in the Petition of Right and the other good Laws of this Land? Are any of our lives, limbs, liberties or goods to be taken from us more than from men, but by due process of Law?[6]

We don't know who actually wrote these words, but the female petitioners answered their critics orally and spontaneously, so charges that the petition must have been written by a man are not warranted. It is also difficult to find out exactly what kind of women petitioned, for contemporary accounts are generally hostile, and refer to them as fishwives or oysterwomen, in other words, lower-class women who were stepping outside their proper place in the class as well as gender order. They were also labeled "bawds and whores," reflecting the common notion that women speaking in public must be of questionable sexual virtue. The content of their arguments was never seriously debated, with newspaper articles urging husbands to exert tighter control over their wives and increase their domestic duties so they would not have the time to worry about politics.

The petitions by women to governmental authorities that *did* get a favorable hearing in the early modern period were those about strictly economic matters, such as the ability to work at a certain trade, and which used language that emphasized the women's domestic responsibilities and reflected the authorities' ideas about the proper roles of women and men. Women who were successful always stressed their

---

[6] Quoted in Ellen A. McArthur, "Women petitioners and the Long Parliament," *English Historical Review* 24 (1909), p. 708.

obligations to their children or parents, their helplessness and the strength – tempered by charity – of the rulers. They did not couch their arguments in terms of rights, or demand that their request be extended to other women, thus enabling authorities to simultaneously bend or break rules restricting women's actions while still feeling they were enforcing them. The frequency with which women brought individual petitions or cases to courts or other governmental bodies gradually declined during the early modern period, but women never stopped completely. Thus though they had no political rights in theory, and were never part of the bodies that decided such cases, women were actually to be found in courts and city council meetings much more often than we might expect.

Women's legal dependence might actually have been a factor increasing their participation in certain types of political activities, particularly riots and popular protests. A husband was legally responsible for many of his wife's actions in most parts of Europe, leading people to think women could not be prosecuted for rioting. For example, a crowd in Holland in 1628 protesting the renting out of what they viewed as common land, chased the renter into the town hall, and then the women of the group cried, "Let us sound the drum and send our husbands home. We will catch the villain and beat him, as we cannot be tried for fighting."[7] Criminal records reveal that women actually were tried and even executed for their part in disturbances, but this did not lessen their participation. They were often the instigators of food riots, protesting scarcities of food and high prices, and took part in iconoclastic and other types of religious riots, threatening clergy, plundering churches, and carrying information.

Women also played a role in more purely political riots, for example, those over taxes in Holland and France in the seventeenth and eighteenth centuries. The women who led such riots were generally older, with reputations for strength and strong connections to other women in their neighborhoods or through their occupations. In terms of the distinctions made above between power and authority, these women had power, but no legitimate political authority. Because they did not demand authority or political rights, or in fact make any specific demands as women, their actions were less disturbing to authorities than those of the English female petitioners. Riots were also clearly extraordinary situations in which female leadership might occur without dis-

---

[7] Translated and quoted in Rudolf M. Dekker, "Women in revolt: popular protest and its social basis in Holland in the seventeenth and eighteenth centuries," *Theory and Society* 16 (1987), p. 345.

turbing gender expectations; both the women activists and the authorities who responded to them were familiar with biblical and historical examples of women who took over in emergencies, but then deferred again to men once the crisis had passed, a model all participants expected would be followed again.

When women's participation in political disturbances went beyond short-term riots to larger and more extensive political rebellions, male authorities were extremely threatened and the response to such rebellions could be particularly brutal. William Palmer has demonstrated, for example, the English men were horrified at Irish women's support of revolts against the English conquest of Ireland in the sixteenth century, and used such women's influence over their husbands as a sign of Irish inferiority. Like the later English female petitioners, Irish women were accused of sexual misconduct, of being, in the words of the English observer William Camden in 1610, "more lewd than lewdness itself."[8] English military actions against the Irish were specifically directed at women as well as men, and their violence was justified with comments about the women's central role as instigators.

Though women's subjection to their husbands may have made some women in early modern Europe more willing to participate in revolts because they might not be held legally liable for their actions, it made others critical of marriage as an institution. Mary Astell, for example, built on the ideas of Anna Maria van Schurman and Bathsua Makin in advocating women's education, but viewed the institution of marriage as well as women's inferior education as a prime cause of their secondary status:

Though a Husband can't deprive a Wife of Life without being responsible to the Law, he may, however, do what is much more grievous to a generous Mind, render Life miserable, for which she has no Redress, scarce Pity, which is afforded every other Complainant, it being thought a Wife's Duty to suffer every thing without Complaint. . . How can a Man respect his Wife when he has a Contemptible Opinion of her and her Sex?[9]

This theme was also part of the writings of Jane Barker, Sarah Fyge, Lady Chudleigh, and Anne Finch (later Lady Winchelsea), who wrote poetry and polemics supporting women's rights to autonomous thought and celebrating female friendship.

---

[8] William Camden, *Britain, or a Chorographical Description of England, Scotland, and Ireland* (London, 1610), p. 144.

[9] Mary Astell, *Some Reflections on Marriage* (1706), quoted in Moira Ferguson (ed.), *First Feminists: British Women Writers 1578–1799* (Bloomington, Indiana University Press, 1985), p. 193.

Negative opinions about marriage were not limited to England, for Maria de Zayas y Sotomayor (1590?–1661?) in Madrid also wrote stories in which the main female character asserted her independence by deciding to go into a convent rather than marry. This option was not open to women in Protestant areas such as England, and Astell's proposal to open a religious retreat for unmarried women was attacked as "Popish." In general, though they criticized marriage, English female writers recognized that most women would be forced to marry for economic reasons, and so also gave suggestions about how to choose a husband wisely. They did note that those few who could afford to remain single should, and suggested that such women should move to rural retreats to avoid other institutions that would compromise their independence.

Women such as Mary Astell and Maria de Zayas y Sotomayor have generally been termed "feminists" for their recognition and deploring of ideas and institutions that hindered women. They are also some of the first individuals to exhibit what we would call a consciousness of gender, that is, the realization that women as a group shared certain characteristics that resulted not from biology or "nature" but from social patterns. Early modern feminists recognized that such patterns could be changed, but also came to feel the power of tradition and the force of misogyny. Marie de Gournay, for example, the protégée of Michel de Montaigne and editor of his works, asserted the equality of men and women in *L'Egalité des hommes et des femmes* (1622). Four years later, after being ridiculed and belittled, she realized its calls for equality would never be taken seriously, and wrote despairingly in *L'Ombre (The Shadow):* "Be happy, reader, if you are not of that sex to which is forbidden all good things inasmuch as it is forbidden liberty."[10] She went on to suggest that she and her male readers should simply separate to avoid arguing.

Men who otherwise broke with tradition in early modern Europe did not change their ideas about the proper roles of men and women, as we have seen with Martin Luther. In England, even the most radical groups in the Civil War did not call for extending political rights to women or suggest that ending the power of the monarch over his subjects should be matched by ending the power of husbands over their wives. The former was unjust and against God's will, while the latter was "natural," as the words of the radical Parliamentarian Henry Parker make clear: "The wife is inferior in nature, and was created for the assistance of man, and servants are hired for their Lord's mere attendance; but it is otherwise in

---

[10] Translated and quoted in Constance Jordan, *Renaissance Feminism: Literary Texts and Political Models* (Ithaca, Cornell University Press, 1990), p. 285.

the State between man and man, for that civill difference. . . is for. . .
the good of all, not that servility and drudgrery may be imposed upon
all for the pompe of one."[11] Women such as Mary Astell may have been
inspired by revolutionary writings to question existing social relationships, but they realized that no general discussion of the "rights of the
citizen" ever concerned itself with women, so they generally remained
loyal to the monarchy. Mary Astell, in fact, specifically criticized the parliamentarians for "not crying up Liberty to poor female slaves," eloquently pointing out the irony of their demands for rights in the second
of the quotations that opens this chapter.[12]

By extending political power to a somewhat larger group of men, parliamentary governments in the early modern period in fact heightened
the importance of sex as a determinant of political power. Once the decision of an all-male parliament became the most important factor in
determining who would rule, women even lost the uncontrollable power
over political succession they had through bearing children. (The fact
that parliamentary power over the choice of a monarch freed men from
being dependent on women's biology was not lost on early modern
advocates of limited monarchy.)

The models that men were encouraged to follow increasingly included
responsible use of political power and were cast in secular terms, while
women's virtues remained domestic and Christian. As Jean Bodin put it,
"To be a good man is also to be a good citizen";[13] to be a good woman
was still to be a good Christian. Though in the sixteenth century
Christian virtues such as piety, charity, and humility were regarded as
equal to or more important than secular ones, by the eighteenth century
secular qualities such as reason, good judgment, and comradeship were
clearly more significant. Christian virtues were privatized and feminized,
no longer viewed as important in the public actions of rulers or political
leaders, though their private lives were still to give evidence of religious
convictions. Qualities such as reason which were becoming the most
important public virtues were characteristics that had long been viewed
as masculine, making it even more difficult for women to play a public
role. As we saw in Chapter 3, in the sixteenth and seventeenth centuries
groups such as craft and journeymen's guilds began to use more explic-

---

[11] [Henry Parker], *Observations upon some of his Majesties Late Answers and Expresses*
[1642], p. 14

[12] Mary Astell, *A Serious Proposal to the Ladies* (1694), quoted in Hilda Smith, *Reason's
Disciples: Seventeenth-century English Feminists* (Urbana, University of Iliinois Press,
1982), p. 10.

[13] Bodin, *Six Books*, in Fauré, *Democracy*, p. 39.

itly masculine words such as "brotherhood" and "fraternity" when describing their aims, words that were extended in the late eighteenth century to discussions of more general public political goals. The importance of gender continued to increase in the nineteenth century, when the word "male" was used for the first time in many voting rights' provisions.

Though spiritual equality and other religious arguments remained important into the twentieth century as grounds for extending rights to women or improving their legal situation, a few early modern feminists also recognized the growing secularization of European culture and began to argue that women and men were equal in their rational as well as spiritual capacities. The Duchess of Newcastle gained this insight, she wrote, from self-contemplation, Mary Astell from reading Descartes and other Cartesian thinkers such as Poulain de la Barre and Jacques Du Bosc, and the anonymous author (probably Judith Drake) of *An Essay in Defence of the Female Sex* (1696) from reading Locke.

Of all early modern political philosophers, John Locke appears to have offered the greatest possibilities for women, for he described marriage as a voluntary compact which could be terminated and whose conditions could be set by the two spouses; as long as the children were cared for, Locke did not see any natural necessity for following traditional patterns of authority in a marriage. This possibility of equality within marriage did not translate into a possibility of political equality for Locke, however, because he did not see the family as analogous to civil society. Rather than basing the rights of a citizen on a man's power as head of household, he based it on the ownership of property, which just as effectively excluded most women. Though in a few cases, such as the early United States, Lockean principles were strictly followed and unmarried female property owners were allowed to vote, these anomalies did not last long because they were not an intentional extension of voting rights to women, but simply accidental. Not until property was also thrown out as the basis for political rights, that is, by some thinkers in the most extreme phase of the French Revolution, did women such as Olympe de Gouges and Mary Wollstonecraft explicitly call for an extension of political rights to both sexes, though they generally discovered that the revolutionaries of 1789 were no more accepting of this idea than those of the seventeenth century had been.

In a similar way, the thought of Thomas Hobbes could have offered women the possibility of greater political rights, because he based male authority on social custom and agreements between the parties involved (what he terms a "contract") rather than on a notion of natural male superiority. In the *Leviathan*, Hobbes noted that in the state of nature, that is, before the development of civil society, mothers had absolute authority over their children; fathers' authority derived from the fact that men were the ones to have formed governments, and not vice versa as Bodin and Filmer had argued. Hobbes does not consider the implications of this line of reasoning for the relationship between husband and wife, however, nor discuss how or why mothers had given up their authority and let men become sovereign within the household as well as the state. In his discussion of implicit contracts as the basis for the authority structure within a household, he refers only to a man and his children or a man and his servants and does not take into consideration the roots of women's inability freely to make contracts. Thus both Locke and Hobbes are simply unable (or unwilling) to consider the implications of their thoughts for women.

Though we can clearly see the importance of gender when looking at women's political role during the early modern period, it is perhaps less apparent when focusing on men. Men's level of participation in government ("political" in the narrow sense) appears to have been based on factors unrelated to gender – class, age, station, occupation, place of residence, and so on. Recent research has suggested, however, that concepts of masculinity were also important determinants of access to political power. The dominant notion of the "true" man in early modern Europe was that of the married head of household, so that men whose class and age would have normally conferred political power but who remained unmarried did not participate to the same level as their married brothers; in Protestant areas, this link between marriage and authority even included the clergy. As we have seen, unmarried women were increasingly suspect in early modern Europe, but unmarried men were as well, for they were also not living up to what society viewed as their proper place in a gendered social order. Some of these men, such as journeymen in Germany and France, recognized that they could never become heads of household, so created alternative concepts of masculinity and masculine honor clearly distinct from the dominant one. They came to view their unmarried, unattached state, which had originally been forced on them by guild masters, as a positive thing, and emphasized their freedom from political duties rather than their lack of political rights. They regarded loyalty to the all-male journeymen's organization as extremely important, making a "true" man, for them, one with few contacts to women who proved his masculinity through drinking and fighting. Masters and journeymen thus had different ideas about masculinity, a split that can be seen in other contexts as well. The English Civil War, for example, is often portrayed as a battle between Royalist cavaliers in their long hair and fancy silk knee-breeches opposing Puritan parliamentarians with their short hair and somber clothing, clearly two conflicting notions of masculinity. Parliamentary criticism of the court was often expressed in gendered and sexualized terminology, with frequent veiled or open references to aristocratic weakness and inability to control the passions. Thus ideas about masculinity were to some degree class-specific, defined in relation not only to ideas about femininity, but also to notions of manhood developing among other male groups. They also appear to have differed in various parts of Europe, and changed across the life-cycle, with honor, sexual prowess, honesty, reason, physical strength, self-mastery, authority over others, and reputation all part of manhood, but varying in their importance.

Notions of masculinity were also important symbols in early modern political discussions. Queen Elizabeth was not the only ruler to realize that people expected monarchs to be male, and that qualities judged masculine by her peers – physical bravery, stamina, wisdom, duty – should be emphasized whenever a monarch chose to appear or speak in public. The more successful male rulers recognized this as well, and tried to connect themselves whenever possible with qualities and objects judged male, though sometimes with ironic results. Jeffrey Merrick has demonstrated, for example, that French monarchs and their supporters used the image of a beehive under a "king bee" as a model of harmony under royal rule and a community whose existence depended on the health of its monarch; even scientists spoke of the beehive in this way, for they regarded nature as the best source of examples for appropriate political structures, which they then termed "natural". When the invention of the microscope made it clear the king bee was a queen, both royal propagandists and scientists tried to downplay her sex as long as possible, embarrassed that nature would provide such a demonstration of "unnatural" female power. (By the eighteenth century the sex of the queen bee was no longer ignored, but her role was now described as totally maternal, a symbol of motherhood rather than monarchy.)

A concern with masculinity, and particularly with demonstrating the autonomy expected of a man, pervades the political writings of Machiavelli, who used "effeminate" to describe the worst kind of ruler. Effeminate in the sixteenth century carried slightly different connotations than it does today, however, for strong heterosexual passion was not a sign of manliness, but could make one "effeminate" (i.e., dominated by as well as similar to a woman). English commentators, for example, described Irish men as effeminate and inferior because they let both their wives and their sexual desires influence their actions. Strong same-sex attachments, on the other hand, were often regarded as a sign of virility, as long as they were accompanied by actions judged honorably masculine, such as effective military leadership, and not accompanied by actions judged feminine, such as emotional outbursts. Manliness, the best quality in either ruler or government, was demonstrated by the ability to use reason to take advantage of every situation; as Machiavelli commented in *The Prince*, "Fortune is a woman, and if you want to keep her under, you've got to knock her around some."[14]

Gender and the social order

Once we begin to investigate all relationships of power ("political" in its broadest sense) we find that gender was a central category in the thinking of early modern Europeans. Not only did the maintenance of proper power relationships between men and women serve as a basis for and a symbol of the larger political system, but also for the functioning of society as a whole. Relations between the sexes often provided a model for all dichotomized relations that involved authority and subordination, such as those between ruler and subject. Women or men who stepped outside their prescribed roles in other than extraordinary circumstances, and particularly those who made a point of emphasizing that they were doing this, were seen as threatening not only relations between the sexes, but the operation of the entire social order. They were "disorderly," a word that had much stronger negative connotations in the early modern period than today, and two somewhat distinct meanings – outside of the social structure and unruly or unreasonable.

Women were outside of the social order because they were not as clearly demarcated into social groups as men. Unless they were members of a religious order or guild, women had no corporate identity at a time when society was conceived of as a hierarchy of groups rather than a collection of individuals. One can see women's separation from such groups in the way that parades and processions were arranged in early modern Europe; if women were included, they came at the end as an undifferentiated group, following men who marched together on the basis of political position or occupation. *The Athenian Mercury*, a periodical designed to provide scientific knowledge for the general public, noted that its mission was to "all men and both sexes"; by "all" it meant all classes, ages, stations, and occupations, divisions that were not essen-

---

[14] Niccolo Machiavelli, *The Prince*, tr. Leo Paul S. de Alvarez (Prospect Heights, Illinois, Waveland, 1980), p. 149.

tial when reaching out to include women, for whom sex was the only significant variable.

Rather than deny that women were less divided by class or occupation than men, a few feminist authors celebrated it. The Venetian writers Moderate Fonte and Lucrezia Marinelli both created models of societies based on cooperation and egalitarian relationships, which they saw as the essence of relationships between women; a feminized society, in their opinion, would be one without rank, and infinitely preferable to the hierarchies that prevailed among men. For most authors, however, such lack of hierarchy was a threat. When a few women in London appear to have adopted slightly masculine dress in the early seventeenth century – wearing shorter gowns, cutting their hair, and perhaps carrying small daggers – a host of pamphlets immediately attacked them for being "Men-women" and James I ordered the preachers of London to preach against the practice. The pamphlets were not especially concerned with the women's sexuality – they regarded them as aggressive man-chasers, not lesbians – but that such dress would lead to a breakdown in distinctions of social class as well as gender, because a woman in man's clothing did not reveal her class affiliation the way she would with her normal dress. To male eyes, middle-class wives and noblewomen all looked the same in doublet and hose.

Women were also more "disorderly" than men because they were unreasonable, ruled by their physical body rather than their rational capacity, their lower parts rather than upper. As we saw in Chapter 7, this was one of the reasons they were more often suspected of witchcraft; it was also why they were thought to have non-diabolical magical powers in the realms of love and sexual attraction. At the same time that the number of witchcraft accusations grew, there was also an increase in accusations and trials for love magic, another way in which women could gain power over men's bodies and minds. This same period saw an increase in accusations and punishment of women for scolding, name-calling, and other types of verbal abuse, particularly when it was directed against their husbands. Through these legal sanctions, communities disciplined women who used words to gain power in their households or neighborhoods.

Disorder in the proper gender hierarchy was linked with other types of social upheaval. Groups and individuals intent on some alteration in political or social hierarchies were also charged with wanting to change the proper hierarchy of the sexes. This charge was leveled at Anabaptists speaking about spiritual equality, Levellers advocating fewer economic disparities, and Quakers unwilling to take off their hats for social superiors. Only in the case of the Quakers was this charge justified at all, for, as we have seen, most Anabaptists on the Continent and revolutionary groups in England had very traditional views on gender roles. In cases where it was clear the group did not advocate equality between the sexes, charges of destroying the proper gender structure were still often made, but in these instances the charge was holding or wanting to hold wives in common. "Community of wives" appeared even more shocking to early modern Europeans than community of goods, requiring harsh suppression in the few instances it actually did appear – such as the Anabaptist community at Münster – and provoking scandal when simply mentioned as part of a mythical utopia – such as Tommaso Campanella's *City of the Sun* (1602). ("Community of husbands" would be still more shocking, of course, which is perhaps why even those attacking Campanella could not mention that the arrangements for procreation in his utopia would have meant this as well.)

Women dominating men were connected with other ways in which the expected hierarchy might be overturned – the unlearned leading the learned, the young controlling the old – in both learned and popular literature and popular festivals. Carnival plays frequently portrayed domineering wives in pants and henpecked husbands washing diapers alongside professors in dunce caps and peasants riding princes. These figures appear in woodcuts and engravings, and in songs, stories, and poems. Shakespeare and other learned authors used gender inversions, especially women in men's clothing, as plot devices with both serious and comic intent, but by the end of the plays the women are back in women's clothing, generally happily married, and the proper social order has been restored.

Gender hierarchies were also linked with developing notions of racial difference, which grew out of earlier ideas about religious and class difference, all of which were conceptualized as "blood." People were regarded as having blood that was Jewish, Muslim, or Christian – or after the Reformation Protestant or Catholic – noble or commoner; marriages across these groups were often prohibited or regarded as threatening because they involved the mixing of unlike blood. In early modern Spain, "purity of the blood" – having no Jewish or Muslim ancestors – became an obsession, and throughout Europe children born of religiously mixed Christian marriages were often slightly mistrusted, for one never knew whether their Protestant or Catholic blood would ultimately triumph. Blood was also used to describe national boundaries, with those having "French blood" distinguished from those having "German blood," "English blood," or "Spanish blood." Describing differences as blood naturalized them, making them appear as if they were created by God in nature.

As Europeans developed colonial empires, these notions of blood became a way of conceptualizing race as well as religion, class, and nation. In some cases religious and racial differences were linked. English Protestant authorities, for example, regarded the Catholicism of Gaelic-speaking Irish as one sign of the "natural" barbarity and inferiority of the "Irish race." Christian suspicions of those with "Jewish blood" or members of the "Jewish race" were not limited to Spain, with Jews throughout Europe increasingly regarded as a separate race as well as religion. Religion was also initially a marker of difference in colonial areas outside Europe, where the spread of Christianity was used as a justification for conquest and enslavement. As indigenous peoples converted, however, religion became less useful as a means of differentiation, and skin color became more important. For example, Virginia laws regarding fornication distinguished between "Christian" and "negroe" in 1662, but by 1691 between "white" men and women and those who were "negroe, mulatto, or Indian." Religious affiliation thus came to have no effect on one's blood in the binary racial classification developing in colonial North America (and its mother countries), where "one drop of [black] blood" made one black. In contrast to this binary classification, the Spanish and Portuguese colonies developed more complex racial hierarchies, but these were also based increasingly on skin color in what has been termed a "pigmentocracy." Racial categories in these colonies were to some degree arbitrary, with priests and officials granted the power to declare an individual "white" for the purposes of marriage, entering a convent, or becoming a priest, no matter what his or her ancestry.

The situation in early modern Latin America highlights the fact that like gender, race is socially constructed and historically variable. (Indeed, most scientists who study the human species as a whole, such as biologists and anthropologists, avoid using the word completely.) Because it marked the beginning of Europe's colonial enterprise, the early modern period was a time when Europeans were more concerned with "racial" differences than they had been earlier, when they were actively engaged in creating social meanings for racial categories. They drew on polarities of white and black which had existed in western culture since ancient times to develop a racial hierarchy to parallel hierarchies based on class, gender, and religion, and then worried about the relations among these hierarchies and the ways in which disorder in one might create disorders in the others. It was clear to most Europeans who stood at the top of the hierarchy – white men – and who at the bottom – non-white women – but the middle was more ambiguous. They wondered which hierarchy was more significant, God-given, and natural, that of race or that of gender. Which was easier to overcome, that is, was it easier for a woman to be "manly" or for a non-white man? If social class could outweigh gender as a determinant of social role for a woman like Queen Elizabeth, could gender outweigh race for a man like Shakespeare's Othello?

Because of the possibility of intermarriage and other intergroup sexual relations (which would, of course, erase the differences if they became common enough), gender often entered into these discussions in a sexualized way. European explorers and colonizers described their conquests in sexualized terms, portraying territory and its peoples as feminized, weak, and passive and themselves as virile, powerful, and masculine. The ambiguous middle of the hierarchy – white women and non-white men – was particularly threatening in terms of sexual relations, a threat not lessened by the rarity of such relationships in Europe during this period. With even greater vigor than the boundaries of class and religion, interracial boundaries were described as "natural," making any crossing, particularly a sexual one, unnatural or even demonic. The "debate about race" in early modern Europe has not been studied as extensively yet as the "debate about women," but it is clear the two are closely related.

The most vigorous debate about race took place in the European colonies rather than Europe itself during this period, for in the colonies racial differences were a matter of day-to-day policy and practice as well as theory. For most authors in Europe, and, judging by court cases, popular customs, and family records, for most people, reversals of the gender hierarchy were the most threatening way in which the world could be turned upside down. Literature and art provided examples of strong women, but their independence was usually restricted in the end, or they voluntarily chose to restrict it through marriage or entering a convent. Men and women involved in relationships in which the women were thought to have power – an older woman who married a younger man, or a woman who scolded her husband – were often subjected to public ridicule, with bands of neighbors shouting insults and banging sticks and pans in their disapproval. Adult male journeymen refused to work for widows, though this decreased their opportunities for employment. Fathers disinherited disobedient daughters more often than sons. The derivative nature of an adult woman's authority – the fact that it came from her status as wife or widow of the male household head – was emphasized by referring to her as "wife" rather than "mother" even in legal documents describing her relations with her children. Of all the ways in which society was hierarchically arranged – class, age, rank, race, occupation – gender was regarded as the most "natural" and therefore the most important to defend.

The early modern period appears, then, to be a time of continual rein-
forcement of gender hierarchies and patriarchal structures, which we can
trace in court records, marriage manuals, dramas, paintings, songs, sermons, and a variety of other sources. Just why that message was so strong
during this period has not been fully explained, however. Were women
acting in ways that appeared to be or actually were breaking down these
hierarchies, so that our evidence represents the reverse of what was happening in reality? Were men not doing what was expected of them? Were
economic, political, or intellectual changes – the growth of capitalism,
the rise of the nation-state, the Scientific Revolution – making the old
gender roles obsolete before satisfactory new ones had been created? Do
these changes only make the continuities in patterns of gender and
power seem stronger than they do in other eras? Questions such as these
are now being investigated, and someday we may have an answer. For
the moment, we can safely say only that by looking at the experiences of
women and the role of gender, we have discovered that the changes
which occurred in the early modern period are even more complex than
we had previously assumed, and that at no time or place did they mean
the same for men and women. Our investigations of women's lives have
led us to realize the extent that women's experiences differed from those
of men, the extent that they varied among women, and, most recently,
the extent that men's experiences varied in ways that have received little
attention. Let us hope that our toleration for complexity and ambiguity
exceeds that of our early modern forbears.

Bibliography

The relationship between gender and power has recently been the focus of many
theoretical discussions, though some of these, especially in linguistics and psychology, do not have a historical dimension. Some of the most important theo-
retical works that do include: Mary O'Brien, *The Politics of Reproduction*
(London, Routledge, 1981); Joan W. Scott, "Gender: a useful category of histor-
ical analysis," *American Historical Review* 91 (1986), 1053–75; R. W. Connell,
Gender and Power: Society, the Person and Sexual Politics (Oxford, Polity, 1987); Jeff
Hearn, *The Gender of Oppression: Men, Masculinity and the Critique of Marxism*
(Brighton, Wheatsheaf, 1987); Arthur Brittan, *Masculinity and Power* (London,
Basil Blackwell, 1989). Theoretical discussions of the links between male/female
and public/private include: Eva Gamarnikow, et al. (eds.), *The Public and the
Private* (London, Heinemann, 1983); Janet Sharistanian (ed.), *Gender, Ideology,
and Action: Historical Perspectives on Women's Public Lives* (Westport, Conn.,
Greenwood, 1986); Sherry Ortner, *Making Gender: The Politics and Erotics of
Culture* (Boston, Beacon, 1996); Joan Landes (ed.), *Feminism, the Public and the
Private* (Oxford, Oxford University Press, 1998). Sharistanian contains several
essays that discuss the public/private split in the early modern period, and for

further specific studies, see Joan Kelly, "Did women have a Renaissance?," in Renata Bridenthal and Claudia Koonz (eds.), *Becoming Visible: Women in European History* (Boston, Houghton Mifflin, 1977 and 1987), pp. 137–64 (1977) and 175–201 (1987); Natalie Davis, "Boundaries and the sense of self in sixteenth-century France," in Thomas C. Heller, et al., (eds.), *Reconstructing Individualism: Autonomy, Individuality, and the Self in Western Thought* (Stanford, Stanford University Press, 1986), pp. 53–63 and 332–35; Merry E. Wiesner, "Women's defense of their public role," in Mary Beth Rose (ed.), *Women in the Middle Ages and the Renaissance: Literary and Historical Perspectives* (Syracuse, Syracuse University Press, 1986), pp. 1–27; Susan Cerasano and Marion Wynne-Davies (eds.), *Gloriana's Face: Women, Public and Private in the English Renaissance* (Detroit, Wayne State University Press, 1992); Retha Warnicke, "Private and public: the boundaries of women's lives in early Stuart England," in Jean R. Brink (ed.), *Privileging Gender in Early Modern England* (Kirksville, Mo., Sixteenth Century Journal Publishers, 1993), pp. 123–40; Robert Shoemaker, *Gender in English Society 1650–1850: The Emergence of Separate Spheres?* (London, Longman, 1998). For a review of Habermas's ideas, see Dena Goodman, "Public sphere and private life: toward a synthesis of current historiographical approaches to the Old Regime," *History and Theory* 31 (1992), 1–20.

The debate about female rulers has been surveyed in: Paula Louise Scalingi, "The scepter or the distaff: the question about female sovereignty, 1516–1607," *The Historian* 41 (1978); Constance Jordan, *Renaissance Feminism: Literary Texts and Political Models* (Ithaca, Cornell University Press, 1990); Amanda Shephard, *Gender and Authority in Sixteenth-Century England: The Knox Debate* (Keele, Keele University Press, 1994); Susan M. Felch, "The rhetoric of Biblical authority: John Knox and the question of women," *Sixteenth Century Journal* 26 (1995), 805–22; Lisa Hopkins, *Women Who Would be Kings: Female Rulers of the Sixteenth Century* (London, St. Martin's, 1991) discusses both ruling queens and queen consorts from all over Europe, while Louise Olga Fradenburg, *Women and Sovereignty* (Edinburgh: Edinburgh University Press, 1992) includes essays on many medieval and early modern female rulers.

Because of her peculiar status as an unmarried queen, Elizabeth I has merited the most attention, both in the early modern period and today. Important discussions of the reality and symbols surrounding her reign include: Allison Heisch, "Queen Elizabeth I: Parliamentary rhetoric and the exercise of power," *Signs* 1 (1975), 31–55; Louis Montrose, "Shaping fantasies: figurations of gender and power in Elizabethan culture," *Representations* 1 (1983), 61–94; P. Berry, *Of Chastity and Power: Elizabethan Literature and the Unmarried Queen* (London: Routledge, 1989); Carole Levin, "Power, politics, and sexuality: images of Elizabeth I," in Jean R. Brink, et al. (eds.), *The Politics of Gender in Early Modern Europe*. Sixteenth Century Essays and Studies, 12 (Kirksville, Mo., Sixteenth Century Journal Publishers, 1989), pp. 95–110, "'Would I could give you help and succour': Elizabeth I and the politics of touch," *Albion* 21 (1989), 191–205 and *The Heart and Stomach of a King: Elizabeth I and the Politics of Sex and Power* (Philadelphia, University of Pennsylvania Press, 1994); J. N. King, "Queen Elizabeth I: Representations of the Virgin Queen," *Renaissance Quarterly* 43 (1990), 30–74; Susan Frye, *Elizabeth I: The Competition for Representation* (Oxford, Oxford University Press, 1993); Margaret Christian, "Elizabeth's

preachers and the government of women: defining and correcting a queen,"
Sixteenth Century Journal 24 (1993), 561–76; Helen Hackett, *Virgin Mother, Maiden Queen: Elizabeth I and the Cult of theVirgin Mary* (NewYork, St. Martin's, 1996); Susan Doran, *Monarchy and Matrimony: The Courtships of Elizabeth I* (NewYork, Routledge, 1996). Recent biographies include: Wallace MacCaffrey, *Elizabeth I* (London, Edward Arnold, 1994), AlisonWeir *The Life of Elizabeth I* (New York, Ballantine Books, 1998) and Alison Plowden's four-volume Elizabethan quartet, published by Sutton. Whether Elizabeth actually gave the Tilbury speech quoted at the beginning of this chapter has been debated in Susan Frye, "The myth of Elizabeth at Tilbury," *Sixteenth Century Journal* 23 (1992), 95–114 and Janet M. Green, "'I My Self': Queen Elizabeth I's oration at Tilbury camp" *Sixteenth Century Journal* 28 (1997), 421–45.

For discussions of other female rulers, see: Marvin Lunenfeld, "Isabella I of Castile and the company of women in power," *Historical Reflections* 4 (1977), 207–29; Michael Lynch (ed.), *Mary Stewart: Queen in Three Kingdoms* (Oxford, Basil Blackwell, 1988); John Carmi Parsons (ed.), *Medieval Queenship* (New York, St. Martin's, 1993); Bethany Aram, "Juana 'the Mad's' signature: the problem of invoking royal authority, 1505–1507," *Sixteenth Century Journal* 29 (1998), 331–58; Magdalena S. Sánchez, *The Empress, the Queen, and the Nun: Women and Power at the Court of Philip III of Spain* (Baltimore, The Johns Hopkins University Press, 1998); Alison Plowden, *Tudor Women* (Rochester, N.Y., Sutton Books, 1998) and *Two Queens in One Isle:The Deadly Relationship of Elizabeth I and Mary Queen of Scots* (Rochester, N.Y., Sutton Books, 1999); Susan E. James, *Kateryn Parr:The Making of a Queen* (NewYork, Ashgate, 1999); Jayne Elizabeth Lewis, *The Trial of Mary Queen of Scots: A Brief History with Documents* (Boston, Bedford, 1999); Kathleen Crawford, "Catherine de Medicis and the performance of political motherhood," *Sixteenth Century Journal* (forthcoming). Lois Schwoerer, *Lady Rachel Russell (1637–1723): "One of the Best of Women"* (Baltimore, The Johns Hopkins University Press, 1988) and Barbara Harris, "Women and politics in early Tudor England," *Historical Journal* 33 (1990), 259–81 discuss upper-class women's informal political role.

Links between public political power and the power of the male head of household have been explored most innovatively by Sarah Hanley, "Engendering the state: family formation and state building in early modern France," *French Historical Studies* 16 (1989), 4–27, "Women in the body politic of early modern France," *Proceedings of the Annual Meeting of the Western Society for French History* 16 (1989), 408–14, "The monarchic state in early modern France: marital regime government and male right," in Adrianna Bakos (ed.), *Politics, Ideology, and the Law in Early Modern Europe: Essays in Honor of J.H.M. Salmon* (Rochester, University of Rochester Press, 1994), and "Social sites of political practice in France: lawsuits, civil rights, and the separation of powers in domestic and state government, 1500–1800," *American Historical Review* 102 (1997), 27–52. Kristin Zapalac, *"In His Image and Likeness": Political Iconography and Religious Change in Regensburg, 1500–1600* (Ithaca, Cornell University Press, 1990), pp. 135–66 discusses paternal imagery in German cities.

Women's participation in revolts and extraordinary political activities during times of unrest have been discussed in: Ellen A. McArthur, "Women petitioners and the Long Parliament," *English Historical Review* 24 (1909), 698–709; Patricia

Higgins, "The reactions of women, with special reference to women petitioners," in *Politics, Religion and the English Civil War* (London, Edward Arnold, 1973), pp. 178–222; Ralph Houlbrooke, "Women's social life and common action in England from the fifteenth century to the eve of the Civil War," *Continuity and Change* 1 (1986), 171–89; Lois Schwoerer, "Women and the Glorious Revolution," *Albion* 18 (1986), 195–218; Rudolf M. Dekker, "Women in revolt: collective protest and its social basis in Holland in the seventeenth and eighteenth centuries," *Theory and Society* 16 (1987), 337–62; William Palmer, "Gender, violence and rebellion in Tudor and early Stuart Ireland," *Sixteenth Century Journal* 23 (1992), 685–712; Rachel Weil, "The politics of legitimacy: women and the warming-pan scandal," in Lois Schwoerer (ed.), *The Revolution of 1688–89: Changing Perspectives* (Cambridge, Cambridge University Press, 1992), pp. 65–82; Dagmar Freist, "The king's crown is the whore of Babylon: politics, gender, and communication in mid-seventeenth-century England," *Gender and History* 7 (1995), 443–65; Sharon L. Jansen, *Dangerous Talk and Strange Behavior: Women and Popular Resistance to the Reforms of Henry VIII* (New York, St. Martin's, 1996); Alison Plowden, *Our Women All on Fire: The Women of the English Civil War* (London, Sutton Books, 1999). Representations of women during times of revolt have been analyzed in a special issue, "Gender, literature and the English Revolution," *Women's Studies: An Interdisciplinary Journal* 24 (1994), 1–188. See the bibliography that follows Chapter 6 for further works about women in the English Civil War.

Discussions of gender in early modern political theory include: Gordon Schochet, *Patriarchalism in Political Thought: The Authoritarian Family and Political Speculation and Attitudes especially in Seventeenth Century England* (New York, Basic Books, 1975); Mary Lyndon Shanley, "Marriage contract and social contract in seventeenth-century English political thought," in Jean Bethke Elshtain (ed.), *The Family in Political Thought* (Amherst, University of Massachusetts Press, 1982), pp. 80–95, 313–316; Catherine Gallagher, "Embracing the absolute: the politics of the female subject in seventeenth-century England," *Genders* 1 (1988), 24–39; Hilda Smith, "'All men and both sexes': Concepts of men's development, women's education and feminism in the seventeenth century," in Donald C. Mell, Jr., et al. (eds.), *Man, God, and Nature in the Enlightenment* (East Lansing, Mich., Colleagues Press, 1988) and "Intellectual bases for feminist analyses: the seventeenth and eighteenth centuries," in Elizabeth D. Harvey and Kathleen Okruhlik (eds.), *Women and Reason* (Ann Arbor, University of Michigan Press, 1992), pp. 19–38; Carole Pateman, "'God hath ordained to man a helper': Hobbes, patriarchy and conjugal right," *British Journal of Political Science* 19 (1989), 445–64; Christine Fauré, *Democracy Without Women: Feminism and the Rise of Liberal Individualism in France*, trans. Claudia Gorbman and John Berks (Bloomington, Indiana University Press, 1991); Jacqueline Murray, "Agnolo Firenzuola on female sexuality and women's equality," *Sixteenth Century Journal* 22 (1991), 199–213; Elizabeth D. Harvey and Kathleen Okruhlic, *Women and Reason* (Ann Arbor, University of Michigan Press, 1992); Gisela Bock and Susan James (eds.), *Beyond Equality and Difference: Citizenship, Feminist Politics and Female Subjectivity* (London, Routledge, 1992); Erica Harth, *Cartesian Women: Versions and Subversions of Rational Discourse in the Old Regime* (Ithaca, Cornell University Press, 1992);

Patricia Crawford, "Public duty, conscience and women in early modern England," in John Morrilll, Paul Slack, and Daniel Woolf (eds.), *Public Duty and Private Conscience in Seventeenth-Century England* (Oxford, Oxford University Press, 1993); Genevieve Fraisse, *Reason's Muse: Sexual Difference and the Birth of Democracy* (Chicago, University of Chicago Press, 1994); Gabriella Slomp, "Hobbes and the equality of women," *Political Studies* 42 (1994), 441–52; Jodi Mikalachki, *The Legacy of Boadicea: Gender and Nation in Early Modern England* (London, Routledge, 1998).

Studies that focus on women's own ideas about their political position include Hilda L. Smith, *Reason's Disciples: Seventeenth-century English Feminists* (Urbana, University of Illinois Press, 1982); Ruth Perry, *The Celebrated Mary Astell: An Early English Feminist* (Chicago, University of Chicago Press, 1986); Christine Mason Sutherland, "Outside the rhetorical tradition: Mary Astell's advice to women in seventeenth-century England," *Rhetorica* 9 (1991), 147–63; Sophia B. Blaydes, "Nature is a woman: the Duchess of Newcastle and seventeenth century philosophy," in Mell, *Man, God*, pp. 51–64; Hilda L. Smith (ed.), *Women Writers and the Early Modern British Political Tradition* (Cambridge, Cambridge University Press, 1998); Megan Matchinske, *Writing, Gender and State in Early Modern England: Identity Formation and the Female Subject* (Cambridge, Cambridge University Press, 1998). Editions of women's feminist works include: Moira Ferguson (ed.), *First Feminists: British Women Writers 1578–1799* (Bloomington, Indiana University Press, 1985); Mary Astell, *The First English Feminist: Reflections on Marriage and and Other Writings,* ed. Bridget Hill (New York, St. Martin's, 1986) and *Astell, Political Writings,* ed. Patricia Springborg (Cambridge, Cambridge University Press, 1996); Moderata Fonte (Modesta Pozza) *The Worth of Women: Wherein Is Clearly Revealed Their Nobility and Their Superiority to Men,* ed. and trans. Virginia Cox (Chicago, University of Chicago Press, 1997); Lucrezia Marinella, *The Nobility and Excellence of Women and the Defects and Vices of Men,* introduction by Letizia Panizza and Anne Dunhill, trans. Anne Dunhill (Chicago, University of Chicago Press, 2000); Marie de Gournay, *The Equality of Men and Women and Other Writings,* ed. and trans. Richard Hillman and Colette Quesnal (Chicago, University of Chicago Press, 2001).

Relations between gender and the social order have been discussed in Natalie Davis, "Women on top," in her *Society and Culture in Early Modern France* (Stanford, Stanford University Press, 1975), pp. 124–51; Thomas Robisheaux, *Rural Society and the Search for Order in Early Modern Germany* (Cambridge, Cambridge University Press, 1989); Hannah Pitkin, *Fortune Is a Woman: Gender and Politics in the Thought of Niccolò Machiavelli* (Berkeley, University of California Press, 1984); David Underdown, "The taming of the scold: the enforcement of patriarchal authority in early modern England," in Anthony Fletcher and John Stevenson (eds.), *Order and Disorder in Early Modern England* (Cambridge, Cambridge University Press, 1985), pp. 116–36; Susan Dwyer Amussen, *An Ordered Society: Gender and Class in Early Modern England* (London, Basil Blackwell, 1988); Carole Pateman, *The Sexual Contract* (Stanford, Stanford University Press, 1988) and *The Disorder of Women* (Stanford, Stanford University Press, 1989); Mary Elizabeth Perry, *Gender and Disorder in Early Modern Seville* (Princeton, Princeton University Press, 1990);

Mary Beth Rose, "Women in men's clothing: apparel and social stability in *The Roaring Girl*," *English Literary Renaissance* 14 (1984), 367–91; Jeffrey Merrick, "Royal bees: the gender politics of the beehive in early modern Europe," *Studies in Eighteenth Century Culture* 18 (1988), 7–37, "Fathers and kings: patriarchalism and absolutism in eighteenth-century French politics," *Studies on Voltaire and the Eighteenth Century* 308 (1993), and "The cardinal and the queen: sexual and political disorders in the Mazarinades, *French Historical Studies* 18 (1994); Jean Howard, "The theatre, cross-dressing and gender struggle in early modern England," *Shakespeare Quarterly* 39 (1988), 418–40; several of the essays in Marilyn Migiel and Juliana Schiesari, *Refiguring Woman: Perspectives on Gender and the Italian Renaissance* (Ithaca, Cornell University Press, 1991); Anthony Fletcher, *Gender, Sex, and Subordination in England 1500–1800* (New Haven, Yale University Press, 1995); Julie Hardwick, *The Practice of Patriarchy: Gender and the Politics of Household Authority in Early Modern France* (University Park, Pennsylvania State University Press, 1998); Pavla Miller, *Transformations of Patriarchy in the West, 1500–1900* (Bloomington, Indiana University Press, 1998); Judith C. Brown and Robert C. Davis (eds.), *Gender and Society in Renaissance Italy* (New York, Longman, 1998); Nancy Shields Kollman, *By Honor Bound: State and Society in Early Modern Russia* (Ithaca, NY, Cornell University Press, 1999).

The best discussion of the links between racial and gender hierarchies in this period is Tessie Liu "Teaching the differences among women from a historial perspective: rethinking race and gender as social categories," *Women's Studies International Forum* 14 (1991), 265–76. See also: Winthrop Jordan, *White Over Black: American Attitudes Toward the Negro, 1550–1812* (Chapel Hill, University of North Carolina Press, 1968); Paul Edwards, "Representations of blacks and blackness in the Renaissance," *Criticism* 35 (1993), 499–528; Margo Hendricks and Patricia Parker (eds.), *Women, "Race" and Writing in the Early Modern Period* (London, Routledge, 1994); Kim F. Hall, *Things of Darkness: Economies of Race and Gender in Early Modern England* (Ithaca, Cornell University Press, 1995). For further readings, see the suggestions in my *Christianity and Sexuality in the Early Modern World: Regulating Desire, Reforming Practice* (London, Routledge, 2000).

The social construction of masculinity has become an extremely hot topic in historical research within the last five years. For general works, see: George Mosse, *The Image of Man: The Creation of Modern Masculinity* (New York: Oxford University Press, 1995); R. W. Connell, *Masculinities* (Berkeley, University of California Press, 1995); Stephen B. Boyd, et al. (eds.), *Redeeming Men: Religion and Masculinities* (Louisville, KY: Westminster/John Knox, 1996). For studies that focus on the medieval or early modern period, see: Stanley Chojnacki, "Political adulthood in fifteenth-century Venice," *American Historical Review* 91 (1986), 791–810; Merry E. Wiesner, "Wandervogels and women: journeymen's concepts of masculinity in early modern Germany," *Journal of Social History* 24 (1991), 767–82; David Kuchta, "The semiotics of masculinity in Renaissance England" in James Grantham Turner (ed.), *Sexuality and Gender in Early Modern Europe: Institutions, Texts, Images* (Cambridge, Cambridge University Press, 1993), pp. 233–46; Clare Lees (ed.), *Medieval Masculinites: Regarding Men in the Middle Ages* (Minneapolis, University of Minnesota Press, 1994); Susan

Amussen, "'The part of a Christian man': the cultural politics of manhood in early modern England," in Susan Amussen and Mark Kishlansky (eds.), *Political Culture and Cultural Politics in Early Modern England: Essays Presented to David Underdown* (Manchester, Manchester University Press, 1995); Lyndal Roper, "Stealing manhood: capitalism and magic in early modern Germany" and "Blood and codpieces: masculinity in the early modern German town," both in her *Oedipus and the Devil: Witchcraft, Religion, and Sexuality in Early Modern Europe* (London, Routledge, 1996); Mark Breitenberg, *Anxious Masculinity in Early Modern England* (Cambridge: Cambridge University Press, 1996); Elizabeth Foyster, *Manhood in Early Modern England: Honour, Sex and Marriage* (London, Longman, 1999); Tim Hitchcock and Michele Cohen (eds.), *English Masculinities* (London, Longman, 1999).

Index

Abelard, Peter, 18
abortion, 62–3, 78
Acidalius, Valens, 22
adultery, 40, 66, 73, 78, 297
aging, 91–3
Agrippa von Nettesheim, Cornelius, 13, 21–2, 27, 296
d'Albret, Jeanne, 156, 224
Ambrose, Saint, 51
Anabaptists, 226–7, 294, 307
anchoresses, 218
Anguissola, Sofonisba, 180–1
Anne, Saint (grandmother of Jesus), 219, 228, 237
apprenticeship. See guilds
Aquinas, St. Thomas, 18, 67, 146
Arbaleste, Charlotte, 197, 213–4, 249
Aristotle, 14, 18, 25–6, 30–1, 272
Arnold, Gottfried, 249
artists, 177–85
Askew, Anne, 226
Astell, Mary, 143, 163, 165, 214, 300–3
asylums for women, 65–6, 238, 296
Augustine, Saint, 17, 67, 122, 273
Austria, 128
autobiographies and memoirs, 195–7, 242–3
Aylmer, John, 292

Bacon, Francis, 200, 272
baptism, 83–4
Barker, Jane, 300
Bassi, Laura, 199

Baulacre, Elizabeth 130
beatas, 236–7
Beausoleil, Baroness Martine de, 199
beehives, 305
begging, 109–110, 220. See also women, poor.
Beguines, 77, 217–8
Behn, Aphra, 194
Bejart, Madeleine, 188
Belta, Martha Salome von, 197
Bentley, Thomas, 152
Bernard of Clairvaux, Saint, 19, 219
Bible, 14, 26, 144–5, 150–1, 223, 227, 245, 247
Bijns, Anna, 77
birth control. See contraception
Boccaccio, Giovanni, 20, 24
Bodin, Jean, 25, 268, 292, 302, 304
Boleyn, Anne and Mary, 156
Boothby, Francis, 194
Bourignon, Antoinette, 246, 254
breast-feeding, 87–8

Caccini, Francesca, 187–8
Calvin, John, 26–7, 156, 220, 224, 225
Camden, William, 300
Campanella, Tommaso, 308
Capellanus, Andreas, 20
capitalism, 3, 111–13, 129–33, 310. See also domestic industry.
Carlini, Benedetta, 68
Carriera, Rosalba, 177, 181–2
Carvajal y Mendoza, Luisa de, 233–5

Cary, Elizabeth, 195
Castiglione, Baldassar, 22, 164
Catherine de Medici, 156, 165, 291
Cavendish, Margaret, Duchess of
    Newcastle, 175, 194, 196–7,
    199–200, 203
celibacy, 17, 27, 58, 72, 158, 228,
    273. *See also* women, unmarried
Cellier, Elizabeth, 201
Cereta, Laura, 154
Chantal, Jeanne de, 234
Châtelet, Madame du, 199
childbirth, 28, 63–4, 79–86, 92, 229,
    250; death in, 85–6
childhood, 52–4
Christianity, Catholic: ideas about
    women in, 55, 57, 86, 94;
    midwives in, 85; in seventeenth-
    century France, 247–8. *See also*
    Council of Trent; Reformation,
    Catholic.
Christianity, pre-Reformation: ideas
    about witchcraft in, 265–6; ideas
    about women in, 16–19, 58, 293;
    role of women in, 215–220
Christianity, Protestant: ideas about
    women in, 26–9, 75, 104;
    midwives in, 85; in seventeenth-
    century England, 242–7; in
    seventeenth and eighteenth-
    century Germany, 242, 248–9. *See
    also* Reformation, Protestant;
    Puritans
Christina of Sweden, 165, 170
Chudleigh, Lady Mary, 70, 300
churching of women, 86–7
Civil War, English, 3, 191, 197, 242,
    244–5, 253, 297–8, 301, 304–5
clitoris, 56, 67
Clitherow, Margaret, 239
cloth production. *See* spinning
Collier, Mary, 102, 114
Colonna, Vittoria, 193
composers, 185–7
confession, 238–9
consumption, 129, 133
contraception, 85, 87

convents, 65, 215–17, 237; closing
    of, 228–31; education in, 149,
    166; and Jansenism, 248; music in,
    187–8; Protestant, 230–1.
cookbooks, 152, 195
Council of Trent, 187, 232–3, 239,
    240
Court of Chancery and Court of
    Requests, 38
courtly love, 19–20
courts, royal, 164–6
crime. *See* law, criminal
cross-dressing. *See* transvestism
Cujas, Jacques, 13, 22

Daughters of Charity, 239–40
debate about women, 20–4, 291–3
Delany, Mary, 177
Denmark, 277, 280
Dentière, Marie, 223, 226
depictions of women, visual, 24–5,
    178–9, 183, 308
devil. *See* Satan
divorce, 52, 73
domestic industry, 112–13, 118–22,
    134
Douglas, Lady Eleanor, 191, 243,
    254
dowries, 37–40, 74–6, 110, 224, 250

education, 53–4, 143–67; advanced,
    159–63; basic, 145–52; at court,
    163–6; humanist, 152–8, 166–7;
    ideas about, 143–5; Protestant
    effects on, 146–9; at salons, 166–7
Eliakim, Isaac ben, 30
Elisabeth of Braunschweig
    (Brunswick-Calenburg), 89, 224
Elizabeth I, Queen of England, 154,
    165, 226, 239, 291, 305, 310
Elizabeth of Bohemia, 170
Elyot, Thomas, 21
embroidery, 178–9
England: childbirth in, 78, 81;
    education in, 150, 152–5, 159;
    homosexuality in, 67; ideas about
    women in, 24, 291–2, 300; laws in,

38–40; religion in, 222, 228, 239, 242–7; scientists in, 200–1; witchcraft in, 279–80; women petititoners in, 245, 297; women's economic role in, 90, 110, 130; writers in, 190–5. *See also* Civil War, English; Puritanism
Erasmus, Desiderius, 21, 155
Erauso, Catalina de, 68
Eve, 15–19, 21–2, 26

Fallopia, Gabriele, 30
Fedele, Cassandra, 154
feminism, early modern, 300–1, 307
Filmer, Robert, 292, 304
Finch, Anne, Vicontess Conway, 199, 300
Finland, 110, 275
Fontana, Lavinia, 181
Fonte, Moderata [Modesta da Pozzo], 24, 307
Fontenelle, Baron de, 198
Fox, John, 245
Fox, Margaret Fell, 245
France: artists in, 179; education in, 155–9, 166–7; ideas about women in, 16–20; laws in, 295–6, 299; marriage in, 91; midwives in, 81; musicians and composers in, 188; religion in, 224, 233, 248; scientists in, 199; writers in, 189
friendship, 70, 300
Fyge, Sarah, 300

Gaeledochter, Claesken, 227
Galen, 30–3
Galizia, Fede, 181
Gambara, Veronica, 193
Geiler of Kaisersberg, 132–3
Gentileschi, Artemesia, 175, 182–5
Germany: education in, 146–7 homosexuality in, 67; midwives in, 81; religion in, 222–31; scientists in, 200; witchcraft in, 281–2; women's economic role in, 90, 108, 110, 115, 130 ; writers in, 186.

Glickl bas Judah Leib, 102, 130–1
Gosynhille, Edward, 22
de Gouges, Olympe, 303
de Gourney, Marie Jars, 1, 9, 24, 301
de Gras, Mademoiselle, 239
Grumbach, Argula von, 222–3, 295
Grymeston, Elizabeth, 89
guardianship, 36–7, 132–3
de la Guerre, Elisabeth-Claude Jaquet, 187
guilds, 104–5, 125–9
du Guillet, Pernette, 193
Guyon, Madame 246–7, 254

Harvey, William, 31–2
Hemessen, Caterina van, 179
Henry VIII, King of England, 152, 155
Heyssin, Elisabeth, 102, 116
Hippocrates, 30
Hobbes, Thomas, 303–4
Holy Roman Empire. *See* Germany
homosexuality, 66–70, 253, 296
honor, 40–1, 60–4, 73, 127–9, 153–6
Hoyer, Anna Owen, 193, 247
Hroswitha of Gandersheim, 216
Hugh of St. Victor, 18
humanism, 20, 152–8
humoral theory 32–3
husbands, 37–9, 52, 74, 293–99. *See also* marriage; women, married
Hutchinson, Lucy, 197

infanticide, 63, 63–4, 71, 283
Inquisition, 235–6, 249, 267–8, 278–9
Ireland, 110, 225, 228, 239, 300, 309
Islam. *See* Muslims
Italy: artists in, 179, 181, ; education in, 149, 152–5, 164, 138; foundling homes in, 65; musicians in, 186–8; religion in, 218, 251; witchcraft in, 278–9; women's economic role in, 115, 124, 130; writers in, 193

James I, King of England and
    Scotland, 7, 201, 293
James, Elinor, 295
Jansenism, 242, 247–8
Jerome, Saint, 17, 273
Jesuits, 232, 240, 248
Joseph, Saint (husband of Mary), 238
journeymen. *See* guilds
Judaism: ideas about women in,
    15–16, 22, 30, 55, 58–9, 66; role
    of women in, 15, 130–1, 146,
    249–52; traditions in, 72, 294, 308
Judith, 15, 183
Julian of Norwich, 218

Kempe, Margery, 218
Knox, John, 288, 292
Krämer, Heinrich, 266, 273–4

Labé, Louise, 143, 156, 193
Lafayette, Madame de, 196
law, criminal, 39–40, 124–5, 297,
    299; and witchcraft, 267–8
law, Roman, 36–40
law codes, 12, 35–40, 295–7
Lead, Jane, 246, 247
Leeuwenhoek, Anton von, 31
Leigh, Dorothy, 89, 195
Leon, Luis, de, 29
Lenclos, Ninon de, 124
Lery, Jéan, 277
lesbianism. *See* homosexuality
letters, 28, 189–90
lettres de cachet, 295–6
Levellers, 243, 244, 298, 307
Leyster, Judith, 182–3
Line, Anne, 239
Lister, Margaret, 276
literacy. *See* education, reading
    material
Locke, John, 303
Louis XIV, King of France, 66, 126,
    165
Loyola, St. Ignatius, 232
Lussan, Marguerite de, 197
Luther, Martin, 7, 13, 26, 58, 220,
    224, 264, 272, 301

Machiavelli, Niccolo, 305–6
maids. *See* servants, domestic
Makin, Bathsua, 162–3, 300
Malleus Maleficarum, 264, 266,
    272–4, 279
Margaret of Austria, 22
Margaret of Parma, 165
Marguerite of Navarre, 156, 223, 224
Maria of Antwerp, 68–70
Maria de Medici, 170
Marinella, Lucrezia, 307
Marot, Jean, 1153
marriage, 37–41, 71–8; men's ideas
    about, 17–18, 27–31, 57–8, 185,
    293; patterns of, 71–5, 85–91, 241,
    295; sermons on, 27–8; women's
    ideas about, 28, 57–8, 194–5,
    300–1. *See also* husbands; women,
    marrried; women, unmarried
Mary, Saint (mother of Jesus), 19,
    179, 218–19, 228, 237, 240
Mary I, Queen of England, 153,
    165, 226
Mary Magdalene, 16, 65
masculinity, 304–6
Mathesius, Johannes, 27
medical ideas and practices, 30–3,
    34–7, 78–81, 269. *See also*
    childbirth; medical practitioners;
    midwives
medical practitioners, 116–17, 134
Medici, Anna Maria Luisa de, 168–9
Medum, Anna von, 192
memoirs. *See* autobiographies
menopause, 92–3, 273
menstruation, 31, 54–6, 93, 276
Merian, Maria Sibylla, 199
Merici, Angela, 232, 235
midwives, 53, 78–85, 134, 252; male,
    81, 201; training of, 78–84, 201;
    and witchcraft, 274–5. *See also*
    childbirth
mining, 111–12
misogyny, 20–26, 59, 269. *See also*
    Christianity, ideas about women
    in; debate about women; sexuality,
    ideas about; witchcraft

Moerloose, Isabella de, 55
More, Thomas, 154–5
Munda, Constantia, 24
Murat, Comtesse de, 196
Muscovy. See Russia
musicians, 185–9
Muslims, 252–3, 294, 308
mysticism, 218, 236, 246–7, 251

Nasi, Gracia, 250
Netherlands: artists in, 179, 181–2;
    education in, 160; religion in,
    228–9, 231, 247; riots in, 299;
    witchcraft in, 280
Neuber, Caroline, 188
Newton, Isaac, 33
niddah, 250
Nippers, Doritte, 277
Nogarola, Isotta, 154, 158
Norway, 60, 63, 106, 107, 224
nuns. See convents

Old Believers, 241
order, ideas of, 276, 306–11
orphanages, 65
Orthodoxy, Eastern, 55, 57, 67, 72,
    86, 111, 217, 240–2

painting. See artists
Paracelsus (Theophrastus von
    Hohenheim), 25, 276
Paré, Amboise, 67
Parker, Henry, 301–2
patrilineality, 74–5
patronage, 167–71, 289
Paul, Saint, 1, 67, 152, 222, 245
Paul, Saint Vincent de, 239
Peeters, Clara, 181
Peter I, Tsar, 241
Petersen, Eleanore, 248–9
petitions, women's, 244–5, 297–9
Philadelphian Society, 247
Philips, Katherine, 190
pietism, 248–9
Pizan, Christine de, 20–1
Plato, 18
playwrights, 193–5

poets, 192–3
Poland, 117
Polwhele, Elizabeth, 194
Pompadour, Madame de, 165
Poole, Elizabeth, 243
popular culture and literature,
    19–20, 22–6, 59, 176, 178, 186,
    251, 272, 308
pornography, 57, 59, 67
Portugal, 250, 278–9
poverty. See women, poor
preaching, women's, 222–3, 243
pregnancy, 4, 54, 60–3, 78–9. See
    also childbirth
property owners, 129–33
prophecies, 243–4
prostitutes, 58, 122–4, 238, 283
proto-industrialization. See domestic
    industry
public/private dichotomy, 289–90
Puritans, 26, 74, 86–7, 192, 225,
    242–5, 293
putting-out system. See domestic
    industry

Quakers, 192, 242, 244–6, 307
queens. See rulers, female
querelle des femmes. See debate
    about women
quietists, 242, 246

race, ideas about, 35, 308–9
Rambouillet, Madame, 166
rape, 40, 57, 60, 63, 182
reading material, women's and girls',
    150–2
Reformation, Catholic, 29–30;
    cloistering of women in, 232; and
    education 146, 149; and
    witchcraft, 266; women's actions
    in support of, 231–40. See also
    Christianity, Catholic
Reformation, Protestant, 5, 26–9,
    72–3, 118, 123, 220–30, 293; and
    education, 146–9; and witchcraft,
    266–7; women's actions in support
    of, 222–31. See also: Christianity,
    Protestant

Renaissance, 5, 152–8, 175–7
riots, 299–300
rituals, women's 81, 86, 251
Roches, Madeleine and Catherine des, 157–8, 166, 193
Roper, Margaret More, 154–5, 158
Roser, Isabel, 232, 234
Rossi, Camilla di, 187
Rossi, Properzia dé, 179
Royal Society of England, 33, 198, 201
rulers, female, 21, 25, 165–6, 168, 224, 226, 230, 291–3
Russia, 41, 110, 131, 241, 275. *See also* Orthodoxy, Eastern
Ruysch, Rachel, 181

saints, 219
salons, 166–7, 289
San Gerónimo, Madre Magdalena de, 65
Satan, 265–6, 274, 279, 282
schools. *See* education
Schurman, Anna Maria van, 143–4, 160–2, 300
Schwarz, Sibylle, 193
Scientific Revolution, 5, 30–5, 187–202, 310
Scot, Reginald, 279
Scotland, 60, 62, 64, 280
Scudéry, Madeleine de, 194
Sera, Beatrice del, 193
servants, domestic, 60, 110–11, 113–15
Sévigné, Madame de, 189
sexuality: control of female, 59–68; ideas about, 13–14, 18–19, 27–9, 56–9; and witchcraft, 274–5. *See also*: homosexuality
Shakespeare, William, 51, 93, 308, 310
Sidney, Mary, 191
silk production, 108, 111
Sisters of the Common Life, 218
slaves and slavery, 110–11, 114, 132
Smith, Thomas, 292, 296

Sophie Charlotte of Prussia, 168
Sowernam, Esther, 24
Spain: education in, 149; religion in, 249–50, 252–3, 309; witchcraft in, 278–9
Speght, Rachel, 1, 8, 24
spinning, 111–12, 118–22
spinsters. *See* women, unmarried
Stampa, Gaspara, 183
Stolberg, Anna von, 230
Strozzi, Allesandra, 92
Strozzi, Barbara, 187
Sullam, Sarra Copia, 251
Sweden, 110, 229, 247, 280
Swetnam, Joseph, 24
Switzerland, 294

Teresa of Avila, Saint, 213, 235–7, 243
Terracina, Laura, 24
Tertullian, 17, 213, 273
traders. *See* work, sales and trading
transvestism, 68–70, 307

Ursulines, 149, 232–3
uterus, 33–5

Vasari, Giorgio, 176
Velten, Catherina Elisabeth, 198
Vesalius, Andreas, 30, 32, 56
Vives, Juan Luis, 21, 153

wages, 108–10, 113–15, 119–20
Ward, Mary, 233–5, 254
Wecker, Anna, 151
Weir, Johann, 279
wet nurses, 87–8
Weyda, Ursula, 222–3
widows, 36–7, 89–91, 224, 310; economic role of, 89–91, 104, 125–6, 132; remarriage of, 90–1; and witchcraft, 270, 272
Wife of Bath, 14
wife beating, 296–7
Wight, Sarah, 243
Wilson, Bessie, 264

Winkelmann, Maria, 201–2
witchcraft, 58, 64, 227, 264–83, 307;
    demonology of, 265–6, 273–4; and
    language, 279; legal treatment of,
    278–82; social change and, 268–9;
    women and, 270–7
wives. See women, married
Wollstonecraft, Mary, 303
women, married: legal rights of,
    36–40, 295–7, 299; as queens,
    292. See also marriage
women, poor, 109, 116, 118, 124–5,
    126, 129, 224
women, unmarried, 75–7, 115;
    giving birth, 63–5; defending their
    status, 77; legal rights of, 36–40,
    132; viewed as a problem, 76–7;
    and witchcraft, 269
work, agricultural, 106–13
work, sales and trading, 117–19,
    129–33

work identity, 103–6, 134
writers, women, 156–8, 160–3, 169,
    189–97; of advice books, 193–5; of
    history, 197; religious, 192–3,
    222–3, 243–4, 247; scientific, 199.
    See also playwrights; poets
Wroth, Lady Mary, 195

Xantippe, 25

Yahya, Gedaliah ibn, 22

Zayas y Sotomayor, Maria de,
    194–5, 301
Zell, Katherine, 223
Zevi, Sabbatai, 251
Zinzendorf, Count Nikolaus and
    Erdmuthe von, 248–9
Zwingli, Ulrich, 26, 220

NEW APPROACHES TO EUROPEAN HISTORY

1 MERRY E. Wiesner   Women and Gender in Early Modern Europe Second edition
  see below

2 JONATHAN SPERBER   The European Revolutions, 1848–1851
  0 521 38526 1 hardback
  0 521 38685 3 paperback

3 CHARLES INGRAO   The Habsburg Monarchy 1618–1815 Second edition
  see below

4 ROBERT JÜTTE   Poverty and Deviance in Early Modern Europe
  0 521 41169 6 hardback
  0 521 42322 8 paperback

5 JAMES B. COLLINS   The State in Early Modern France
  0 521 38284 X hardback
  0 521 38724 8 paperback

6 CHARLES G. NAUERT, JR   Humanism and the Culture of Renaissance Europe
  0 521 40364 2 hardback
  0 521 40724 9 paperback

7 DORINDA OUTRAM   The Enlightenment
  0 521 41522 5 hardback
  0 521 42534 4 paperback

8 MACK P. HOLT   The French Wars of Religion, 1562–1629
  0 521 35359 9 hardback
  0 521 35873 6 paperback

9 JONATHAN DEWALD   The European Nobility, 1400–1800
  0 521 41512 8 hardback
  0 521 42528 X paperback

10 ROBERT S. DUPLESSIS   Transitions to Capitalism in Early Modern Europe
  0 521 39465 1 hardback
  0 521 39773 1 paperback

11 EDWARD MUIR   Ritual in Early Modern Europe
  0 521 40169 0 hardback
  0 521 40967 5 paperback

12 R. PO-CHIA HSIA   The World of Catholic Renewal 1540–1770
  0 521 44041 6 hardback
  0 521 44596 5 paperback

13 ROGER CHICKERING Imperial Germany and the Great War, 1914–1918
0 521 56148 5 hardback
0 521 56754 8 paperback

14 W. R. WARD Christianity under the Ancien Régime, 1648–1789
0 521 55361 X hardback
0 521 55672 4 paperback

15 SIMON DIXON The Modernisation of Russia 1676–1825
0 521 37100 7 hardback
0 521 37961 X paperback

16 MARY LINDEMANN Medicine and Society in Early Modern Europe
0 521 41254 4 hardback
0 521 42354 6 paperback

17 DONALD QUATAERT The Ottoman Empire, 1700–1922
0 521 63328 1 hardback
0 521 63360 5 paperback

18 REX A. WADE The Russian Revolution, 1917
0 521 41548 9 hardback
0 521 42565 4 paperback

19 JAMES R. FARR Artisans in Europe, 1350–1914
0 521 41888 7 hardback
0 521 42934 X paperback

20 MERRY E. WIESNER Women and Gender in Early Modern Europe Second edition
0 521 77105 6 hardback
0 521 77822 0 paperback

21 CHARLES INGRAO The Habsburg Monarchy 1618–1815 Second edition
0 521 78034 9 hardback
0 521 78505 7 paperback